teach yourself...

CorelDRAW!

VERSION 2.0

PAUL WEBSTER

MIS:
PRESS

P.O. Box 5277
Portland, Oregon 97208-5277

First Printing
ISBN 1-55828-123-1

Printed in the United States of America

TRADEMARKS

Adobe Illustrator is a trademark of Adobe Systems, Inc.
AutoCAD is a trademark of Autodesk Corporation
CorelDRAW! is a trademark of Corel Corporation
CorelTRACE! is a trademark of Corel Corporation
GEM is a trademark of Digital Research Inc.
IBM AT is a trademark of International Business Machines Corporation
IBM PC is a trademark of International Business Machines Corporation
IBM PIF is a trademark of International Business Machines Corporation
HPGL is a trademark of Hewlett-Packard Company
LaserJet is a trademark of Hewlett-Packard Company
Lotus 1-2-3 is a trademark of Lotus Development Corporation
Macintosh is a trademark Apple Computer, Inc.
Mosaic is a trademark of Corel Corporation
MS-DOS is a trademark of Microsoft Corporation
PageMaker is a trademark of Aldus Corporation
PANTONE® and PANTONE MATCHING SYSTEM are registered trademarks of Pantone, Inc.
PostScript is a trademark of Adobe Systems, Inc.
OS/2 is a trademark of International Business Machines Corporation
SlideShow is a trademark of Corel Corporation
Ventura Publisher is a trademark of Xerox Corporation
Windows is a trademark of Microsoft Corporation
WordPerfect is a trademark of WordPerfect Corporation

Acknowledgements

The author would like to acknowledge the assistance of the following people who helped in the production of this book:

- Carrie Webster, for the creation of some of the exercises.
- Tony Webster, for his proofreading and editing.
- David Webster, who helped with the introduction and the screen shots.
- Barbara Larter and Wayne Clarke, for additional editing.

Contents

Introduction

This two-part book makes it easy to learn CorelDRAW! so that you can create your own professional graphics. Part 1 provides a general overview of major CorelDRAW! features. The extensive use of illustrated screens enables you to easily understand the concepts. Part 2 contains exercises for you to use on your own.

What This Book Teaches You

This book teaches you about the CorelDRAW! features and how you use them in the Microsoft Windows or OS/2 environment. You will learn

- the major concepts of CorelDRAW!
- how to use the menus, screens, and dialog boxes
- how to use the tools in the toolbox so that you can
  - draw
  - select graphics
  - move and resize objects
  - mirror, rotate, and skew objects
  - outline graphics and fill them with patterns
- how to input text and arrrange it with your graphics
- how to use the two additional programs that are packaged with CorelDRAW!.

Additionally, the self-paced exercises in Part 2 of this book give you the hands-on experience that will help you to fully understand CorelDRAW! and to maximize its capabilities. The 15 exercises move from simple to complex operations and provide step-by-step details.

What This Book Does Not Teach You

This book does not teach you how to operate a PC. It assumes that you are familiar with PC operations and that you are at least somewhat comfortable using your machine's operating system.

What You Need to Use This Book

To use this book, you need a personal computer, Microsoft Windows, Version 3.0 (or above) or the OS/2 operating system, and CorelDRAW!, Version 2.0.

Part 1

CorelDRAW! Overview

Chapter 1

Using CorelDRAW!

This chapter teaches you the basics of CorelDRAW!, including the screen, menus, and other tools. You will see how these are used together to create, modify, close, and open graphics files.

These basics include:

- Microsoft Windows environment
- OS/2 operations
- Screen
- System Menu
- Title Bar
- Arrows
- Scroll Bars
- Status Line
- Tools
- Working Area
- Menu Bar
- Menu Commands
- Dialog Boxes
- Preview Screen.

CorelDRAW! Version 2.0 operates in a graphics operating environment known as Microsoft Windows, Version 3.0 and above (see Figure 1-1), as well as the OS/2 operating system.

Before you begin using CorelDRAW!, briefly look at the Windows and OS/2 environments.

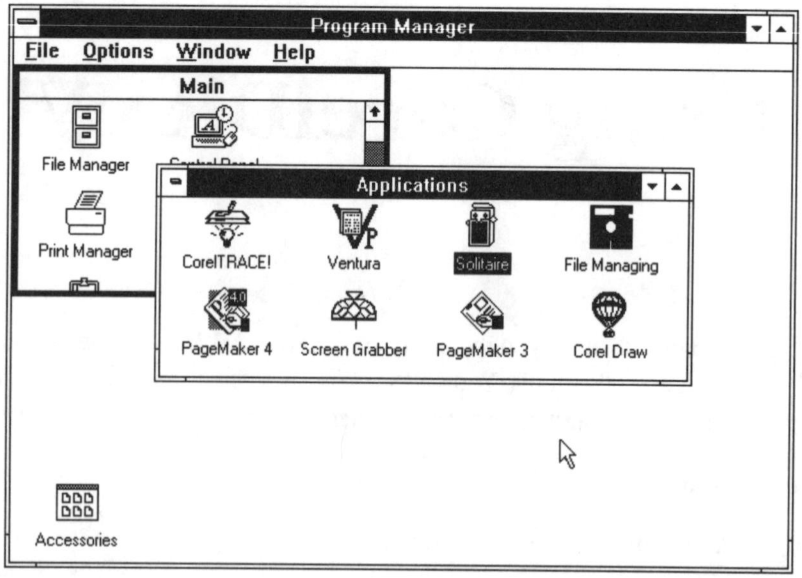

Figure 1-1. The CorelDRAW! Icon with Microsoft Windows, Version 3.0.

Microsoft Windows Environment

Microsoft Windows is an operating environment that allows several programs to be opened together, and allows you to easily swap information between these programs (see Figure 1-2).

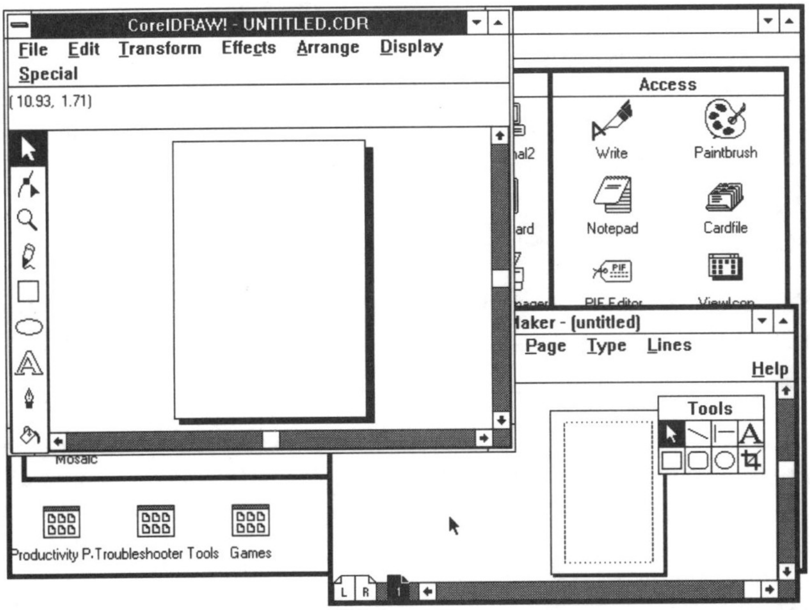

Figure 1-2. Microsoft Windows with Several Programs, Each One in a Separate Window.

Microsoft Windows has another advantage over other graphic environments, in that it operates much like the Presentation Manager of OS/2. This makes it very easy to swap from the MS-DOS or PC-DOS operating environments into OS/2, without extensive retraining.

You can start CorelDRAW! in one of many ways on your computer, depending on how it is set up on your particular machine. You may be able to select it from a menuing system, such as Direct Access or VS Menu. You can also open CorelDRAW! from within Windows 3.0, by double-clicking on the CorelDRAW! icon.

Alternatively, you can start CorelDRAW! from the DOS prompt by typing in the following command:

```
C:\WIN C:\CORELDRW\CORELDRW.EXE
```

When you type this command and press the Enter key (assuming that you substitute the correct Windows and CorelDRAW! directories) you open Windows, and a CorelDRAW! window. You can also open a CorelDRAW! file directly by appending a CorelDRAW! file name to the DOS command on the previous page.

OS/2 Operation

OS/2 looks and operates almost identically to Microsoft Windows 3.0. In general, CorelDRAW! operates in the same way under OS/2 as it does for Windows 3.0.

This book describes CorelDRAW! Version 2.0 for Windows. Your version of CorelDRAW! for OS/2 may not include features such as Mosaic, color bitmap importing, text importing, symbol library, or many new object manipulation features contained in the **Effects** menu.

The Screen

This section introduces you to the various parts that make up the CorelDRAW! screen (see Figure 1-3). It also includes a brief overview about the function and use of each part of the screen.

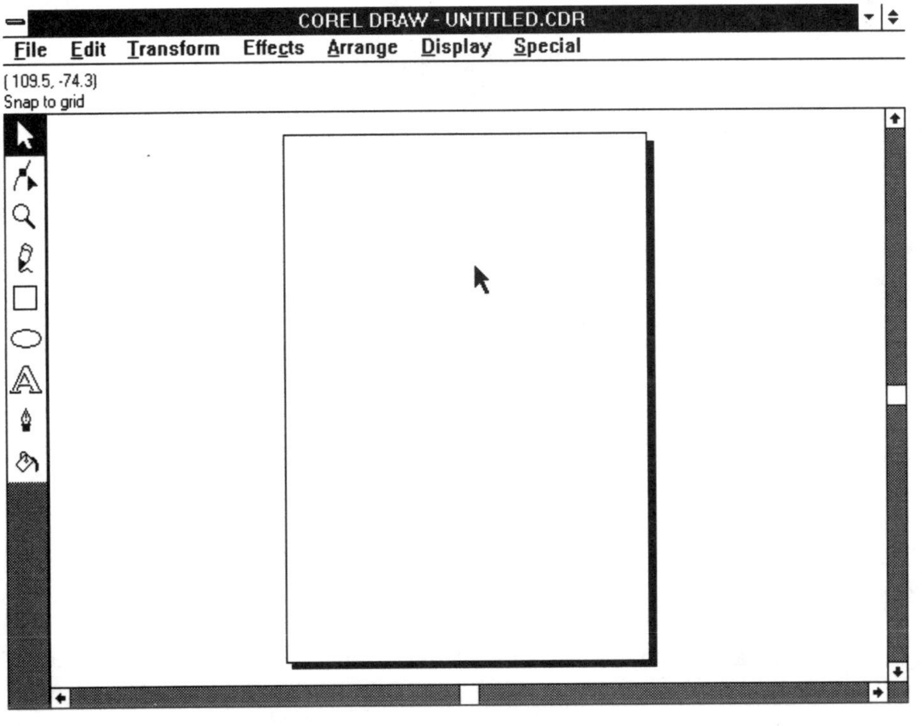

Figure 1-3. The CorelDRAW! Screen.

System Menu

The Windows **System** menu is common to the majority of Windows applications. It is an icon in the top left-hand corner of the CorelDRAW! window (Figure 1-4), just above the **File** menu. It contains commands (Figure 1-5) that control the size of the window that CorelDRAW! occupies, as well as a *Close* command, which terminates and exits from CorelDRAW!, and closes its window.

Figure 1-4. The Windows System Menu Icon Above the File Command.

Figure 1-5. The Windows System Menu that is Common to All Windows Applications.

Title Bar

The Title Bar, across the top of the screen, tells you two things — first the application that you are in, and second, the name of the file currently open within that application. When there is no file open, this title bar reads "CorelDRAW - UNTITLED" (Figure 1-6).

Figure 1-6. The CorelDRAW! Title Bar.

Figure 1-7 illustrates the Title Bar after a file called DEBBIE.CDR has been opened. In this case, the file would be displayed on the screen as well.

Figure 1-7. The CorelDRAW! Title Bar Reflecting the Name of the New File.

Arrows (Minimize and Maximize Boxes)

The Minimize and Maximize boxes (Figure 1-8) are at the top right-hand corner of the CorelDRAW! window.

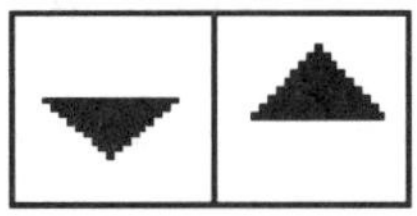

Figure 1-8. The Minimize and Maximize Boxes.

The icon on the left (down-pointing arrow), or the Minimize box, reduces the currently open window to a small icon, which is displayed along the bottom of the screen. When running CorelDRAW! alone, there is no need to use this arrow. However, when you open CorelDRAW! in conjunction with other Windows programs, reducing one of the programs to an icon can increase available memory and reduce screen clutter. You can reduce several programs to icons, making it very simple to identify, locate, and reload the closed window on the screen.

The up-pointing arrow, or the Maximize box, has two functions, depending on how it looks currently (compare Figure 1-8 to Figure 1-9). Upon initially starting CorelDRAW!, it expands the CorelDRAW! window to its maximum size possible, filling the screen. Clicking on this arrow is a good idea, particularly if CorelDRAW! is the only application you are running, as you will have more area to work with, and no wasted space on the screen.

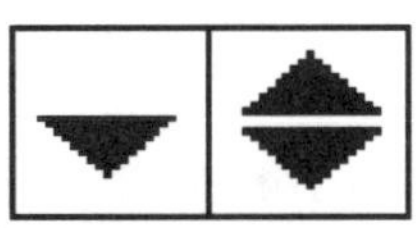

Figure 1-9. The Minimize and Maximize Boxes, After the Maximize Box has been Clicked On.

Once you click on this arrow, you find that it changes appearance (Figure 1-9). It is displayed as two arrows: an up- and a down-pointing arrow. This indicates to you that the window is at full size. If you click on this arrow now, the window that contains CorelDRAW! returns to whatever size it was. This allows applications like CorelDRAW! to run at full size, and permits you to quickly swap into other applications at full size if you wish.

Scroll Bars

The scroll bars are down the right-hand side and along the bottom of the screen (Figure 1-10). You use these bars to look at an enlarged view of your work when you cannot see the entire job in the screen area. The scroll bars let you move around the picture to see different sections.

Figure 1-10. The CorelDRAW! Scroll Bars.

The two scroll bars, each with a directional arrow at either end, enable you to move precise distances in any direction.

Initially, you may find the scroll bars a little difficult to operate. With a little practice, however, they become almost second nature to use. One advantage of working with a large screen is that you do not need the scroll bars as often.

Scroll bars are common to virtually all Windows graphics-type software, and are used in virtually all WYSIWYG (What You See Is What You Get) programs.

Status Line

The Status Line is below the Title and Menu Bars in CorelDRAW! (Figure 1-11). When operating CorelDRAW!, this optional line provides vital information about the objects currently selected on the screen, such as size, angle, and color.

The value of this Status Line becomes far more visible as you start working with CorelDRAW!.

The Status Line also tells you the exact position of your mouse on the working page, and whether the *Snap to grid* feature is currently activated.

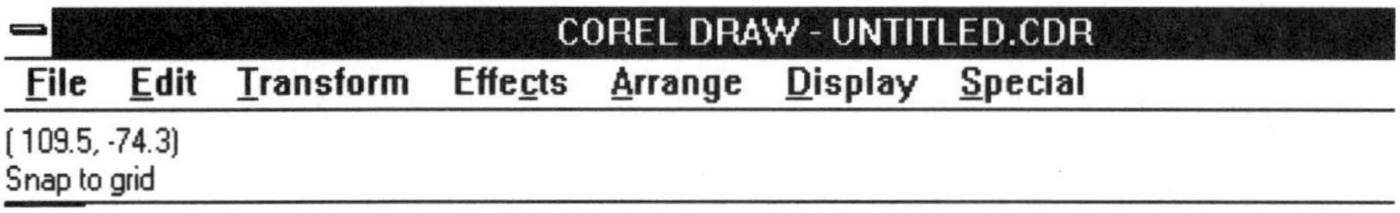

Figure 1-11. The Status Line.

The Tools

The tools that you use in CorelDRAW! are down the left-hand side of the screen (Figure 1-12). Each of these tools has separate and distinct functions, and you can select one at any time. The tools are discussed in the next two chapters, and in detail throughout the exercises in Part 2 of this book.

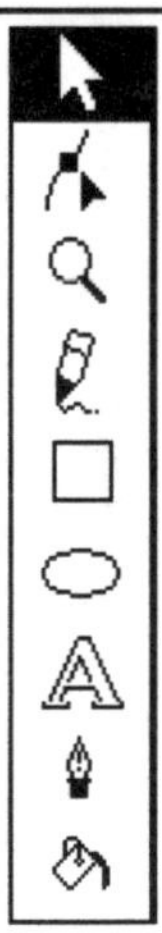

- The **Pick** Tool, which is generally used to select objects.
- The **Node** or **Shape** Tool for editing lines and individual text characters.
- The **Zoom** Tool, which directly changes viewing size and area of screen.
- The **Pencil** Tool, which you use for freehand drawing.
- The **Rectangle** Tool for drawing squares and rectangles.
- The **Ellipse** Tool for drawing circles and ellipses.
- The **Text** Tool for placing text on your page.
- The **Outline** Tool, which gives outlines to objects.
- The **Fill** Tool to apply fills to objects.

Figure 1-12. The CorelDRAW! Toolbox.

The Working Area

The area in the center of the page is where you do all your work in CorelDRAW! (Figure 1-13). You will see a "page" in the center of the screen, representing the page that you eventually produce through your output device. This representation of your printed page makes it very easy to use CorelDRAW! by allowing you to place and move objects in precise relation to this page. You can alter the size of the page at any time.

As you can see, the screen in CorelDRAW! remains relatively uncluttered, making it much easier to draw and view your work.

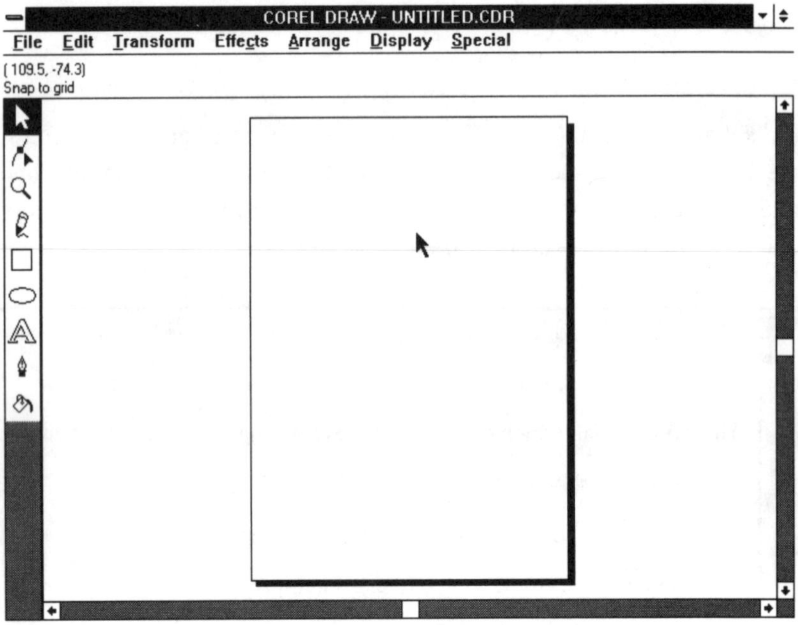

Figure 1-13. The CorelDRAW! Working Area.

Menu Bar

The series of names below the Title Bar (such as **File**, **Edit**, **Transform**, Figure 1-14) are menu names located in the Menu Bar. These menus, discussed in detail in **Chapter 5: Menu Commands**, allow easy access to the commands, which form the basis of CorelDRAW! operation.

Many packages use menus to provide quick access to a relatively large number of commands without cluttering the screen. If you have not used a program that employs the theory of drop-down menus before, it will not take you long before you are an expert at using them. These menus operate very similarly to all other Windows software, and similarly to many non-Windows programs.

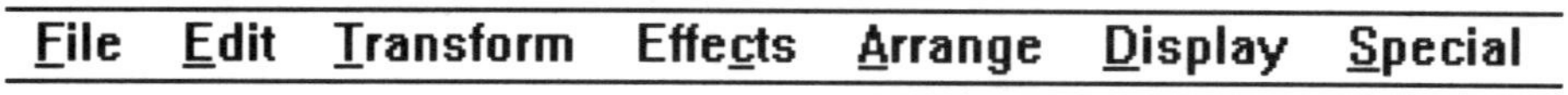

Figure 1-14. The CorelDRAW! Menu Bar.

Menu Commands

In any particular menu, there are a varying number of commands listed. Some of these commands display in black, while others are shown in gray (see Figures 1-15 and 1-17). If a command is in gray, you cannot select it. You must perform some other function before you can select this command.

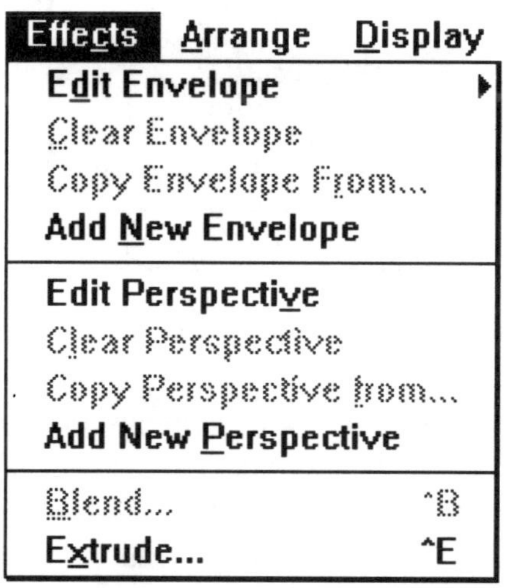

Figure 1-15. Gray Menu Commands that Cannot Be Selected.

A check mark or tick next to a menu command indicates that you have selected this command, and it is currently active. Not all menu commands require a tick beside them.

You can select the commands listed in black by positioning the mouse cursor over the command name and clicking the left mouse button. The command you click on becomes selected. Another way is to hold your finger on the mouse, and move it down the menu until you highlight the command you want. Once you do this, release your finger from the mouse and again the command is selected. For example, the *Page Setup* command has been selected in Figure 1-16.

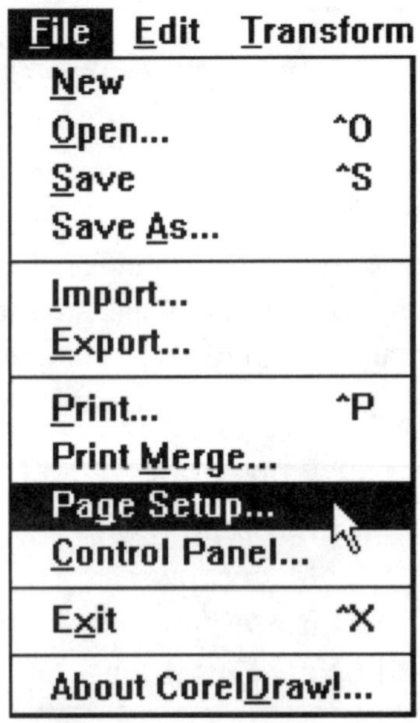

Figure 1-16. A Selected Menu Command.

SHORTCUT

You can invoke some commands using shortcut keyboard commands. This is indicated by a key sequence displayed next to the command name in the menu, as shown in Figures 1-15 through 1-17. If, for example, you wish to select the *Show Preview* command from the **Display** menu in Figure 1-17, it is as simple as pressing the Shift + F9 keys when no menu has even been invoked. Although you cannot select all commands this way, you can save time for commands that you need to select quite often. Many command names have three ellipses following them. This indicates that if this command is selected, a dialog box will follow (Figure 1-16).

One of three things may happen after you select a command in a menu. First, it may seem like nothing has happened. In this case, you may have activated a command that does not become apparent until you perform a certain task. Second, a visible change may take place on screen. Third, you may see a dialog box (Figure 1-18).

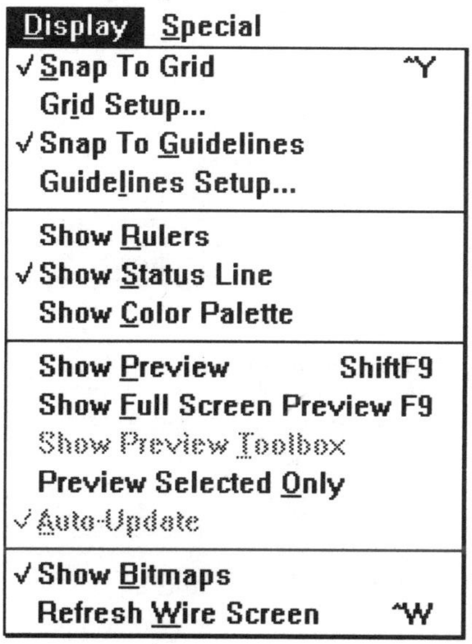

Figure 1-17. Menu Options with Grayed-out Commands, Keyboard Shortcuts, Ellipses Marks, and Tick Marks.

Dialog Boxes

You use a dialog box to customize the results of a selected command. The program displays a window on the screen, most often listing a series of choices associated with this command (Figure 1-18). Most dialog boxes take on a different appearance to one another; however, they all have fundamental and operational similarities.

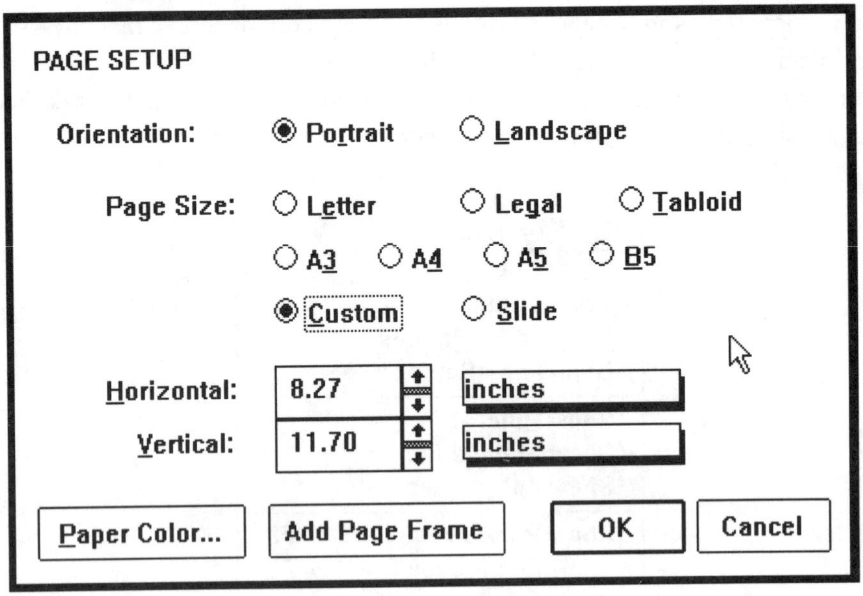

Figure 1-18. A CorelDRAW! Dialog Box.

All dialog boxes contain a *Cancel* button, and an *OK* button (normally near the bottom right-hand corner of the box). Clicking the mouse in either of these buttons removes the dialog box from the screen. Cancel, however, ignores any changes you may have made to this box. Clicking on OK indicates to CorelDRAW! that you would like to execute the selected command using newly entered parameters. In some dialog boxes, the OK button may be replaced by options, such as *Open, Save,* or *Import*.

There are three different types of choices you may be asked to make within a dialog box. The first is a series of choices, each with a small circle to the left of them (see Figure 1-19). This indicates that you can select any one, but only one, of these options by clicking inside a circle. As you select a new option, the previous option is deselected. These options are mutually exclusive. A dot inside one of the circles indicates which option you have selected.

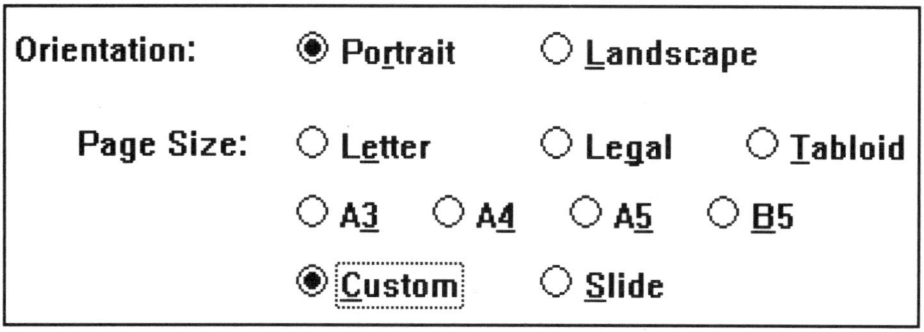

Figure 1-19. Mutually Exclusive Options in a Dialog Box.

You can select choices in a dialog box that have a square box to their left by clicking inside the correct box or boxes. The boxes then have a check mark in them (Figure 1-20). In a list of such options, you can select any number. These options are not mutually exclusive.

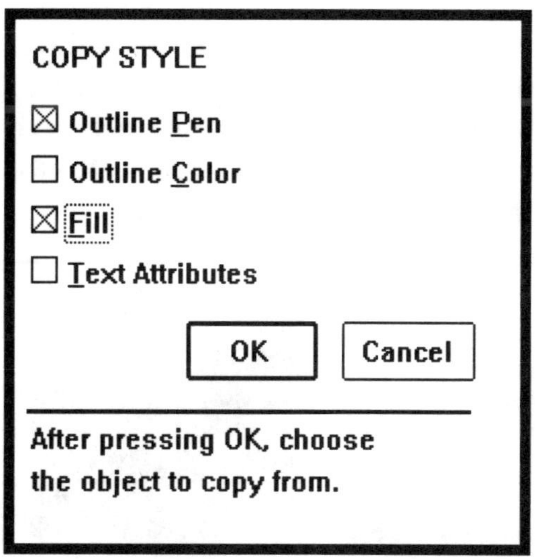

Figure 1-20. A Dialog Box with More Than One Check Box Option.

You may also be required to select a dialog box that needs a numerical figure (Figure 1-21). These are easy to spot. The program usually displays a default figure inside a rectangle. The rectangle has a small up-and-down-arrow on its right-hand side. If you click the mouse button on the up arrow, you increase the value of the figure. If you click on the down arrow, you decrease the value of the figure. Optionally, you may also click the cursor inside these boxes, delete the current figures, and type in the new ones.

There are also measurement frames in many dialog boxes. In Figure 1-21, the current unit of measurement is in inches. To get access to the other measurement styles, you click on the frame that contains the word "inches" with your mouse, and one-by-one, the other measurement units become available.

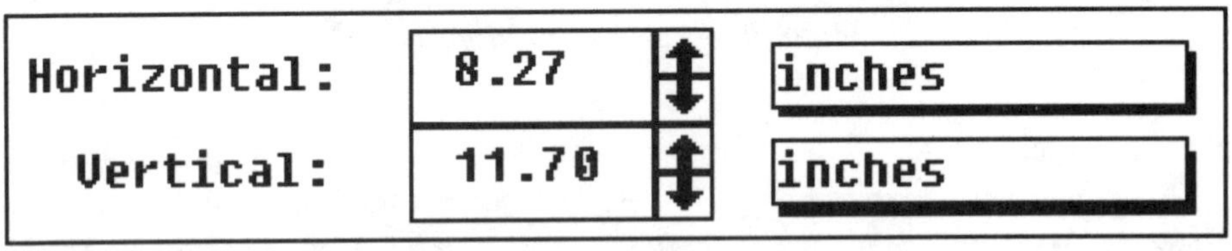

Figure 1-21. Numerical Options in Some Dialog Boxes.

Some dialog boxes, such as the color dialog boxes, have scroll bars that you can use to change certain settings. As well as these horizontal scroll bars, some of the color dialog boxes have *Visual Selectors* that you use in conjunction with the mouse to change the color settings (Figure 1-22). For more information on color dialog boxes, see **Chapter 3: The Outline and Fill Tools**.

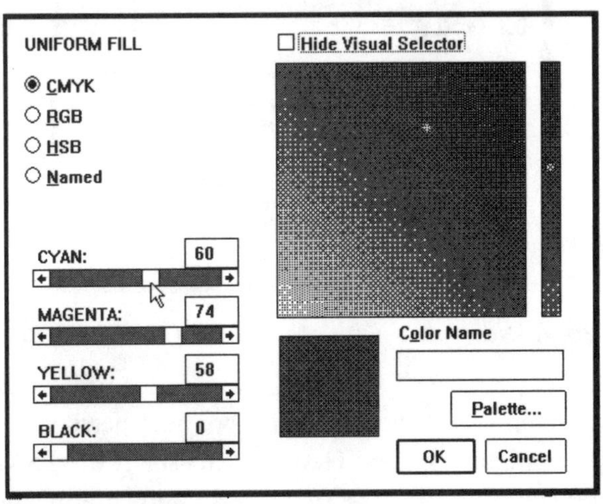

Figure 1-22. A Color Dialog Box Where You Change Settings.

The Preview Screen

The Preview Screen in CorelDRAW! allows you to view the file that is currently open in an additional window. The image in this window shows all fills and outlines you may have applied to objects on the page (except PostScript fills). It lets you view the file before you output to a printer or a bureau for color separations. If you only have a black and white screen, any color fills or outlines you apply are displayed in shades of gray.

You activate the Preview Screen by selecting the *Show Preview* command from the **Display** menu (Figure 1-23).

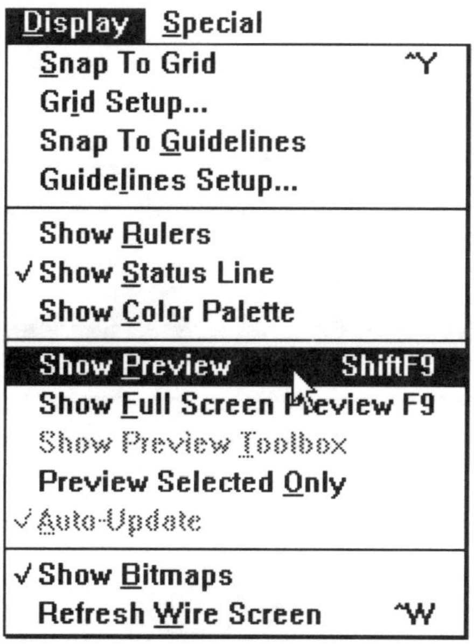

Figure 1-23. The Show Preview Command from the Display Menu.

Figure 1-24 shows the Preview Screen to the right of the working screen. You can also resize the Preview Screen (Figure 1-25) by holding the mouse down on the left-hand wall of the Preview Screen window, and dragging it across to the left or right. If you have enlarged it, as in Figure 1-25, you can then toggle between the Preview Screen and the working screen by pressing the Shift + F9 keys. This lets you check on the progress of your drawing, without having the

Preview Screen activated the whole time. This latter screen can sometimes slow you down because certain fills and complex images can take some time to redraw.

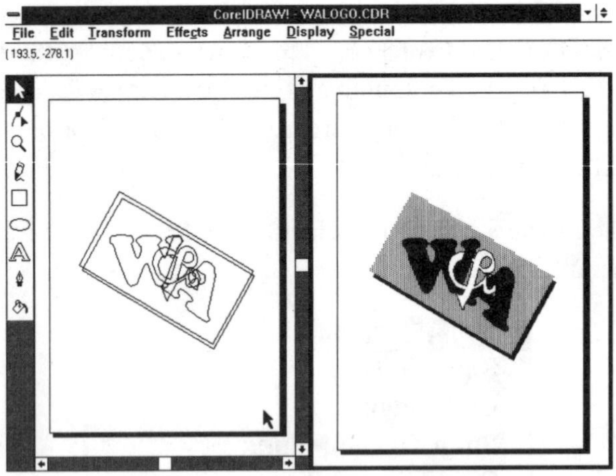

Figure 1-24. The Preview Screen (Left) Running Beside the Working Screen (Right).

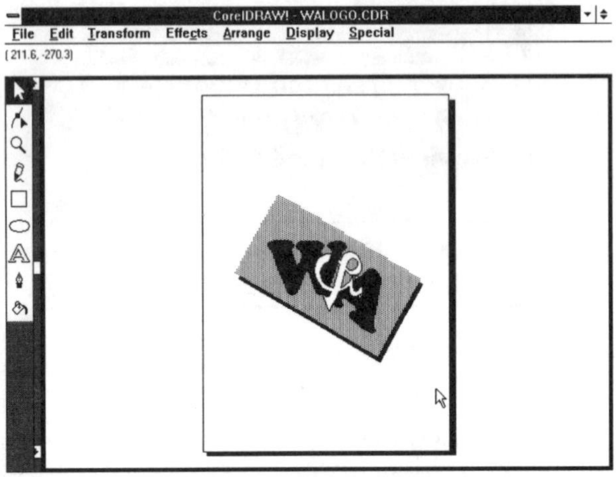

Figure 1-25. The Enlarged Preview Screen that Covers the Working Screen.

In addition to the Preview Screen shown in Figures 1-24 and 1-25, CorelDRAW! provides the *Show Full Screen Preview* command, which you also access through the **Display** menu (Figure 1-23). This command displays the image without the restrictions of the page border, menus, Toolbox, or window edges. You can use the Preview Screen extensively in the exercises in Part 2 of this book.

Summary

This chapter introduced you to the basics of CorelDRAW!. You learned about selecting and operating CorelDRAW! in a Windows environment. You also learned about how you use the System menu, the Title Bar, arrows, scroll bars, and the working area.

Chapter 2

The Toolbox

The Toolbox contains the tools you use to create and manipulate graphics in CorelDRAW!. You also use the tools to perform a variety of other tasks. The Toolbox is along the left side of the CorelDRAW! screen.

This chapter explains the use for each of the following tools:

- Pick
- Rectangle
- Ellipse
- Pencil
- Node (or Shape)
- Zoom
- Text.

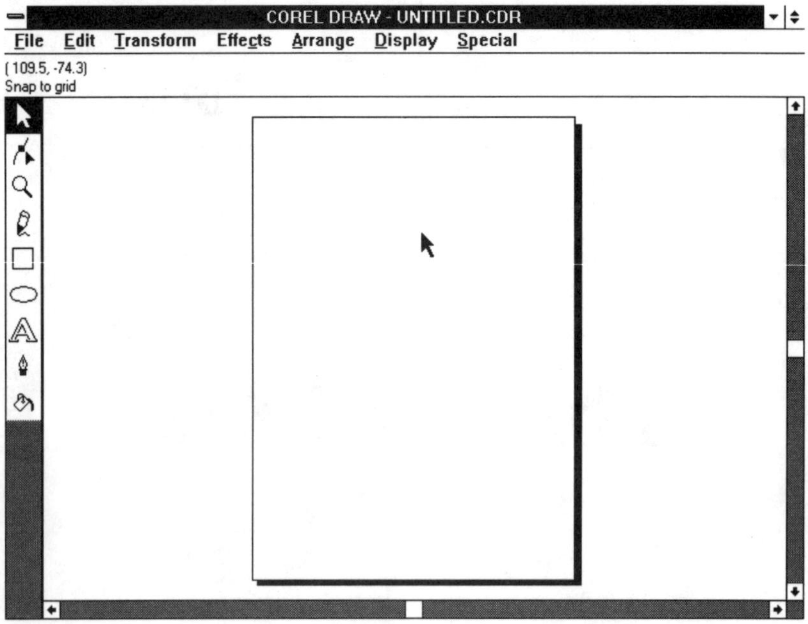

Figure 2-1. The Corel DRAW! Toolbox Along the Left Side of the Window.

The Pick Tool

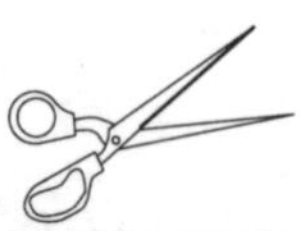

SHORTCUT

You use the Pick Tool to manipulate and select graphics on the screen (Figure 2-2). This tool is selected by default when you start CorelDRAW!, and it is probably the tool you will use most of all. You will create graphics using this tool. To move quickly to the Pick Tool, if you have any other tool selected, press the space key.

Figure 2-2. The Pick Tool.

Using the Pick Tool

The basic use of this arrow-shaped tool is to "select" an object on the page to perform some operation on it. It may be to delete it, resize it, move it, color it, or some other function. You must select an object, using this tool, before you can perform any of these operations.

Using the Pick Tool to select a graphic

Selecting a graphic is very easy. First, decide which graphic you would like to select. Then position the mouse cursor somewhere over the outline of this graphic, and click the mouse button once as shown below:

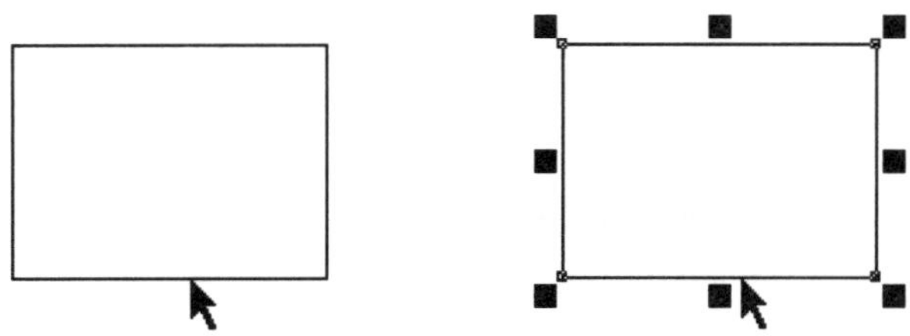

That graphic is now selected — denoted by the eight black boxes (called selection handles) around the outside edge of the graphic.

This can sometimes be a very precise task. You must be exact in where you are placing the mouse cursor on screen, particularly when there are several graphics on display, that may be very close together. If you have drawn several graphics on the screen, and you select one of them, the status line displays only the dimensions of the one you selected. Figure 2-3 shows a screen with several graphics.

Caution: If you need to delete one of several graphics on a screen make sure that you have selected the correct one to delete, or you might delete another one.

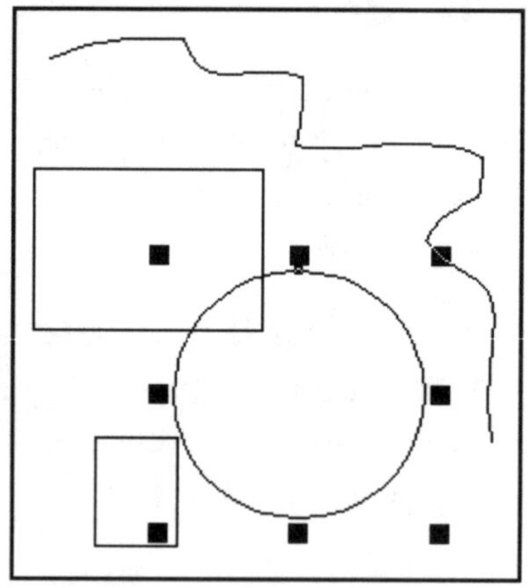

Figure 2-3. A Screen with Several Graphics.

After selection, a graphic has eight handles around it. Any command then used only affects the selected graphic.

If you want to delete that graphic, it is simple. First, select a graphic that you would like to remove from the page. Then, choose the *Clear* command from the **Edit** menu (Figure 2-4).

The graphic is immediately removed from the page.

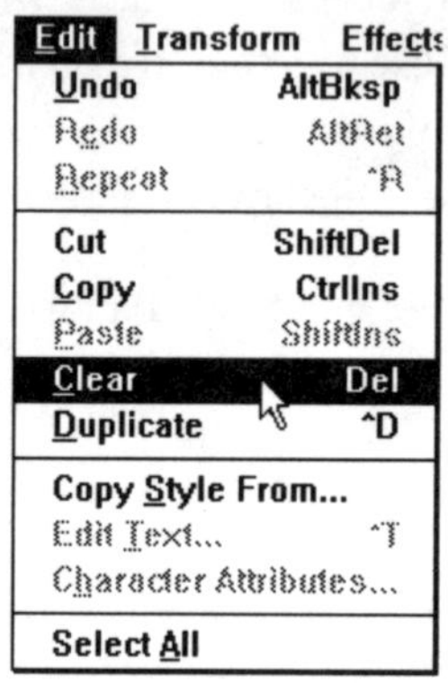

Figure 2-4. The Clear Command from the Edit Menu.

Once you select a graphic, you can click on and select any other graphic. When you select a new graphic, any previous graphic that was selected becomes "deselected" (the selection handles around it are removed).

Other methods for selecting graphics

There is a simple method that allows you to select more than one graphic at a time. Choose the Pick Tool and select the first graphic as described above. Then, hold down the [⇧ Shift] key on your keyboard, keep it held down, and click on another graphic. This graphic, as well as the original graphic, will be selected.

The next method is very handy for selecting either large groups of graphics, or individual graphics. It involves drawing an imaginary box around one or more graphics. This method is described in conjunction with illustrations.

In this method, you draw an imaginary rectangle around the graphic or graphics you wish to select. To do this, position the mouse cursor (with the Pick Tool selected) outside the top left-hand corner of the graphic like this:

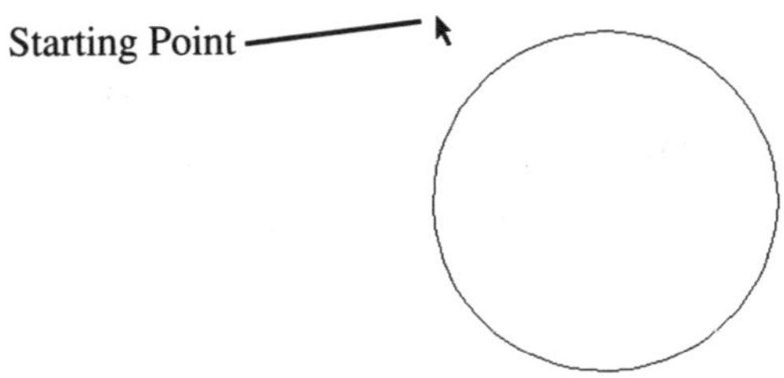

Then, hold down the mouse button, and pretend you are drawing a rectangle that will totally enclose the graphic like this:

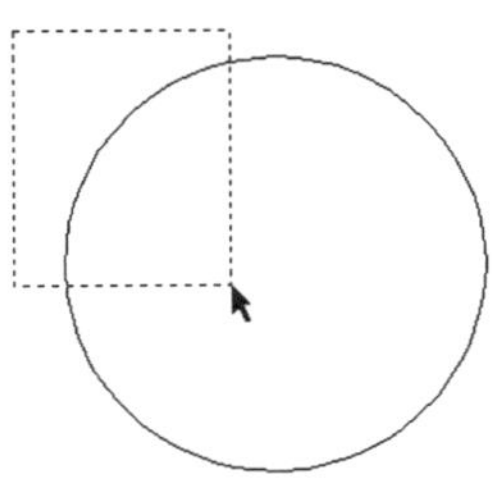

Note that the dotted line is displayed as you hold down the mouse button and move the mouse — much like the line that would be displayed if you were drawing a rectangle. This dotted rectangle indicates the area in which all graphics will be selected. Make sure that the imaginary rectangle you draw completely encloses the graphic(s) you would like to select like this:

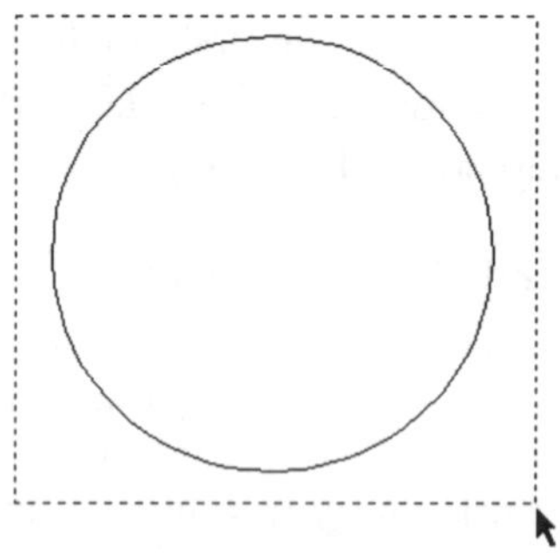

Note: This approach works equally well for multiple graphics. Just make sure that the rectangle you draw covers all of the graphics to be selected.

Release the mouse button when you have totally enclosed the graphic within the dotted rectangle. The graphic will then be selected with the selection handles around it. This is called the Marquee selection method. This is how the selection handles look:

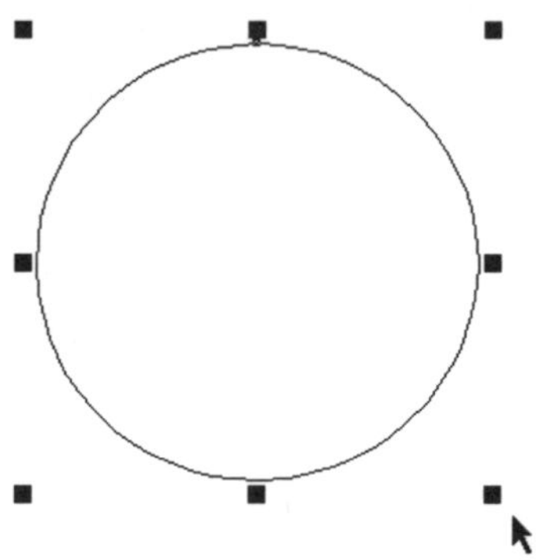

You can select multiple graphics, as mentioned before, by using this same method (Figure 2-5).

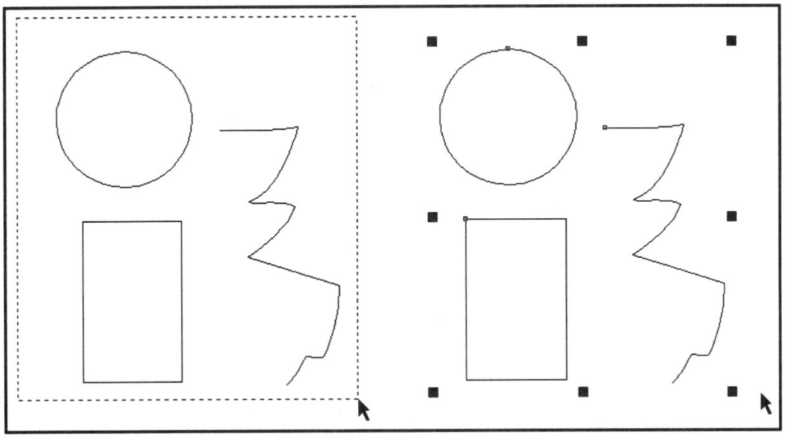

Figure 2-5. Selecting Multiple Graphics (Left) and Selection after Releasing the Mouse (Right).

Note that there are selection handles around multiple graphics. The Status Line, instead of reading "Ellipse" or "Rectangle," now reads "3 objects selected."

Moving objects

You move an object by holding the mouse down on the object with the Pick Tool selected, and dragging it to the new position. If you want to move more than one object at a time, select them as shown in Figure 2-5, and hold the mouse down on any of the objects, and drag it to the new position. The mouse turns into a four-sided arrow and, after a second or two, a copy of the object you are moving is displayed in the dotted frame that moves with the mouse like this:

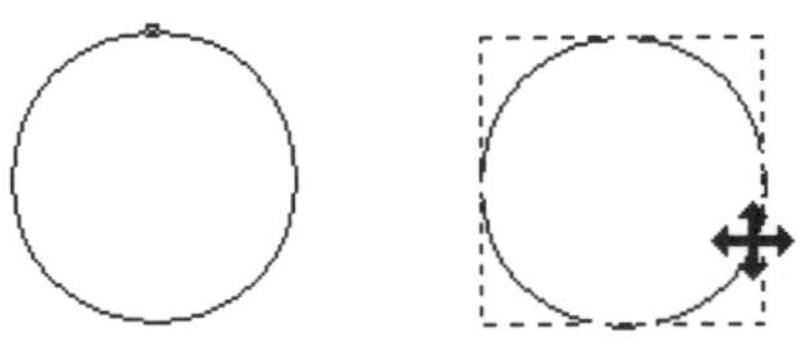

If you keep your finger on the mouse, you can move the object around like this to see how it will look in different positions.

Resizing objects

You can also use the Pick Tool to resize objects. You do this by holding the mouse down on one of the eight selection handles surrounding an object until it becomes a crosshair like this:

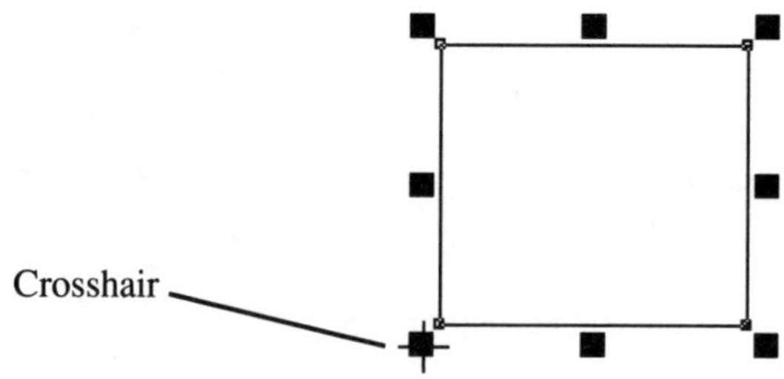

Then to resize the object in proportion, so as not to distort it, drag one of the four corner handles and release the mouse like this:

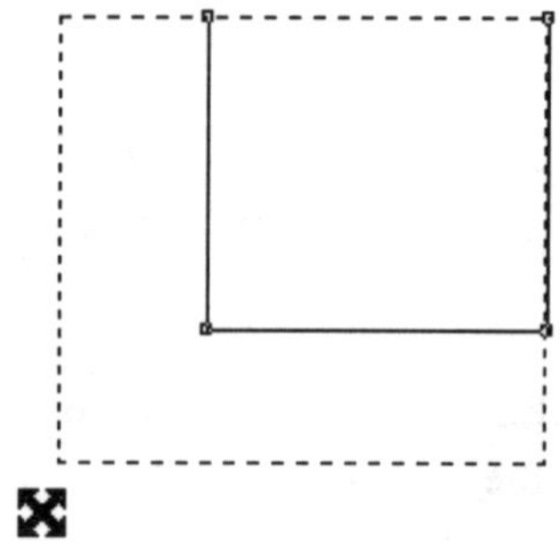

The following illustration shows the object being resized horizontally, using the middle handle on the left vertical side. This obviously distorts the graphic.

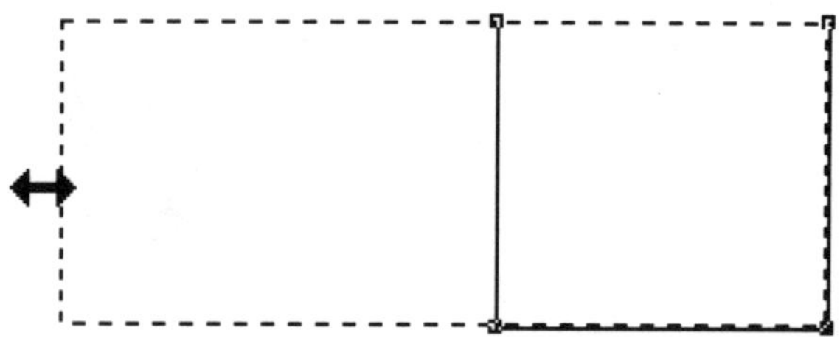

Rotating and skewing objects

You use the Pick Tool to rotate and skew objects. To do this, click once on a selected object, or twice on an unselected one. If you do this accurately, you will get the Rotate and Skew handles as shown in the following illustration:

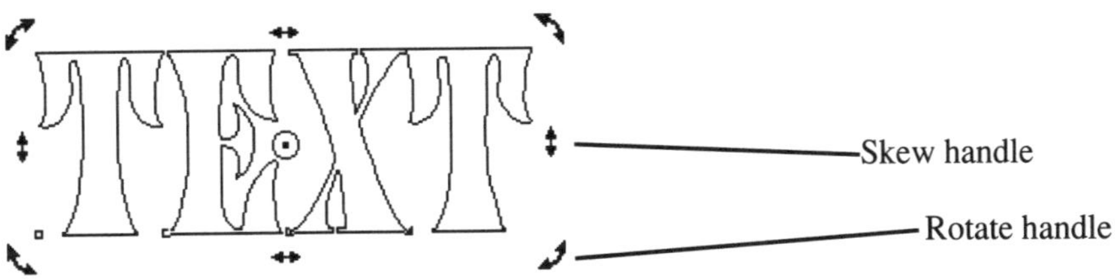

Hold the mouse down on one of the four corner rotation handles and drag it clockwise or counterclockwise to rotate the object like this:

Position the mouse over the center of rotation until you see a crosshair. Hold the mouse down and drag it to a new position like this:

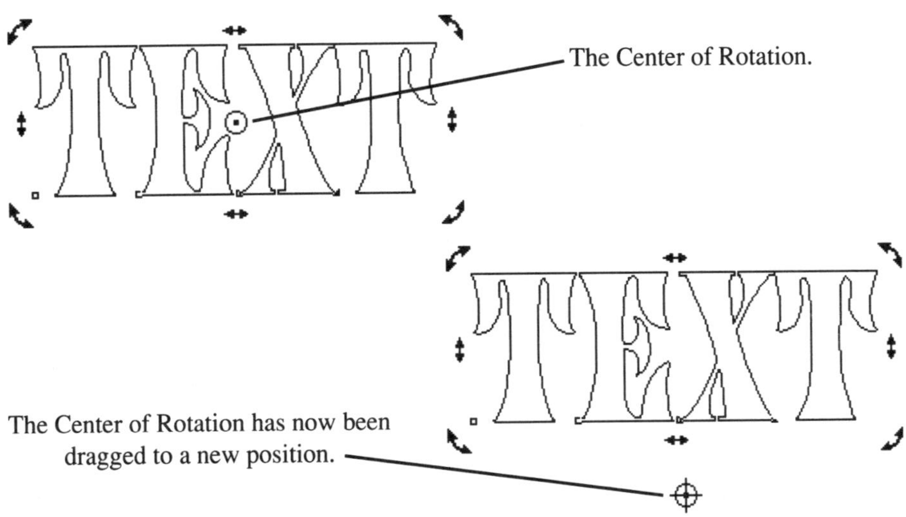

You can also alter the object to rotate on a different axis like this:

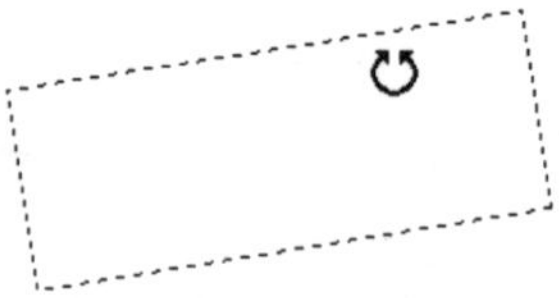

The four handles in between the rotation handles are for skewing. You can hold the mouse down and drag it to the left or right (for the horizontal skew handle), or up or down (for the vertical skew handle), to skew the object. The following illustration shows the mouse positioned over the right skew handle (left) and text skewed (right) after holding down the mouse and dragging.

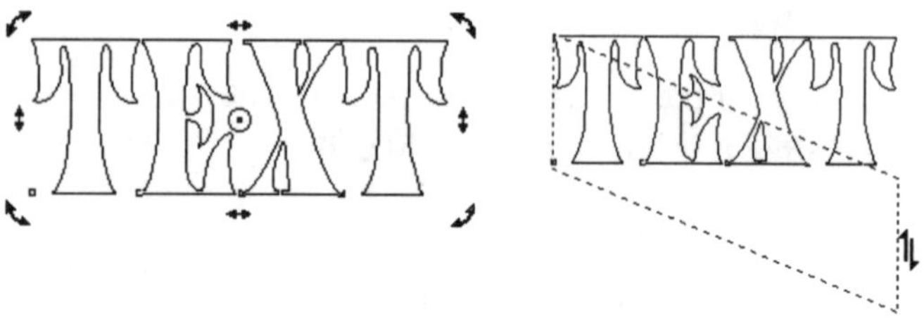

This illustration shows the reformatted text in a skewed position.

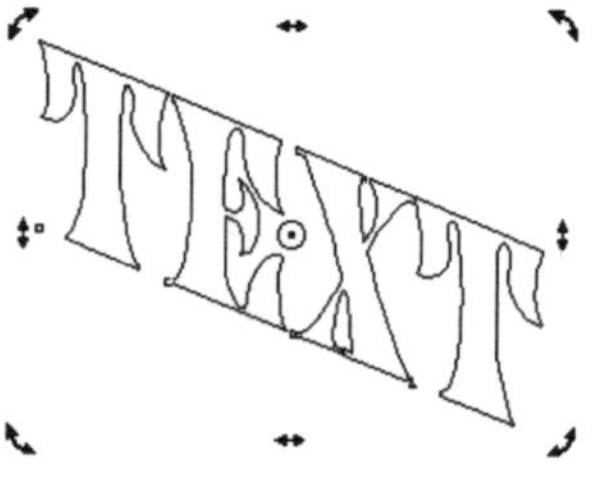

The Status Line always tells you the correct proportions, measurements, positions, and degrees, of objects you are skewing, rotating, resizing, and moving with the Pick Tool.

If you press the [+] key on the numeric keypad while resizing, rotating, skewing and mirroring, you leave behind an original of the object.

GOOD IDEA

The Rectangle Tool □

You use The Rectangle Tool, [F6], to create rectangles and squares of any type on the screen (Figure 2-6). This tool is simple to use.

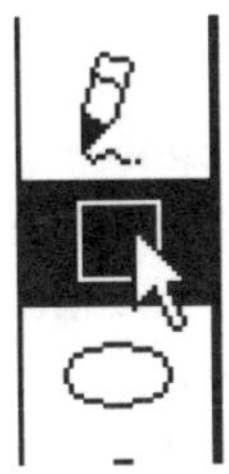

Figure 2-6. The Rectangle Tool.

You must select a tool to use it. It is simple to select a tool. Move the mouse cursor over the tool you need, and click the left mouse button once. The tool will be highlighted in reverse video, indicating that it is now selected (Figures 2-6 or 2-7).

After you select the Rectangle Tool, you find that the mouse cursor changes shape as it is moved over the working area. It now looks like a crosshair indicating that you have selected the Rectangle Tool. You can now create a rectangle on the screen (Figures 2-7 and 2-8).

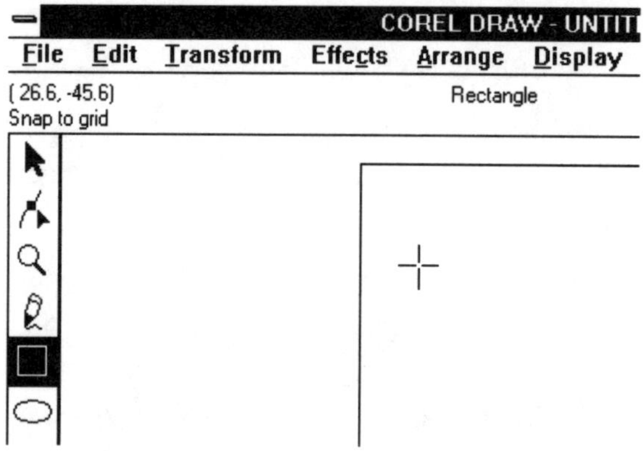

Figure 2-7. The Rectangle Tool in the Shape of a Crosshair After Selection.

To create a rectangle, make sure the mouse cursor is positioned over the working area, and hold the mouse button down. Move the mouse cursor slowly in any direction. As you do, you can see that you are creating a rectangle on the screen. When this rectangle is the size you want, release the mouse button. The program displays the rectangle on the screen like this:

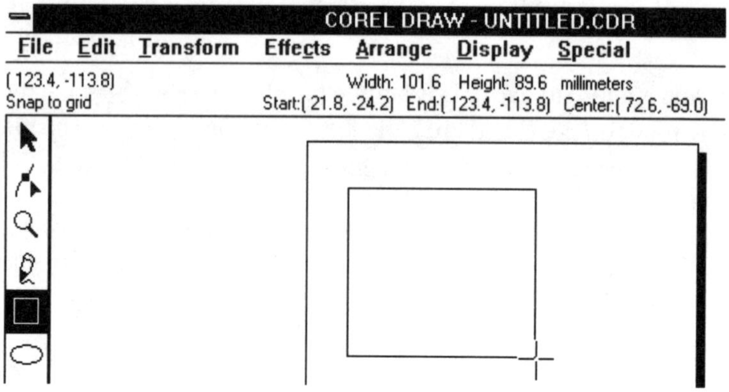

After you release the mouse button, the Status Line reflects the size of the graphic and its center, and shows exactly what type of graphic it is (Figure 2-8).

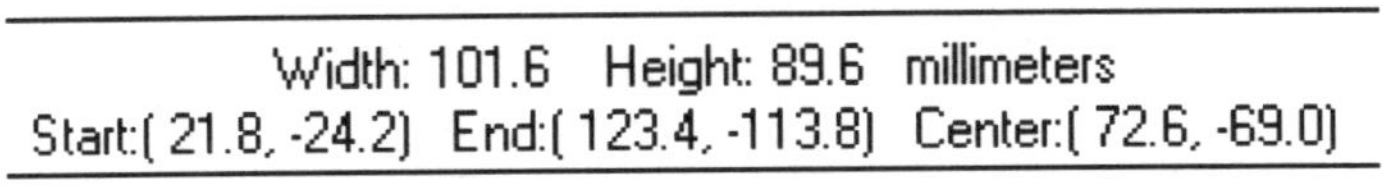

Figure 2-8. Rectangle Size Displayed on the Status Line.

Once you have created a rectangle, and the name "Rectangle" is in the Status Line, the rectangle on the screen has a small dot in each corner.

You can create as many rectangles as you like. The Rectangle Tool remains selected after you create a rectangle, allowing you to immediately add more rectangles to the page, if you desire.

The Ellipse Tool

The Ellipse Tool, F7, works like the Rectangle Tool. Select the tool (Figure 2-9), and move the mouse cursor out onto the page. The mouse cursor remains as a crosshair.

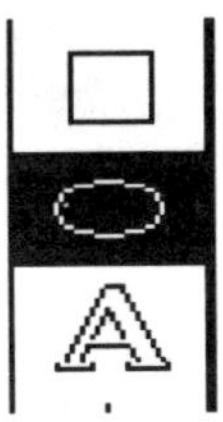

Figure 2-9. The Selected Ellipse Tool.

Draw some ellipses using the same technique as described for drawing rectangles. Hold down the mouse button with the cursor on the page somewhere, move the mouse, and release the mouse button. You have created an ellipse on screen. Watch the Status Line again. It constantly reflects exactly the size and position of the ellipse while you create it, as shown in the following illustration:

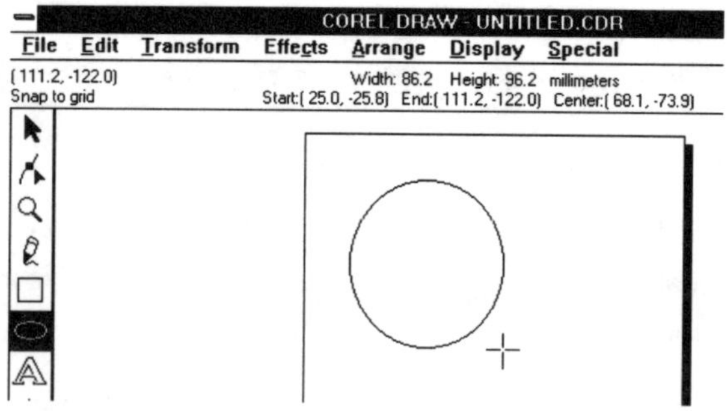

The Pencil Tool

The Pencil Tool, F5, (Figure 2-10) works similarly to the tools described previously. However, you can use this tool in one of two ways. The way in which you use this tool depends on exactly what you want to draw.

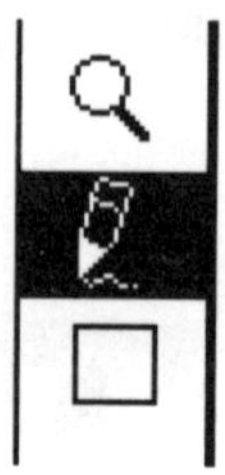

Figure 2-10. The Pencil Tool for Creating Curved and Straight Lines.

The two options for drawing with the Pencil Tool are Freehand Mode and Bezier Mode. You can swap between the alternate drawing modes in the *Preferences* dialog box available from the **Special** menu. From this dialog box, click on the *Lines & Curves* button to activate the associated dialog box. The *Drawing Mode* command in this dialog box lets you select either Bezier or Freehand. The explanations follow.

Freehand Mode

Use the Pencil Tool to create freehand drawings, much like you use a pencil or pen (Figure 2-11). However, in this mode, you can also use this tool to draw perfectly straight lines or graphics that are constructed from a series of straight lines.

To draw curved lines in Freehand Mode, perform these tasks:

Select the Pencil Tool by clicking on it. The Status Line now tells you that you are drawing in Freehand Mode. (The mouse cursor becomes a crosshair as you move it onto the page.) Move the mouse cursor out onto the page, and hold the mouse button down where you want to start drawing a freehand line.

Move the mouse freely in any direction (although fairly slowly), and change the direction as you wish. When you have created a line of the desired length, release the mouse button (Figure 2-11).

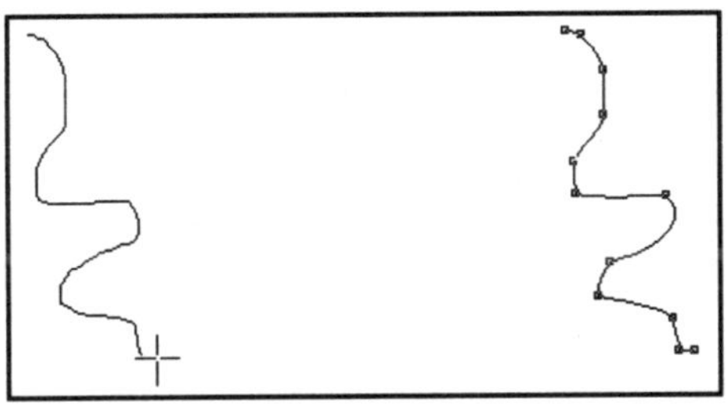

Figure 2-11. A Freehand Curve Before (Left) and After (Right) the Mouse Button Release.

You have created a freehand line. This line is plotted as a series of points by CorelDRAW!. You can edit these points later using other CorelDRAW! tools.

To draw straight lines in Freehand Mode, perform these tasks:

Select the Pencil Tool. Move the mouse cursor out onto the page. Click and release the mouse button once when the mouse cursor is positioned where you want to start drawing the line.

Move the mouse cursor where you would like the line to end. You will see that a line stretches from where you initially clicked the mouse to the current position of the mouse. To keep drawing straight lines that are connected, double-click the mouse at each point where the line is to change direction. The following illustration shows how a straight line looks (left) and how connected lines look (right).

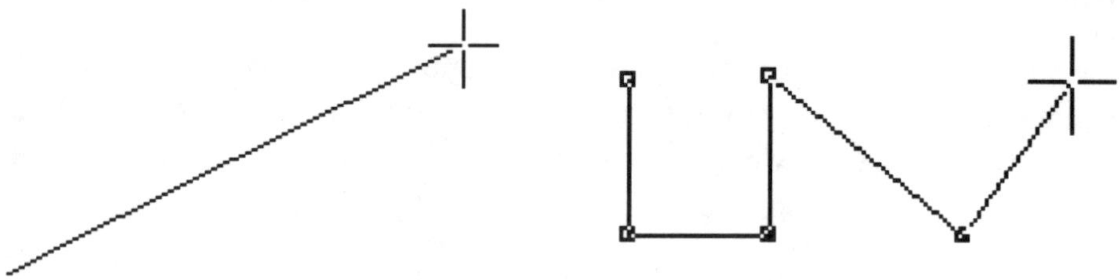

Bezier Mode

You can also use the Pencil Tool to draw lines in Bezier Mode. This lets you determine where nodes are placed along your line. To draw in Bezier Mode, you must select the Bezier Mode option from the *Preferences* command in the **Special** menu. After you make the changes in the *Preferences* dialog box and select the Pencil Tool, the Status Line displays “Drawing in Bezier Mode.”

To draw curved lines in Bezier Mode, perform these tasks:

Hold the mouse down on the page where you want to begin the drawing, and the program will display a node. Begin dragging the mouse and you will see two control points moving away from this node in adverse directions like this:

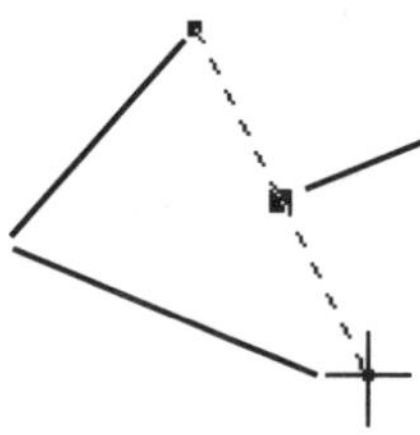

The distance between the control points, which is controlled by your dragging the mouse, determines the height and depth of the curve. The angle of the control points determines the slope of the curve.

Once you have maneuvered the control points to the desired angle and position, release the mouse. Now move the mouse to where you want the next node or the end of the line to be.

Hold the mouse down in the new position, and there will now be a curved line between the two nodes as shown below:

Keeping your finger on the mouse, drag it again so that the control points move in opposite directions like this:

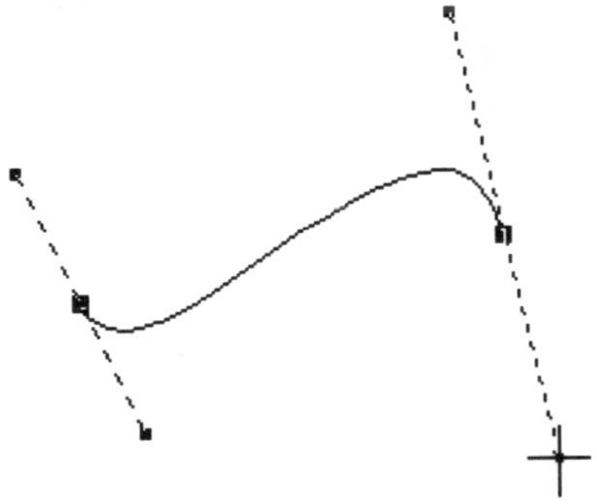

Release your finger from the mouse and click it where you want the next line to be, and another curved line will join the two nodes like this:

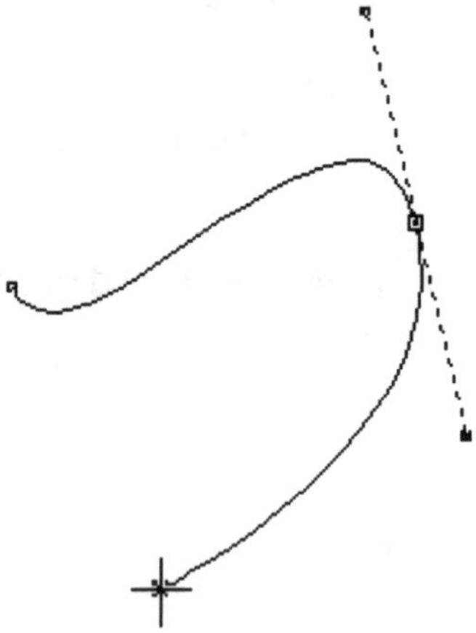

Note: Remember that the curve and angle of the line are determined by the placement of the control points.

Use the above steps to create any shape you like. To close off an object, click on the node you used to begin the drawing. To start drawing another object, press the [space] key twice, and you can place another node on the page ready to draw a new object.

To draw straight lines in Bezier Mode, perform these tasks:

Click the mouse once on the page without holding it down, or you will draw a curved line. The following illustration shows the node that is displayed when you click the Mouse in Bezier Mode.

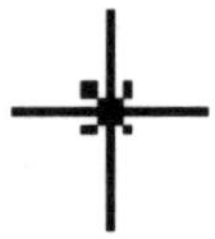

Move the mouse to where you want the line to go to, and click the mouse again. There will now be a straight line between the two points that you clicked the mouse like this:

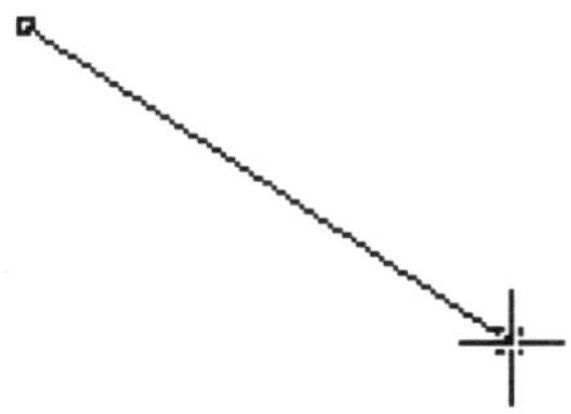

After the second click, move the mouse to the next position, and click again. You can do this as many times as you like. To close off an object, click the mouse on the first node of the object.

If you have clicked the mouse at the wrong point at any time, you can use the *Undo* command from the **Edit** menu. To begin drawing a new object, press the [space] key twice, and the next click you make with the Pencil Tool will not be connected with the previous one.

AutoTracing Bitmaps

The Pencil Tool automatically traces a bitmap or scanned image. When a bitmap is traced, it becomes an actual object that you can edit like any other CorelDRAW! object. You can trace bitmaps in CorelDRAW! and CorelTRACE!.

Tracing bitmaps is beneficial because a bitmap suffers in quality when resized, but a traced image does not. You can edit a traced image in CorelDRAW!, but not a bitmap.

To trace an image, first import it into CorelDRAW!. Scanned images usually have a file extension of .TIF or .PCX. Make sure the *For Tracing* option is selected in the first *Import* dialog box.

Once the bitmap is on your page, you might find it easier to magnify the area you are working on with the Zoom Tool. Select the frame surrounding the bitmap with the Pick Tool, as you would select any other object in CorelDRAW! The eight selection handles will appear around the frame like this:

Now activate the Pencil Tool to automatically activate the AutoTrace feature. Note that the cursor changes to a cross on its side like this:

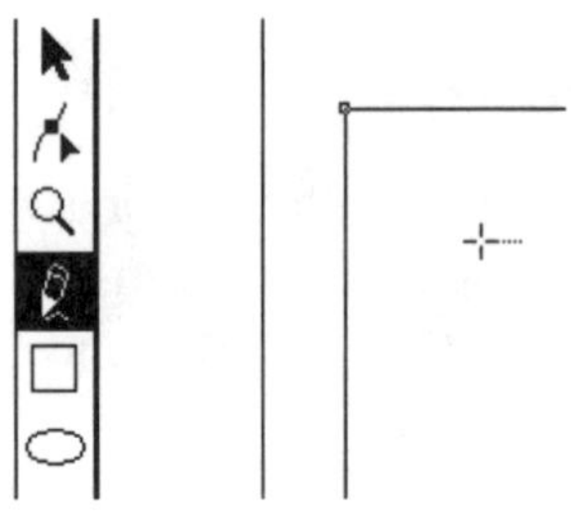

Place this crosshair just to the left of the area of the bitmap you want to trace like this:

Click the mouse. CorelDRAW! will now trace the area to the right of the crosshair like this:

Continue to click the mouse to the left of all sections of the bitmap you want to trace until the drawing looks like this:

Sometimes when you click the mouse, it does not trace anything. When this happens, move the crosshair closer to the section you are trying to trace as shown here:

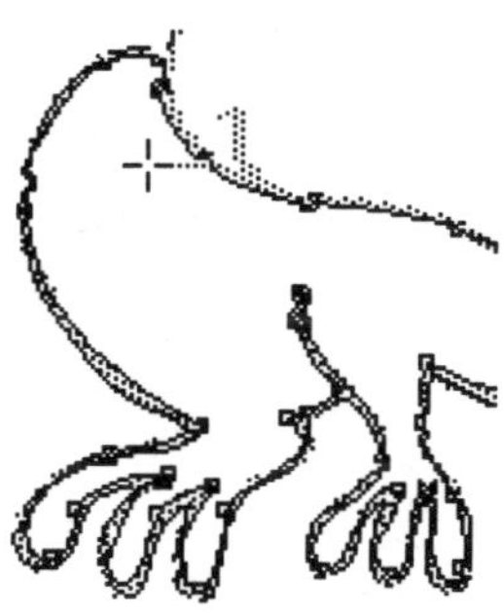

The bitmap is now fully traced.

When you have finished tracing the bitmap, you can delete it by selecting the frame with the Pick Tool and pressing the [delete] key. The following illustration shows the remaining traced image after the bitmap is deleted.

The traced lines will still be there after the bitmap is deleted. There is also a command in the **Display** menu called *Show Bitmaps*. This lets you hide the bitmap to speed up drawing time. Use this command if you do not want to delete the bitmap, but just want to hide it. Now, you can fill, edit, move, and manipulate the traced bitmap like any CorelDRAW! drawing.

If you have a bitmap that you want to crop before you trace it, you can crop it with the Node Tool. Activate the Node Tool and click it on the frame containing the bitmap. Eight cropping handles will be displayed around the frame. If you hold the mouse on one of these cropping handles, and drag the mouse in the desired position, you will crop or cut off the section of the bitmap concerned. Furthermore, you can rotate, skew, move, and resize bitmaps using the Pick Tool.

The Node or Shape Tool

The Node Tool, F10, is below the Pick Tool. You use this tool (often called the Shape Tool) to manipulate objects. On freehand-drawn and curved objects, you change the object's shape through its nodes and control points. Once you select a line with the Node Tool, the nodes become larger (Figure 2-12). This makes them easier to select and maneuver.

When used on text, this tool interactively kerns text and text blocks. It also maneuvers individual letters away from the other text. Additionally, it can change the attributes of a single character within a word or block of text.

The exercises in Part 2 of this book cover the uses of the Node Tool.

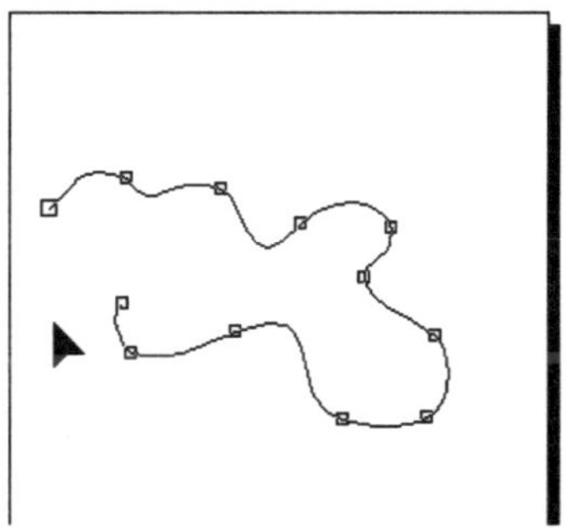

Figure 2-12. Use of the Node Tool for Manipulating Freehand Lines and Curved Objects.

You can select each section of a freehand drawn line separately by clicking on it with the Node Tool like this:

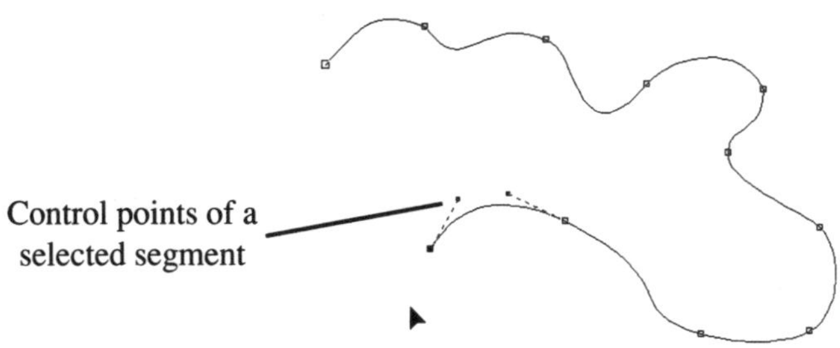

Once you select a segment of a line, the associated nodes of the line will have control points highlighted. You can change the shape of the line by holding down the Node Tool on one of these control points, and dragging it in the desired position like this:

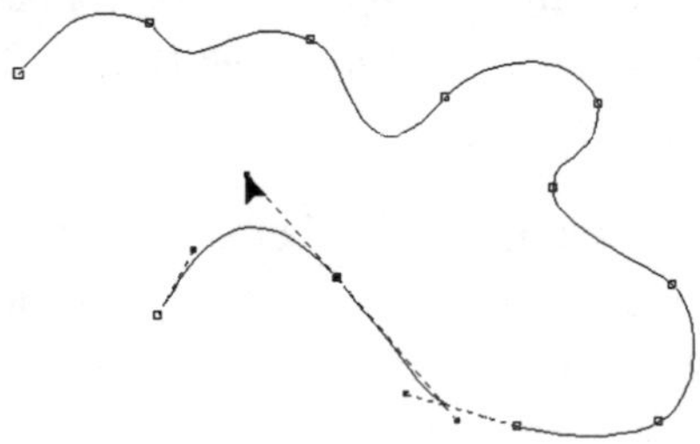

You can also select the actual nodes. To select one node, simply click inside it with the Node Tool and it takes on a black fill. To select more than one node, use the Node Tool to draw a frame around the nodes you would like to select like this:

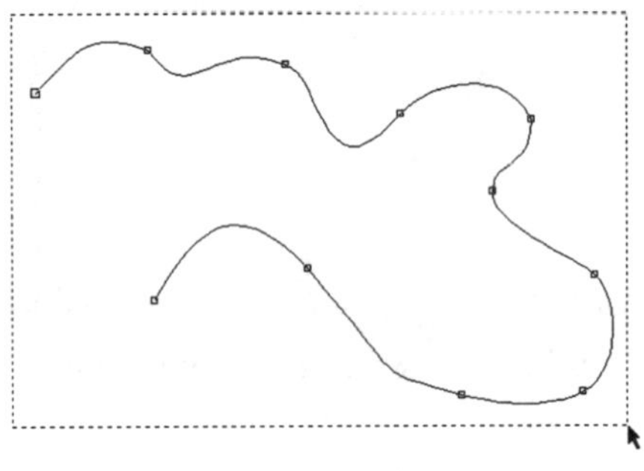

All nodes are black after the selection process like this:

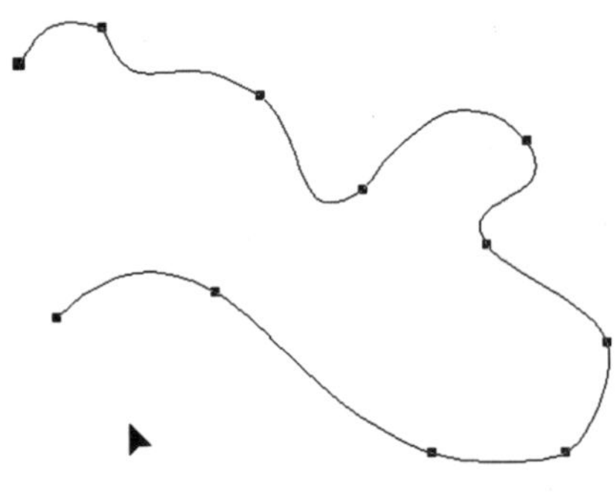

To change the attributes of a selected node or nodes, you need to activate the *Node Edit* dialog box (Figure 2-13). You do this by clicking twice on a node with the Node Tool. Once the program displays this dialog box, you can add and delete nodes, change a line to a curve, smooth out a line, or straighten it.

The Node Edit Dialog Box

Figure 2-13. The Node Edit Dialog Box.

Figures 2-14 through 2-22 explain the options available in the *Node Edit* dialog box. Figure 2-14 shows a node that is selected (left) and deleted (right).

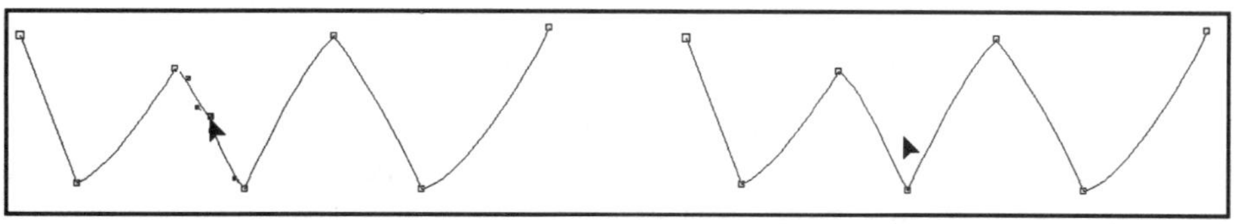

Figure 2-14. Removing Nodes with the Delete Option.

If you choose Break from the dialog box, the selected node or nodes become two separate nodes that you can manipulate individually (Figure 2-15).

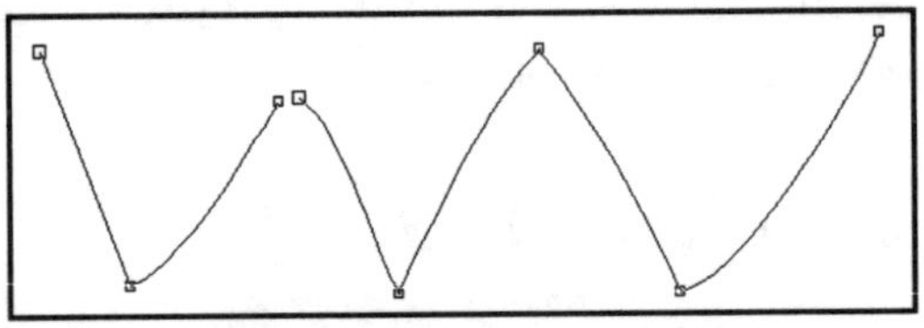

Figure 2-15. Two Separate Nodes that Can Be Manipulated Individually.

You can turn a curved line into a straight by using the *toLine* command. To achieve this, select the line you wish to straighten, or the node which follows it, by double-clicking with the Node Tool. Then select the *toLine* command.

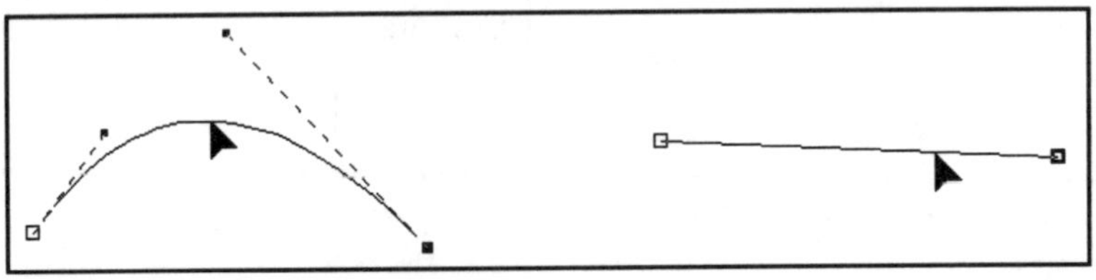

Figure 2-16. Using the toLine Command to Turn a Curved Line (Left) into a Straight Line (Right).

The *Cusp* command changes the attributes of the selected node, so that the two segments on either side of the node can be moved independently from each other. On selecting this command, no apparent change occurs with the line until you begin to manipulate the affected segments.

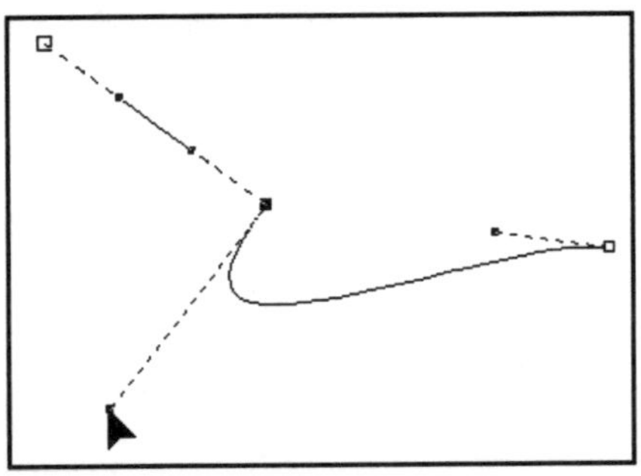

Figure 2-17. Using the Cusp Command.

The *Align* command activates the *Node Align* dialog box. You can only use this option when more than one node is selected. From the *Node Align* dialog box, you can align selected nodes horizontally, vertically, or through the control points. In (a) of Figure 2-18 two nodes are selected, in (b) the *Align Horizontal* option in the *Node Align* dialog box is chosen, and after clicking on OK, the two selected nodes have aligned horizontally (c).

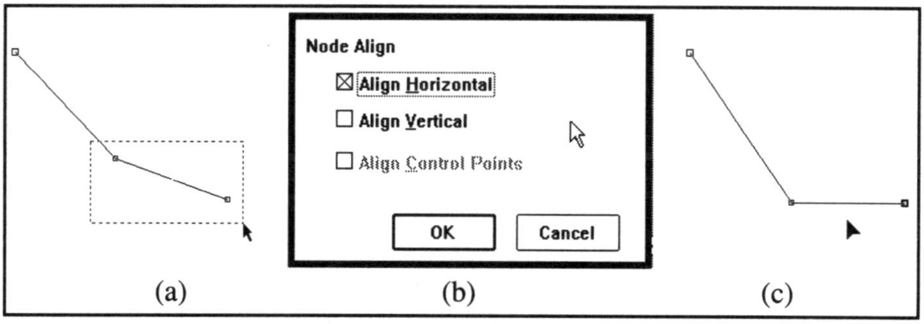

Figure 2-18. Using the Align Command.

The *Add* command places another node along the selected segment

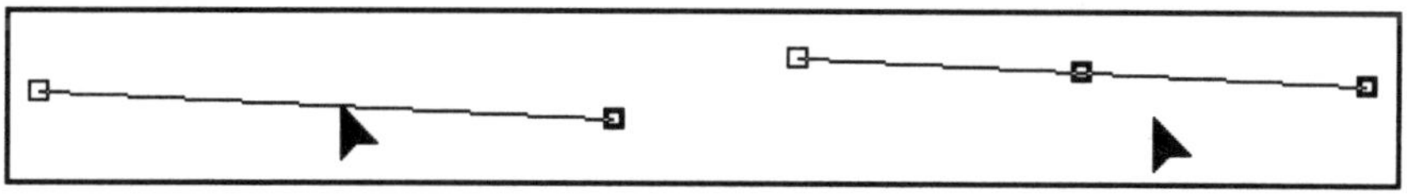

Figure 2-19. Before (Left) and After (Right) the Add Command.

The *Join* command joins two end nodes at the end and beginning of a drawing. You select them both, and double-click in one of the selected nodes (Figure 2-20a). Once the *Node Edit* dialog box is on screen, you select the *Join* command. The result is shown in Figure 2-20b.

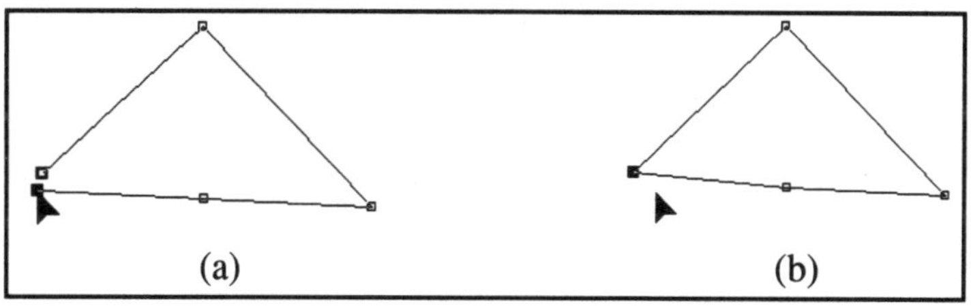

Figure 2-20. Using the Join Command.

The *toCurve* command gives a selected segment or node curved attributes (Figure 2-21). In other words, a straight line (a) is allotted two control points, one from each node that allow you to curve the line (b).

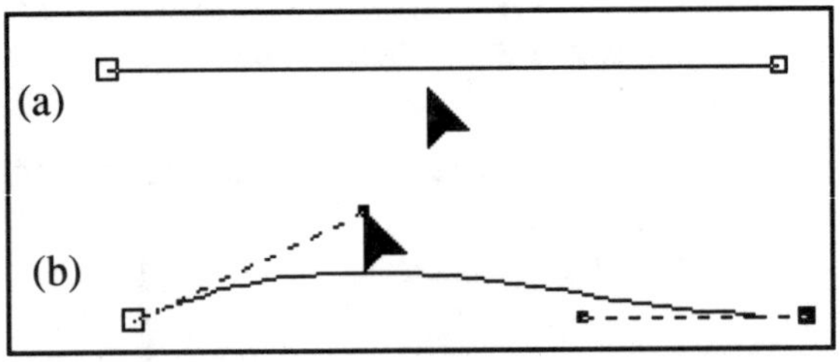

Figure 2-21. Using the toCurve Command.

The *Smooth* command turns all selected segments or nodes that end in a sharp point to smooth. Also the sections of line on either side of a Smooth node are affected when manipulating the control points. This is the opposite to *Cusp*, where either side of the node can be affected independently.

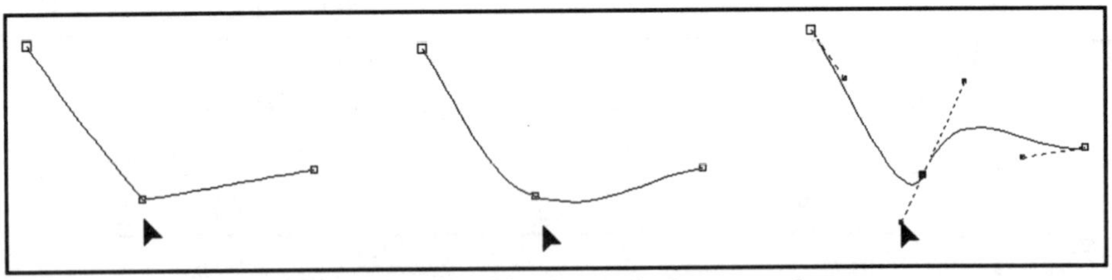

Figure 2-22. The Smooth Command.

The *Symmet* command gives a selected node and its segments symmetrical attributes (Figure 2-23). The two segments on either side of the symmetrical node move in opposite directions and in equal lengths. Only curved lines can become symmetrical. This option is similar to the *Smooth* option, but the control points of a symmetrical node move in opposite directions and in equal lengths. In the previous example, the middle node is the *Symmet* one, and the control points are the same distance from the node, but at adverse angles. This causes the lines on either side of the node to move in equal proportions but in opposite directions.

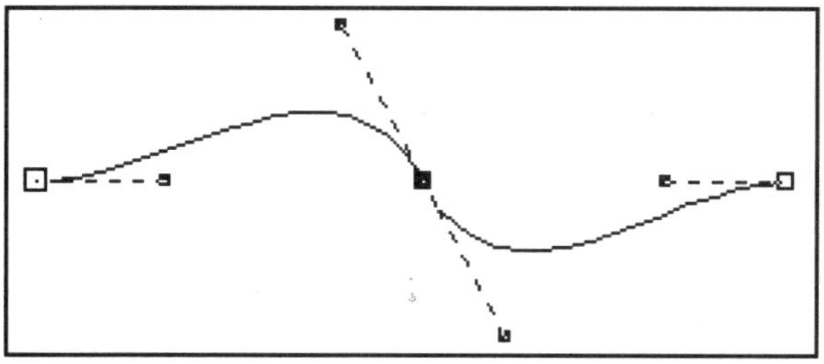

Figure 2-23. The Symmet Command.

You can also use the Node Tool to move individual text pieces away from a text string (Figure 2-24). By holding the Node Tool down on a letter node and dragging the mouse in any direction, the letter follows. To move several characters at once, simply select more than one by clicking inside the nodes, holding the mouse on one of the selected nodes, and dragging them away. Holding down the Ctrl key, while moving the letters, limits the movement to the nearest baseline.

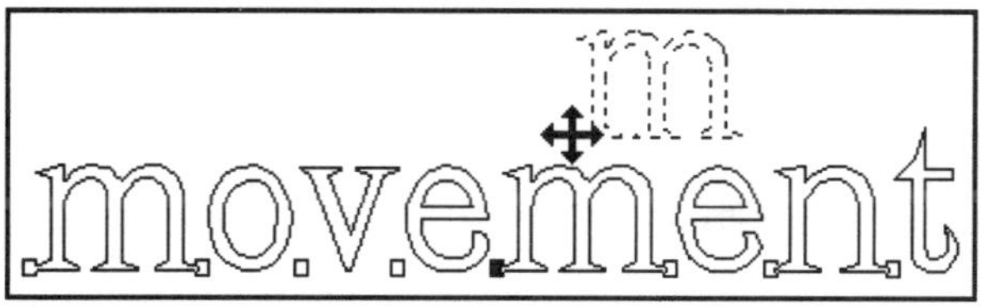

Figure 2-24. Text Nodes while using the Node Tool.

Whenever you select a piece of a text or text string with the Node Tool, it will have markers at the baseline at either end of the string. The marker to the right (right facing arrow) controls inter-character spacing. Moving the mouse over this marker changes it to a crosshair. Holding down the mouse button changes this crosshair to a two-sided arrow; dragging it to the right or left, increases or decreases the amount of spacing between the letters of the selected text string (Figure 2-25). For inter-word spacing changes, hold your finger on the Ctrl key while you are dragging the right-hand marker.

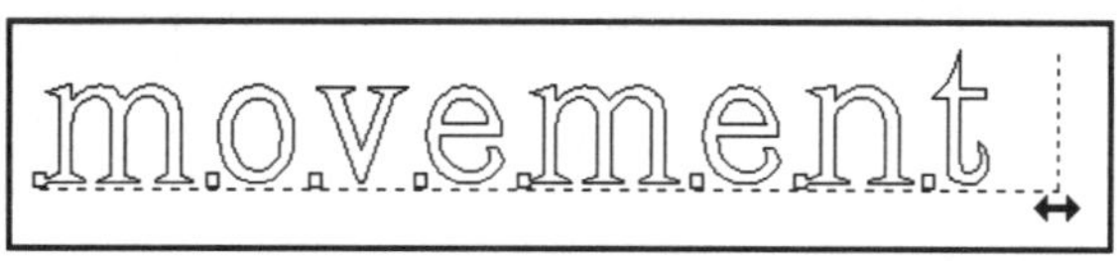

Figure 2-25. Dragging the Right-Hand Marker.

The marker to the left of the text string (down facing arrow) controls the inter-line spacing, and is effective only when there is more than one line in the text block. Holding the mouse down on this marker, and dragging it up or down, increases or decreases the spacing between the lines of the selected text block (Figure 2-26).

Figure 2-26. Increasing the Inter-Line Spacing.

The Zoom Tool

The Zoom Tool changes the view of your page. This tool lets you magnify any section of your page, or instantly swap from actual size to a view that shows whatever is on the page or to the original whole-page view.

The first choice from the Zoom Tool fly-out is the option with the Plus symbol (Figure 2-27). To use this tool, select it, then hold your finger on the mouse and draw a frame or box around the section of your page you would like to magnify. Once you release your finger from the mouse, the section inside the frame you have just drawn takes up the whole screen. You will use this first tool extensively throughout the exercises contained in this book. To activate this first option in the Zoom Tool fly-out, press the F2 key. This specific tool is discussed in detail in the exercises in Part 2 of this book.

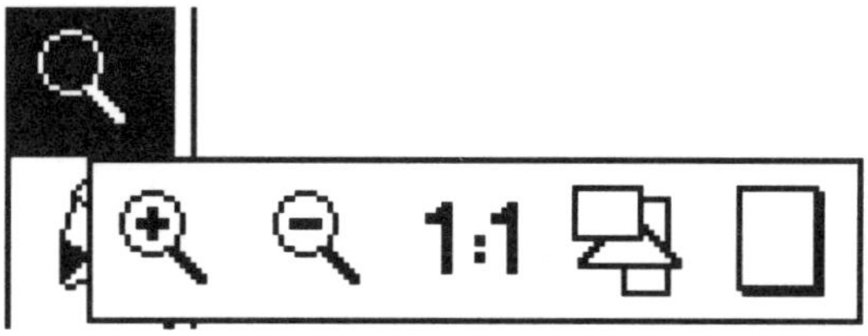

Figure 2-27. The Zoom Tool Fly-Out.

There are five options from the zoom tool fly-out. They are as follows:

This option magnifies selected sections of the page.

This option changes the view size on your screen to approximately the size the page will print.

1:1

On selecting this tool, the page returns to the view where you were previously before you magnified a section.

This is the Fit In Window option and it displays every object you have placed or drawn on the screen.

The whole page shows if you select this last option.

The Text Tool

You use the Text Tool to place text onto the page. You select it by clicking the mouse on the icon in the Toolbox, or by pressing the F8 key (Figure 2-28). Once you select this tool, click the current icon on the page, or draw a frame with your finger on the mouse where you would like the text to begin. The placement of the text is not important at first because you move it once it is on the page.

Once you have clicked the Text Tool on the page, the *Text* dialog box is displayed. This dialog box is for typing in the required text and changing things such as font and point size. The *Text* entry dialog box is discussed in detail in **Chapter 4: Text Input Capabilities**.

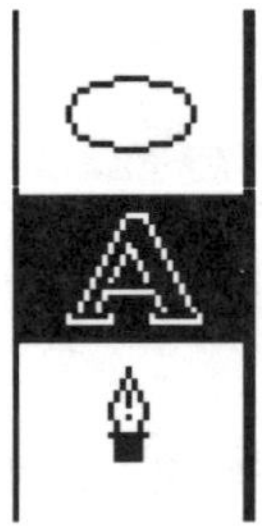

Figure 2-28. The Selected Text Tool.

Tips for Creating Simple Graphics

There are several keys that you can use to help create a graphic. You hold these keys down as you create any one of these graphics, causing these objects to be created with slightly different properties.

If, for example, you want to create an ellipse, follow these steps:

1. Select the Ellipse Tool.
2. Move the mouse cursor out onto the page.
3. Hold down the ⇧ Shift key.
4. Hold down the mouse button to create the ellipse on screen.
5. Release the mouse button after creating the ellipse.
6. Release the ⇧ Shift key.

Holding down different keys as you create a graphic causes these results:

The Shift key: If you hold down the Shift key, when you are using the Ellipse Tool or the Rectangle Tool to create a graphic, that graphic will be created from the center outwards, rather than from a corner. In other words, the spot where you initially click the mouse becomes the center of the ellipse or rectangle, rather than a corner.

If you hold down the Shift key, when you are using the Freehand Tool to create a curve (keep the mouse button held down as you draw), it has the effect of letting you backtrack over a line, and deletes parts of the line as you do this. If you release the Shift key, while still holding the mouse button down, you can continue drawing.

The Ctrl key: If you hold down the Ctrl key, as you draw a rectangle or an ellipse, you can draw a square or a circle. It has the effect of a constrain key, forcing a perfect square (as opposed to a rectangle) or a circle (as opposed to an ellipse) to be created.

If you hold down the Ctrl key while drawing straight lines (using the Freehand Tool, clicking once and moving the mouse), all straight lines that are created snap to fifteen degree increments on the screen making it far easier to create perpendicular or horizontal lines. You can hold down the Shift key and the Ctrl key in conjunction, if you wish. Both results occur together.

Mirroring Objects

To mirror an object, hold the mouse down on one of the middle selection handles until it becomes a crosshair. Drag the mouse across the object completely pass it, and release the mouse.

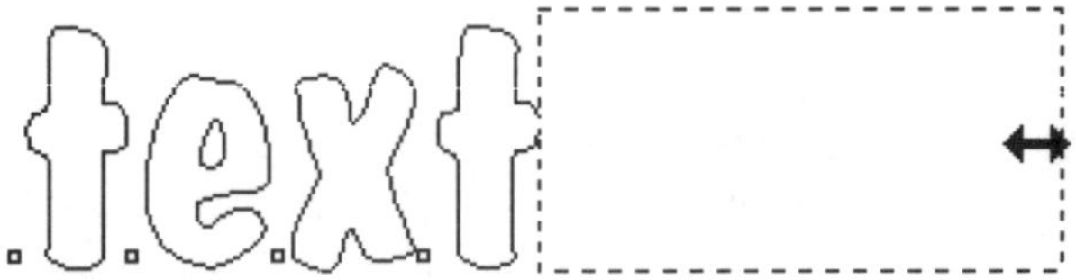

The text will now be mirrored like this:

To get a reflection the same size as the original, hold down the Ctrl key while you are dragging the mouse. When using the Ctrl key, you must release the mouse before the Ctrl key, so it works properly. To get a perfect reflection, and leave the original behind, press the + key on the numeric keypad, while dragging the mouse, and then hold down the Ctrl key.

Summary

This chapter explained how you use the Pick, Rectangle, Ellipse, Pencil, Node (or Shape), Zoom, and Text tools. You learned how to use these tools to select graphics and text to manipulate them. You also learned how to draw lines, rectangles, and circles. Finally, the chapter provided some tips for creating simple graphics.

Chapter 3

The Outline and Fill Tools

The Outline and Fill Tools in CorelDRAW! enable you to customize and control the fill pattern, color, and outline of any object for your own specific needs. This chapter teaches you about these features:

- Outline Tool
- Colors (Spot and Process)
- CMYK Method
- RBG Option
- HSB Option
- Named Option
- Fill Tool
- Bitmap Patterns
- Vector Patterns
- Fountain Fills.

The Outline Tool

You activate the Outline Tool by clicking on the pen-shaped icon in the Toolbox, which activates the Outline Tool fly-out (Figure 3-1).

The top row of the Outline Tool fly-out contains a range of line thicknesses that you can apply to a selected object's outline. The bottom row of the fly-out contains white, black, or a choice of a percentage of gray that you can apply to a selected object's outline.

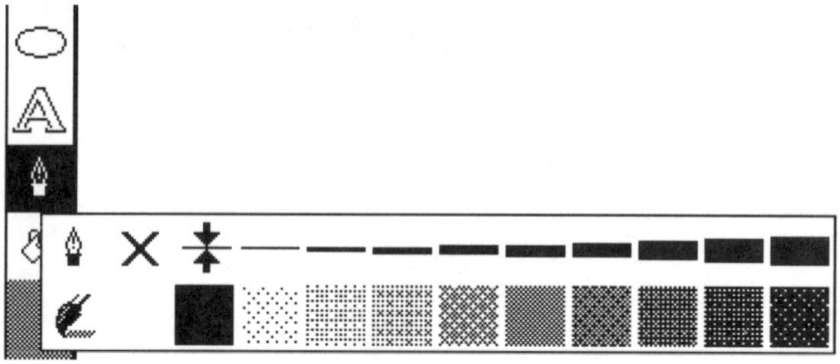

Figure 3-1. The Outline Tool Fly-Out.

In addition, there are a number of dialog boxes available from the Outline Tool fly-out, which let you create and apply a color to an outline, and determine the outline's width, shape, style, end, and beginning.

The first dialog box you can choose from the Outline Tool fly-out is the *Outline Pen* dialog box. Here you can customize the width and shape of an outline, create dashed or dotted lines, and apply an arrowhead to the beginning or end of a line. To activate the *Outline Pen* dialog box (Figure 3-3), select the pen shaped icon, which is the first icon available from the fly-out (Figure 3-2). You can also activate this dialog box by selecting an object with the Pick Tool and pressing the F12 key.

Figure 3-2. Icon for the Outline Pen Dialog Box.

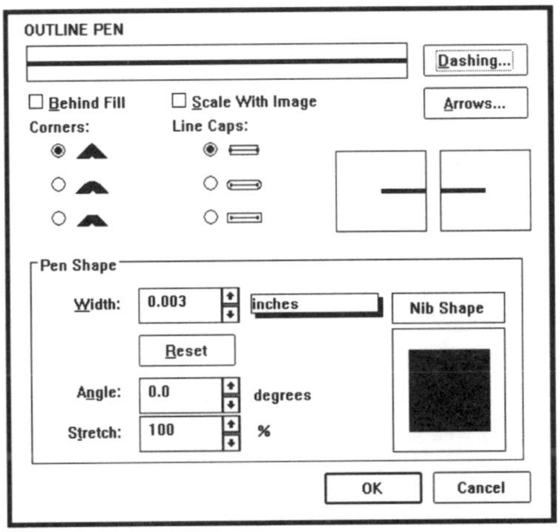

Figure 3-3. The Outline Pen Dialog Box.

The first option available in the *Outline Pen* dialog box is the *Dashing* option. Clicking on this option displays the *Dashed & Dotted Line Styles* dialog box of Figure 3-4. Clicking on a style from this dialog box applies that particular style to a selected line.

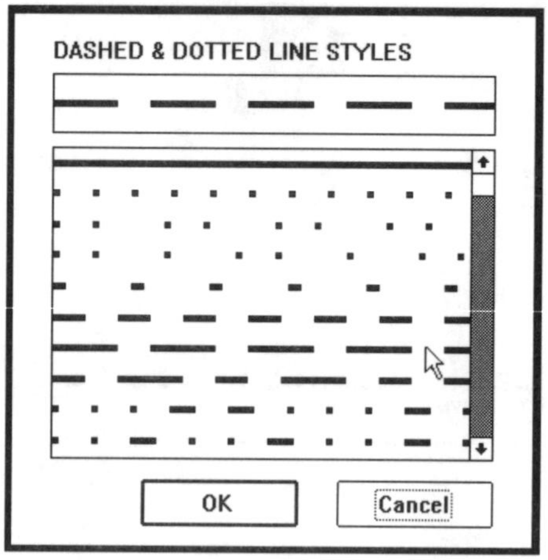

Figure 3-4. The Dashed & Dotted Line Styles Dialog Box.

When you click on the *Arrows* option in the *Outline Pen* dialog box, you activate the *Arrowhead Selection* dialog box (Figure 3-5). Here you can give a line a certain end or beginning from the choices available. The arrowheads available here come with CorelDRAW!, but you also have the option of creating your own arrowhead (see the *Create Arrow* command, from the **Special** menu, in **Chapter 5: Menu Commands**).

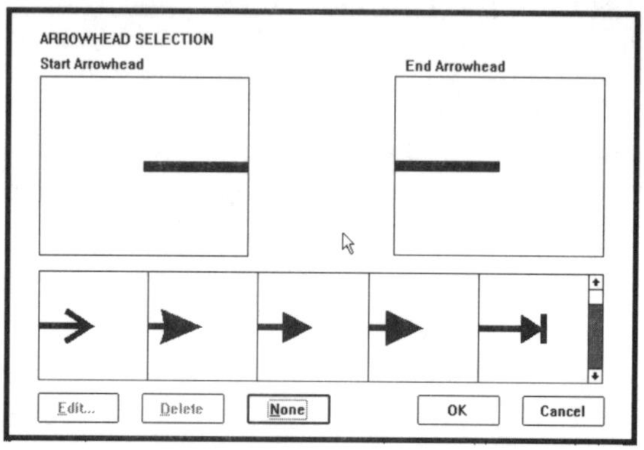

Figure 3-5. The Arrowhead Selection Dialog Box.

Use the scroll bar to the right of the frame containing the arrowheads to view each arrowhead available. The boxes that have the diagonal line through them are empty, so you can add arrowheads you create yourself.

To apply an arrowhead to the start of a line (the start of a line is determined by the larger node), select an arrowhead from the options available with the left mouse button. Select your choice with the right mouse button to determine the end of the line. The size of the arrowhead is determined by the thickness of the line. You can view arrowheads only on the Preview Screen. Figure 3-6 shows some examples of arrowheads.

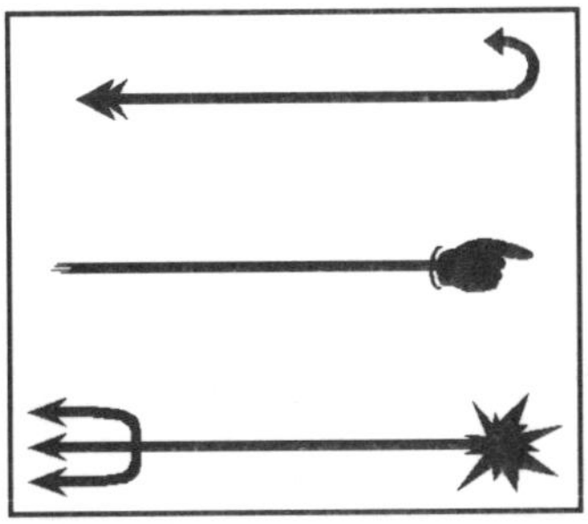

Figure 3-6. Some Examples of Arrowheads Applied to Lines.

You can also edit existing arrowheads in the *Arrowhead Selection* dialog box (Figure 3-5). To do this, select the arrowhead you wish to edit and click on the *Edit* Button at the bottom left of the dialog box. This activates the *Arrow Head Editor* dialog box (Figure 3-7).

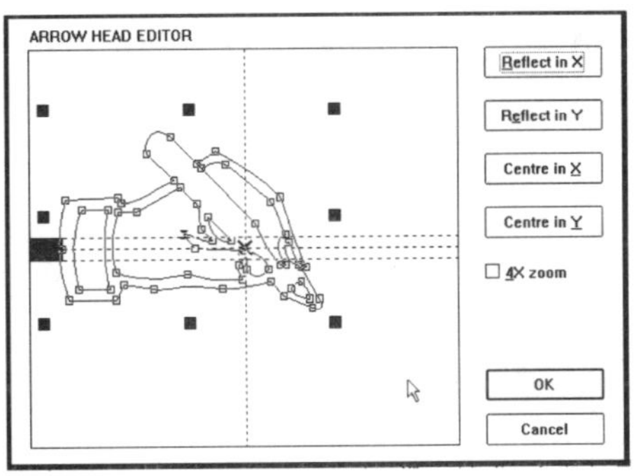

Figure 3-7. The Arrow Head Editor Dialog Box.

From the *Arrow Head Editor* dialog box, you can change the size, positioning, and direction of the arrowhead. To change the size of the arrowhead, hold the mouse down on one of the eight black markers, and drag it as you would when resizing any object in CorelDRAW!. You change the position of the arrowhead by holding the mouse down on one of the hollow markers that is displayed in certain points along the outline of the object.

To change the horizontal direction of an arrowhead, click on the *Reflect in X* option at the top right of the dialog box. The *Reflect in Y* option changes the arrowhead vertically on the guideline. The *Center in X* and *Center in Y* options move the object so that it is centered over the cross in the center of the *Arrowhead Editor.* These options affect the object if you have moved, scaled, or stretched the object, thus changing its center.

The *4X zoom* option enlarges the arrowhead four times for more accurate sizing and positioning. After you have made all the changes in the *Arrow Head Editor* dialog box, click on OK to return to the *Arrowhead Selection* dialog box (Figure 3-5). The two frames below *Start Arrowhead* and *End Arrowhead* show any arrowheads you may have selected for the start and end of your lines. You can remove any arrowheads you no longer want in the *Arrowhead Selection* dialog box by selecting the arrowhead you want to remove and clicking on the *Delete* button. The *None* option ensures that no arrowheads are applied to a selected line. After making your choices in this dialog box, click on OK to return to the *Outline Pen* dialog box (Figure 3-3).

The *Behind Fill* option in the *Outline Pen* dialog box, by default, is not selected, and generally is only effective when you are working with thick lines. When this option is not selected, any outline you have applied to a line is drawn on top of the object, regardless of the fill.

If you select the *Behind Fill* option (clicking inside the square to the left of the option), the outline of an object is drawn partly behind the fill of the object. Therefore, the outline does not appear as thick as you have specified because half the outline is behind the fill.

When you select the *Scale With Image* option, the outline of an object changes in size when the object is stretched or scaled. When you increase the size of the object, the outline increases in thickness; when you decrease the object, the outline becomes thinner. If you have not selected this option and, for example, you decrease a thick outlined object in size, the thick outline remains thick and possibly distorts the object in some way. This option also affects calligraphic outlines when an object is rotated. If you have the *Scale With Image* option selected, rotating an object with a calligraphic outline, does not affect this outline as it would when this option is not selected.

The *Corners* option affects the corners of objects or where two lines meet at a point (Figure 3-8). The first option available is the Miter option. This means the two lines meet at the corner in a sharp point. The middle option is the Round option, where the corners of an object has no sharp point but a rounded curve. The last option is the Bevel option, where the corner has a flattened end.

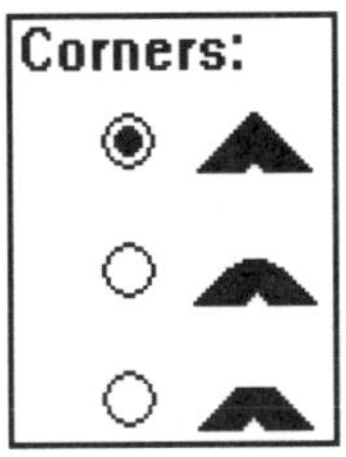

Figure 3-8. The Corners Option.

The *Line Caps* option (Figure 3-9) affects the ends of a line drawn with the Pencil Tool. By default, the first option is selected, which means the start and end of a line will be squared off. The second option is the rounded option. Selecting this applies a rounded end to all lines you draw. The third option squares off the ends of a line as in the first option, but there is an extra section of line that is equal to half the line's thickness. These three options also affect dashed and dotted lines, with each dash or dot reflecting the choice you have made from the Line Caps option.

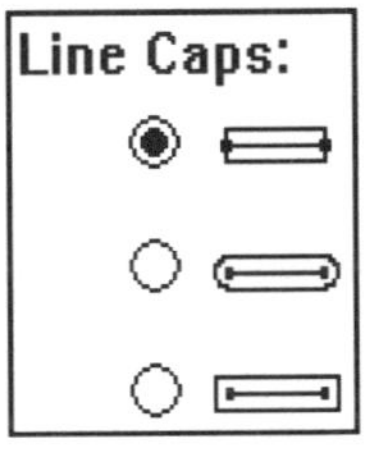

Figure 3-9. The Line Caps Option.

The bottom half of the *Outline Pen* dialog box holds the *Pen Shape* options (Figure 3-10). The first setting you can alter here is the *Width* setting. You can change the measurement by clicking in the frame holding the current measurement. For example, click on the word "inches" to reveal the other measurement systems available.

The figure in the *Width* box changes to reflect the current measurement system you select. To change this figure, double-click over it so that it is reflected in reverse video, then type in the new figure. Alternatively, you can click on the arrows to the right of the box containing the current figure, until the desired number shows in the box.

The *Angle* and *Stretch* options affect the *Nib Shape*. You can use these options to apply a calligraphic outline to an object or line. Altering the figures in the relevant frames for these options is reflected in the *Nib Shape* frame to the right. The black or colored square (whatever color the outline is) changes in shape, to reveal the settings you give to the *Angle* and *Stretch* options.

The *Reset* button quickly returns the *Angle* and *Stretch* options back to their default values if you have altered them. You can view the results of altering these options only in the Preview Screen. For an example of calligraphic outlines, see the **Exercise 6: Calligraphic Outlines and Bitmap Fills** in the second part of this book.

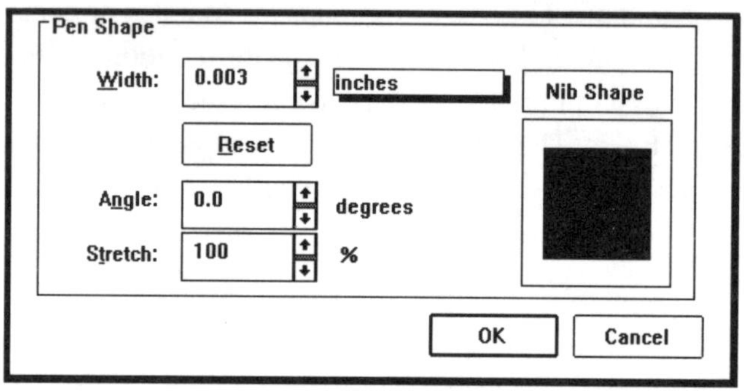

Figure 3-10. The Pen Shape Options.

The other dialog boxes available directly from the Outline Tool fly-out (Figure 3-1) are the color dialog boxes, which you activate by clicking on the paint brush icon in the Outline Tool fly-out (Figure 3-11). When you press the Shift + F12 keys, while an object is selected, you activate the color dialog box that you use to apply the object's outline color, discussed next.

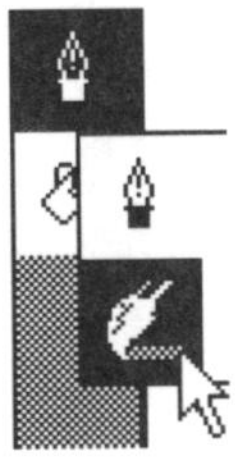

Figure 3-11. The Paint Brush Icon.

There are six dialog boxes with CorelDRAW! that you can use to apply color to an outline. If you are using CorelDRAW! for the first time, the *Outline Color* dialog box (Figure 3-12), is the first one you will see. From here, or any other color dialog box, it is easy to make your way into all other color dialog boxes.

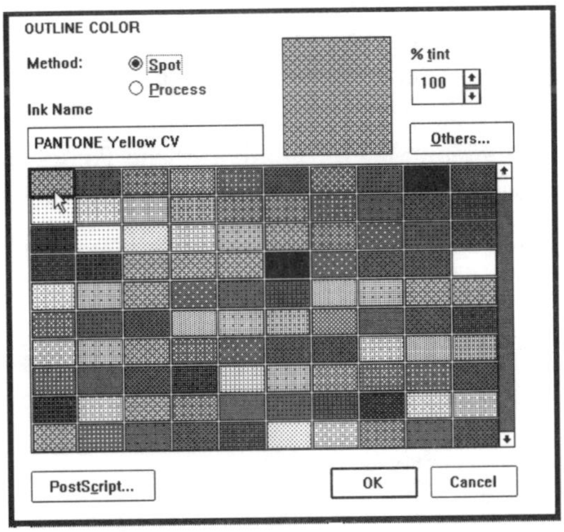

Figure 3-12. The Outline Color Dialog Box.

At the top of the *Outline Color* dialog box (Figure 3-12), is the *Method* option, which is either Spot or Process. To move between the two, simply click inside the relevant circle with the mouse. This dialog box, whether on Spot or Process, has a palette full of colors that, when clicked on, applies the chosen color to a selected object's outline.

When you select a color from the palette, the name of the color is displayed in the *Color Name* frame (or *Ink Name* if using the Spot method) above the palette, and an example of the color is displayed in the frame to the right of this. The *tint* option, at the top right of the dialog box, lets you lighten the selected color. The scroll bar to the right of the palette gives you access to the remaining colors on the palette. You can move colors around the palette by holding the mouse on the square containing the color, and dragging it to a new position on the palette.

Spot Colors

When you select the *Spot color* option from the *Outline Color* dialog box, the palette will be full of registered Pantone colors, which are used and recognized by commercial printers worldwide. When you color separate a file that has been colored with Pantone colors, a new color separation is made for each color used. Therefore, when you use Pantone colors on a file that is going to be commercially printed, it is best to use no more than four different colors.

To select the Pantone color you want, click on it from the color palette. The scroll bar to the right of this palette, when clicked on, gives you access to the rest of the palette. When you have selected the color, the Pantone name appears in the *Ink Name* frame, and an example of the color is displayed in the frame to the right of this. If you know the name and/or number of the Pantone color you wish to use, click on the *Others* button below the *tint* option, in the top right of the box (Figure 3-12). This activates the *Ink Colors* dialog box (Figure 3-13).

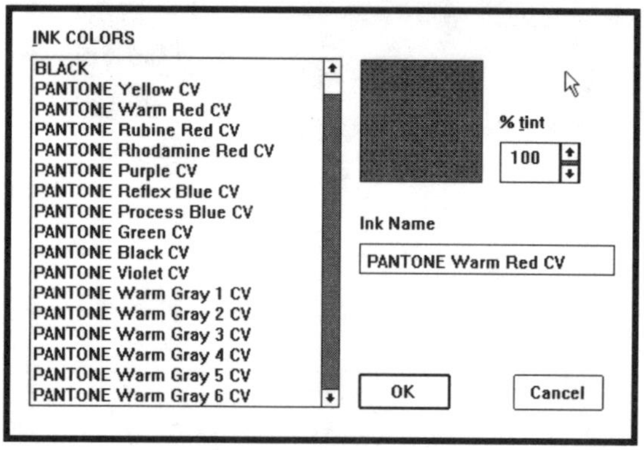

Figure 3-13. The Ink Colors Dialog Box.

The *Ink Colors* dialog box lets you select the Pantone color by name and/or number. The scroll bar, to the right of the frame containing the list of colors, gives you access to all Pantone colors available, by their name. You can alter the *tint* of the selected Pantone color in either the *Outline Color* dialog box (Figure 3-12) or the *Ink Colors* dialog box (Figure 3-13).

If you change the tint of a Pantone color, you can save it on the palette for future use. This obviates the need for readjusting the tint each time a color is required. You can do this from the *Outline Color* dialog box of Figure 3-12. If you wish to follow this method, and are currently in the *Ink Colors* dialog box, press OK or Cancel to get back to the *Outline Color* dialog box, and make sure the Spot method is still active.

Using the scroll bar, move down the palette until you see the squares with the diagonal line through them. These are empty squares, where you can save defined colors. To save a specified tint of a Pantone color, double-click on an empty square to display the *Ink Colors* dialog box. From here, select the color you want to change, alter the tint to whatever you want, and click on the OK button. This color is now displayed in the square you double-clicked on in the *Outline Color* dialog box palette.

Process Colors

Process colors are made up of the four colors used in printing color publications. These colors are made up of percentages of cyan, magenta, yellow, and black. The color combinations available through the Process method are almost endless. To apply Process colors, select the Process *Method* from the *Outline Color* dialog box (Figure 3-12). You select colors from this palette in the same way you selected Spot colors. You simply click on the square in the palette containing the color you want to apply to a selected object. There are 99 colors named and included as standard in the color palette.

As in the Spot palette, you can move colors you use to the top by holding the mouse on the square and dragging it to the new position.

It is also possible to create your own process colors to add to this palette. To do this, click on the *Others* button toward the top right of the *Outline Color* dialog box while the Process method is active.

Clicking on this button takes you to a further *Outline Colo*r dialog box, where you have four options for setting and applying colors (Figure 3-14). The three top options, CMYK, RGB, and HSB, each provide a different method for defining process colors.

CMYK

The first option available is the CMYK method, which lets you define a color using cyan, magenta, yellow, and black (Figure 3-14). To specify a color using the CMYK method, you have to adjust the settings for each of the four colors. One way to do this is to click the mouse on the horizontal scroll bars, underneath each color, as you would any scroll bar. Alternatively, double-click over the current figures in the frames containing the numbers, and type in the new figure.

The defined color is now displayed in the frame to the right of the horizontal scroll bars, so you can view the color before applying it to a selected object.

You can also adjust the color using the *Visual Selector*. This has the large and small color boxes in the top right of the dialog box. Dragging the little black marker around in these boxes also adjusts the color: cyan and magenta for the large box, and yellow for the smaller one. The black selection changes automatically.

After defining the color you want, you can click the mouse in the frame under the words *Color Name*, and type in your own name for the color you have just specified. After you select OK, the color is saved in the color palette (Figure 3-12), and the name is added to the list that is displayed when you select the *Named* option, which is the fourth option (Figure 3-14).

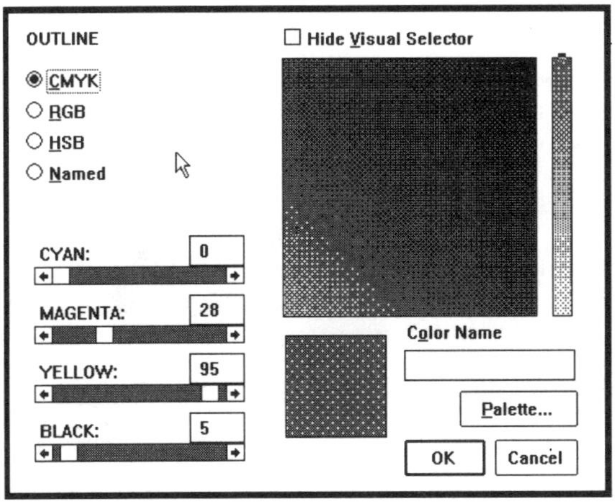

Figure 3-14. The Outline Dialog Box.

As with the HSB and RGB color options, you can hide the two color frames or *Visual Selectors* (Figure 3-14), by clicking in the *Hide Visual Selector* box above the frames.

RGB

The RGB option, when selected (Figure 3-15), also has two *Visual Selector* frames that can be hidden or used to define the colors, the same as explained for the CMYK option. The RGB option uses percentages of red, green, and blue to make colors. One hundred percent of each color produces white, while zero percent produces black.

The large *Visual Selector* Frame represents red and green, while the thin frame represents blue. You can either define your colors here, by dragging the markers around the frame, or by changing the settings at the left of the dialog box. Altering the horizontal scroll bars, or changing the figures in the settings, adjusts the colors.

As with CMYK, an example of the specified color is displayed in the preview box, and you can name your color, which again is displayed in the Process palette and the *Named* dialog box. If you are using the RGB method to produce color separations, CorelDRAW! converts the colors you have used to the CMYK equivalents.

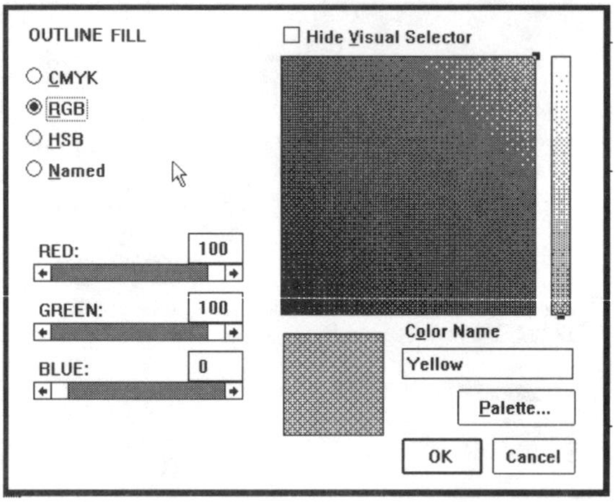

Figure 3-15. The RGB Option.

HSB

The HSB option has a different look all together (Figure 3-16). The Hue selection represents a whole color including its shades and tints. For example, the Hue of blue includes light blue and dark blue, and all the shades in between. The Saturation represents the lightness and darkness of a color. Brightness refers to the amount of black in the color, with 0 being black, and 100 being white.

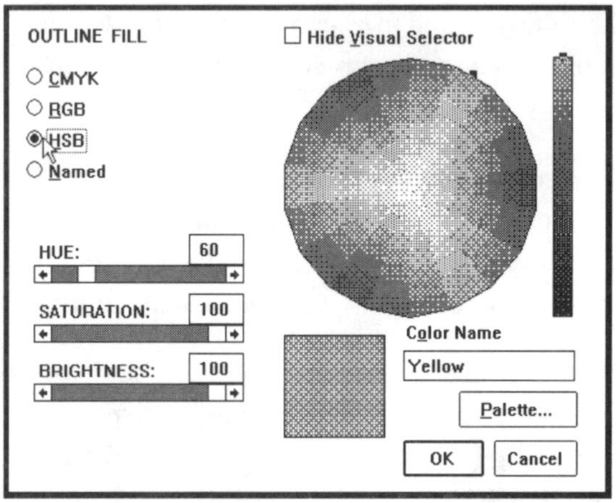

Figure 3-16. The HSB Color Option.

To define a color in this dialog box, you first drag the marker, on the *Visual Selector*, into the area of the color you want. The outside of the wheel has the colors in their purest forms, whereas the center of the wheel displays the colors with less intensity or lighter in color. The brightness of the color (the amount of black) is determined by the long thin *Visual Selector* frame to the right.

Of course, you can also adjust the Hue, Saturation, and Brightness of the color through the settings at the left of the dialog box. As with the other *Visual Selectors*, the changes you make with the marker are reflected in the settings to the left, and you can turn the *Visual Selector* off or on again at any time.

You can also name and save the colors defined with the HSB. If you are going to use these colors for color separations, CorelDRAW! converts them as best as it can to CMYK colors, since the HSB and CMYK methods do not create colors in the same way.

Named

Selecting the *Named* option activates the *Outline* box (Figure 3-17). This dialog box contains a list of named colors already predetermined by CorelDRAW!, as well as any you may have saved yourself. These are the same colors that are displayed in the Process palette, although this dialog box makes it easier to find and select them. When you click on the color from the list it is displayed in the preview box.

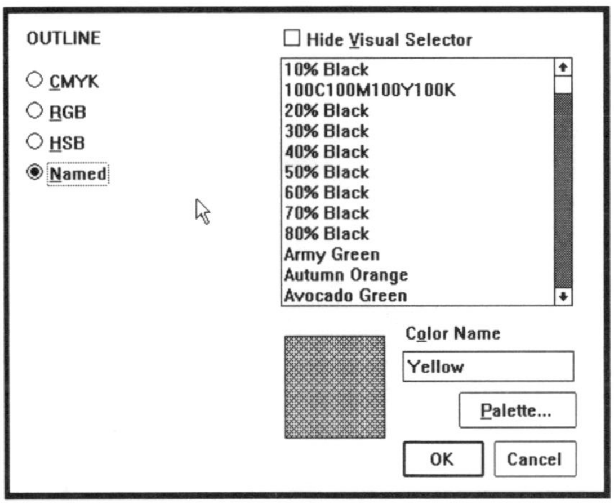

Figure 3-17. The Outline Dialog Box Where Process Colors are Named.

Note that in every color method dialog box that you have just seen, there is a *Palette* button toward the bottom right of the box. Clicking on this gives you access to the Process palette, and from there you can get to the Spot palette.

Whenever you define a color in any of the available color dialog boxes, and you swap to another color method, CorelDRAW! converts the color to the new method selected. Since some of the methods produce colors in a different way, the conversion is not always accurate.

If you have a Spot color you want to convert to a Process color, first select the Pantone color from the palette. Next, select the Process option and click on the *Others* button. This activates the CMYK option, where you can see the color as near to it as possible, made up of the four colors: cyan, magenta, yellow, and black. Finally, name the color in the manner described above, and click on OK.

PostScript

Toward the bottom left of the *Outline Color* dialog box (Figure 3-12), there is a *PostScript* button that activates the *PostScript Controls* dialog box (Figure 3-18). The options available in this dialog box are only effective if you have a PostScript printer. The *PostScript Halftone Screen* options only work when you are using Spot colors. There is a list of options available in *Screen Type*, which you can see by using the scroll bars. You can apply these to an object to obtain a certain effect. These include spots, lines, and diamonds, among other things.

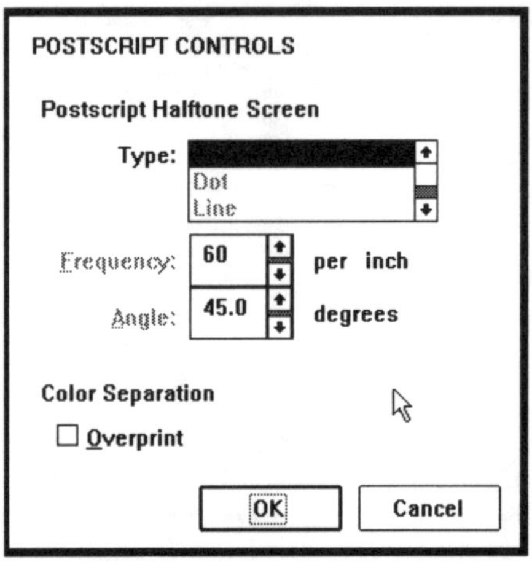

Figure 3-18. The PostScript Controls Dialog Box.

The *Frequency* option determines how many dots or lines occur per inch. The *Angle* option determines at what angle these dots or lines will be. You cannot see changes you make in this dialog box in the Preview Screen. You must print them to see the result. The *CorelDRAW! Users Manual* provides printed examples on varying the *Screen Type*, *Frequency,* and *Angle.*

The *Color Separation Overprint* option, when checked, prints a spot color on top of another one, when there is a knockout or a gap where the colors overlap. (This option only applies to fills, not outlines, of objects.) This has the effect of blending the two colors. The result depends on what two colors you use. You cannot see this process until you print a proof from the color separations. You can also use this feature to stop gaps in uneven registration around a colored object that is sitting on top of another colored object.

The Fill Tool

You can apply a fill to any closed object on your page. CorelDRAW! includes numerous sorts of fills, and you can create your own fills. When you apply a fill to a selected object, this fill is only visible in the Preview Screen. However, you can see an example of the fill of a selected object on the right-hand side of the Status Line.

To apply a fill to an object, you must first select it with the Pick Tool. Once you select it, activate the Fill Tool fly-out by clicking on the paint bucket icon from the Toolbox. This fly-out offers simple fills of black, white, none, and tints of gray from 10% to 80% in 10% increments. More complex fills are also available for Bitmaps, Vector Patterns, Fountain, and PostScript fills. In addition, the paint bucket icon provides access to the range of color dialog boxes. Figure 3-19 shows the options available from the Fill Tool fly-out.

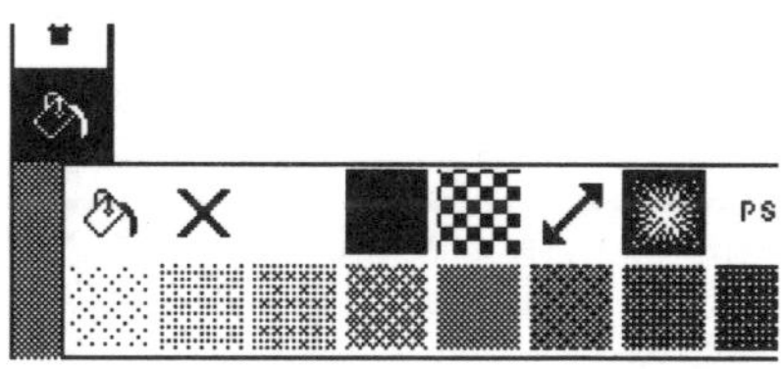

Figure 3-19. The Fill Tool Fly-Out.

The first option available from the Fill Tool fly-out is the *Uniform Fill* color dialog box option. If you select this paint bucket icon from the left-hand top row of Figure 3-19, you have access to the numerous spot and process color dialog boxes. These color dialog boxes are identical to the color dialog boxes used to apply color to an outline, explained in the first part of this chapter. The other dialog boxes are discussed below.

Bitmap Patterns

The next available dialog box is the *Bitmap Fill Pattern* dialog box, which you activate by clicking on the checkered icon from the Fill Tool fly-out. The *Bitmap Fill Pattern* dialog box (Figure 3-20) gives you access to the numerous bitmap fills that you apply to a selected, closed object.

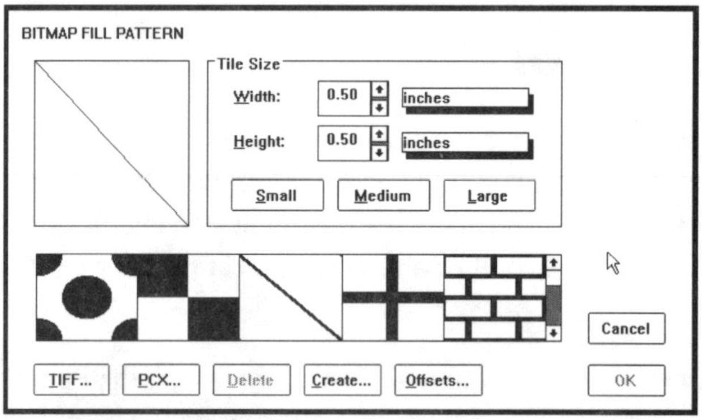

Figure 3-20. The Bitmap Fill Pattern Dialog Box.

To view all the bitmap fills available (Figure 3-20), use the scroll bar to the right of the frame holding the patterns, to move up or down the list. The squares to the bottom of this scrolled list with the diagonal lines through them are empty. Any bitmap patterns you create or import will go there. Select a pattern from the list, by clicking the mouse on the square holding your desired pattern. This pattern is displayed in the large square to the left of the dialog box. This is the pattern that is then applied to any object(s) you can select. Before you click on OK, there are a number of adjustments you may make.

The *Tile Size* options (Figure 3-21) determines at what size the Bitmap Pattern will be displayed inside the object you are filling. There are already three pre-set sizes available in this section of the dialog box: *Small, Medium,* and *Large*. When you click the mouse on each of these options, one at a time, you can see that the Bitmap Pattern in the square to the left changes in size, according to which option you select.

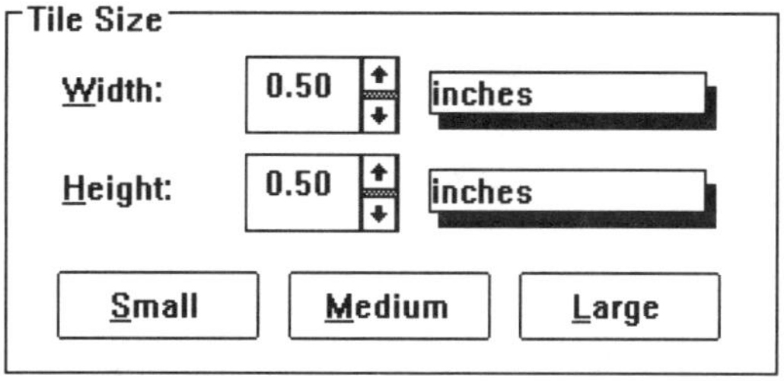

Figure 3-21. The Tile Size Section of the Bitmap Fill Pattern Dialog Box.

You can also type in your own sizes in the *Width* and *Height* frames, but be careful. Bitmaps lose quality when the size is increased or decreased too drastically. For custom sizes, use the scroll arrows, or double-click in the boxes to type in your own figures. You can alter the system of measurement by clicking the mouse on the current unit of measurement.

Click on the TIFF or PCX buttons at the bottom left of the *Bitmap Fill Pattern* dialog box to see the *Import Bitmap* dialog box (Figure 3-22). Here you can import a .TIF or .PCX image that you may have created in an outside paint program, or an image that you have scanned.

The *Import Bitmap* dialog box gives you access to your machine's disks and directories where you may have .TIF or .PCX images saved. Select the .TIF or .PCX image you want from the list, and click on *Open*. This .TIF or .PCX image is now saved in the *Bitmap Fill Pattern* dialog box, where you can use it for filling objects. If the image you are importing is color, it is converted to black and white.

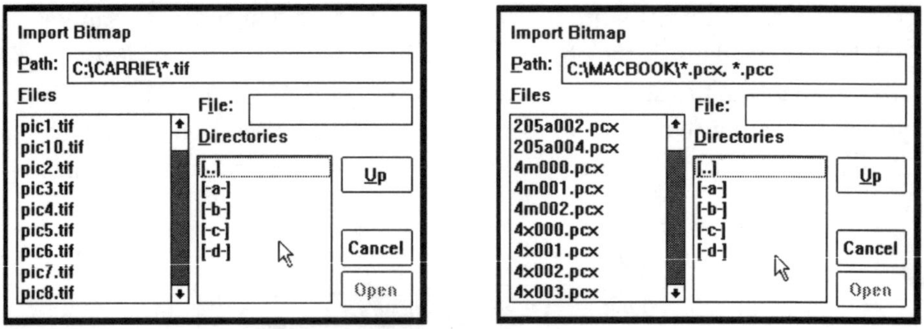

Figure 3-22. The Import Bitmap Dialog Box.

If there is a Bitmap Pattern in the dialog box that you no longer want, you can select it and click on the *Delete* button. You can use this option on a created or imported Bitmap Pattern that you no longer need.

The *Create* button, when clicked on, activates the *Bitmap Pattern Editor* dialog box. This is one way of creating your own Bitmap Pattern; the other way being through the *Create Pattern* command from the **Special** menu.

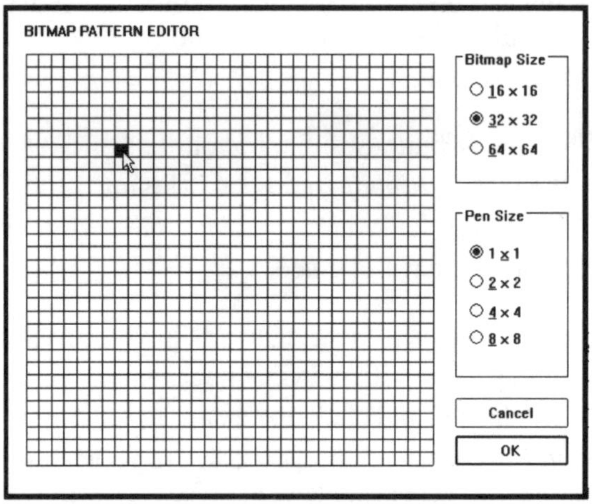

Figure 3-23. The Bitmap Pattern Editor Dialog Box.

This dialog box contains a grid and some sizing options to the right of the grid. The *Bitmap Size* option, which determines the size the bitmap is displayed in the *Bitmap Fill Pattern* dialog box. This in turn determines the resolution of the bitmap pattern. The first and smallest size creates rectangular patterns. The last two sizes are best suited for diagonal and curved lines. If you swap between sizes in the middle of a drawing, the current drawing is deleted.

STOP

The *Pen Size* option determines how many squares or pixels that one click of the mouse shades. The 1 x 1 option obviously colors one square at a time, and the choices then double in value up to 8 x 8. To draw your pattern, click the left mouse button for black squares, and the right mouse button for white squares.

After creating the pattern, click on OK, and the pattern will be included with the other *Bitmap Fill Patterns*, which you can then apply to a selected object.

For more information see the *Create Pattern* command in the **Chapter 5: Menu Commands**, and **Exercise 12: Creating and Saving Patterns**.

Now return to the original *Bitmap Fill Pattern* dialog box. The *Offsets* button activates the *Tile Offsets* dialog box (Figure 3-24). The changes you make in this dialog box affect the currently selected Bitmap Pattern. This dialog box lets you alter the placement of the tiles, so that they do not have to start at the same spot, or run exactly side by side horizontally and vertically.

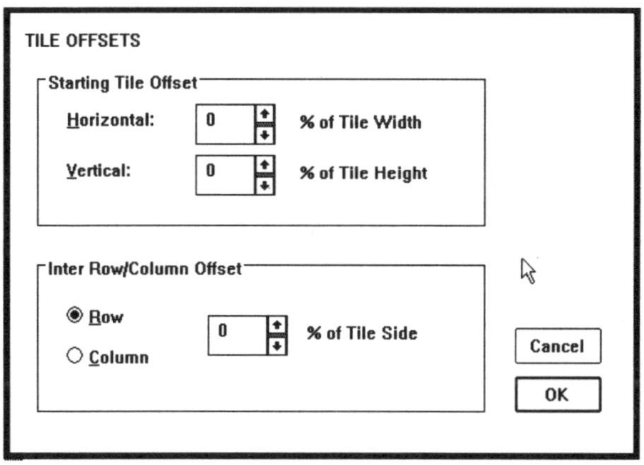

Figure 3-24. The Tile Offsets Dialog Box.

Changing the settings in *Starting Tile Offset* moves the whole pattern either horizontally or vertically, depending on which setting you alter. The size you specify is a percentage of the tile size. For example, placing 25 in either the *Horizontal* or *Vertical* options shifts the whole pattern one quarter of the tile size. Figure 3-25 shows The Bitmap Pattern Tile Offset option unaltered (left) and altered (right) by 15% for both Horizontal and Vertical.

Figure 3-25. The Bitmap Pattern, Tile Offset Option Unaltered (Left) and Altered 15% (Right).

The *Inter Row/Column Offset* option shifts alternate rows or columns. Again, the amount of shift that occurs is a percentage of the tile size. After making changes in this dialog box, click on OK to return to the *Bitmap Fill Pattern* dialog box. Figure 3-26 shows an example of the *Inter Row Offset* of a bitmap pattern that has been altered by 75%.

Figure 3-26. The Bitmap Pattern with its Inter Row Option Setting Changed to 75%.

After you select the Pattern you want from the *Bitmap Fill Pattern* dialog box (Figure 3-20), and make any necessary changes, you then click on OK. The *Bitmap Pattern Color* dialog box (Figure 3-27) is now displayed. Here you can specify a color for both the foreground and the background of the *Bitmap Fill Pattern* you have selected. This color dialog box works in the same way the *Outline* and *Fill Color* dialog boxes work, except that here you choose two colors.

The palette to the left represents the actual color of the bitmap fill. Clicking on a color here is shown in the preview frame at the right of the dialog box. The palette to the right alters the color behind the pattern; selecting a color here also shows in the preview frame. Once you have chosen the appropriate colors here, click on OK to return to the screen. Bitmap fills are only displayed in the Preview Screen.

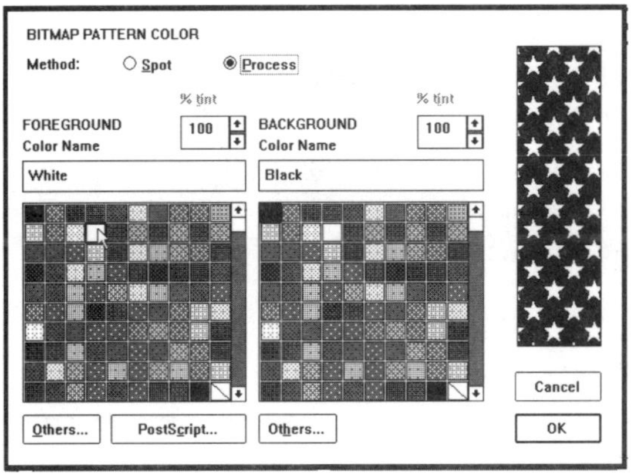

Figure 3-27. Bitmap Pattern Color Dialog Box.

Vector Patterns

The next dialog box that is available through the Fill Tool fly-out is the *Load Vector Pattern* dialog box. You activate this by selecting the arrow icon from the fly-out (Figure 3-28).

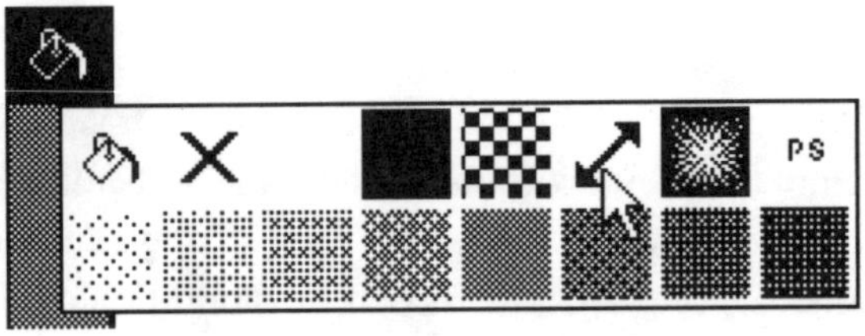

Figure 3-28. The Icon for Activating the Load Vector Pattern Dialog Box.

CorelDRAW! has a wide range of Vector patterns that can, like Bitmap fills, be applied as a fill for a selected object. Selecting the relevant icon, as in Figure 3-28, activates the *Load Vector Pattern* dialog box (Figure 3-29). The *Load Vector Pattern* dialog box is filled with the patterns that come with CorelDRAW! and the files have an extension of .PAT. Selecting a pattern from this list displays a black and white version in the frame to the right of the dialog box.

You can also create Vector patterns within CorelDRAW!. (See **Exercise 12: Creating and Saving Patterns**, in Part 2.)

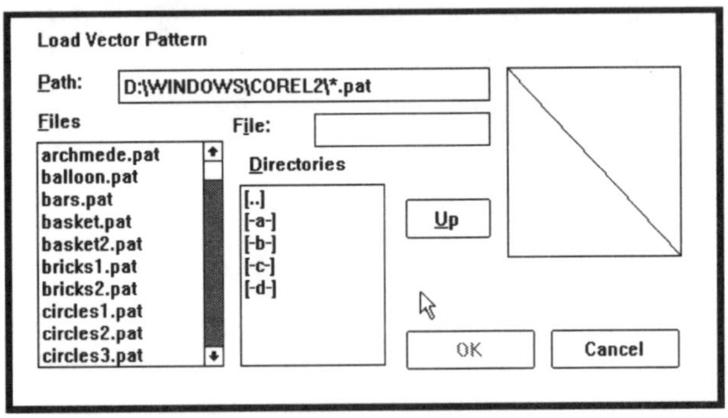

Figure 3-29. The Load Vector Pattern Dialog Box.

Vector patterns are full color. To see their color before you apply them to an object, select from the list of files and click on the OK button in the *Load Vector Pattern* dialog box. This takes you to the *Vector Fill Pattern* dialog box (Figure 3-30), for full color display.

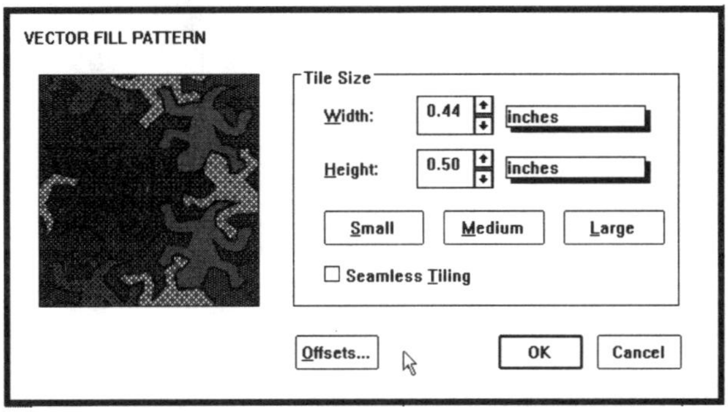

Figure 3-30. The Vector Fill Pattern Dialog Box.

The options available in the *Vector Fill Pattern* dialog box mainly show the size of the pattern tiles. To alter the size of the tiles, change the settings in the *Tile Size* section of the dialog box. You can increase the tile size to 3 x 3 inches. Vector patterns do not lose quality when resizing, as bitmaps do, but the more tiles you have in a Vector pattern, the more complex the drawing becomes, slowing down printing time.

Just below the sizing choices is the *Seamless Tiling* option. Clicking on this prevents any gaps occurring between tiles in the Preview Screen and when using a printer that is not PostScript.

The *Offsets* option takes you to the *Tile Offsets* dialog box, which is identical to the one described for Bitmap patterns.

You can edit a Vector pattern the same way you would edit any CorelDRAW! file. To do this, select the *Open* command from the **File** menu when you are inside CorelDRAW!. In the *Open Drawing* dialog box, change the file extension to .PAT. The Vector patterns are now available, to open from the directory that holds the patterns. Open a Vector pattern by double-clicking on the file name or clicking once, which allows you to view the pattern, and then click on *Open* (Figure 3-31).

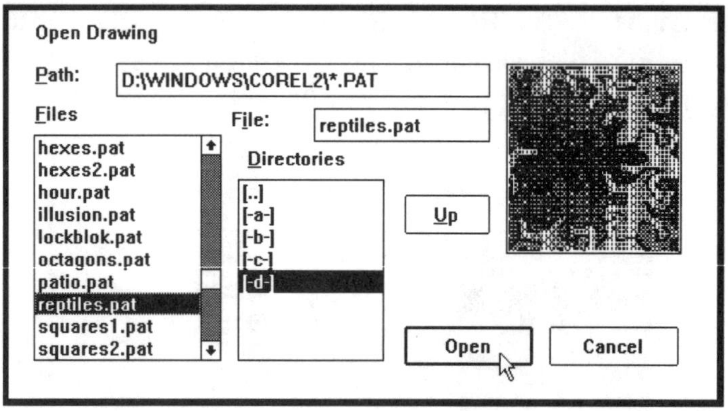

Figure 3-31. Opening a Vector Pattern in CorelDRAW!.

The Vector pattern is now open and you can edit it like any other CorelDRAW! file (Figure 3-32). The pattern is displayed as a group of objects that have to be ungrouped, before you can edit individual tiles.

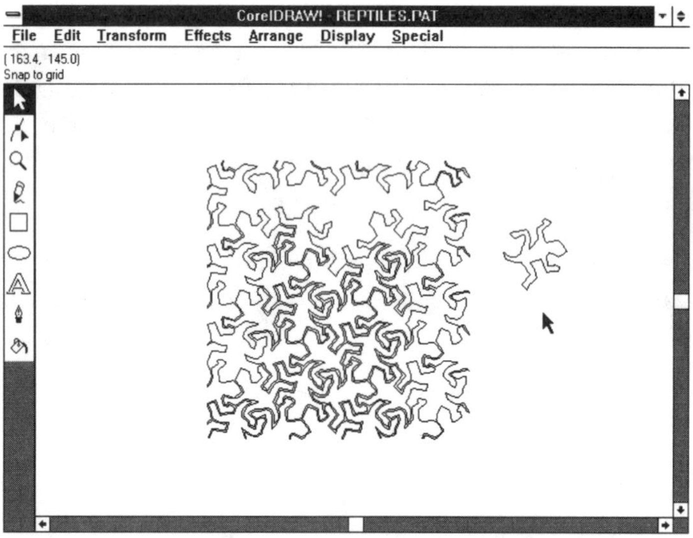

Figure 3-32. Editing the Vector Pattern.

Fountain Fills

The next Vector Pattern option on the Fill Tool fly-out is the *Fountain Fill* option. This dialog box lets you define two colors that will merge together for a fill. Clicking on the *Fountain Fill* icon, from the Fill Tool fly-out, activates the *Fountain Fill* dialog box.

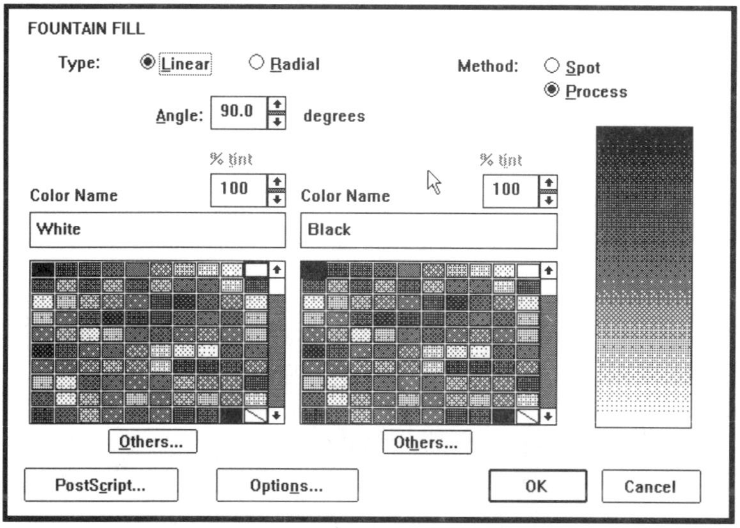

Figure 3-33. The Fountain Fill Dialog Box.

The first option available in the *Fountain Fill* dialog box is the *Type* of fill. The two options available here are *Linear* and *Radial*. The *Linear* type fill an object with the two colors in lined steps in the direction that you specify. The *Radial* option fills an object in circular steps from one color to another. Making the change from *Linear* to *Radial* is reflected in the preview frame at the right of the dialog box. This preview frame gives you an example of the fill you are choosing before you apply it to the selected object.

The option below the *Type* of fill is *Angle*. This option is only available when the *Type* of fill you choose is *Linear*. Changing the setting in the *Angle* frame changes the angle of the fill, which you can see in the preview frame at the right.

You must select two different colors (one from each palette) in the *Fountain Fill* dialog box for the effect to be successful. The methods available for choosing colors are the same as in the *Outline* and *Fill* color dialog boxes, described earlier, except that you choose two colors.

The choice of the Spot or Process method of coloring is determined at the top right of the dialog box. To activate the other dialog boxes associated with each of these methods, click on the *Others* button below each palette. After you select or create colors in one of these other dialog boxes, click on OK to return to the original *Fountain Fill* dialog box (Figure 3-33). Any changes to the color you have made are again reflected in the preview frame to the right. The palette to the left of the dialog box determines the start color, and the palette to the right determines the end color.

The *Options* button below the palettes, when clicked on, activates the *Fountain Fill Options* dialog box (Figure 3-34). The Edge Pad option can have a percentage of up to 45 inserted in the relevant frame. This increases the section of color at the start and the end of the fill you have specified. This feature is useful for obscure-shaped objects, where the end and beginning steps of the *Fountain Fill* could fall outside the object.

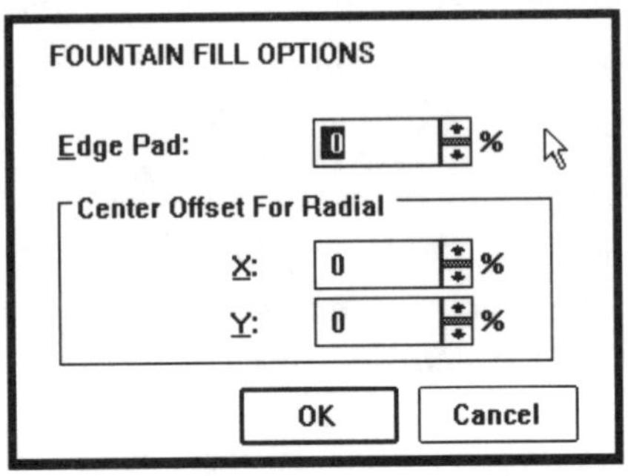

Figure 3-34. The Fountain Fill Options Dialog Box.

You can also change the center of a *Radial* Fill through the *Fountain Fill Options* dialog box. Entering a plus figure in either the X or Y settings shifts the center of the fill up and to the right, and a minus figure, the opposite. Whenever you fill an object with a *Radial Fountain Fill*, the circular steps begin from the center of the object. Altering the figures in the *Center Offset For Radial* section of the *Fountain Fill Options* dialog box alters this.

PostScript Textures

The last dialog box available from the Fill Tool fly-out is the *PostScript Texture* dialog box. You activate it by clicking on the PS square at the end of the fly-out. This box allows you to fill an object with interesting and unusual fills.

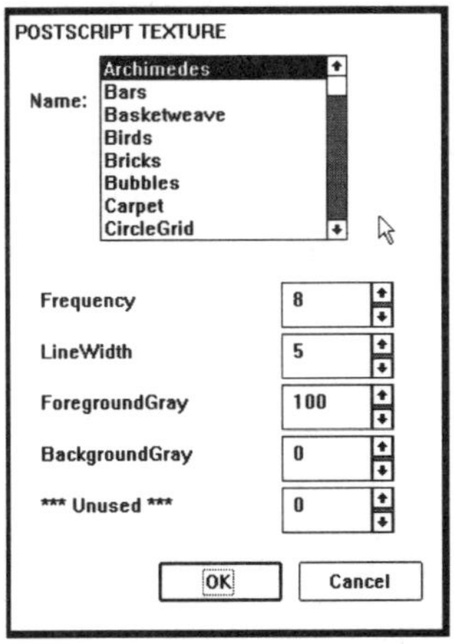

Figure 3-35. The PostScript Texture Dialog Box.

Coloring Bitmaps

You color bitmaps using the color options that are displayed in the second row of the Fill Tool fly-out. These are the shades of gray and black and white options. If you choose the X option for the selected bitmap, it is not displayed in the Preview Screen or on the printed page. You can also use the *Outline Color* dialog boxes to change the color of your bitmaps, including the *PostScript Halftone Screen frequency.*

You can fill or change the box surrounding a bitmap in color using the Fill Tool color dialog boxes. The fill you give the surrounding frame only shows through a black and white bitmap. Color or gray-scale bitmaps are not transparent, and are not affected by any changes made in the Fill Tool color dialog boxes.

New Object Default Settings

Whenever you choose any of the options from the Outline or Fill Tool fly-outs, and no object is currently selected, the *New Object* dialog box (Figure 3-36) will be displayed. Selecting one of the three options here, lets you set a default fill and/or outline for all objects you draw or place on the page, just text, or all objects other than text.

After you select the appropriate option you want and click on OK, the fill or outline you choose in the following dialog boxes apply to everything from then on. You can change any fill or outline default setting at any time, by following the same steps. If, by mistake, you choose one of the fill or outline options without having an object selected, select Cancel from the *New Object* dialog box. Figure 3-36 shows the *New Object* dialog box for *Outline Color*, but every fill and outline option has one.

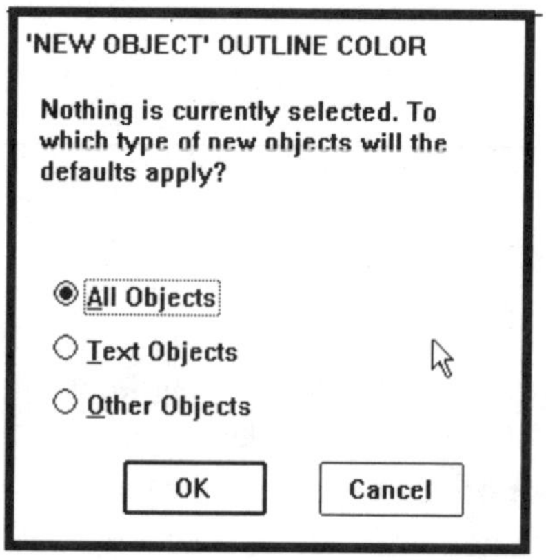

Figure 3-36. The New Object Dialog Box.

Summary

This chapter introduced you to the Outline and Fill Tools that you can use to outline and fill any object you create. You learned about spot and process colors, and how to apply them to your graphic. Additionally, this chapter explained bit map and vector patterns, and how you can use them.

Chapter 4

Text Input Capabilities

This chapter teaches you about the Text Tool in CorelDRAW!. The Text Tool lets you type text on the page so that you can manipulate it and use it for special effects and headings. Additionally, you can use it as body or paragraph text. You will learn about:

- Text strings
- Paragraph text
- Text attributes
- How to import text
- How to manipulate text
- Symbols.

Text Strings

To apply strings of text to your page, select the Text Tool from the Tool box (Figure 4-1), and click it once on the page. It is not important where you click the Text Tool, since you can move strings of text around once they are on the page.

When you have clicked the Text Tool on the page, the *Text* dialog box (Figure 4-2) will be displayed. After typing in the required text and changing the attributes, click on the OK button to display the text on the page. You can also paste text into this dialog box using the *Paste* button. The remaining features of this dialog box are explained after next discussing the *Paragraph Text* option.

Figure 4-1. The Text Tool.

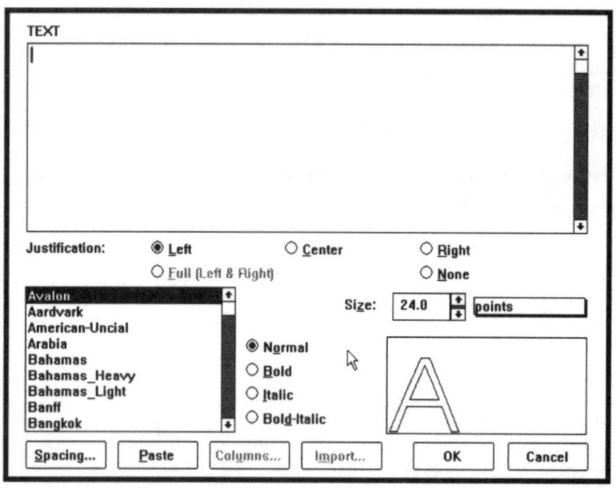

Figure 4-2. The Text Dialog Box.

Paragraph Text

To apply lengthy text blocks, select the Text Tool as in Figure 4-1, and draw a frame on the page with your finger on the mouse (Figure 4-3).

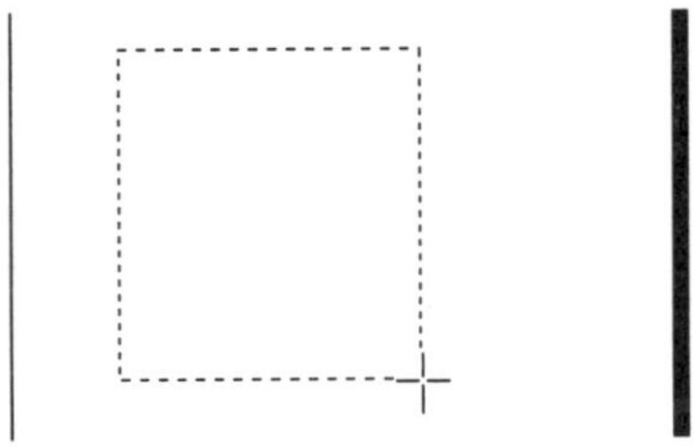

Figure 4-3. Drawing a Frame with the Text Tool.

Once you release your finger from the mouse, the *Paragraph Text* dialog box (Figure 4-4) is displayed. This dialog box is almost identical to the *Text* dialog box (Figure 4-3). Since you drew the frame first with the Text Tool, you can now enter up to 4000 characters.

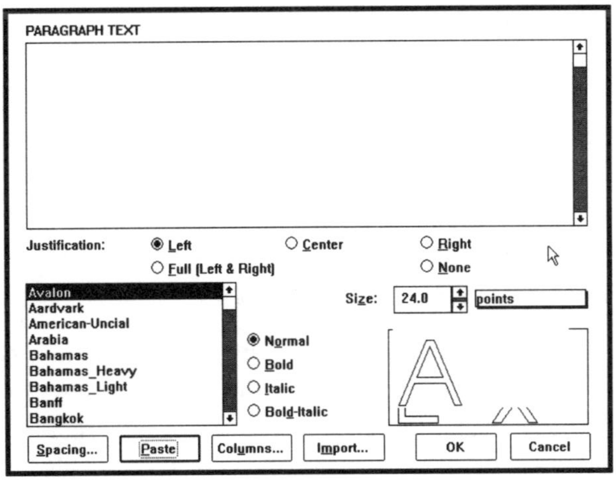

Figure 4-4. The Paragraph Text Dialog Box.

In addition, you can select the *Import* and *Columns* options, (Figure 4-4) which are discussed later in this chapter. Once you type, import, or paste in the required text and change the attributes, select OK. The text is now inside the frame that you drew with the Text Tool (Figure 4-5). If all the text is not displayed in this frame, enlarge the frame as you would any other frame, box, or object in CorelDRAW!.

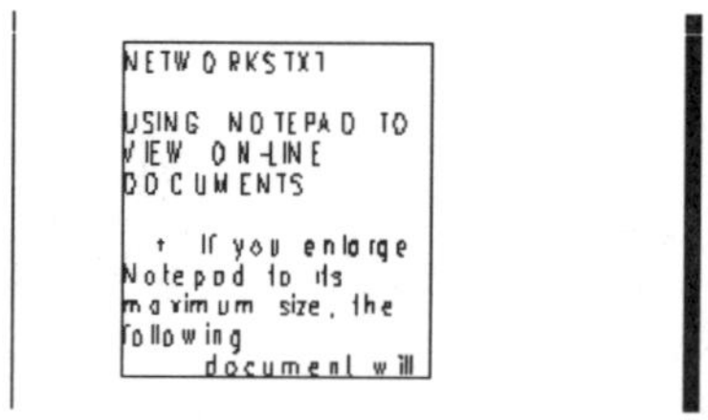

Figure 4-5. Text Created from the Paragraph Text Dialog Box.

The following two sections describe the various options contained in the Figure 4-2 *Text*, and the Figure 4-4 *Paragraph Text* dialog boxes.

Text Attributes

The window at the top of the Figures 4-2 or 4-4 dialog boxes is for typing in, or importing the text. The flashing cursor in this window is ready for the text to be typed. If it is not there, it is just a matter of clicking the mouse once inside this window. Type the text in the window as you would in any word processor. In the *Text* dialog box, text can be typed or pasted in. In the *Paragraph Text* dialog box, you can type, paste, or import text. Importing text is discussed in this chapter.

After you click the Text Tool on the page, the *Text* dialog box holds up to 250 characters. If you draw a frame with the Text Tool, the *Paragraph Text* dialog box holds up to 4000 characters. Once you have entered the required text, you can then set the attributes of the text.

The first option you have is *Justification* (Figure 4-6). The choices here are *Left*, *Center*, *Right*, *Full* (*Left & Right*), and *None*. The justification occurs in relation to where you click the Text Tool on the page. When there is only one line of text, the *Justification* option is not necessarily important, since you can move the text around. When there is more than one line of text, the *Justification* is effective. The *Full (Left & Right)* option is only available for paragraph text.

Figure 4-6. The Justification Option.

There is an extensive range of fonts packaged with CorelDRAW!, and it is simple to select and change them. The frame containing the list of fonts is at the bottom left of the dialog box (Figure 4-7). There is a scroll bar to the right of this frame, that gives you access to the remaining typefaces. To select the typeface you want, simply click on it once. To the right of the typeface frame are the style options. Not all fonts can have all these styles applied to them. For example, the Dawn Castle font can only have *Normal* or *Bold*. To select one of the style options, click inside the circle to the left of (or on) the actual option (Figure 4-7).

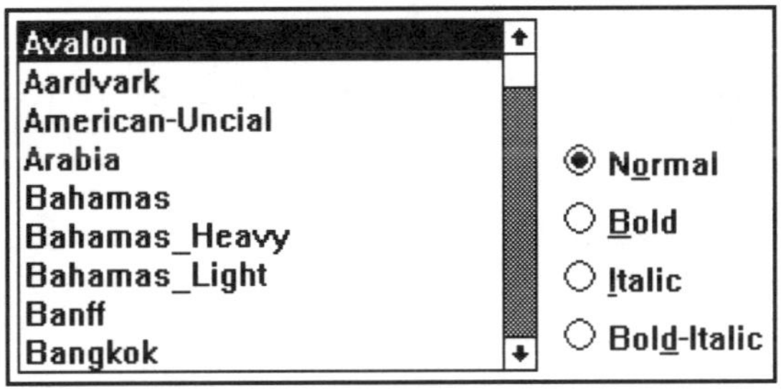

Figure 4-7. Typefaces and Styles.

To the right of the typeface frame is another frame that, on the first activation of the *Text* or *Paragraph Text* dialog box, contains the letter "A." (See Figure 4-2 or 4-4.) On typing text in the window at the top of the dialog box, the letter "A" changes to the first two letters you have typed. Also, whenever the style of the font is altered, the letter or letters in this frame change to reflect the new attributes you have selected.

To change the size of the text you are planning to place on the page, use the *Size* option (Figure 4-8). Its location in the dialog box is highlighted. The choices available for the size of the text are points, inches, millimeters and picas. To change the current measurement system, click on the measurement frame until your measurement type is activated.

Figure 4-8. The Size Section of the Text Dialog Box.

You change the actual size of the text by altering the current figure in the *Size* frame. To do this, double-click over the figure, so that it is selected in reverse video, and type in the new number. Alternatively, click on the up or down scroll buttons to the right of the frame, until you reach the required number.

You can always change the size of the text once it is on the page, by manipulating it with the Pick Tool. You can change the size of the paragraph text only through the *Text* dialog box. The size you can apply to text is from 0.7 points to 1440 points.

Along the bottom of the *Text* or *Paragraph Text* dialog boxes is a series of buttons. The first button is the *Spacing* button, which activates the *Text Spacing* dialog box (Figure 4-9).

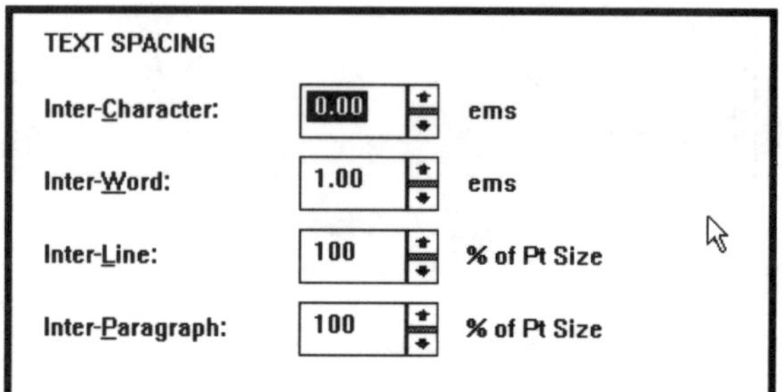

Figure 4-9. The Text Spacing Dialog Box.

The options in the *Text Spacing* dialog box apply to all text you type on the page. The unit of measurement is "ems" for the first two options. This size is equal to a capital M of the current point size of the current font. When you are scaling the text, any changes you have made in this dialog box, are still effective, as the "em" measurement is relative rather than absolute. If you change the point size, for example, you do not have to readjust these figures.

The first option available in the *Text Spacing* dialog box (Figure 4-9) is the *Inter-Character* option. Making any changes here increases or decreases the space between all text characters. The *Inter-Word* option affects the spacing between the words in your text string or paragraph text. Positive values increase and negative values decrease the spacing.

The *Inter-Line* (leading) option controls the amount of space between lines. Altering the figure in the *Inter-Paragraph* frame affects the spacing between paragraphs, and only applies to paragraph text. That is, text that has been typed inside the frame drawn with the Text Tool (see Figures 4-3 and 4-4). New paragraphs are distinguished by an empty line (made with the Enter key) between lines of text.

If you have changed any settings in the *Text Spacing* dialog box, and if you want these changes to apply to all text from now on, you can click on the *Save as Default* button. You can change this whenever necessary.

The next option after Spacing is *Paste*. Clicking on this button pastes text into the window, at the top of the dialog box, from the Windows clipboard. You must first copy text into the clipboard from a word processing program, or any program that can use the Windows clipboard.

All the same rules apply with pasted text, that apply when you are typing text yourself. That is, a maximum of 250 characters fits when you click the Text Tool on the page (Figures 4-1 and 4-2), and a maximum of 4000 characters if you draw a frame with the Text Tool (Figures 4-3 and 4-4). Any extra text is not displayed. Figure 4-10 shows the *Paragraph Text* dialog box with pasted text in the window.

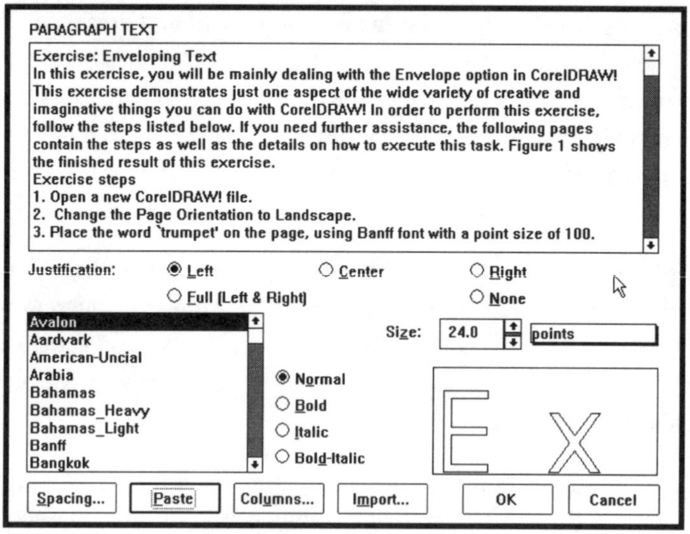

Figure 4-10. Pasted Text in the Text Entry Window.

The *Columns* button activates the *Text Columns* dialog box of Figure 4-11. You can apply columns to paragraph text. There are eight columns available, and the *Gutter Width* option determines the space between the columns. You change the settings in this dialog box as you would in any dialog box.

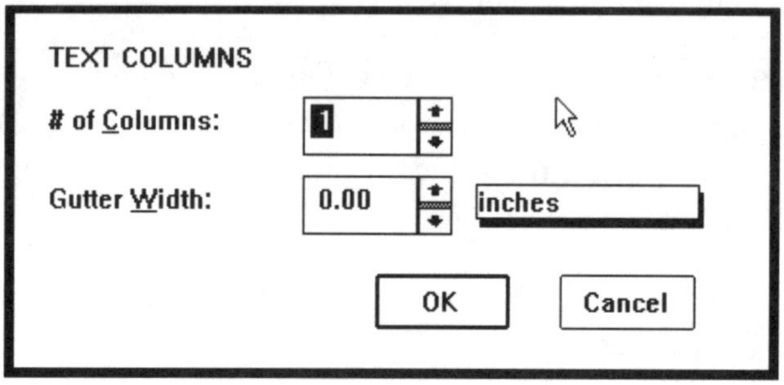

Figure 4-11. The Text Columns Dialog Box.

Importing Text

In addition to pasting text, you can import text. Click on the *Import* button to get the *Import Text* dialog box (Figure 4-12). You can activate the *Import* button only when you have drawn a frame with the Text Tool.

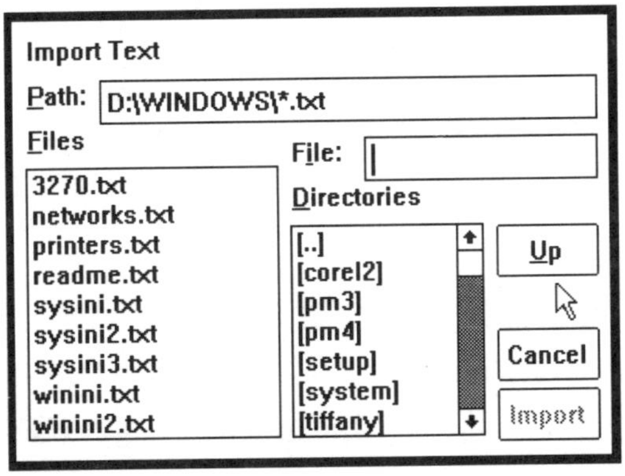

Figure 4-12. The Import Text Dialog Box.

Any text that you created in any word processing program, and saved as an ASCII file, can be imported into the *Paragraph Text* dialog box. The file extension initially active in the *Import Text* dialog box is .TXT. You can also change this file extension in the Path field to suit the format of the file you want to import.

Through the *Import Text* dialog box (Figure 4-12), you have access to your computer's drives and directories, enabling you to search anywhere on your disk to find the necessary file. Once you find it, either double-click on the name in the *Files* frame, or click on it once and then click on the *Import* button. The text is then displayed in the window at the top of the *Paragraph Text* dialog box (Figure 4-13). You can then apply any of the attributes available to this text as described earlier. Once you click on OK, the text is displayed on the page in the frame you originally drew (Figure 4-3).

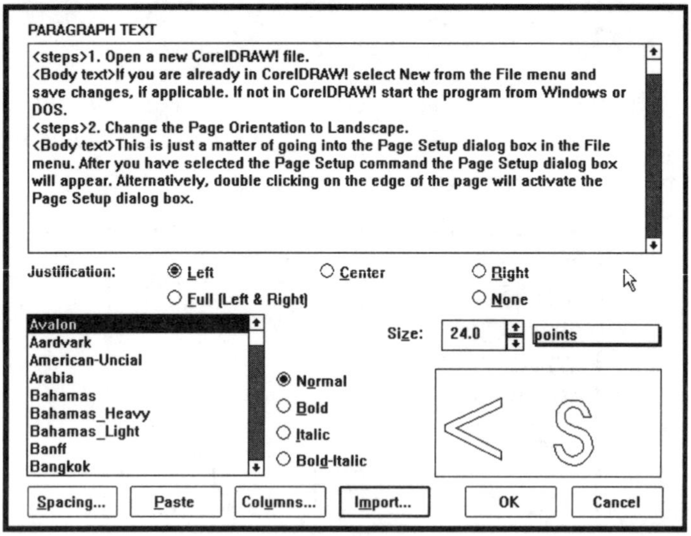

Figure 4-13. Text Imported into the Paragraph Text Dialog Box.

Editing text with the Node Tool (explained in **Chapter 2: The Toolbox**) still applies to paragraph text. You select paragraph text by clicking on the frame surrounding the text. This applies for both the Pick Tool and the Node Tool. To edit paragraph text, follow the same steps as you would with text strings. You can also rotate and skew paragraph text like you would any other text string or object on your page.

On the working screen, the typeface style you apply to paragraph text is not displayed. The Figure 4-14 shows paragraph text typeface in the screen font (left) and how it looks on the Preview Screen (right).

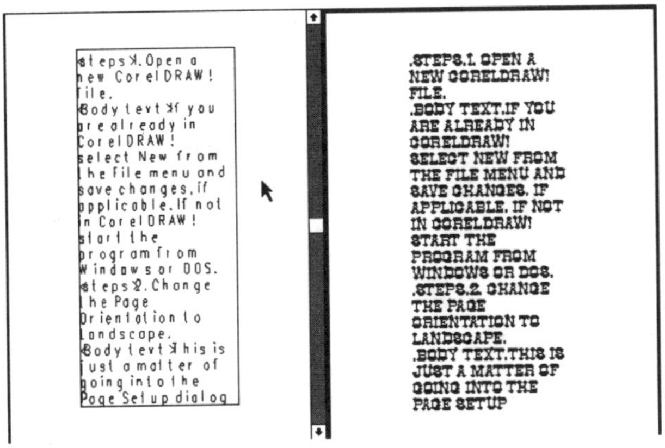

Figure 4-14. Paragraph Text in the Screen Font and on the Preview Screen.

Manipulating Text

You can use text in many different ways in CorelDRAW!. The following pages show brief explanations of how to manipulate text.

This first bit of text is a text string. After typing it on the page in a single line, activate the Node Tool with the text still selected. Then move the letters around by placing the Node Tool inside the nodes to the bottom left of each letter, holding the mouse down, and dragging the letters to their new positions like this:

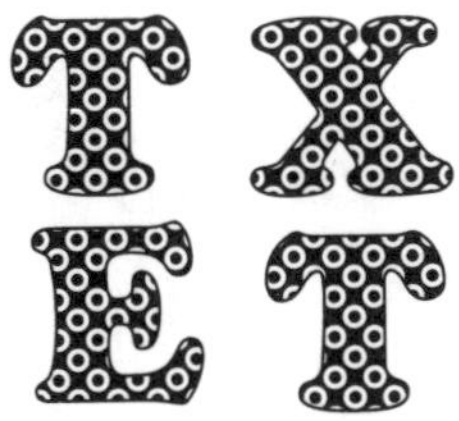

For more information on this process, see **Exercise 4** in Part 2 of this book. A *Bitmap Fill Pattern* is applied to this text (see **Exercise 6**), as well as a thick black outline from the Outline Tool fly-out.

The following text string has the *Extrude* command from the **Effects** menu applied to it.

For more information on extruding, see the **Effects** menu in **Chapter 5: Menu Commands**, and **Exercises 9**, **11**, and **15**.

The following text string was created by clicking the Text Tool on the page, which activated the *Text* dialog box. The text was then typed in the window at the top of the dialog box, the font and size options were changed, and then the OK button was clicked on.

> **This text string was created by clicking the Text Tool on the page which activated the Text dialog box. The text was keyed into the window at the top of the dialog box. The font and size options were changed and the OK button was clicked on.**

In CorelDRAW!, you can flow text along any shape or curve. Here it is flowed around a circle, which is explained in detail in **Exercise 1.**

Once you place text on the page, you can alter it in size both horizontally and vertically, as well as scale it in its correct proportions. For the following example, hold the mouse down on the middle right selection handle with the Pick Tool, and drag it slightly to the right. The result is stretched text. To change the size of text, or any other object for that matter, while keeping it in its correct proportions, hold the mouse down on any corner selection handle, and drag it in the desired direction.

You can rotate text in CorelDRAW! just like you can rotate any other object. You select the text with the Pick Tool and click the mouse once or double-click on the text. This activates the Rotate and Skew handles (see The Pick Tool in **Chapter 2: The Toolbox**). Once these handles are activated, hold the mouse down on the bottom left handle, and drag the mouse in a counterclockwise direction. Release the mouse when the text is rotated to the desired position. The Status Line shows the degree of rotation.

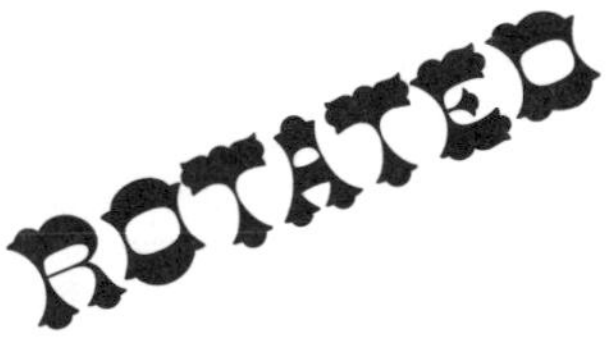

You use the *Blend* command in the **Effects** menu on two text strings. Whenever two different objects are blended, the blend steps are sometimes not whole fillable objects. But when the two objects are the same (not necessarily the same size), the blend steps can be filled. If these two objects are different colors, the steps also change from one color to the other. For more information on blending, see **Chapter 5: Menu Commands** and **Exercise 15**.

The individual pieces of the following text string were altered in the *Character Attributes* dialog box, which you activate from the **Edit** menu when you select the text with the Node Tool. For more information on this option, see **Exercise 2**.

jumbled

The following text paragraph was created by drawing a frame on the page with the Text Tool. After typing the text into the *Paragraph Text* dialog box, changing the text attributes, and clicking on OK, the text was displayed in the frame. This frame surrounding the text was then selected with the Pick Tool, and clicked on once more to activate the Rotate and Skew handles. The mouse was then held down on the top middle handle, which was dragged to the right. After releasing the mouse, the frame surrounding the text was skewed, and the text reformatted to accommodate this.

This text paragraph was created by drawing a frame on the page with the Text Tool. The Paragraph Text dialog box then appeared, and the text was keyed in. The font and size of the text was changed and then the OK button was clicked on. The frame surrounding the text was then selected with the Pick Tool and then clicked on once more to activate the Rotate and Skew handles. The mouse was then held down on the top middle skew handle and dragged the mouse to the right, skewing the text.

The following paragraph text was created by drawing a frame on the page with the Text Tool. The paragraph was given two columns in the *Text Columns* dialog box (Figure 4-11), which is activated by clicking on the *Columns* button at the bottom of the *Paragraph Text* dialog box.

This paragraph text was
also created by drawing
a frame on the page with
the Text Tool. The font
and size of the test was
altered and two
columns was selected
from the Text Columns

dialog box, which w
activated by clicki
on the Columns butt
at the bottom of t
Paragraph Text dial
box. For Justificati
we selected the Full (L
& Right) option.

The following text has the *Edit Perspective* command in the **Effects** menu applied to it (see *Edit Perspective* in **Chapter 5: Menu Commands** and **Exercises 9** and **11**). Text that has had the *Edit Perspective* command applied to it remains as text and can be edited as such.

As with the *Edit Perspective* command, you can edit text that has been enveloped. For more details on applying the *Edit Envelope* command from the **Effects** menu to text, see **Chapter 5: Menu Commands** and **Exercise 10**.

Once text has been converted to curves, you can change the shape of each text character with the Node Tool (see **Exercises 3** and **8**). Text that you have converted to curves cannot be changed back to text again, therefore the *Edit Text* and *Character Attributes* dialog boxes no longer apply. The advantage of converting text to curves, is that you can manipulate and change the shape of the individual text characters as shown below.

Symbols

You place symbols using the Text Tool. The Clip Art catalog that comes with the package displays the available Symbols. You choose symbols from the *Symbols* dialog box, which is activated when you click the Text Tool on the page with the [Shift] key pressed.

Once the *Symbols* dialog box is displayed (Figure 4-15), there are approximately 3000 symbols from which you can select a wide range of subjects. The way to access a certain symbol is to scan through the topic choices in the rectangle at the top right of the *Symbols* dialog box (Figure 4-15). Use the scroll bars, if necessary, to select other topics. Once you click on a different topic, you can see the first ten symbols of the topic displayed in the horizontal row at the bottom of the dialog box.

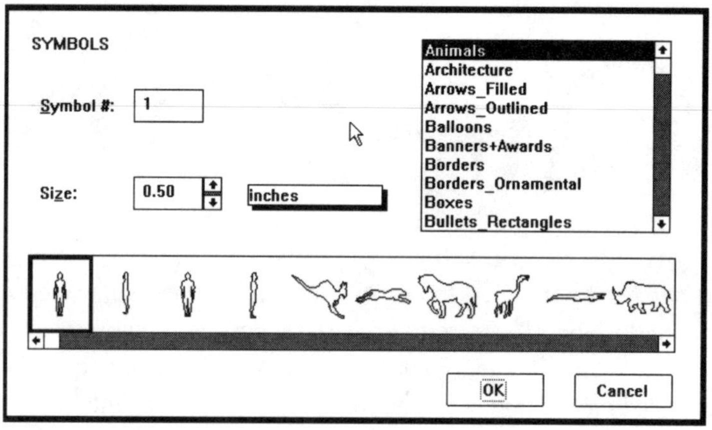

Figure 4-15. The Symbols Dialog Box.

After selecting the topic, use the scroll bar at the bottom of the horizontal frame containing the symbols, to view the whole range of symbols for this topic. When you find the required symbol, click on it once with the mouse. The number of the symbol is displayed in the *Symbol #* frame. Every symbol has a number, so if you find a symbol from the Clip Art Catalog, you can type in this number instead of wasting time scrolling through the full range.

SHORTCUT

You can also specify the size you want the symbol to appear on the page. To do this, change the setting in the *Size* frame. You change this as you would in any other dialog box. It does not necessarily matter what size you place the symbol on the page because you can always resize it later unless you want a specific size.

Click on OK in the *Symbols* dialog box (Figure 4-15) to return to the screen. The symbol is now on the page. If the symbol has more than one part to it, it is combined. Symbols are always displayed on the page with a white fill and a thin black outline. If you want to edit a symbol, or apply a fill and/or an outline to the separate parts of it, select the symbol with the Pick Tool and choose the *Break Apart* command from the **Arrange** menu.

Any symbol you place on the page can be resized, rotated, skewed, filled, and manipulated, like any other object in CorelDRAW!. See Figure 4-16 for examples of symbols that are placed on the page, broken apart, and have fills applied to them. The banner symbol (bottom left) also has some text placed on top of it. The text is enveloped to fit the curve of the banner. The buildings are extruded separately to give them a three-dimensional appearance.

Figure 4-16. CorelDRAW! Symbols.

Summary

This chapter explained how to use text in CorelDRAW!. You learned how to activate the *Text* and *Paragraph Text* dialog boxes so that you can change the text's shape and size. Also, you learned how to import and paste text, and how to use symbols.

Chapter 5

Menu Commands

The CorelDRAW! menu commands enable you to work in the files and manipulate text and graphics to suit your needs. You choose the commands from the easy-to-use pop-down menus that are displayed horizontally across the top of the screen. This chapter teaches you about these command menus:

- File
- Edit
- Transform
- Effects
- Arrange
- Display
- Special.

File Menu

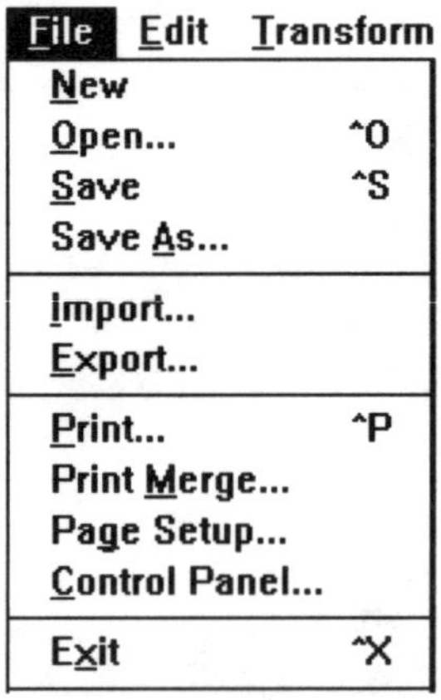

Figure 5-1. The File Menu.

New

The first command from the File menu is the *New* Command. When you select this command, the program opens a new CorelDRAW! file.

If you have made any changes to the existing file, CorelDRAW! asks whether you want to save these changes. If you choose to save the changes of a current untitled file, the *Save Drawing* dialog box is displayed (see the *Save* command, also in the File menu).

Open

The *Open* command gives you access to previously created CorelDRAW! files. On selecting this command, the *Open Drawing* dialog box (Figure 5-2) is displayed. This dialog box lets you scroll through the computer's drives and directories to where you have saved your drawings. To open a saved drawing, select it from the list of files and click on *Open*. CorelDRAW! files use an extension of .CDR. All files that have been created in CorelDRAW! version 2.0, on being selected in the list of files, will be displayed in a very low resolution format in the box at the right of the dialog box.

If you select the *Use Mosaic* option in the *Preferences* command in the **Special** menu and then choose *Open*, you will load the Mosaic program. See **Chapter 7: Mosaic** for more details.

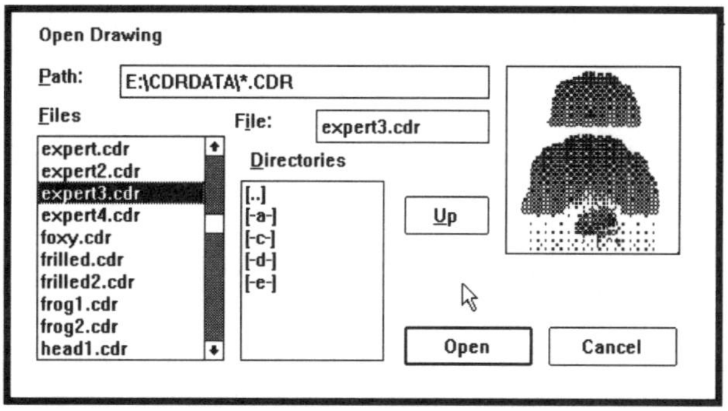

Figure 5-2. The Open Drawing Dialog Box.

Save

The *Save* command saves whatever you have done since last using this command. If you have not used this command before, the *Save Drawing* dialog box (Figure 5-3) is displayed. You cannot save a drawing without naming it. In this dialog box, you give the current file a name and decide where you want to save it (see *Save As*). Once you have done this, you can use the *Save* command without displaying the *Save Drawing* dialog box.

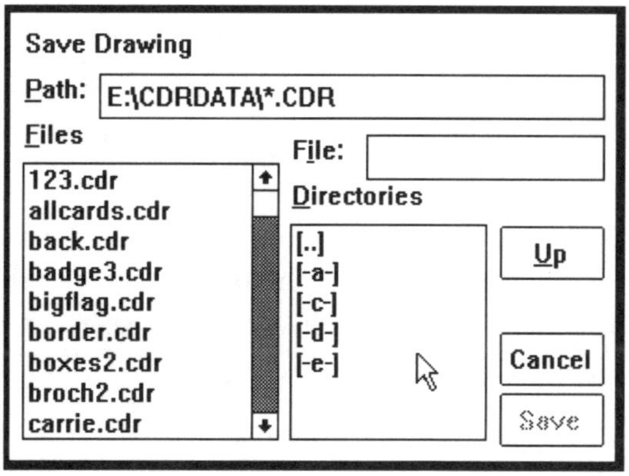

Figure 5-3. The Save Drawing Dialog Box.

Save As

You use the *Save As* command when you want to rename the current file, or save it to a different drive or directory. You can also use this command if you want to alter the graphic, but keep the original. When you select this command, you will again see the *Save Drawing* dialog box. Once you have entered the name of the file in the File box, click on *Save*.

Import

The *Import* command lets you bring in graphics and bitmaps created in other programs. The dialog box (Figure 5-4) that is displayed when you select this option, lets you select the format of the file you would like to import.

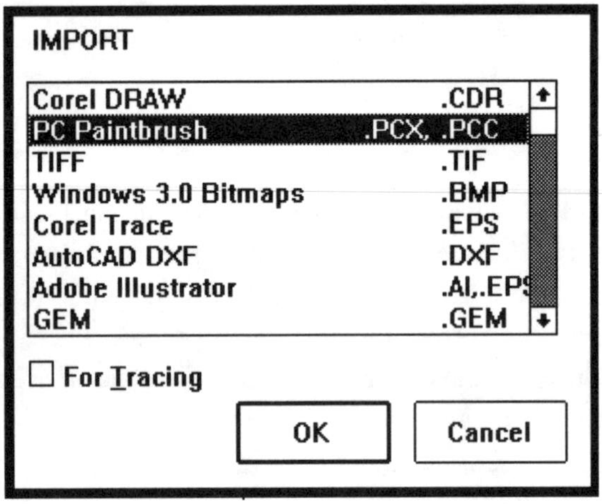

Figure 5-4. The Import Dialog Box.

Once you have selected the format, click on OK, and another *Import* dialog box is displayed. This second dialog box is similar to the *Open Drawing* dialog box, where you can scroll through your drives and directories to find the image that you would like to import. Only images in the format selected in the first *Import* dialog box are displayed in the list of Files.

You can select the *For Tracing* option in the *Import* dialog box (Figure 5-5) if you decide to import a bitmap, and would like to trace that bitmap. If you select this option, the bitmap imported will be of a higher screen resolution than if you did not select it. You can still trace a bitmap if you do not select this option.

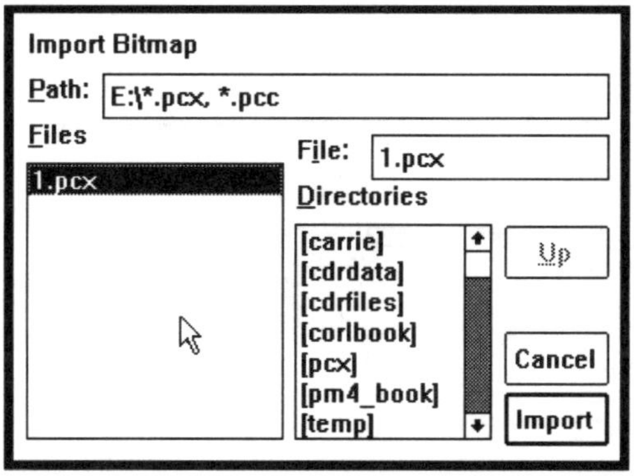

Figure 5-5. The Import Bitmap Dialog Box.

For more details on the *For Tracing* (manually) option see The Pencil Tool, **Chapter 2: The Toolbox**.

Import file types

CorelDRAW! Version 2.0 supports the following import file types:

- CorelDRAW!
- PCX
- .TIF
- Windows 3 Bitmap (BMP)
- AutoCAD DXF
- Adobe Illustrator AI EPS
- GEM
- Lotus 1-2-3 PIC
- IBM PIF (GDF)
- PICT (Macintosh)
- HPGL
- CGM.

Export

The *Export* command allows you to save your drawing in a format other than the CorelDRAW! standard format. This allows you to use a graphic in other programs. The *Export* dialog box (Figure 5-6) is displayed when you select this option.

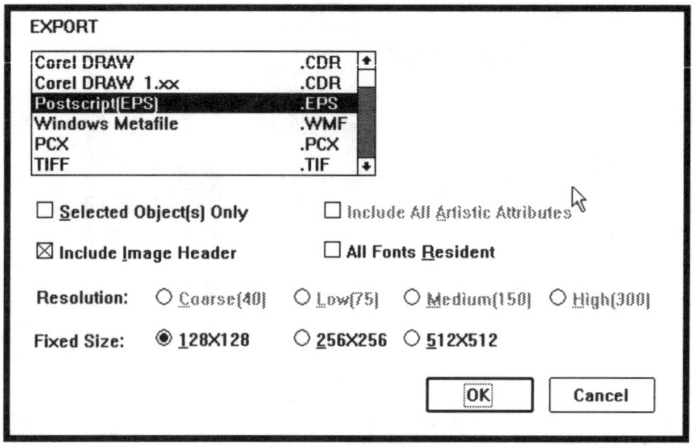

Figure 5-6. The Export Dialog Box.

From the *Export* dialog box, select the option for exporting the file. Once you select a format and click on OK, the second *Export* (file) dialog box is displayed, where you name the file and decide where to save it.

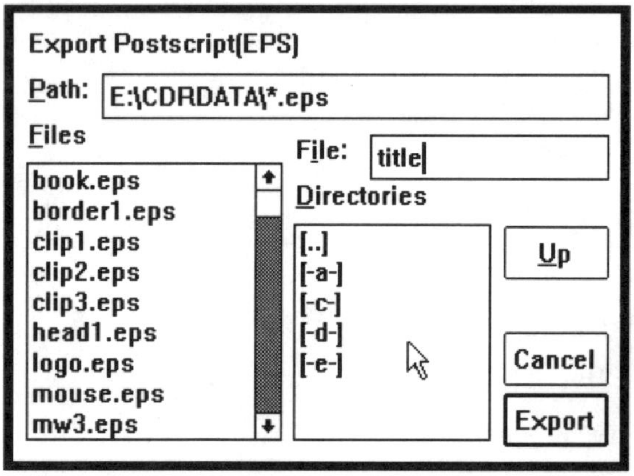

Figure 5-7. The Second Export (File) Dialog Box.

If you check the *Selected Object(s) Only* option, you export only what you have currently selected on your page. The *Include Image Header* option is only available when exporting as an EPS file. If you do have this option checked, the exported graphic contains a TIFF screen image, which is displayed when importing into programs such as PageMaker and Ventura. The *All Fonts Resident* option again is only used for EPS files. If you have it selected, it is assumed that the printer has all the resident fonts needed. If you do not select it, CorelDRAW! downloads the necessary fonts.

The *Resolution* option lets you determine the resolution when exporting PCX or TIFF bitmap files. Use *Fixed Size* when creating a bitmap image header for EPS files. The smallest size is recommended to conserve disk space.

Export file types

CorelDRAW! Version 2.0 supports the following export file types:

- CorelDRAW! Version 2.0
- CorelDRAW! Version 1.xx
- Corel Symbols&Typeface (WFN)
- Encapsulated PostScript (EPS)
- Windows Metafile (WMF)
- DXF (outlines only)
- PCX, TIFF, CGM
- Adobe Illustrator (AI)
- WordPerfect (WPG)
- GEM
- IBM PIF (GDF)
- PICT (Macintosh)
- HPGL
- SCODL (SCD)
- SlideShow (PIC).

Print

The *Print* command activates the *Print Options* dialog box (Figure 5-8). This dialog box lets you print your graphic as is, or lets you apply extra commands that affect the way the graphic is printed.

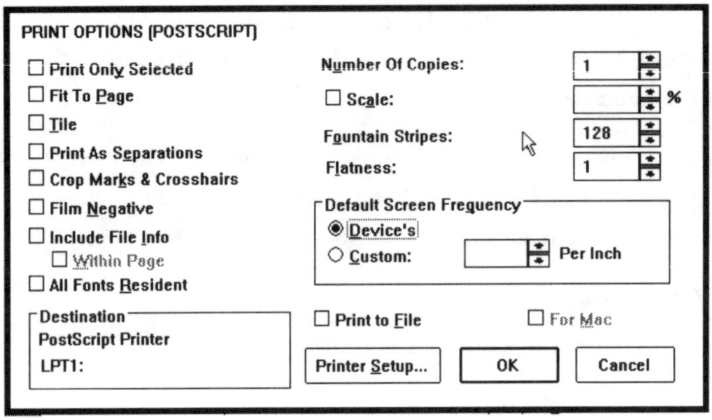

Figure 5-8. The Print Options Dialog Box.

The *Print Only Selected* option prints only what is selected on your page with the Pick Tool.

The *Scale* choice lets you shrink or increase the graphic when printing. The actual size is set at 100%, and values set higher or lower than this change the graphic size, respectively. Use the *Fit To Page* option to resize your graphic to fit the entire page.

The *Tile* option prints graphics larger than the page size of your printer. Any section of the image that does not fit on the initial page is printed on additional pages.

When you select the *Print As Separations* option, your image prints out on a number of pages. The number of pages depends on what colors you have assigned to the objects on your page.

If you have used Process colors (Cyan, Magenta, Yellow, and Black), the page prints as four separate outputs. If you have used Spot colors (Pantone) for your objects, you get a different printout for every color you have used.

If you want crop marks on your page, select the *Crop Marks & Crosshairs* option. The *Page Setup* command, also under the **File** menu, lets you alter the position of the crop marks. You can use this option only if you have a PostScript printer.

The *For Mac* command is used in conjunction with the *Print to File* option. The *Print to File* option contains certain characters that do not allow the file to be printed on Macintosh-controlled printers. Selecting the *For Mac* option removes these characters.

If you have the *Print As Separations* option checked, the *Color Separations* dialog box (Figure 5-9) is activated every time you go to print. This dialog box has a list of every color used in your graphic. Each of these colors can be selected separately, or in multiples. Whichever color or colors you select from this box, are the ones that print. The *All Colors* or *Selected Colors* choices, at the bottom of the dialog box, are used when you want all or just the selected color or colors to print.

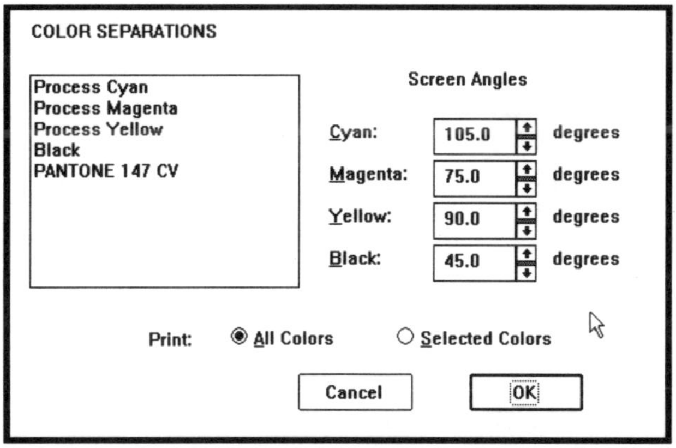

Figure 5-9. The Color Separations Dialog Box.

The *Screen Angles* option available for each color, in the *Color Separations* dialog box, changes the angle that the selected color is printed. The screen angles you select depend on the final printing process you are using.

The *Film Negative* option is only available with a PostScript printer. The image you wish to print with this option selected prints as a negative on film. The image also prints mirrored. Selecting *Include File Info* provides the name of your file, and the day's date and current time, to be printed in 10 point Courier at the side of the page (PostScript only).

If you select the *All Fonts Resident* option, you are assuming the printer has the necessary fonts already loaded. If you do not select this option, CorelDRAW! downloads the relevant fonts enabling your page to print correctly (PostScript only).

Default Screen Frequency relates to the number of lines per inch or gray scales in the final printout, which change depending on the resolution of the printer. It can also depend on the final printing process.

The *Print to File* option prints your image to a disk or directory on your computer. If you have this option selected, then you click on OK in the *Print Options* dialog box (Figure 5-10) to activate the *Print to File* dialog box. Here you are prompted to name the file and select where you would like to save it.

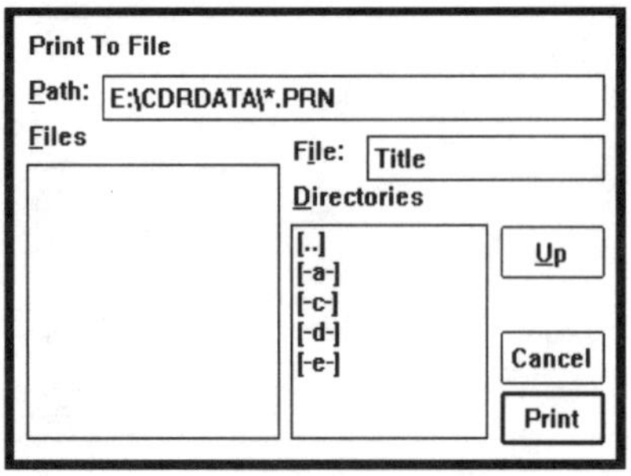

Figure 5-10. The Print To File Dialog Box.

When you select the *Printer Setup* option, you are presented with a *Printer Setup* dialog box (Figure 5-11), which differs depending on your printer and version of Windows. This dialog box is for setting things such as paper size and orientation, how many copies you want printed, resolution, and a list of available printers.

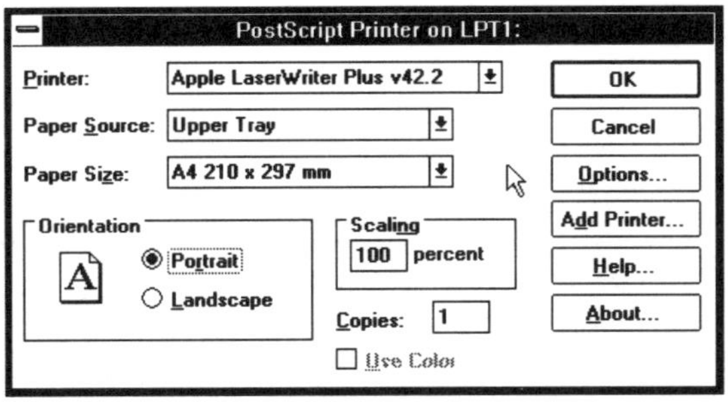

Figure 5-11. The Printer Setup Dialog Box.

Print Merge

The *Print Merge* option activates the *Print Merge* dialog box (Figure 5-12). Here you select a text file you have created in a word processing program. You use this option for things such as certificates or invitations, where the main information or drawing stays the same, and only a name or date, or some small text information, changes. To accurately set up the required information in the word processing program, consult the CorelDRAW! manual.

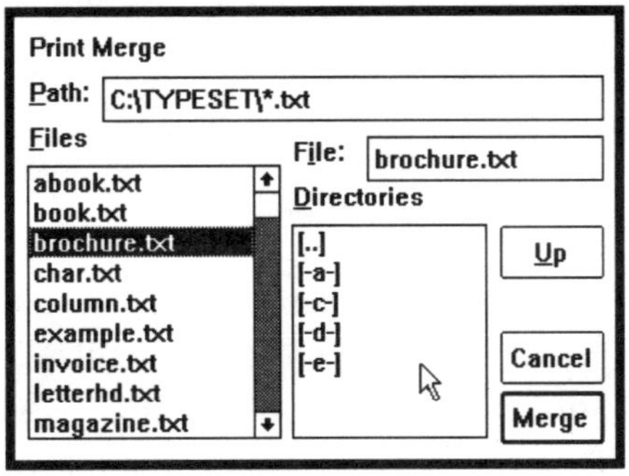

Figure 5-12. The Print Merge Dialog Box.

Page Setup

The *Page Setup* command activates the *Page Setup* dialog box (Figure 5-13). Double-clicking the mouse on the edge of the page also activates this dialog box. The options available in this box alter the *Orientation* and *Page Size* of the page you are working on. The options also affect the next page you use until you change it again. The *Horizontal* and *Vertical* frames reflect the dimensions of the page size you choose. Selecting *Custom* page size allows you to enter your own page dimensions into these frames.

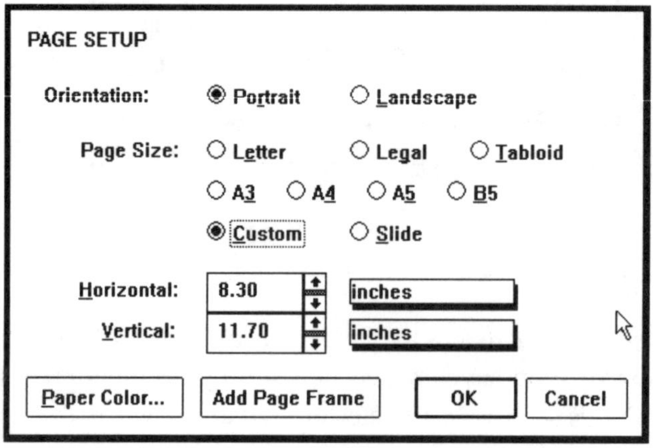

Figure 5-13. The Page Setup Dialog Box.

The *Paper Color* button activates a color dialog box similar to the *Uniform Fill* dialog box. When you select a color from this dialog box, the current page reflects this color. The color you selected does not print. It is only used for printing on color paper when you want to see the actual result on this color. The color you select is displayed only on the Preview Screen.

The *Add Page Frame* button places a frame, the size of the page on the screen, directly on top of the page and behind all objects. The fill and outline of this frame are the current default settings. To change the fill, outline, and/or size of the frame, select it with the Pick Tool as you would any rectangle, square, or object, and make the necessary changes.

Exit

Use the *Exit* command to leave CorelDRAW!. If you have made changes to the current document that have not been saved, a dialog box is activated that asks if you want to save these changes. If you have not yet saved the current document, and you select *Yes* from this dialog box, you will see the *Save Drawing* dialog box (Figure 5-14).

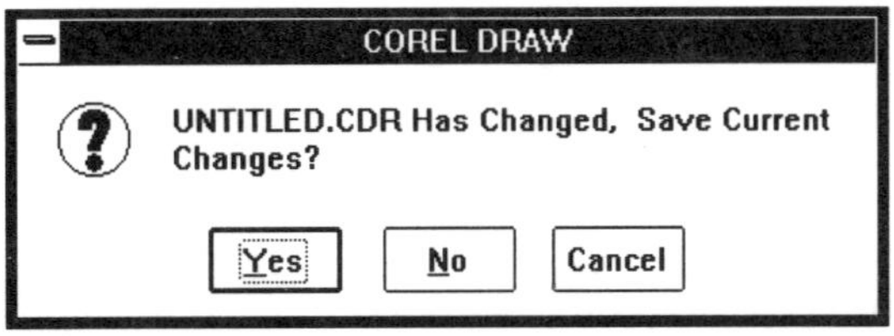

Figure 5-14. The Save Drawing Dialog Box.

Edit Menu

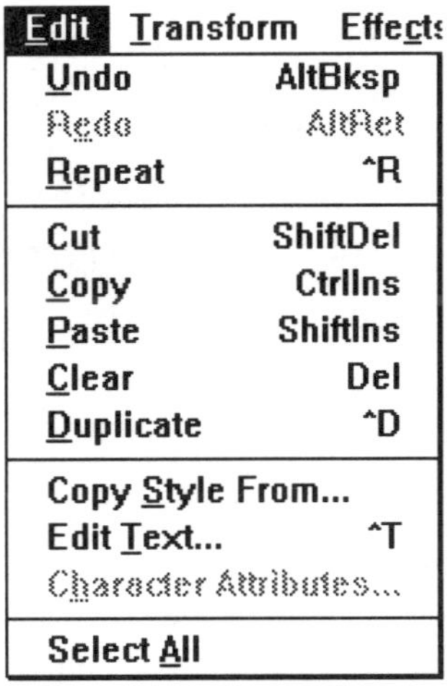

Figure 5-15. The Edit Menu.

Undo

This command changes the graphic to its previous state, and is particularly useful if you have just made a mistake. Most commands can be undone, except for changes made with the Zoom Tool, *Open, Save, Save As, Import* and *Export*, and selecting objects with the Pick Tool or Node Tool.

Redo

The *Redo* command is only available directly after you have used the *Undo* command. On selecting this option, the previous command you have just undone will be redone.

Repeat

If you have performed a task, or applied a command to an object that you want to apply exactly to another object, use the *Repeat* command. Once you have changed the first object, select the next object(s) with the Pick Tool and choose the *Repeat* command.

Cut

The *Cut* command removes a selected object(s) from the page and stores them in the Windows clipboard. You can then paste the cut objects into the same CorelDRAW! file or into another. You can use this command only once if you want to paste the cut object(s) back onto the page at a later stage. Every time you use the *Cut* command, the previous cut object(s) are no longer stored in the clipboard.

Copy

When you apply this command to a selected object, a copy of this object is saved to the Windows clipboard, while the original remains on the screen. You can then paste the copied object into the same or another CorelDRAW! file. As with the *Cut* command, the *Copy* command only saves one object at a time.

Paste

The *Paste* command places an object(s), that has been previously cut or copied, back onto the screen from the Windows clipboard.

Clear

The *Clear* command deletes selected object(s) from your page.

Duplicate

Use the *Duplicate* command to create an object on your page the same as any selected object.

Copy Style From

The *Copy Style From* command enables you to apply certain attributes of one object to another object on your page. The attribute choices available with this command are *Outline Pen*, *Outline Color*, *Fill*, and *Text Attributes*. See **Exercise 14** for more details on how to use this command.

Edit Text

Select the *Edit Text* command to alter a selected text string's attributes. The *Text* dialog box (Figure 5-16) that is displayed when you click the Text Tool on your page will then be activated. You now have the option of making any changes to the text you like.

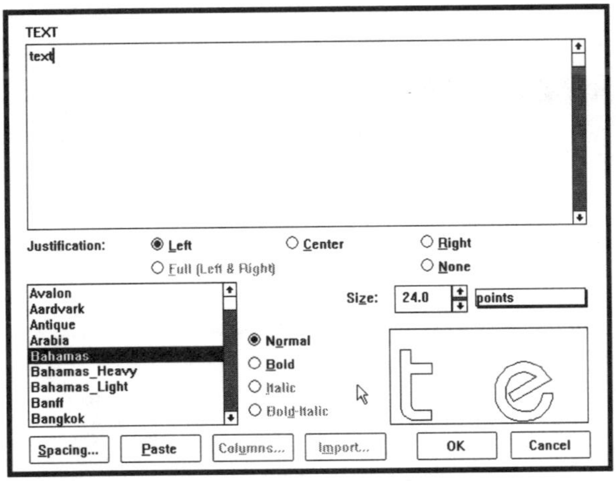

Figure 5-16. The Text Dialog Box.

With this dialog box, as with the *Text* dialog box, the first two letters that you place in the window, at the top of the dialog box, are displayed in the frame at the bottom right of this box. This lets you see what a specific letter will look like, in a certain font, before you place it on the page. This dialog box is explained in more detail in **Chapter 4: Text Input Capabilities**.

Character Attributes

This command is available only when you have selected a text string or text character with the Node Tool. To alter the attributes of just one text piece, either double-click inside its node, or click on it once and select the *Character Attributes* command from the **Edit** menu. To alter the whole text string, do the same, but have all the nodes selected.

Once you have activated the *Character Attributes* box (Figure 5-17), you can alter the *Font*, *Point Size*, *Horizontal* and *Vertical Shifts*, and *Character Angle* of the selected text.

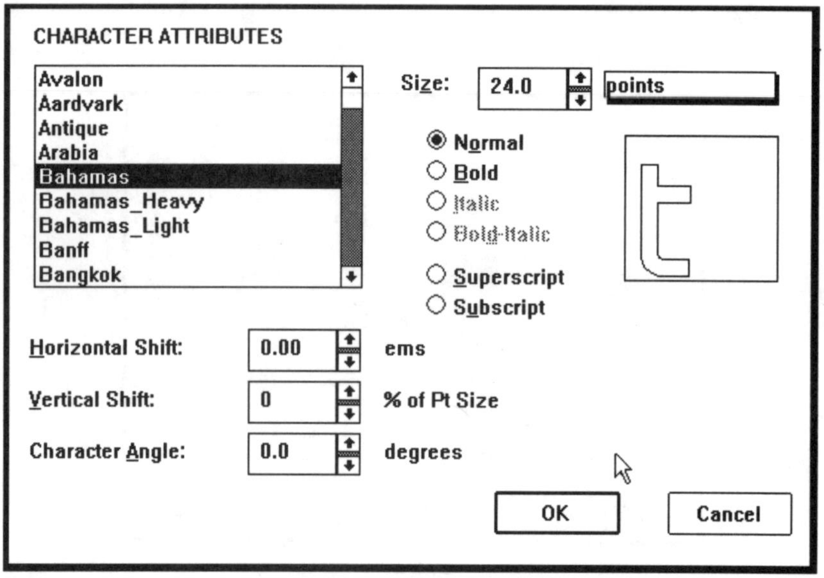

Figure 5-17. The Character Attributes Dialog Box.

For examples on the usage of the *Character Attributes* command and dialog box, see **Exercise 2**.

Select All

On choosing this command, you select every object on your page, as though you have selected each one with the Pick Tool. If you have a command you would like to apply to every object in a complex drawing on your page, the *Select All* command makes it easier than having to select each object one by one, with the [⇧ Shift] key held down. It is equivalent to drawing a marquee (or box) around all objects on the page with the Pick Tool.

Transform Menu

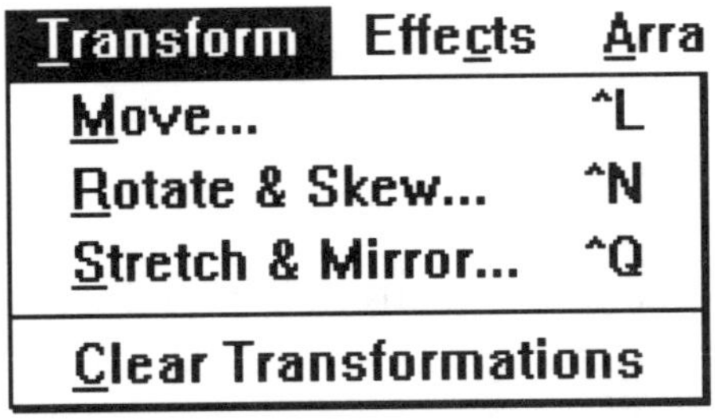

Figure 5-18. The Transform Menu.

Move

The *Move* command and associated dialog box (Figure 5-19) let you set coordinates for moving selected objects to a new position. This procedure is an alternative to dragging an object with the mouse. Using the *Move* dialog box, however, allows you to move an object to an exact measurement. Adding positive figures in the *Horizontal* and *Vertical* frames moves the object up and to the right. Negative values have the opposite effect. To make a copy of the original as you move, click on *Leave Original.*

You can also determine which part of the object will sit on the coordinates you select. The rulers must be turned on for this to work. Make sure the object you want to move is selected, activate the *Move* dialog box, and check the *Absolute Coordinates* option. Now, from the nodes situated at the bottom left of the dialog box, click the mouse inside the node you want situated at the coordinates you set above. For example, if you want the object to be to the right and below the coordinates, select the top left node by clicking inside it with the mouse.

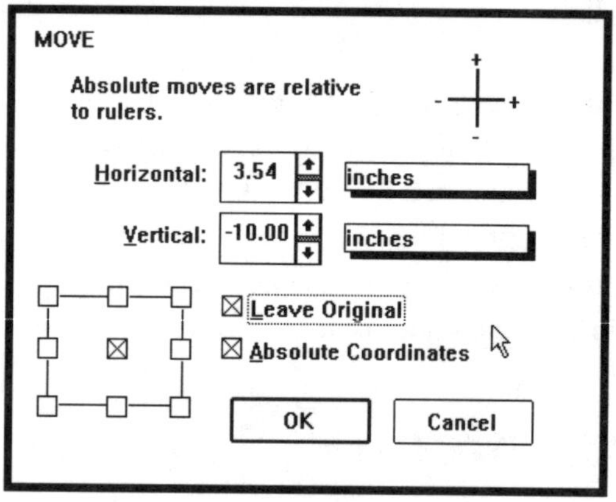

Figure 5-19. The Move Dialog Box.

Rotate & Skew

The *Rotate & Skew* command activates the *Rotate & Skew* dialog box (Figure 5-20). This dialog box gives you the option to either rotate or skew a selected object to a specified degree. You also have the option of leaving the original object behind. **Exercise 13** in Part 2, provides examples of rotating objects. See also "The Pick Tool" in **Chapter 2: The Toolbox.**

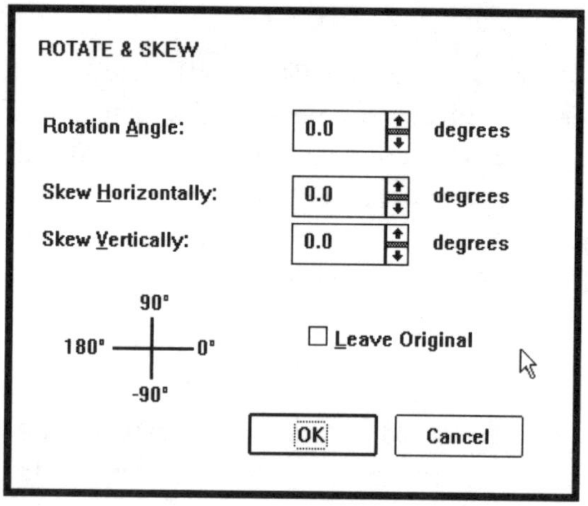

Figure 5-20. The Rotate & Skew Dialog Box.

Stretch & Mirror

The *Stretch Horizontally* and *Stretch Vertically* options in the dialog box (Figure 5-21) that is displayed when you select the *Stretch & Mirror* command, enable you to alter an object's shape by stretching it. The settings are automatically on 100%, and changing this setting either up or down stretchs the object larger or smaller, respectively.

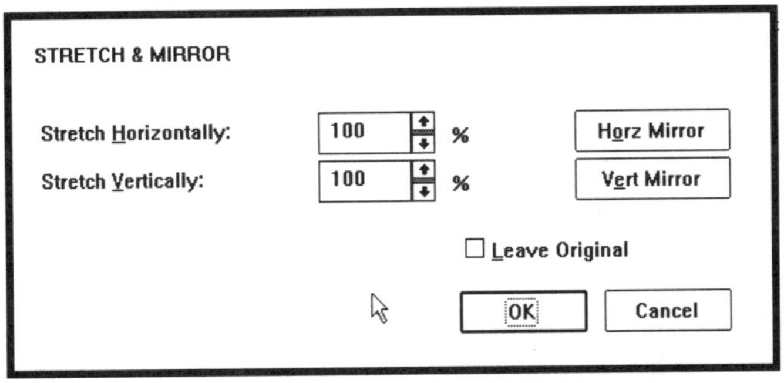

Figure 5-21. The Stretch & Mirror Dialog Box.

You can select the *Horizontal Mirror* and *Vertical Mirror* options when you want to display a mirror image of a selected object on the page. There is also the *Leave Original* option, that when selected, leaves the original object on the page, no matter what changes you make to it in this dialog box. You can also perform *Stretching & Mirroring* manually with the Pick Tool.

Clear Transformations

This command lets you return an object to its original state if it has had any attributes applied to it from either the *Move, Rotate & Skew*, or *Stretch & Mirror* dialog boxes. It also clears an object of all envelope or perspective frames applied through the **Effects** menu.

Effects Menu

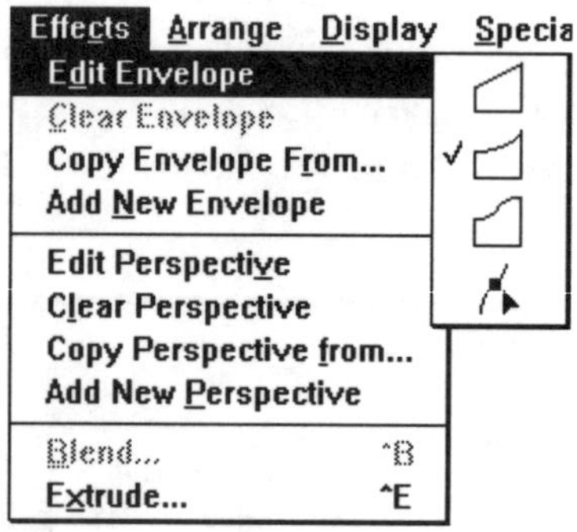

Figure 5-22. The Effects Menu.

Edit Envelope

The *Edit Envelope* command, and associated sub-menu, apply a dashed frame around an object or text, allowing you to distort the object or text in any shape or direction you like. Clicking on this command activates a sub-menu, where you select the way in which you will edit the enveloped object. After selecting one of the styles from this sub-menu, the dashed envelope frame and eight handles are displayed around the selected object, and the Node Tool is automatically activated. **Exercise 10** explains with the enveloping of text.

The four options available in the *Edit Envelope* sub-menu are as follows:

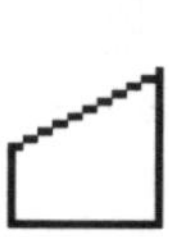

Selecting this top option gives the nodes of the envelopes straight line attributes. You cannot achieve a curved effect of the envelope by using this method. The envelope frame remains in a squared off fashion on all sides like this:

This option is the *Single Arc* option. Each side of the envelope frame remains in an arc shape on moving each of the nodes. The parts of the frame on either side of each node cannot be moved independently of each other.

The *Two Curves* option lets you manipulate the envelope frame so that there is a curve on either side of each node like this:

The last choice (the *Not Constrained* option) gives the nodes control points that you can be use to edit the envelope. You can select more than one node at once with this option, but with the other methods, you can move only one node at a time. This option gives you greater freedom when manipulating enveloped objects.

Clear Envelope

This command deletes the envelope that you have added to an object. The object then reverts to its original state before the envelope was added. The *Clear Envelope* command only clears the last envelope given to an object, if you have applied more than one envelope to it. This command does not work if you have applied the *Edit Perspective* command to an object.

The perspective must first be cleared before the envelope. This removes the perspective of the object. If you do not want this to happen, first make a duplicate of the object. Next, clear the perspective and then the envelope of the original object. To apply the same perspective again, use the *Copy Perspective From* command, to copy the perspective from the duplicated object back to the original.

Copy Envelope From

The *Copy Envelope From* command lets you copy the attributes of an enveloped object to another object. To do this, first use the Pick Tool to select the object that you would like to copy the envelope attributes to, and then select this command. Once you select the *Copy Envelope From* command, you will see a right-facing arrow with the word **From?** in it like this:

You then click this arrow on the enveloped object, that has the attributes you require, and the object you first selected takes on these attributes.

Add New Envelope

This command adds an envelope to a selected object that already has an envelope applied and manipulated. If the object has already been enveloped, the shape does not change and a new envelope frame is displayed around the object ready to be edited at your discretion.

The Ctrl + Shift keys have a certain effect on the way an envelope is edited, but can only be used on the first three options of the *Edit Envelope* sub-menu. If you drag a node while holding down the Ctrl key, you also move the opposite node in the same direction. The Shift key moves the two nodes in the opposite direction. Holding down both keys moves all four sides in opposite directions.

Edit Perspective

The *Edit Perspective* command places a dotted frame around a selected object that is similar to the envelope frame, except that the Perspective frame only has a node in each corner. You cannot edit these nodes in the same way you edit envelope nodes. Altering the perspective is as easy as dragging one of the four corner nodes to a different position and then releasing the mouse button like this:

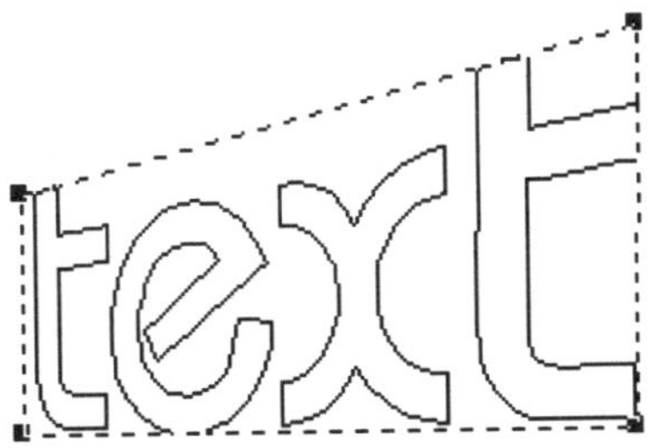

The perspective of the above text was altered by first choosing the *Edit Perspective* command, while the text was selected. Once the perspective frame was around the text, the top right node was dragged upwards. The text has now taken on the appearance that it is coming forward. If the perspective is acute enough, an X mark will be displayed. It represents the vanishing point like this:

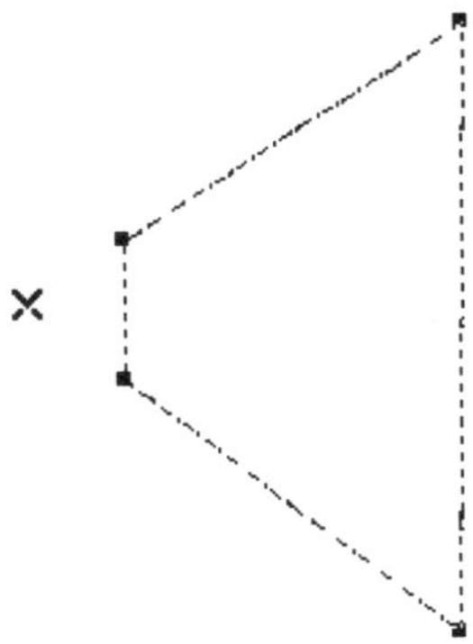

The perspective of the above square is acute enough that the vanishing point is visible, which is symbolized by the X mark to the left of the square.

The Perspective feature gives an object on your page artificial depth. You achieve one point perspective by dragging one of the handles horizontally or vertically.

You achieve two point perspective by dragging a handle closer to, or away from, the center of the object.

The vanishing point that is on either side of the object is the horizontal vanishing point; the one that is above or below represents the vertical vanishing point. You can drag these vanishing points at any time to change the perspective as well. If you move a vanishing point too close to the object, however, it snaps back to its original perspective.

Holding down the Ctrl key, while dragging a perspective handle, constrains the movement of the handle along the horizontal or vertical axes. The Ctrl + Shift keys, held down together, cause the opposing handles to move in opposite directions at the same distance. Text that has had the Perspective feature applied to it, will still be text and can be edited as such.

Clear Perspective

The *Clear Perspective* command reverts an object to the state it was, before its perspective was altered. If you have more than one perspective added to an object, using this command only applies to the last perspective box added. You can use this command if you have not given the object an envelope. See the *Clear Envelope* command discussed previously for information on how to get around this problem. To clear an object of both the envelope and perspective frames, execute the *Clear Transformations* command from the **Transform** menu with the object selected.

Copy Perspective From

This command lets you copy a perspective from one object to another. Use the Pick Tool to select the object you wish to copy the perspective to, then choose the *Copy Perspective From* command. This activates a right facing arrow with the word **From?** in it. Then click this arrow on the object that has the perspective you require.

Add New Perspective

This command adds a new perspective bounding box to an object, without changing its current perspective. This example shows a square that has already had its perspective altered, with a new perspective frame now added.

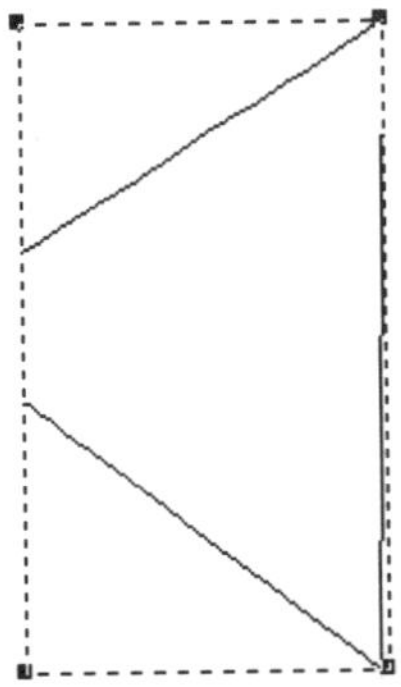

Blend

The *Blend* option joins two selected objects together in a series of steps. The *Blend* dialog box below (Figure 5-23) shows a setting with 20 steps for the joining of a square and a circle.

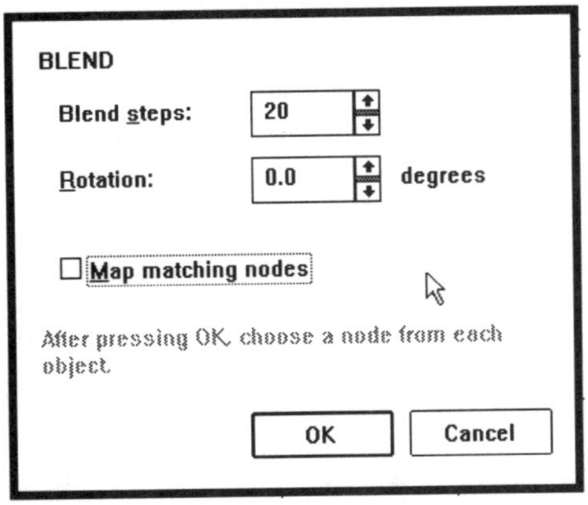

Figure 5-23. The Blend Dialog Box.

The *Blend steps* option, at the top of the dialog box, lets you determine how many steps it will take to blend the two selected objects. The maximum number of blend steps is 200. The more steps you use, the more complex the drawing will be.

You can blend any two objects together. They do not have to be the same shape. Objects with Vector, Bitmap, or Fountain Fills cannot be blended with these fills, thus the fill is replaced with white. Otherwise, two objects with different Spot or Process colors can be blended, and the blend steps change from one color to another. For example, if you blend a white circle with a black circle, the steps will appear as shades of gray from white to black.

In this example, the square and the circle have been joined, or blended together, using the settings established in the *Blend* dialog box.

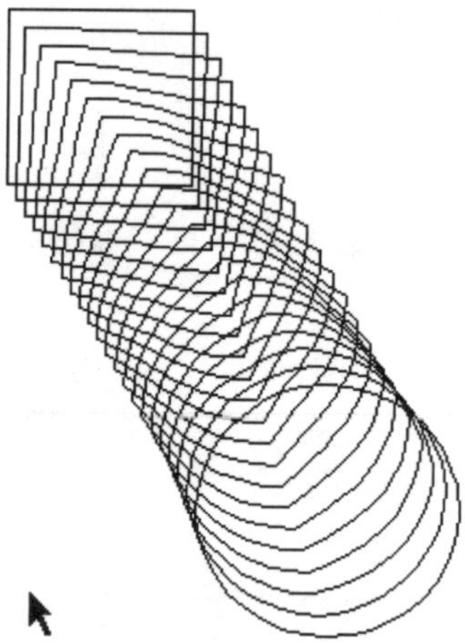

The *Rotation* option lets you determine an angle of rotation that the blend steps will take. If you keep it on 0, there will be no rotation. If you change this figure to 360, the blend steps form a complete rotation before the two objects fully blend. The rotation of the steps normally occurs in a straight line between the two objects.

You can alter this by selecting the two objects with the Pick Tool, and clicking on them once more, so that the *Rotate & Skew* handles are displayed. Then, by holding the mouse down on the Center of Rotation and dragging it to a new position, the blend steps rotate in accordance with the new position of the Center of Rotation, forming an arc, instead of a straight line. For more information on the *Rotate & Skew* handles, and the Center of Rotation, see "The Pick Tool" in **Chapter 2: The Toolbox**.

When you blend objects, the location of the first node of each object is the basis for which the steps are created. This may cause the two objects to blend in a way that you did not want. The *Map matching nodes* option allows you to choose which nodes you wish to have as the first nodes of the objects.

After you select the *Map matching nodes* option and the OK button, the *Blend* dialog box tells you to select a node from each object that you want as the first nodes. You do this, one object at a time, with the two curved arrows, one after the other. Once you have clicked on each node, the objects then blend according to the position of these nodes.The following example shows two circles that were drawn in opposite directions (left). Note that the above circle has a node at the top and the circle below has a node at the bottom. The blended result is shown at the right.

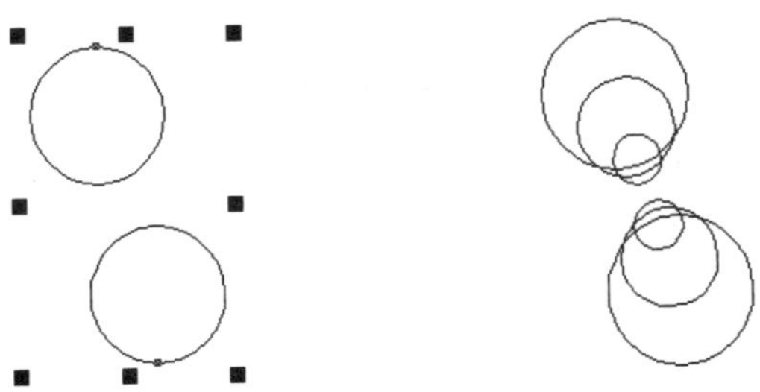

The following example shows the *Map matching nodes* option at work. After selecting the *Map matching nodes* option in the *Blend* dialog box, and clicking on OK, you are asked to select a node from each circle as shown here. The bottom circle's nodes are highlighted first on the diagram to the left. Choose a node by clicking the curved arrow on it. Repeat this process when the top circle's nodes are highlighted (middle diagram). The blended result is shown on the right.

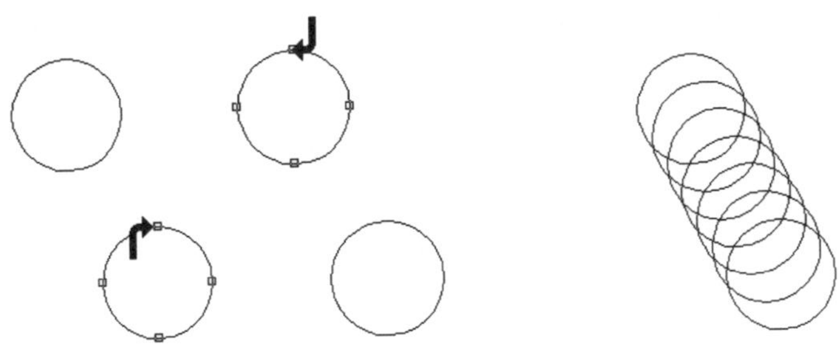

When you blend two objects, the actual steps or shapes that make up the blend will be grouped. That is, if you selected 20 as the blend steps, the 20 steps would be grouped. You can then ungroup and move these around like any normal object.

Extrude

You can use the *Extrude* command on only one selected object (or piece of text) at a time. It gives a selected object a three dimensional appearance. On selecting the *Extrude* command, you see the *Extrude* dialog boxes (Figures 5-24 and 5-25).

Two types of extrusion are possible: Parallel or Perspective. Parallel is simple. You just enter a figure for X and Y, which determines the direction and depth of the extrusion.

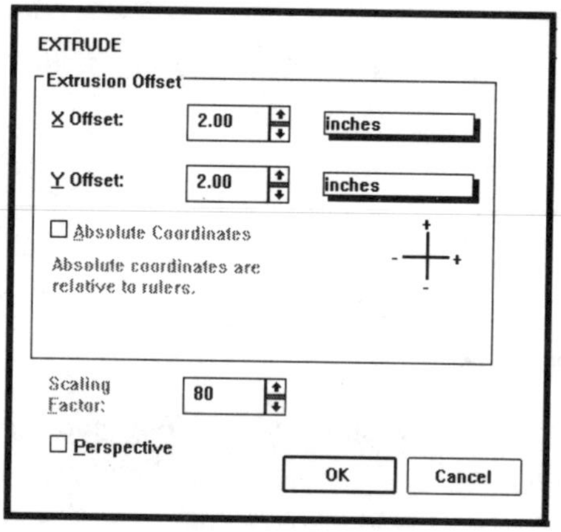

Figure 5-24. The Extrude Dialog Box for Parallel Extrusion.

The following example shows a square that was extruded with the *Perspective* option unchecked (Parallel extrusion). Notice that the extruded parts are running parallel to each other.

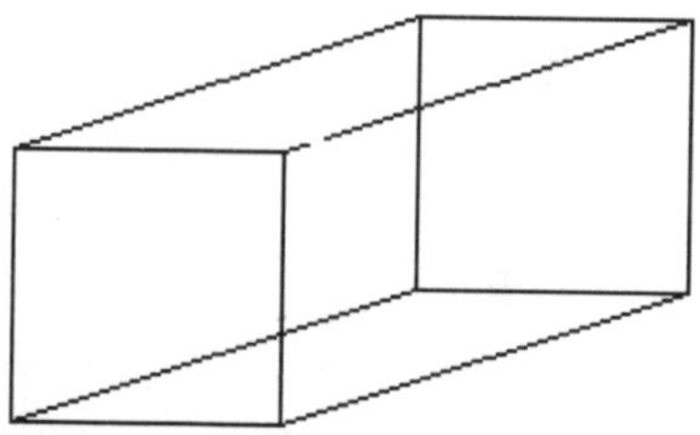

Perspective extrusion requires extra parameters and allows surfaces of the object to be projected towards a vanishing point. The *Absolute Coordinates* option determines the depth of the object, by measuring from the center of the object. The alternative to this is to enter your own X and Y Offset values. When you select the *Perspective* option, you have to either select the *Absolute Coordinates* option, or change the X and Y Offsets figures for it to work.

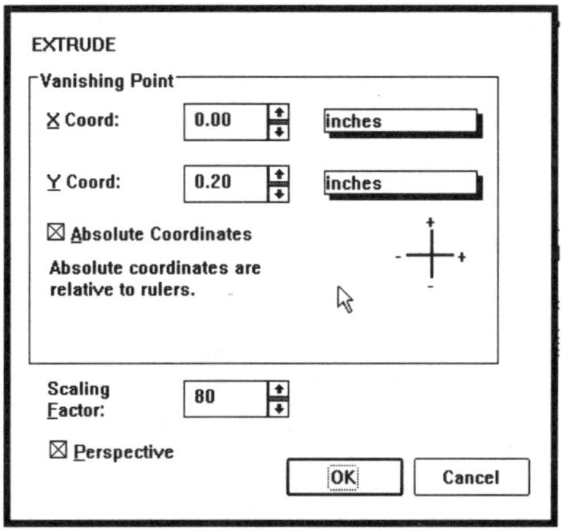

Figure 5-25. The Extrude Dialog Box for Perspective Extrusion.

The following example shows a square that was extruded with the *Perspective* option checked. The extrusion is heading back toward a vanishing point.

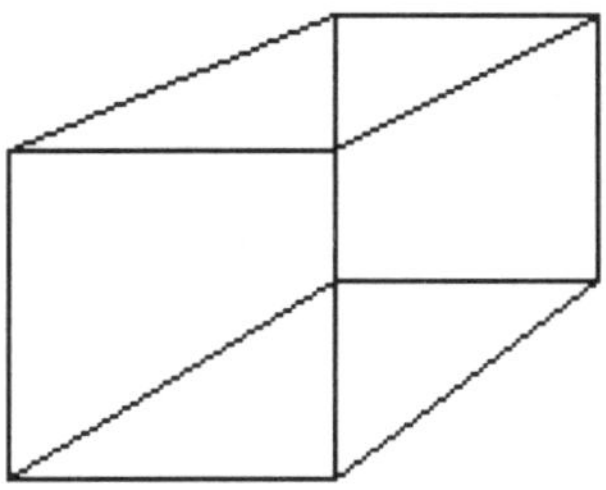

The *Scaling Factor* is only available when you select the *Perspective* option. This lets you put the vanishing point in front of or behind the object. A figure between 0 and 99 puts the extrusion behind the object, however, a figure between 101 and 200 puts the vanishing point in front of the object.

The following example shows text that was extruded, and on moving to the Preview Screen, from the Display menu, you can see the effect achieved. The text and the actual extruded part are two separate objects, and you can edit them separately. In this case, the text has a black fill, and the extruded section a white fill and a thin black outline.

Arrange Menu

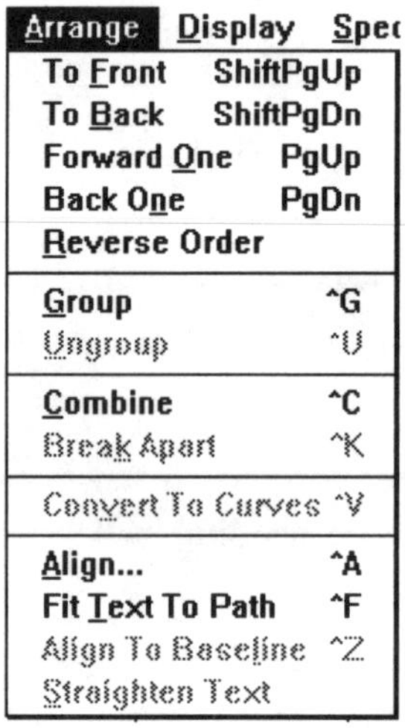

Figure 5-26. The Arrange Menu.

To Front

If you have an object on your page that you want to be on top of all other objects, select it and choose the *To Front* command. Every time you draw a new object on your page, it will be in front of all other objects. If you want the first object you drew to be in front of any other object drawn later, use the *To Front* command to achieve this as well.

To Back

The *To Back* command works in the opposite way to the *To Front* command. You select any object in the front of your drawing that you want to sit behind everything else and choose the *To Back* command.

Forward One

This command brings a selected object(s) forward one place, but not necessarily on top of all other objects on your screen.

Back One

Back One performs the same functions that the *Forward One* command does, but in reverse.

Reverse Order

With this command, you have to select more than one object. When you have, for example, two objects selected on your page, and you choose the *Reverse Order* command, the object that was originally on top will now be on the bottom and vice versa.

Group

When you use the *Group* command, whatever objects you have selected with the Pick Tool, become part of a group of objects. This means from now on, or until you ungroup them, they will be selected together, and any commands such as rotating, will affect the whole group.

If the grouped objects are drawings, you cannot use the Node Tool on them. If you have grouped text with other text or objects, you cannot edit it. Grouping certain objects (such as a complex drawing) that have to remain together, makes it easier to move the objects around on your page. Grouped objects can also be grouped with other grouped objects, to form a much larger group.

Ungroup

The *Ungroup* command ungroups a selected group of objects. It works opposite to the *Group* command. Use it when you want to make certain changes to a drawing or text that is part of a group.

Combine

Combining objects combines selected lines and curves into one curved object. This command also works on objects that were originally drawn separately. Objects such as text are converted to a curved object once the *Combine* command has been applied to them. Combining is a special form of grouping, which is very useful for conserving memory in complex drawings. See **Exercise 13** in this book for one of the uses for combining objects.

Break Apart

This command works in reverse to the *Combine* command. It breaks apart combined objects, whether they are drawings or text, into numerous objects. When breaking apart letters that have two sections to them, such as the letter O, you will have to combine them again if you want the middle to be transparent and not all black.

Convert To Curves

Objects such as squares, circles, and text, are the only objects that do not have the attributes of curved objects. Therefore you cannot manipulate them with the Node Tool the same way you can manipulate curved objects.

This all changes when you select one of these objects and use the *Convert To Curves* command. If you convert a text string to curves, you can manipulate it quite easily because you can individually select each node. Once you convert an object to curves you cannot change it back again. See **Exercises 3** and **8** for a detailed description on the conversion of text to curves, and the manipulation of that text.

Align

Upon choosing this command, the *Align* dialog box (Figure 5-27) is displayed on the screen. You then have the option of aligning the selected objects on your page. If you have two objects on your page you want aligned, you first select them both with the Pick Tool before activating this dialog box. Once in the dialog box, select *Horizontal* and/or *Vertical*, depending on how you would like to align the selected objects.

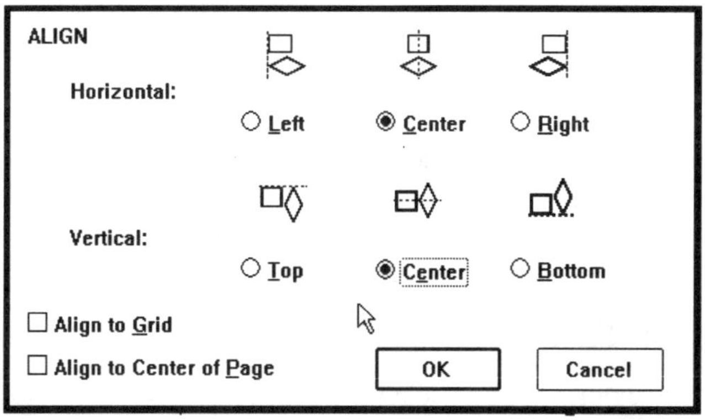

Figure 5-27. The Align Dialog Box with Center Selected.

The following example shows the results of the settings made in the dialog box in the previous example. Multiple squares were drawn on the page at various sizes, and then selected together with the Pick Tool. The *Align* command from the *Arrange* menu was chosen, to activate the *Align* dialog box. Selecting *Center* for *Horizontal* and *Vertical* alignment, and clicking on the OK button, centers the selected squares on the page.

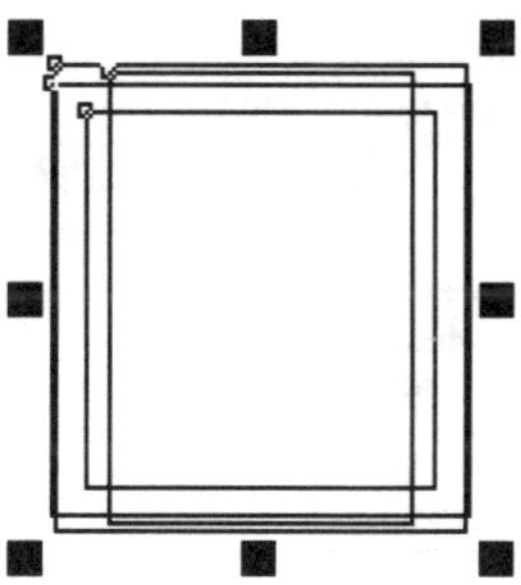

Fit Text To Path

This command enables you to flow text along any path you create on your page, such as a circle or curved line. Once the text and the path are on your page, select them both with the Pick Tool, and choose the *Fit Text To Path* command. For more information on this command, see **Exercise 1** in Part 2 of this book.

Align To Baseline

This feature enables you to straighten text strings that you may have altered through interactive kerning or rotation. A selected text string moves each piece of text back onto the baseline, once you select this command. Text characters that have been moved to the left or right, as well as off the baseline, only move down to the baseline but not back to their original position. The text will sit on the baseline, but to the left or right, depending on where you moved it.

Straighten Text

If you apply this command to a selected text string that has been altered in any way, it returns to its original state. This includes changes to the font and size, as well as rotating and kerning. The whole text string will also be shifted to the baseline.

Display Menu

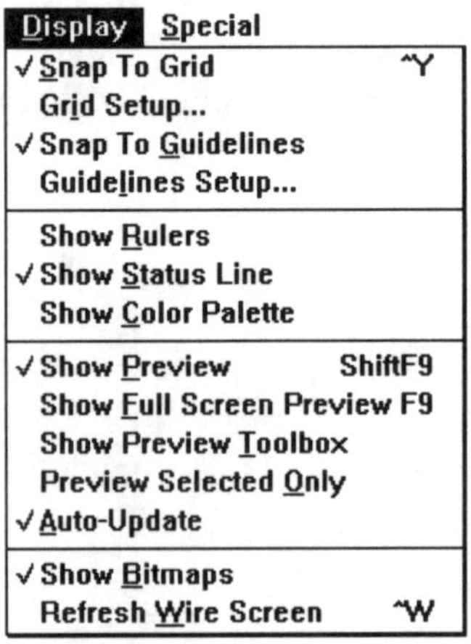

Figure 5-28. The Display Menu.

Snap To Grid

This command activates the grid on your page. The grid frequency and origin is controlled in the *Grid Parameters* dialog box (Figure 5-29). When you select the *Snap To Grid* option, the cursor snaps along the control points except when you are selecting, drawing curves, autotracing, rotating or skewing, or using the Zoom Tool. Everything else you do is affected by this option when it is turned on. The status line shows you when the *Snap To Grid* option is activated.

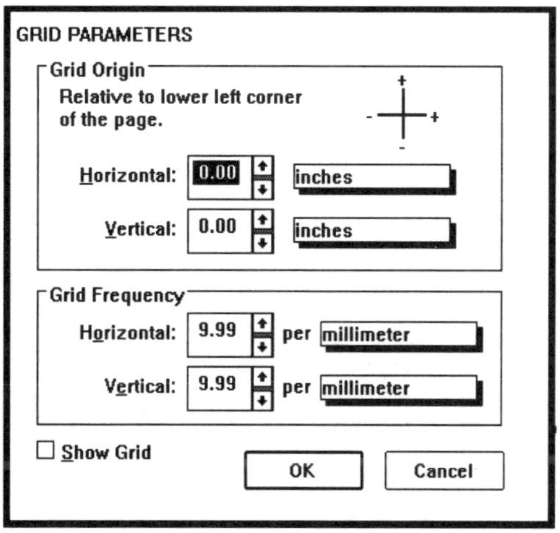

Figure 5-29. The Grid Parameters Dialog Box.

Grid Setup

This command activates the *Grid Parameters* dialog box. The first option available in this dialog box is the *Grid Origin* option. This lets you change the zero points of the horizontal and vertical rulers on the screen, in relation to the bottom left-hand corner of the page. For example, if you put in four inches for the *Horizontal* value and eight inches for *Vertical*, the zero points of the ruler will be four inches in, and eight inches up, from the bottom left-hand corner of the page. The rulers must be displayed for this option to work. A shortcut way to change the zero points of the rulers, is to hold the mouse down in the corner where the rulers join each other, and drag the mouse down and across. Release your finger where you want the new zero point to be.

SHORTCUT

The *Grid Frequency* option determines the spacing of the grid points. When you change the unit of measurement here, the rulers and measurement system in the Status Line reflects this change. The frequency controls how many lines occur per inch, or whatever measurement you are using, so note your preferred measurement before you put in your amount here. If you put in a figure that is too large, you receive an invalid grid frequency message when you click on OK. You then must change it to less than the *maximum* figure. The maximum figures are: inches (1/72), Picas (12), Points (1), and millimeters (approximately 2.80). If the grid settings are changed later, the objects aligned to the old grid do not move to the new one.

The *Show Grid* option at the bottom left of the *Grid Parameters* dialog box, when checked, displays a series of dots on your page, that reflect the frequency of your grid as shown in the following example.

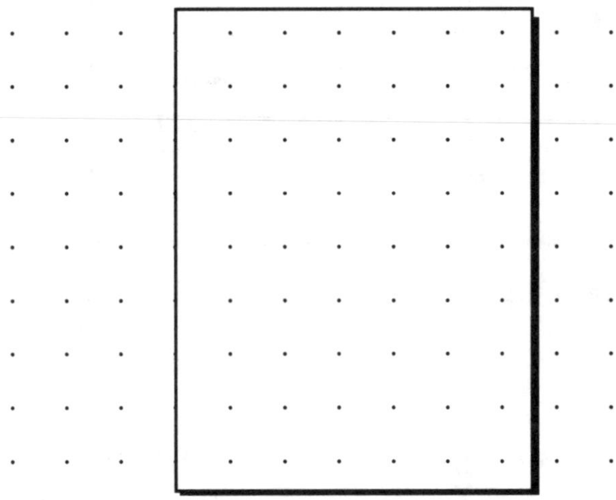

Snap To Guidelines

You can use guidelines to assist in the exact drawing or placement of graphics and/or text on your page. See the description of the *Guidelines Setup* command following for more details on how to draw guidelines. If you have guidelines on your page, and you activate the *Snap To Guidelines* command, objects that you draw or move near a guideline automatically snap to it.

Guidelines Setup

This command and its associated dialog box (Figure 5-30) let you accurately place guidelines on the screen (either horizontal or vertical) by typing in the exact coordinates.

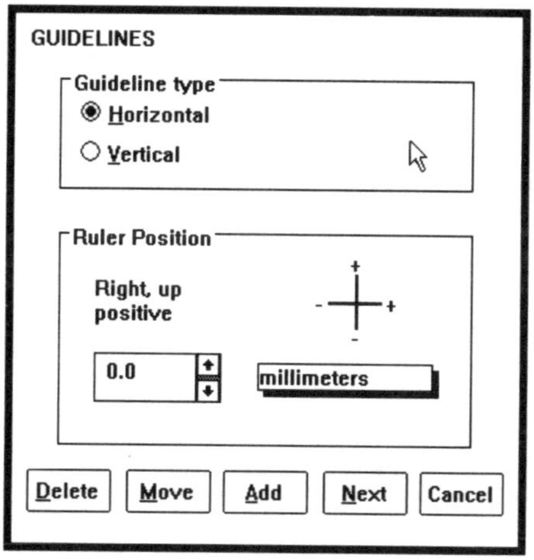

Figure 5-30. The Guidelines Dialog Box.

To add guidelines to your page without using this *Guidelines Setup* command, first select the *Show Rulers* command from the **Display** menu. Once the rulers are displayed, you can drag a guideline down or across from the rulers by holding the mouse down on a ruler and dragging it. Release your finger where you want the guideline to sit. To remove it from the page, hold the mouse down on the guideline with the Pick Tool, drag it back into the ruler, and release your finger.

The *Guidelines* dialog box is the alternative way of adding guidelines to the page. You can place only one guideline at a time through this dialog box. Click on either *Horizontal* or *Vertical* for the *Guideline type*. Next, change the *Ruler Position* option to where you want the guideline to sit along your ruler. Then, click the *Add* button, and the dotted guideline will be displayed on the page.

You can move guidelines by entering the new spot in the *Ruler Position* option and clicking on *Move*. The *Delete* button removes the guideline. If you have a number of guidelines on the page, the *Next* button displays the *Ruler Position* of each guideline, one at a time, so you may perform the *Move* or *Delete* options. If you double-click on a guideline with the Pick Tool, the *Guidelines* dialog box will be displayed, with the correct position of the selected guideline.

The following illustration shows two horizontal and two vertical guidelines that are positioned on the page.

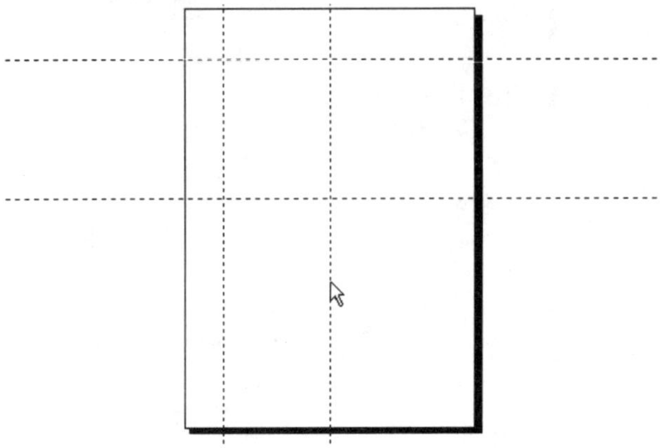

Show Rulers

When you select this command, you activate a set of rulers running both horizontally and vertically at the edge of your page. To deactivate the rulers, select the *Show Rulers* command again. The following illustration shows the *Show Rulers* command activated with the rulers at the edge of the page.

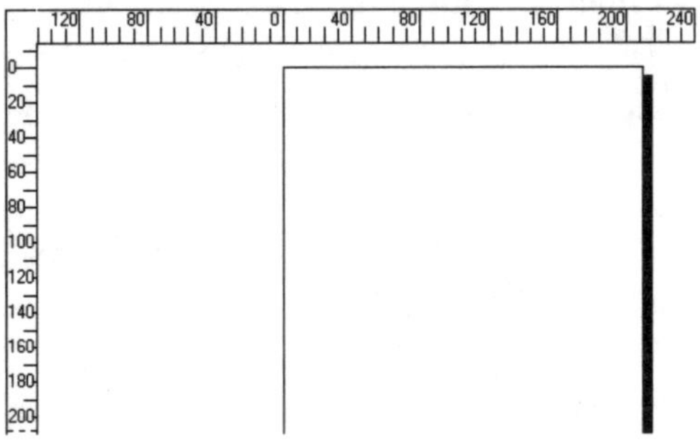

Show Status Line

The *Show Status Line* command makes the Status Line visible or invisible on your screen. Keep the Status Line on because it provides important information while you are creating a graphic. By default, the Status Line is on.

Show Color Palette

If you activate this command, a row of colors is displayed across the bottom of the screen (Figure 5-31), enabling you to change the fill or outline color of a selected object, without having to use the different color dialog boxes. You can choose to display either the Spot or Process color palette.

You can click on the east and west facing arrows, to the left and right of this row of colors to show further options. You can change between Spot or Process palettes by clicking on the *Uniform Fill* option in the Outline Tool fly-out menu with no objects selected. Clicking on OK, moves you to the *New Object Uniform Fill* dialog box. At this point, choose Spot or Process.

Figure 5-31. The Show Color Palette.

Show Preview

This command activates the Preview Screen, which is a separate window that you can optionally display on screen. This second window displays your drawing with its correct outlines and fills, and shows how it will look when printed. To remove the Preview Screen, once activated, select the *Show Preview* command again. The exercises in this book make full use of the Preview Screen. The easier way to get to and from the Preview Screen is to press the [Shift] + [F9] keys.

Under normal circumstances, you do not work with the Preview Screen active, as it slows down screen re-drawing. Use it only as a final check on how your drawing will look when printed. The following illustration shows the Preview Screen in the window on the right.

Show Full Screen Preview

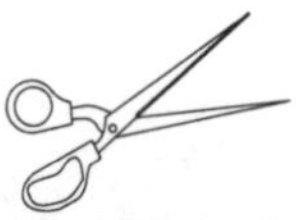

SHORTCUT

This option shows the Preview Screen across the entire screen. This displays your work without the constraints of the Toolbox, Status Line, or Menu Bar of the standard CorelDRAW! window. The easier way to move to and from the Full Preview Screen is to press the F9 key.

Show Preview Toolbox

The Preview Screen has its own Toolbox, which is activated when you select the *Show Preview Toolbox* command. You can select this command only once the Preview Screen is displayed. As soon as this Toolbox is activated, the view of the Preview Screen is controlled separately from the working screen. This Toolbox has its own Zoom Tool, which works the same as the Zoom Tool on the working page. See **Exercise 14** for usage of the Preview Screen Zoom Tool.

Other features of the Preview Screen Toolbox control the way in which the Preview Screen is displayed. By default, the Preview Screen is displayed to the right of the working screen when you select it. With this new Toolbox, you can change the position of the Preview Screen, so that it sits underneath the working screen. The following illustrations show which part of this Toolbox controls this feature. The icon on the left is selected when the Preview Screen is situated alongside the working screen. To make it sit underneath, select the icon on the right.

Preview Selected Only

If you have a large or complex drawing, with numerous fountain fills, it sometimes takes a minute or so to redraw on the Preview Screen. To solve this problem, choose the *Preview Selected Only* command, and only the selected object on the working screen will redraw on the Preview Screen. When you activate the *Preview Selected Only* command, only what you have selected on the working side of the screen is displayed on the Preview side. In this case, only the circle is displayed on the Preview Screen. The following illustration shows a selected part of the graphic (left) redrawn on the Preview screen (right).

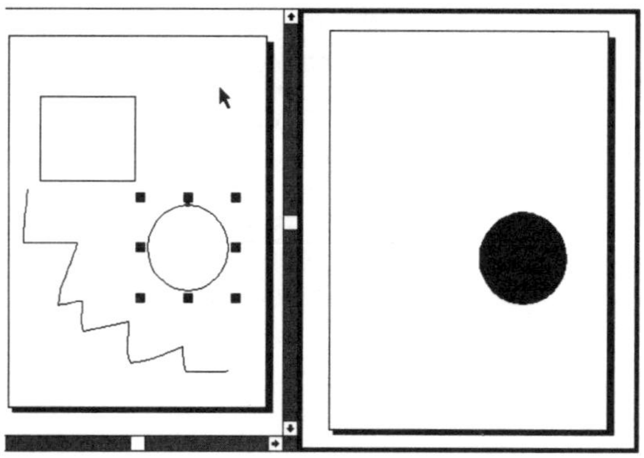

Auto-Update

This command affects the redrawing of your page on the Preview Screen. By default, the *Auto-Update* command is on. If you deselect it in the **Display** menu, and the Preview Screen is currently displayed, any changes that you made to the drawing on the working screen do not appear on the Preview Screen until you click on the Preview Screen with the mouse.

Show Bitmaps

This command gives you the option of displaying your bitmaps on the working screen, since bitmaps may sometimes take a while to redraw. If you select this option, there will be an empty rectangle in place of the bitmap. If the bitmap has been imported to be traced, you can hide the bitmap after it has been traced, to speed up drawing time.

Refresh Wire Screen

You can interupt the redrawing of your image on the Working screen at any time by pressing a key or the mouse button. Then, to redraw the page, select the *Refresh Wire Screen* command.

Special Menu

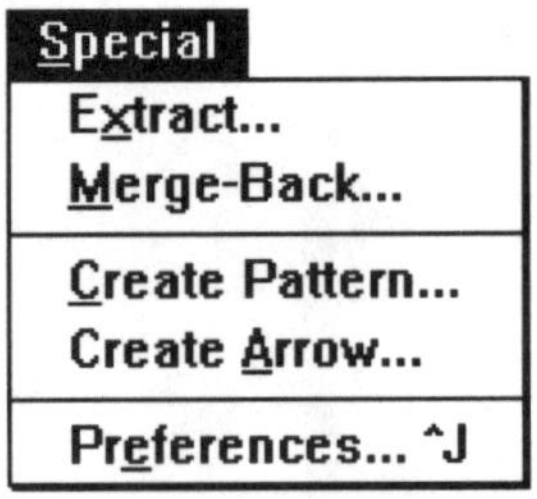

Figure 5-32. The Special Menu.

Extract

You can export all text in CorelDRAW! to a word processor for editing. This is useful if you have a CorelDRAW! file with a large amount of text. The *Extract* command activates the *Extract* dialog box (Figure 5-33). Here you give the file a title, and decide in which drive and directory you are going to save it. Then, click on the *Extract* button.

The file will have an extension of .txt, and you can now open it in any word processing program for editing. When you have opened the file in the word processor, edit only the text you have created yourself. CorelDRAW! has placed a code at the very top of the file, a number before each text block, and the letters CDR after each one, that must not be changed. If any of these items are altered, the file will not come back into CorelDRAW!. Once you have made all the necessary changes to the file, save it as an ASCII file. Then re-enter CorelDRAW!, open the relevant file, and replace the text (see *Merge-Back*).

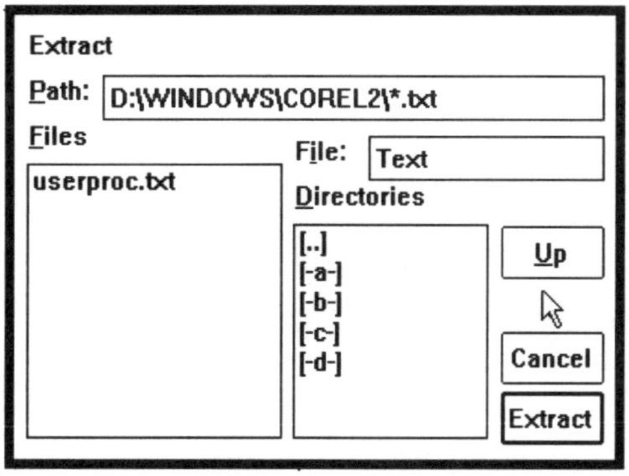

Figure 5-33. The Extract Dialog Box.

Merge-Back

The *Merge-Back* command follows the *Extract* command and returns an extracted file to CorelDRAW!. To do this successfully, open the CorelDRAW! file from which you extracted the text, and select the *Merge-Back* command. The *Merge-Back* dialog box (Figure 5-34) is displayed. Locate the text file that you edited; it will have a .txt extension. Select the file, and click on the *Merge* button. The text file that was edited outside CorelDRAW! now replaces the old one. If any of the text is overlapping, or not in its correct position, you can edit it directly in CorelDRAW!.

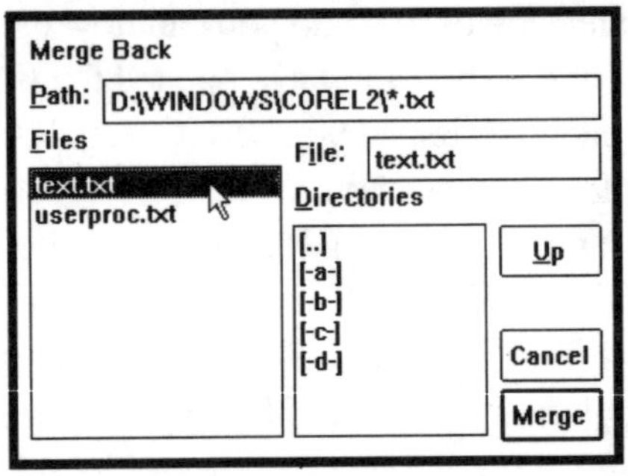

Figure 5-34. The Merge Back Dialog Box.

Create Pattern

The *Create Pattern* command and dialog box (Figure 5-35) let you select an object or a section of your page to save in the *Bitmap Pattern* dialog box or the *Vector Pattern* dialog box (both available from the Fill Tool fly-out). After you select the type of pattern (*Bitmap* or *Vector*, from the *Create Pattern* dialog box), you see a large crosshair, that moves with your mouse and covers the whole screen. Holding the mouse down, select the section on the screen, with the center of the cross, that you would like to save as your pattern. Once you release your finger from the mouse, a screen prompt asks you whether this section you previously selected is, in fact, the section you want to save as the pattern. If it is, click OK.

If you selected *Bitmap* for your type of pattern, it is available as a fill through the *Bitmap Pattern* dialog box. If you choose *Vector*, after dragging the crosshair over the section you wish to save as your pattern, you are asked if the section you just selected is correct. Upon saying OK, the *Save Vector Pattern* dialog box is activated, where you have to name the pattern and decide in which directory you would like to save it. For more information on the *Create Pattern* command, see **Exercise 12**. Also see The Fill Tool in **Chapter 2: The Toolbox,** for information on applying Bitmap and Vector fills to objects.

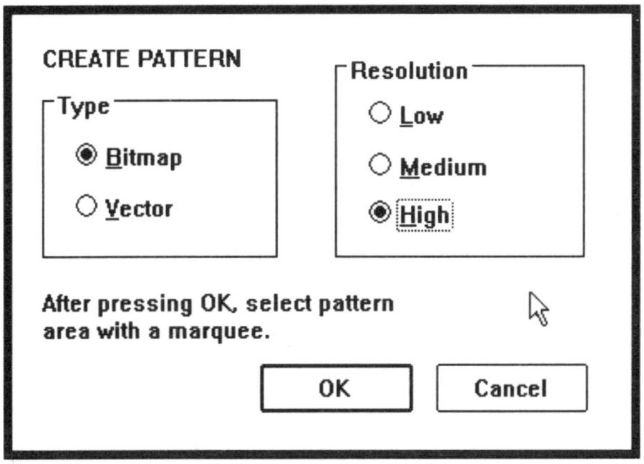

Figure 5-35. The Create Pattern Dialog Box.

Create Arrow

The *Custom Outline Pen* dialog box (available from the Outline Tool fly-out) has an *Arrowhead selection* command, where you can give an arrowhead to lines that are open paths or have patterned endings and/or beginnings. CorelDRAW! has a number of arrowheads already built in, but you can also create your own. To do this, select an object on your page that you wish to use as an arrowhead. Then select the *Create Arrow* command to activate the screen prompt. If the selected object is the correct object, click on OK. The following illustration shows the screen prompt for creating an arrowhead with a selected object:

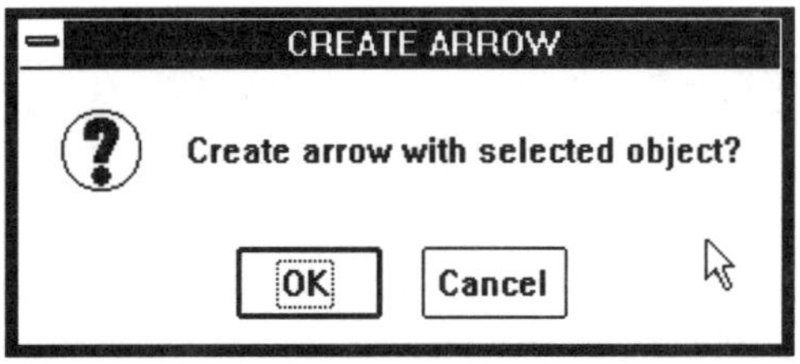

Figure 5-36 shows the Arrowhead Selection box available through the *Custom Outline Pen* dialog box. The arrowhead created was the star. It was first drawn on the page, and then selected with the Pointer Tool. Once it was selected, the *Create Arrow* command was invoked, which activated the *Create Arrow* screen prompt, from which you can choose OK. On going to the *Arrowhead Selection* box, you see the star among the patterns.

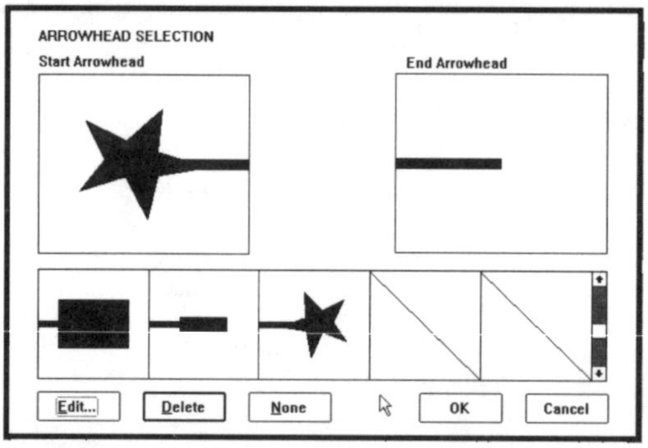

Figure 5-36. The Arrowhead Selection Dialog Box.

Preferences

Selecting the *Preferences* command invokes the *Preferences* dialog box (Figure 5-37). You can alter all options and measurement systems in this dialog box like in any other dialog box in CorelDRAW!.

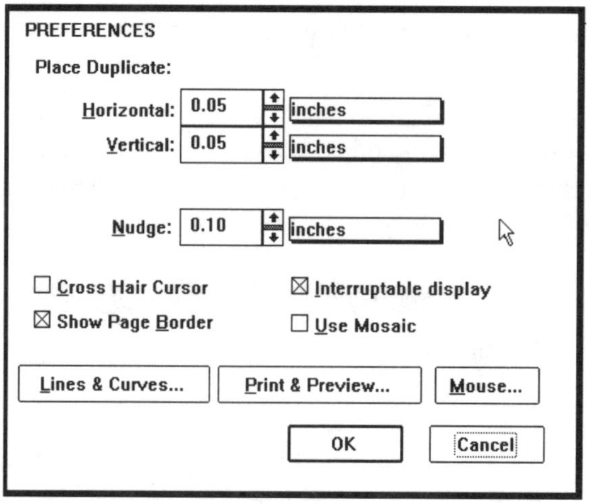

Figure 5-37. The Preferences Dialog Box.

The *Place Duplicate* feature determines where a duplicated object is displayed in relation to the original. See the *Duplicate* command under the **Edit** menu in this Chapter. See also **Exercise 5** for more information on the *Place Duplicate* option.

The *Nudge* option lets you move a selected object on your page a certain distance using the cursor keys on your keyboard. You can hold your finger on any one of the cursor keys to move the object continuously in that direction. The figure you place in the *Nudge* frame determines how far the object will move, with each press of a cursor key.

The *Cross Hair Cursor* choice changes the point of your mouse into a cross that covers the whole screen. The mouse reverts to an arrow when it is off the actual screen, so that you can select tools and/or menus. This crosshair works with all tools except the Zoom Tool. This feature may allow you to draw and place text and other objects more accurately on the page. The following illustration shows the selected *Cross Hair* option.

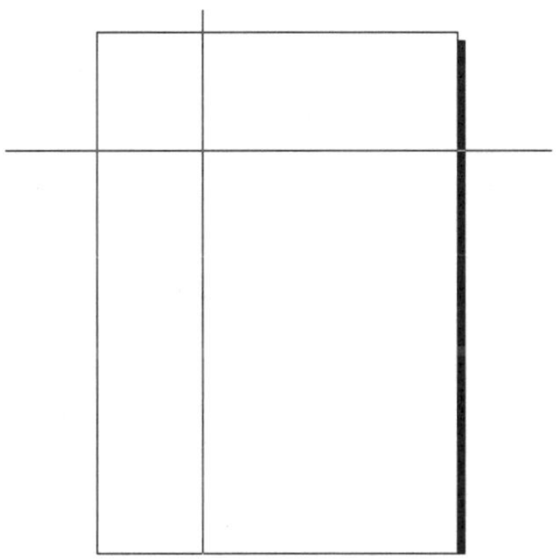

Interruptable display lets you stop the drawing of a large or complex image on the working screen. You do this by clicking the mouse button or pressing a key on the keyboard. You can still select objects even though you cannot see them on the screen. To redraw the screen completely after interrupting it, select the *Refresh Wire Screen* option from the **Display** menu.

The *Show Page Border* is the default selection. If you uncheck this option, the page border and shadow are not displayed on either the Preview or working screens.

The *Use Mosaic* option lets you *Open*, *Import*, *Export*, *Print,* and search for files using the Mosaic utility. This makes it easier to find the file you want, and will only work if you have the *Use Mosaic* option checked. For more information on the Mosaic feature see **Chapter 7: Mosaic**.

If you click on the *Lines & Curves* button, you activate the following dialog box.

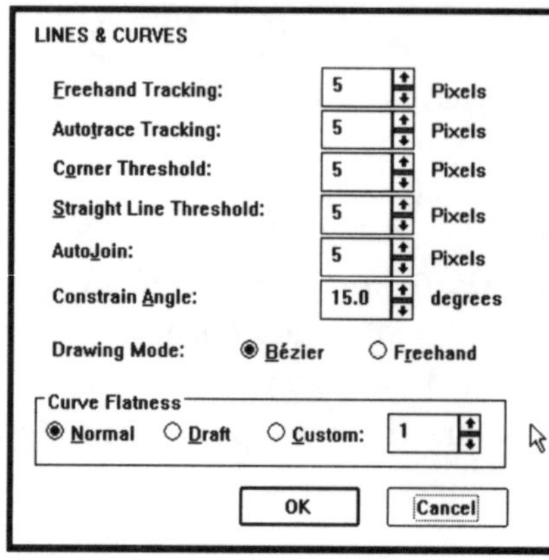

Figure 5-38. The Lines & Curves Dialog Box.

Freehand Tracking is a control over how closely mouse movement is tracked when you create a freehand line. A higher figure causes the mouse to be loosely tracked, meaning less nodes, and often a smoother, if less accurate appearance.

The *Autotrace Tracking* is the same as the *Freehand Tracking* option, yet it controls the amount of nodes that appear when you use the Autotrace function.

The *Corner Threshold* option controls whether a corner is smooth or a cusp. The lower the figure, the more likely it will be sharper or a cusp. If the figure is higher and you are autotracing, the lines do not necessarily follow your bitmap accurately, but will give it a smoother look.

The *Straight Line Threshold* decides whether to make lines straight or curved, when either autotracing or freehand drawing. If the figure is low, it is more likely that the lines will become curves.

AutoJoin decides how far away nodes have to be from each other before they will actually join. If you are drawing an object, such as a triangle, that needs to become a closed object. The smaller the figure in this dialog box, the closer you will have to place your last point of the drawing to the first node.

The *Constrain Angle* option constrains the following actions, while you hold down the Ctrl key, to the angle specified in this frame: rotating and skewing, drawing straight lines in Freehand mode, and adjusting the Control points when drawing curves in Bezier mode.

The *Drawing Mode* option gives you the choice of whether you want the lines drawn by the Pencil Tool to be in Bezier or Freehand mode. See The Pencil Tool in **Chapter 2: The Toolbox**, for more information.

The *Curve Flatness* option controls the amount of segments representing the curves of an object on the screen, and printers that are not PostScript. The higher the number you have here, the faster the drawing and printing time is. Checking the *Normal* option gives you the most accurate and smoothest result, but it is also the slowest. The *Draft* option is the roughest and quickest option. The *Custom* option lets you put in your own figure between 1 and 10.

Clicking on the *Print & Preview* button in the Preferences dialog box activates the Print and Preview dialog box (Figure 5-39).

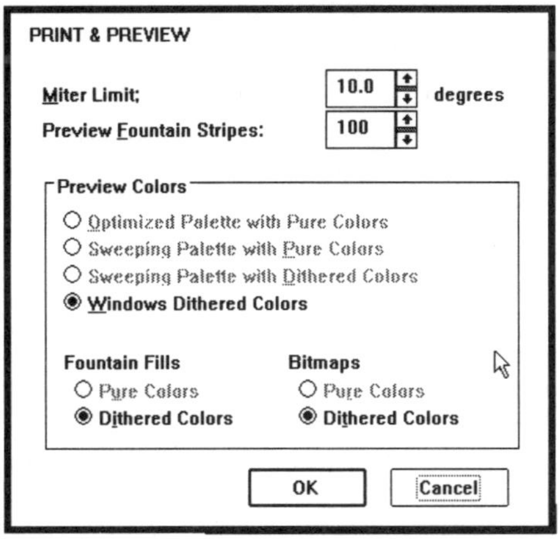

Figure 5-39. The Print & Preview Dialog Box.

The *Miter Limit* option controls the length of your corners. If you have a sharp corner, the *Miter Limit* option ensures that it does not extend out further than the actual corner.

You also have the option here to control the number of sections used to create a *Fountain Fill* on the screen. This is determined by the *Preview Fountain Stripes* option. The higher the figure, the more stripes that occur, and the longer it takes to preview. Use this option if you have a complex drawing with numerous fountain fills. Placing a lower number in this option redraws the image quicker, but the quality will suffer.

The *Preview Colors* option in the *Print & Preview* dialog box determines how the colors will display on the Preview Screen. These options are only available if you have a monitor and a Windows 3 screen driver that allows you to display 256 colors or more.

The difference between *Pure Colors* and *Dithered Colors* is that with *Pure Colors* each pixel on the screen is made up of the color you are using. With *Dithered Colors*, two or more pixels make a color. So orange would be made up of pixels in shades of red and yellow, set closely together, to give the illusion of orange.

The *Optimized Palette with Pure Colors* option displays the drawing on the Preview Screen using the colors contained in the palette of the drawing. When you save a drawing you also save the palette of colors you used for the drawing. If there are not enough colors in this palette to make every color a pure color, CorelDRAW! substitutes these colors for the most appropriate color from the palette. This usually is not very accurate, since the palette can be very limited.

The *Sweeping Palette with Pure Colors* and the *Sweeping Palette with Dithered Colors* options load the palette with a wider range of colors. The *Pure Colors* option uses the closest matching color from your palette of colors. The dithering technique uses as many colors as it can to make the preview as smooth as possible.

Windows Dithered Colors is the only choice you can select when you cannot display 256 colors or more.

At the *Fountain* option, the *Dithered Colors* choice has a better effect on the preview of your drawing if you have any *Fountain Fills* because more colors will be used giving it a smoother look.

For the *Bitmaps* selection, it depends on the bitmap you are working with to determine which option gives the best effect.

Moving again to the *Preferences* dialog box, click on the *Mouse* button to activate the *Mouse* dialog box.

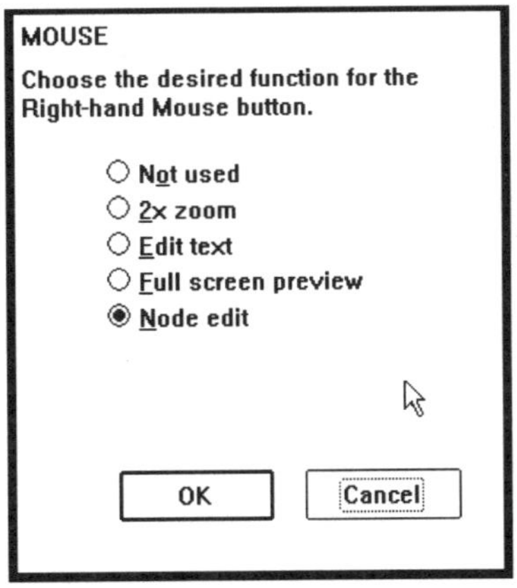

Figure 5-40. The Mouse Dialog Box.

CorelDRAW! gives you the choice of assigning the mostly unused right-hand mouse button to a certain task. When you select a choice here, and move back to the screen, the right-hand mouse button performs the function you selected in this *Mouse* dialog box.

The *Not used* option leaves the right mouse button inactive.

The *2x zoom* option increases the size of the working screen by two. Double-clicking on the right mouse button returns you to the previous view before zooming.

The *Edit text* option works only if you have some text selected. It then activates the *Text Editing* dialog box.

The *Full screen preview* option lets you move to and from the *Full Screen Preview* option by clicking on the right mouse button.

The *Node edit* option activates the Node Tool.

Menu Shortcuts

Some of the menu commands have shortcut keys. This saves time going to and from menus, to perform a command. You can activate the allotted commands directly from the keyboard. To find out which commands have shortcut keys, display each menu, and the shortcut keys will be to the right of the command. Figure 5-41 shows the **File** menu and its shortcut keys.

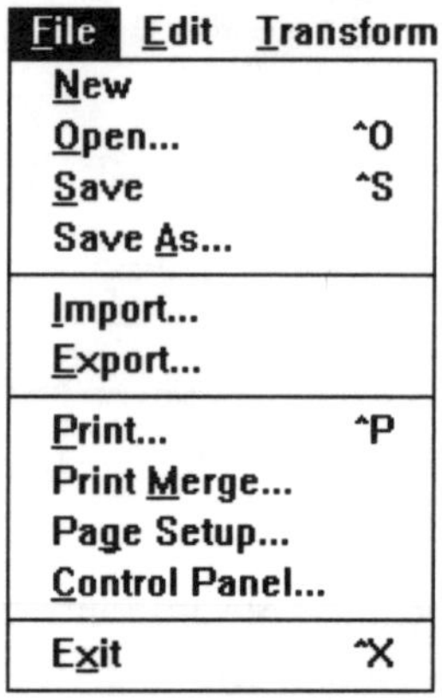

Figure 5-41. The File Menu and Its Shortcut Keys.

Summary

This chapter explained how you use all the menu commands in CorelDRAW!. You learned about all of the options available for each menu and how you use the dialog boxes to manipulate text and graphics.

Chapter 6

CorelTRACE!

CorelTRACE! enables you to trace scanned images and bitmaps so that you can improve the resolution of graphics when you enlarge them. This chapter teaches you how to use the options and dialog boxes from these CorelTRACE! menus:

- Tracing Options
- View Image
- Preferences.

Tracing Bitmaps

Tracing a bitmap changes it from a fixed resolution image to a resolution-independent, object-based graphic. Once you trace this new object you can enlarge it and it always prints at the maximum resolution of the output device.

CorelDRAW! has its own built-in tracing program called AutoTrace. CorelTRACE! is a separate tracing program that provides more accuracy and speed for tracing complex graphics.

CorelTRACE! accepts images with a .TIF or .PCX extension. The best images to trace are black and white line art images with a high resolution. Although CorelTRACE! attempts to trace color or gray scale images with slabs of color that best match the original, solid color images trace a lot better than continuous tone images. Once you trace the image, you can place it into a desktop publishing or word processing program, or into CorelDRAW! for further editing or manipulation.

You start CorelTRACE! from Windows by double-clicking on the relevant icon, like you would start any program from Windows. This activates the main CorelTRACE! window as shown in Figure 6-1.

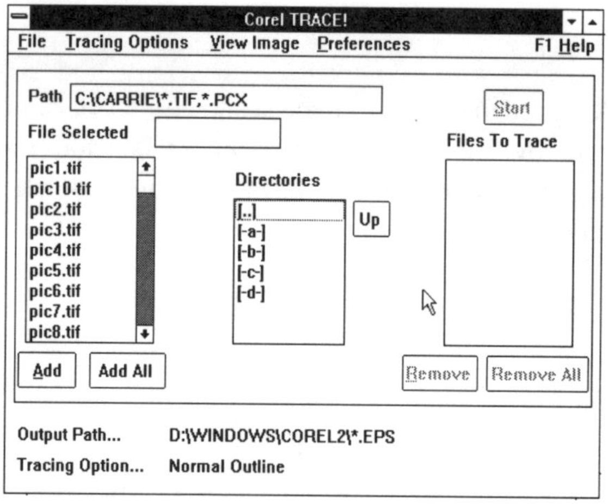

Figure 6-1. The Main CorelTRACE! Window.

Tracing Options Menu

The window in the Figure 6-1 lets you select the files you intend to trace, by giving you access to the computer's hard drives, directories and/or sub-directories. The *Path* frame tells you the drive and directory you are currently in, and it lists the .TIF or .PCX files from here in the *File Selected* box below the *Path* frame. When you select a file from this list, the file name is displayed in the *File Selected* frame.

Note: Floppy disk files are very slow to trace, and it is best to transfer them to the hard disk.

Once you have selected the file you want traced, click on the *Add* button below the list of files to display the file name in the *Files To Trace* frame at the right of the dialog box. The *Add All* button adds all the .TIF and .PCX files in the box to the left to the *Files To Trace* list. If you have added an incorrect file, use the *Remove* button to delete it.

Once you have located the correct drive and directory that lists the file(s) you want traced, select the file from the list in the frame to the left, and click on the *Add* button. It is now displayed in the *Files To Trace* frame at the right of the dialog box as Figure 6-2 shows.

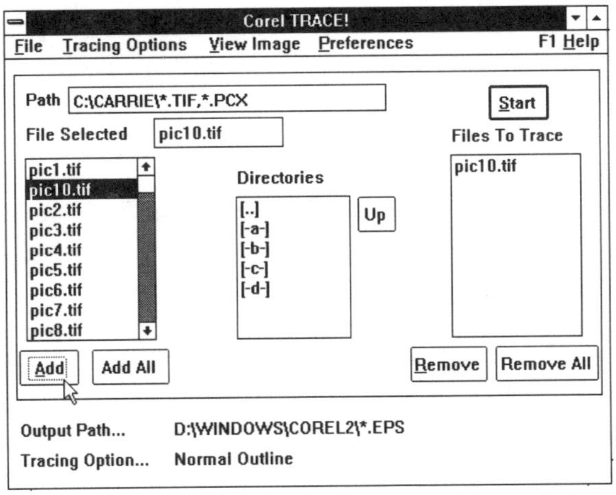

Figure 6-2. The Selected File in the Files To Trace Frame.

The *Remove All* button deletes all the files from the *Files To Trace* frame.

The *Output Path* option at the bottom left of the dialog box indicates the disk and directory locations for the traced files. Traced files have an EPS file extension. To change the *Output Path,* select the *Output Options* command from the **File** menu. This activates the *Output Options* dialog box as shown in Figure 6-3.

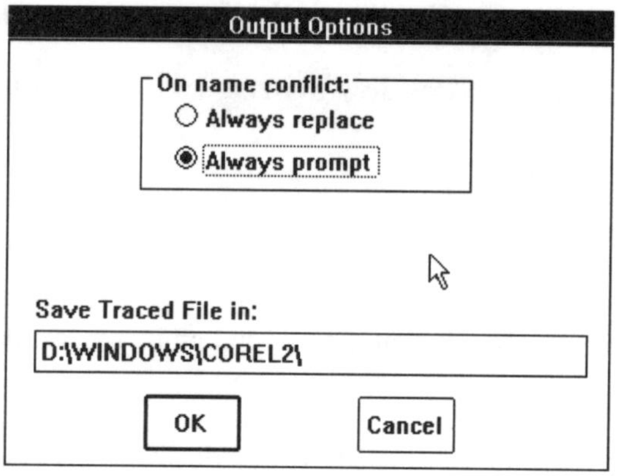

Figure 6-3. The Output Options Dialog Box.

The *On name conflict* section of this dialog box has two options. These are relevant only if the image you are tracing has already been traced and placed in the same directory. The *Always replace* option automatically overwrites any file with the same name. The *Always prompt* option warns you that two files have the same name, and you are given the opportunity to change the name.

The *Save Traced File in* option determines the *Output Path,* for example, where the traced file is saved. To change it, click the cursor in the frame, backspace over the current location, and type the new drive and directory information.

The *Tracing Option* underneath the *Output Path* (Figure 6-2) is determined by any changes made in the **Tracing Options** menu. Further discussions of these options follow. If you wish to trace any files you have selected, which are displayed in the *Files To Trace* frame, you simply click on the *Start* button at the top of the dialog box. CorelTRACE! now automatically traces any or all of the files in this frame.

The **Tracing Options** menu lets you set up your own tracing options. Figure 6-4 shows the **Tracing Options** menu. Clicking on one of the eight sets of three dots that take up the last part of the menu, activates the *Tracing Options* dialog box.

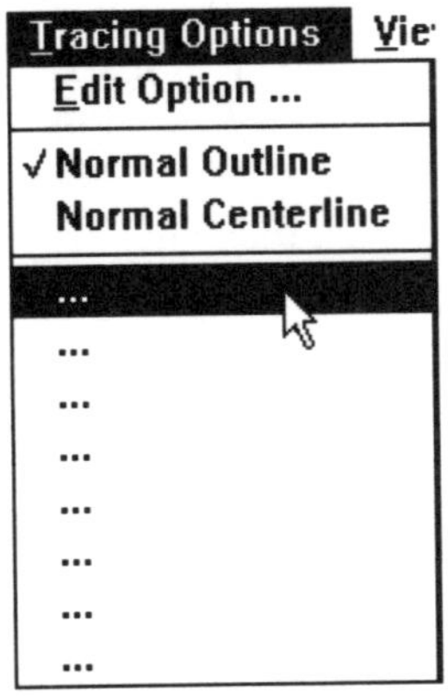

Figure 6-4. The Tracing Options Menu.

Figure 6-5 shows the *Tracing Options* dialog box, where you can set up different ways in which an image is traced.

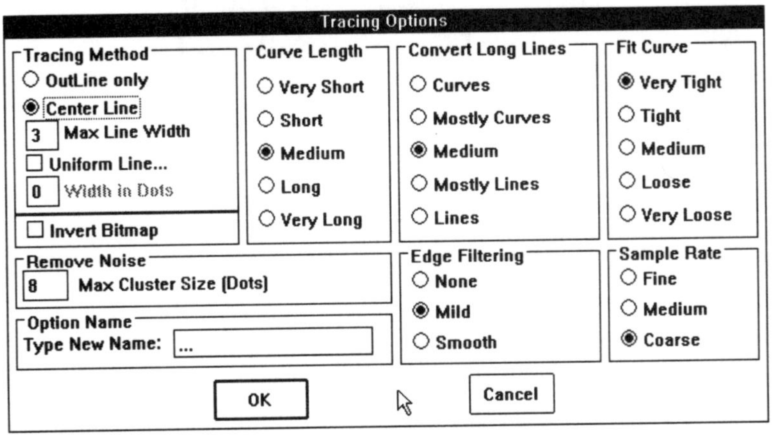

Figure 6-5. The Tracing Options Dialog Box.

The options available in the *Tracing Options* dialog box determine how you can trace an image. For detailed information on the effects these options have, consult the CorelTRACE! manual. Once you have set up this dialog box, click the cursor inside the *Type New Name* frame, and give this tracing option a name. Once you click on OK, the name will be displayed in the **Tracing Options** menu allowing you to select it at any time.

You can create as many styles as you like, but only eight can be saved at once. The *Normal Outline* and *Normal Centerline* options in Figure 6-4 are two styles that are provided with CorelTRACE!. To edit any style from this menu, make sure it is currently active (it will have a tick next to the command in the menu), and select the *Edit Option* command at the top of the menu. To remove a style from the list, replace the name of the style with three dots in the *Tracing Options* dialog box.

View Image Menu

The first option available in the **View Image** menu is the *View File Information* command as shown in Figure 6-6.

Figure 6-6. The View Image Menu.

When you select the *View File Information* command, the dialog box in Figure 6-7 is activated.

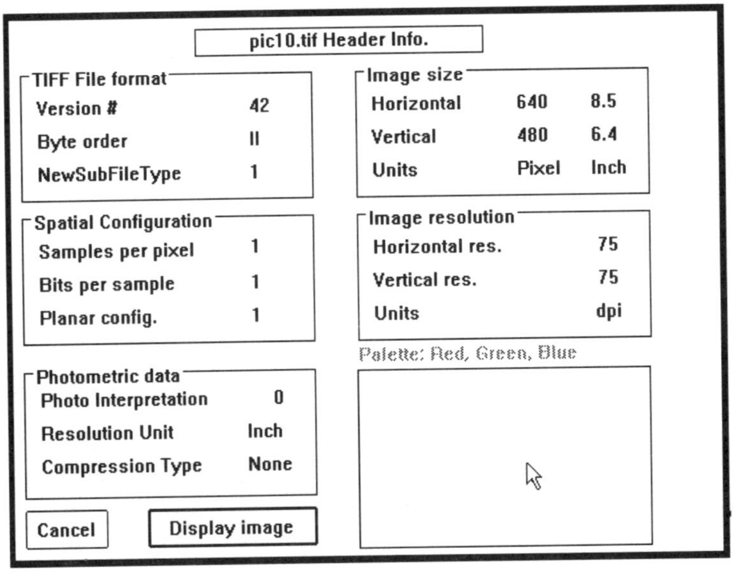

Figure 6-7. The View File Information Dialog Box.

You must select a file from the list of files under the *File Selected* frame of the **CorelTRACE!** menu before you can access this option. The information displayed in this dialog box is technical information about the file. The *Display image* button, toward the bottom left, displays the selected image in a further dialog box or window. The *Cancel* button returns you to the main window of the **CorelTRACE!** menu.

The *Display Image* command from the **View Image** menu displays the selected image in its own window (Figure 6-8). This lets you view the file before you trace it. You can remove this window by selecting the *Close* option from the **System** menu, at the top left of the current window.

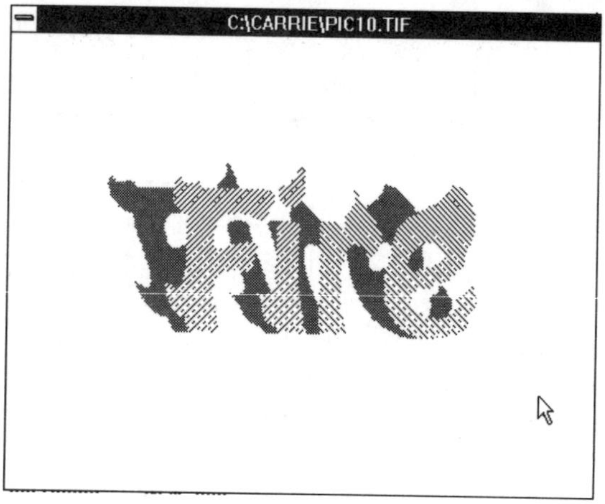

Figure 6-8. A Currently Selected File Displayed in its Own Window.

Preferences Menu

The first option available in the **Preferences** menu is the *Trace Partial Area* command as Figure 6-9 shows. If you have this selected, there will be a tick next to the command.

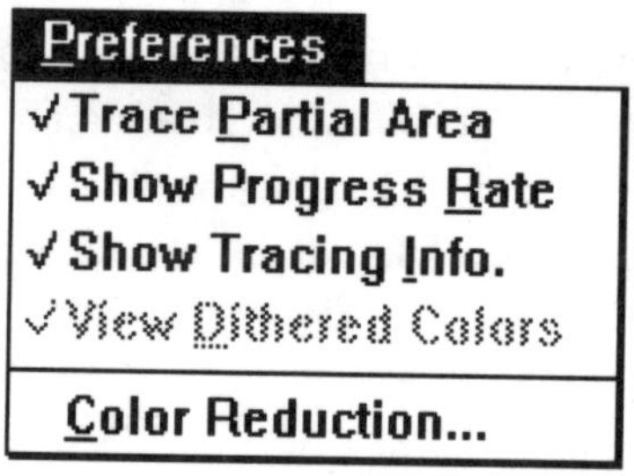

Figure 6-9. The Preferences Menu.

Now, after clicking on the *Start* button to begin tracing, you are given the opportunity to select the section of the image you want traced. The bitmap is displayed in a window, with a selection box and eight selection handles around it like the following illustration shows.

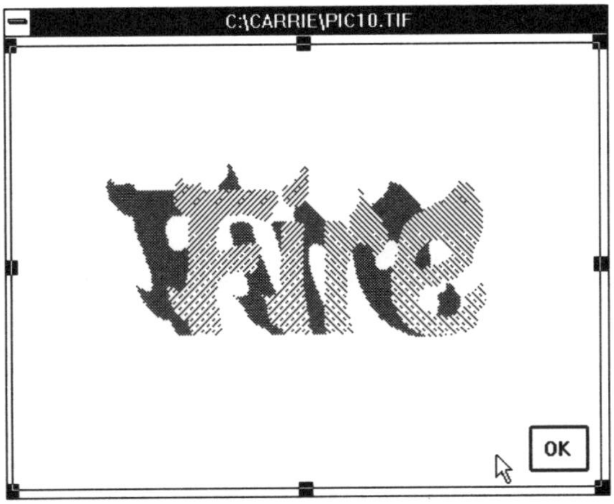

Holding the mouse on a selection handle, you can alter the shape of the box, until it sits over the area you would like traced. Click on the OK button once you have squared off the area to begin tracing. The following illustration shows a squared off area of the bitmap to be the only section traced.

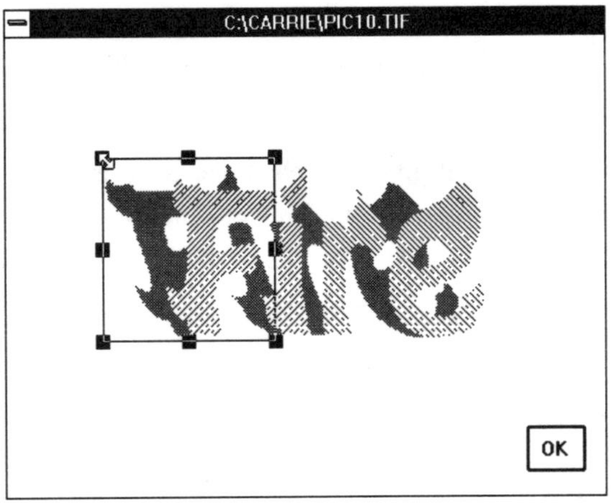

If you want the *Trace Partial Area* option deactivated, select the option from the **Preferences** menu again. You will know it is deactivated, if there is no tick to the left of the command.

The *Show Progress Rate* command displays an indicator at the bottom right of the tracing window. It shows the percentage of the trace as it is occurring. If you do not want this option on, deactivate this command by running the mouse down the menu and selecting the option. Figure 6-10 shows the *Show Progress Rate* command.

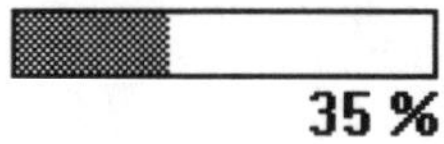

Figure 6-10. The Show Progress Rate Command.

The *Show Tracing Info* command tells you the number of pixels, nodes, and objects that the image has after it has been traced, and the time it took to trace the image (Figure 6-11).

Figure 6-11. The Show Tracing Info Command.

Again, if you do not want this option selected, make sure it has no tick mark next to it in the **Preferences** menu.

The *View Dithered Colors* option of the **Preferences** menu lets you display the traced image in dithered or pure colors. This option only works on gray scale or color images, and only if you have a color screen that can display 256 colors or more. This option does not affect the quality of the final trace.

The *Color Reduction* option activates the *Color Reduction Scheme* dialog box. The options here let you set the number of colors and gray scales your image will have, when traced. Figure 6-12 shows the *Color Reduction Scheme* dialog box.

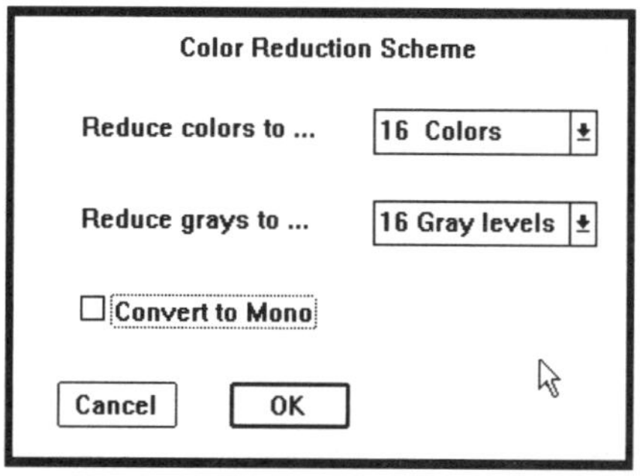

Figure 6-12. The Color Reduction Scheme Dialog Box.

Holding the mouse down on the arrow to the right of the *Reduce Colors to* and *Reduce Grays to* options, activates sub-menus where you select the required number as shown in Figure 6-13.

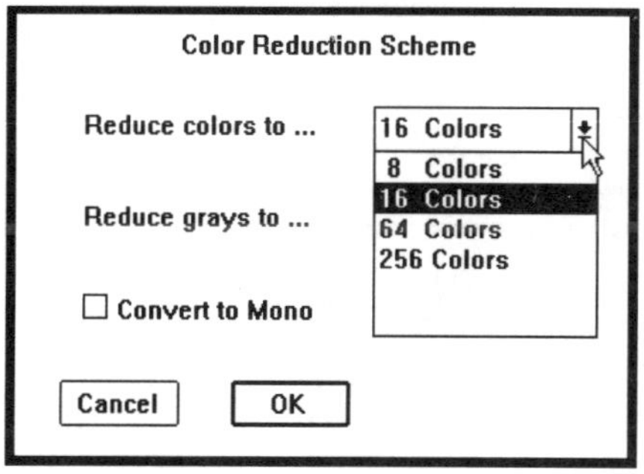

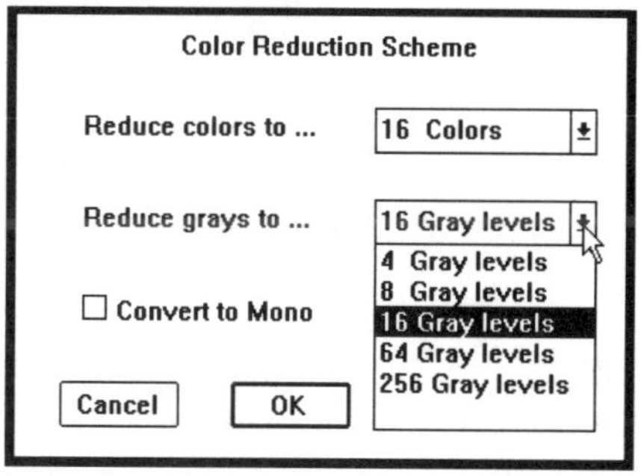

Figure 6-13. Changing the Levels of Color (Left) or Gray Scale (Right) Images.

You can convert colored and gray scaled images to black and white line art images by selecting the *Convert to Mono* option.

Exiting CorelTRACE!

Once you have finished tracing your images, leave CorelTRACE! by selecting the *Exit* command from the **File** menu. You can now import the traced image into any program that accepts EPS files. To import the image into CorelDRAW!, select the CorelTRACE! option from the *Import* dialog box in CorelDRAW! as Figure 6-14 shows.

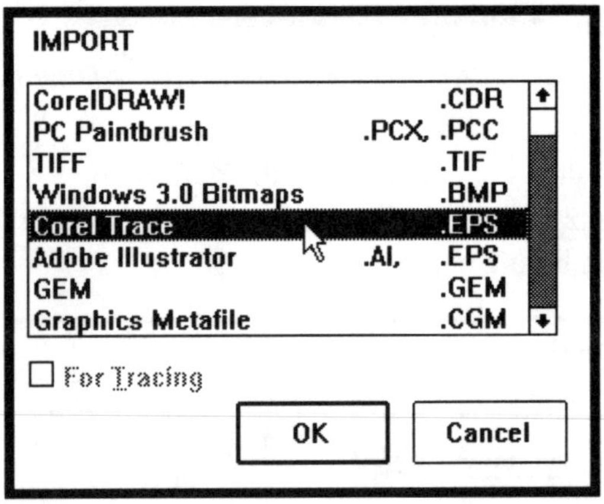

Figure 6-14. The Import Dialog Box with CorelTRACE! Selected.

For programs not accepting EPS files, import the image into CorelDRAW! first, and then export it in a format that the program will accept.

Summary

This chapter explained how you use CorelTRACE! to trace images and bitmaps so that they have better resolution for enlargement. You learned about the three menus and how to use them. Additionally, the chapter explained how you exit CorelTRACE!.

Chapter 7

Mosaic

Mosaic is a separate program that use you in conjunction with CorelDRAW!. The main feature of Mosaic is the visual file selector that displays all the CorelDRAW! Version 2.0 files as small boxes. This chapter teaches you how to perform these tasks:

- Open Mosaic in the two access modes
- Use the visual file selector
- Use the menu options and dialog boxes.

Accessing Mosaic

You can access Mosaic directly from Windows by double-clicking on the appropriate icon or from inside CorelDRAW!. There are slight differences in the program when you access it from Windows, and when you use it from inside CorelDRAW! These two different modes are known as standalone mode and CorelDRAW! mode.

If you have opened Mosaic from Windows (standalone mode), then you open a file by either double-clicking on the box containing the bitmap image of the file, or selecting it by clicking on it once and selecting the *Open* command from the **Mosaic** menu.

When you are in CorelDRAW!, you activate the Mosaic program so that it comes on every time you select *Open* or *Import*. Do this by accessing the **Special** menu and selecting the *Use Mosaic* command in the *Preferences* dialog box. You can turn this option off or on at any time. Once the file is located in the visual file selector, you can load it by selecting *Open* or *Import* and double-clicking on it or clicking on it once, and then clicking on the *Open/Import* menu item. Figure 7-1 shows the *Preferences* dialog box where you select the *Use Mosaic* option.

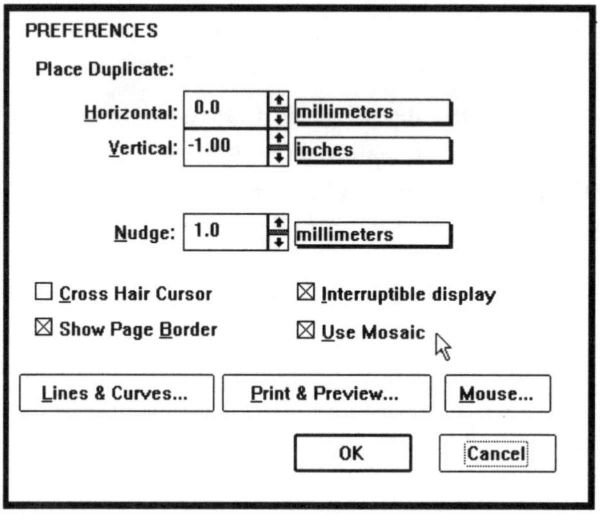

Figure 7-1. The Preferences Dialog Box.

When selecting the files in both standalone and CorelDRAW! modes, you can also use the arrow keys on the numeric keypad. If a certain directory contains more files than can be displayed on the screen, a scroll bar is displayed to the right of the window. You can use the scroll bar in conjunction with the mouse to give you access to the unseen files. You can select more than one file at a time by clicking on the files while holding down the Shift key. Mosaic lets you select more than one file and perform certain functions.

Visual File Selection

The main feature of Mosaic is the visual file selector. It displays, in rows and columns, all the CorelDRAW! Version 2 files as small boxes. These boxes contain a low resolution bitmap version of the CorelDRAW! image. If the file was created in an earlier version of CorelDRAW!, there will be a diagonal line through the box. Figure 7-2 shows the visual file selector of Mosaic, which lets you view CorelDRAW! Version 2.0 files in the currently active directory.

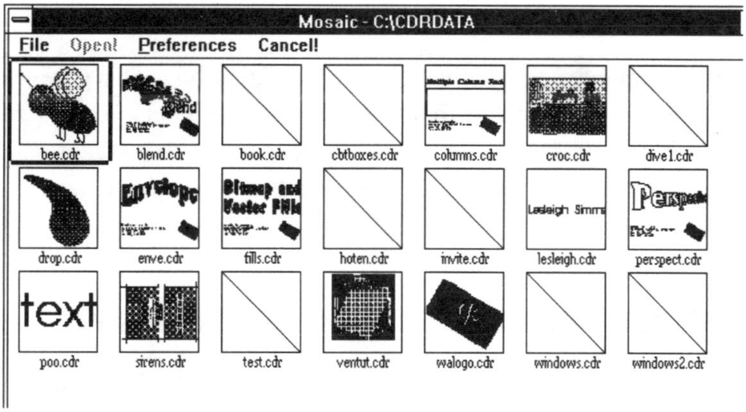

Figure 7-2. The Visual File Selector.

Menu Options

The first option available in the **File** menu is the *Delete* command. This command removes the currently selected file from the drive and directory. Figure 7-3 shows the **File** menu.

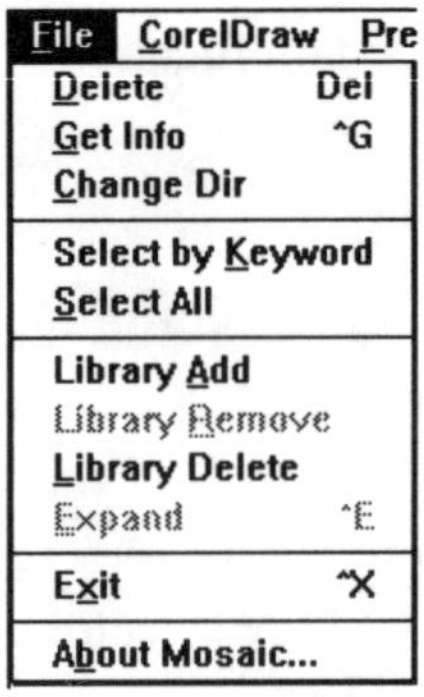

Figure 7-3. The File Menu.

The *Get Info* command displays the *Information* dialog box. This gives you current information on the selected file. The *Keywords* box lets you insert words allowing Mosaic to search and select files in a directory with common keywords. You can place as many words as you like here, but you must separate them by commas. The *Notes* option lets you type in any relevant information about the file as is shown in Figure 7-4.

Figure 7-4. The Information Dialog Box.

The *Change Dir* command activates the *Change Directory* command dialog box. The *Path* frame displays the current drive and directory selected. You change the drive by clicking on the relevant letter in the drive selector frame to the left of the dialog box. You change the directory in the frame to the right of the drive selector box. The CorelDRAW! files are displayed in a third box. The *File Type* option lets you display singular CorelDRAW! files or a library of CorelDRAW! files. Figure 7-5 shows the dialog box that is activated when you select the *Change Dir* command.

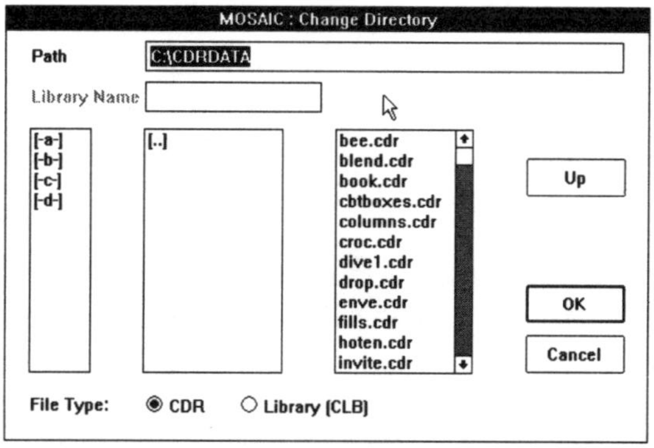

Figure 7-5. The Change Directory Dialog Box.

The *Select By Keyboard* command activates the dialog box in Figure 7-6. You can then put in the keywords you placed in the *Mosaic: Information* dialog box. You must separate the words by a comma, which signifies the word "or" or a + which means "and." Mosaic then searches for the files with matching keywords.

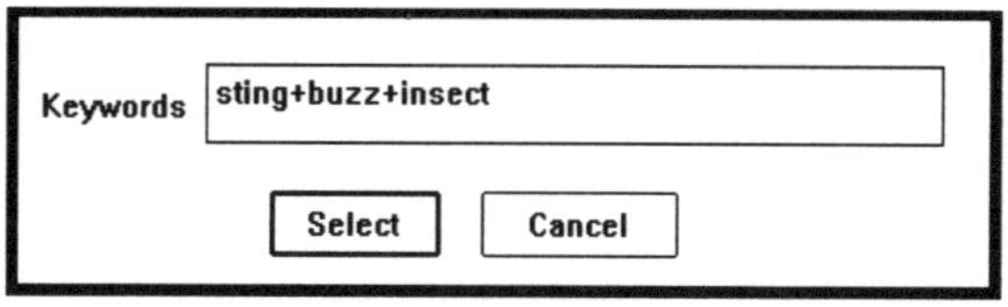

Figure 7-6. The Keyword Dialog Box.

The *Select All* command selects all the files in the current directory.

You can also create libraries of files with Mosaic. This compresses files and saves space on your hard disk. A library can consist of files on different drives and directories. This lets you use some of the features of Mosaic on files in different drives and/or directories.

A library is made up of two files. They have the same name but different extensions, which are .CLB and .CLH. These two files must be in the same directory for the library feature to work.

The *Library Add* command lets you create a new library or add to an existing one. When you create a new library, you must select one or more files in the visual file selector. The dialog box that is displayed after you select this command lets you choose the drive and directory where you are going to save your library. You also have to name your library file here.

When you select OK in the *Add To Library* dialog box (Figure 7-7), you are asked if you want to go ahead and create this library. If you do, the program then reverts to DOS to use an archiving program, the files are compressed, and the library created. Once it is complete, Mosaic returns. Compressing the files in a library does not have any effect on the original CorelDRAW! files.

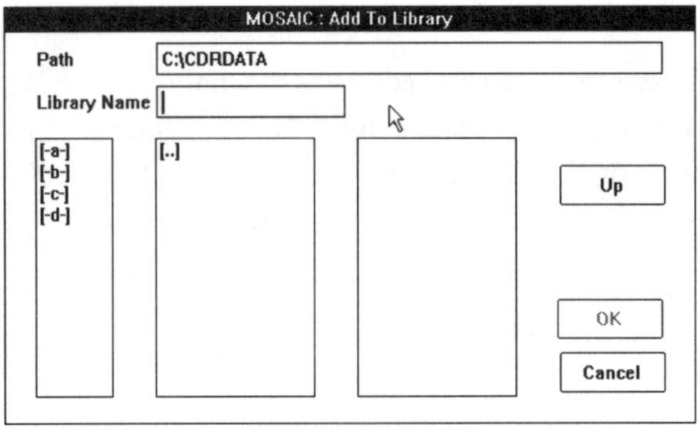

Figure 7-7. The Add To Library Dialog Box.

To add files to a library, use the *Library Add* command again. Locate the chosen directory with the .CDR files. Select the files you wish to add to the library, and then select the *Library Add* command. In the dialog box that is displayed, put in the name of the drive, directory, and library, and select OK. Once again, the archiving program is activated, until the library has been updated.

To use the *Library Remove* command, make sure the relevant library is displayed in the visual file selector. Click once on the files you wish to remove, and then on the *Library Remove* command. A screen prompt asks you to confirm your selection for removal.

To delete an entire library, choose the *Library Delete* command and in the associated dialog box, select the library(s) you want deleted. After you select OK, a prompt asks if you are sure you want to delete these libraries.

The *Expand* command expands a compressed library file and makes it a .CDR file. In the associated dialog box, you select the drive and directory the expanded files will be saved.

The *Exit* command leaves Mosaic.

The **CorelDRAW!** menu in Figure 7-8 is only available when you have opened Mosaic from Windows, not from inside CorelDRAW!.

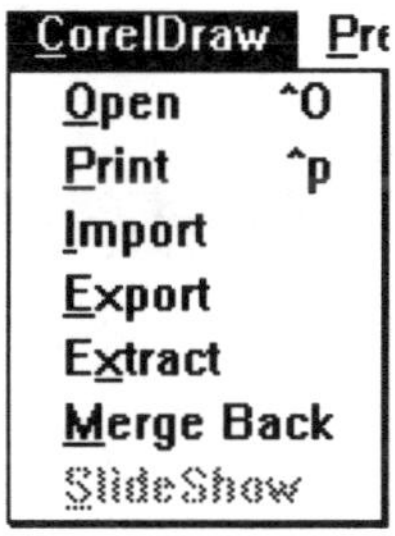

Figure 7-8. The CorelDRAW! Menu.

The *Open* command from the **CorelDRAW!** menu opens CorelDRAW! and loads a selected file. The file can either be a .CDR file selected from the visual file selector, or a compressed library file. If it is a library file, you will be asked to nominate a directory where this file is to be decompressed.

The *Print* command opens CorelDRAW! and prints the selected file or files. You can select any number of files, and the files will be opened in CorelDRAW! and printed one at a time. As with the *Open* command, you must select the directory in which the file is extracted and decompressed if it is a library file.

The *Import* command imports any number of CorelDRAW! files into a new or already existing CorelDRAW! file. The same rules apply for library files that were discussed in the *Open* and *Print* commands.

When using the *Export* command, you can select any number of files in the visual file selector and export them all. After selecting the files, and choosing the *Export* command, CorelDRAW! is opened and the *Export* dialog box is activated. The parameters set in this dialog box apply to all files now selected, prior to choosing the *Export* command. You also must select a directory where the exported files will go.

The *Extract* and *Merge Back* options are explained in **Chapter 5: Menu Commands**. Mosaic simply lets you select a number of files to be extracted and merged back.

The *Slideshow* option leads to the *Mosaic Slide Show* dialog box (Figure 7-9). This command lets you select two or more files and, after you select OK, all the selected files are displayed one at a time in Full Screen Preview Mode. You also have the option to select here the time each slide appears.

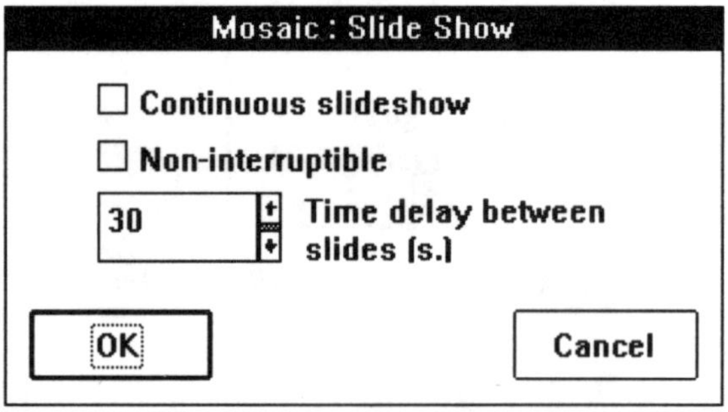

Figure 7-9. The Mosaic Slide Show Dialog Box.

Continuous slideshow keeps the .CDR files you selected displayed in a rotating fashion. To stop this, press any key. The *Non-interruptible* option displays each file only once, and the cycle cannot be interrupted. If you have neither option selected, the slideshow is continuous. However you can interrupt it by pressing any key.

The first option available in the **Preferences** menu in Figure 7-10 is the *Icon display* command, which displays the .CDR files in the directory as icons in the visual file selector.

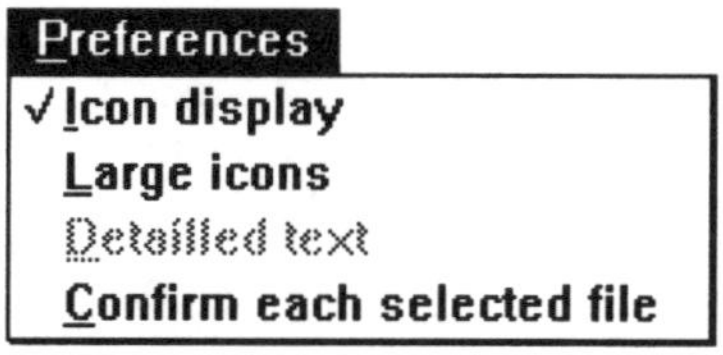

Figure 7-10. The Preferences Menu.

The *Large icons* option increases the size of the icon in the visual file selector. Compare the following icons to those in Figure 7-11.

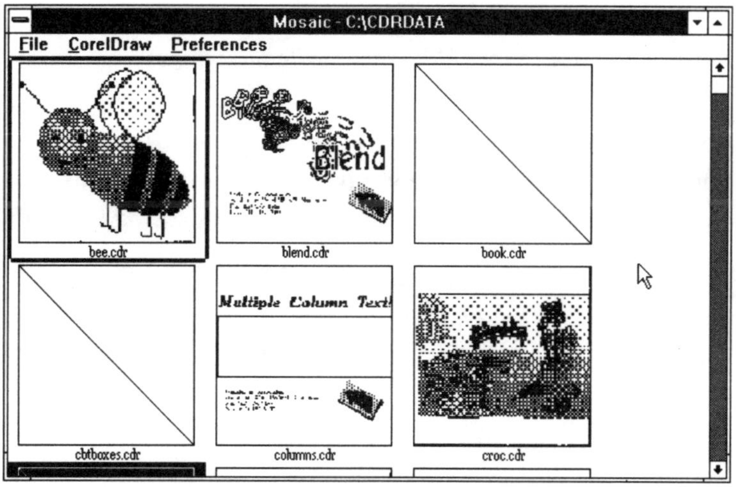

Figure 7-11. Large Icons in the Visual File Selector.

The *Detailed text* option displays all the files as text, giving you the title, date, and size of the file as is shown in Figure 7-12.

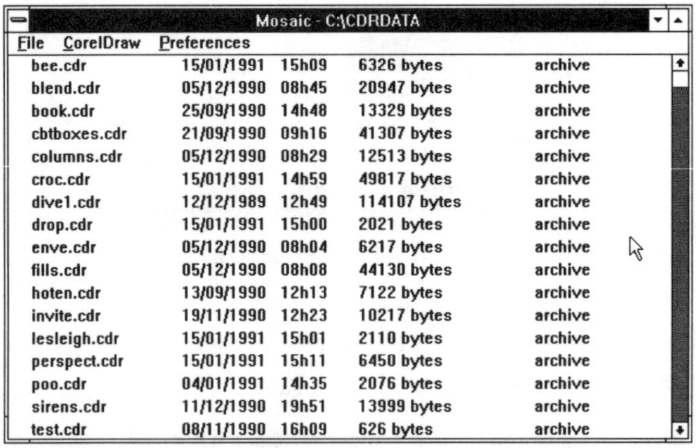

Figure 7-12. Detailed Text Option.

When you activate the *Confirm each selected file* option, a dialog box is displayed asking you to confirm any command you apply to a file. If this option is not activated, any command you choose proceeds without asking for confirmation.

If you have opened Mosaic from inside CorelDRAW!, the **CorelDRAW!** menu item is replaced by the *Open/Import* menu item. When you select the *Open* or *Import* command from the **File** menu in CorelDRAW!, the visual file selector is displayed. After clicking on the file you want, click on the *Open* or *Import* menu item.

Summary

This chapter taught you how to open Mosaic in standalone and CorelDRAW! modes. You learned how to select files from the visual file selector and how to use the menu options and dialog boxes in Mosaic.

Part 2

Self-Paced Exercises

Exercise 1

Flowing Text Around a Circle

This exercise takes you through the steps of flowing text around a circle. Text you type onto your page in CorelDRAW! can be flowed to any object on your page including circles, curved lines, and squares. The following pages contain the steps, as well as the details on how to execute this task.

The Steps in Brief

1. Create a new CorelDRAW! file.
2. Create a line of text on the page that reads “flowing text around a circle” using 50-point Penguin typeface.
3. Underneath the text, draw a circle approximately 2.56" (65mm x 65mm).
4. Flow the text around the circle.
5. Rotate the text and the circle 90 degrees.
6. Delete the circle.
7. Enlarge the text approximately 175%, keeping it in its correct proportions.
8. Activate the Preview Screen and enlarge it so it covers the whole screen.

This illustration shows the result of this exercise.

The Steps in Detail

1. Create a new CorelDRAW! file.

If you are already in CorelDRAW!, select *New* from the **File** menu and save the changes, if applicable. If you are not in CorelDRAW!, start the program from Windows or DOS.

2. Select the Text Tool from the Toolbox and click it on the page where you want the line of text to begin. Now click the Text Tool on the page to activate the *Text* dialog box so that it looks like this:

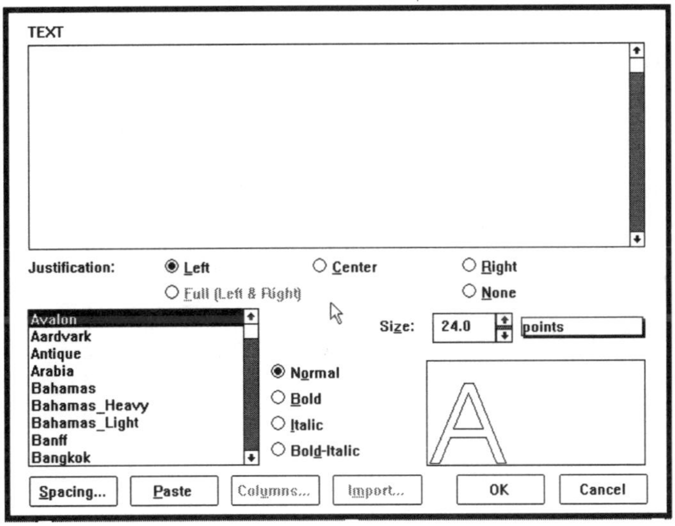

Once the *Text* dialog box is displayed, the flashing text cursor will be in the window at the top of the dialog box. This is where you type the text. If the flashing cursor is not in the window, click the mouse inside the window, and type "flowing text around a circle."

Once you have typed the text, move to the rectangle underneath that contains the list of fonts. Using the mouse, click on the down arrow to the right of the box containing the fonts, until the Penguin is available; then click on it.

Now move to the *Size* box and double-click the current value and type 50 over the reversed out figure.

The screen should now look like this:

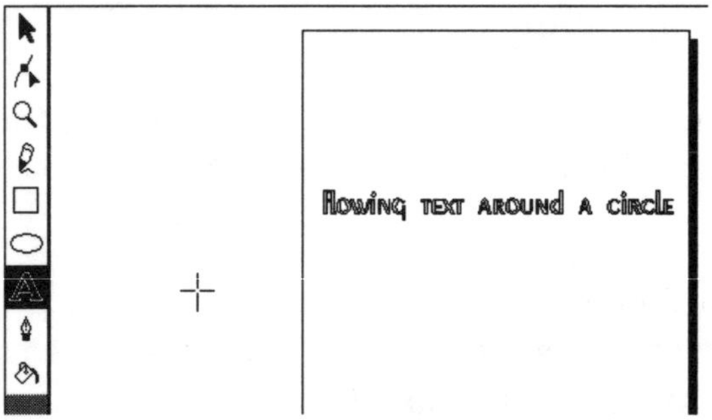

3. Now select the Ellipse Tool from the Toolbox. Move it onto the page, in preparation for drawing a circle underneath the text like this:

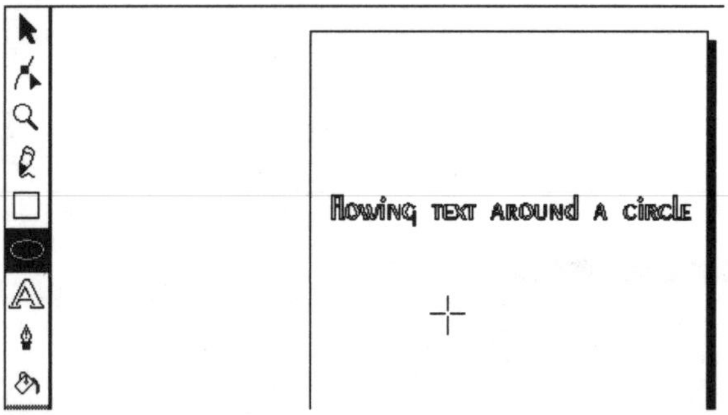

Before you draw your circle, make sure that the Status Line is on. If it is not, select the *Show Status Line* command from the **Display** menu.

Hold your finger on the Ctrl key while you are using the Ellipse Tool. This ensures that a perfect circle is drawn.

To draw the circle, hold your finger on the mouse and drag it down and to the right. Watch the Status Line, and when it reaches approximately 2.56" (65mm x 65mm), take your finger off the mouse and then off the Ctrl key. The circle will now be on the page. You can change the Status Line measurement type (such as inches, or millimeters) through the *Grid Setup* command in the **Display** menu. See the description of this command in **Chapter 5: Menu Commands** if you have any trouble changing the measurement on the Status Line.

The screen should look like this:

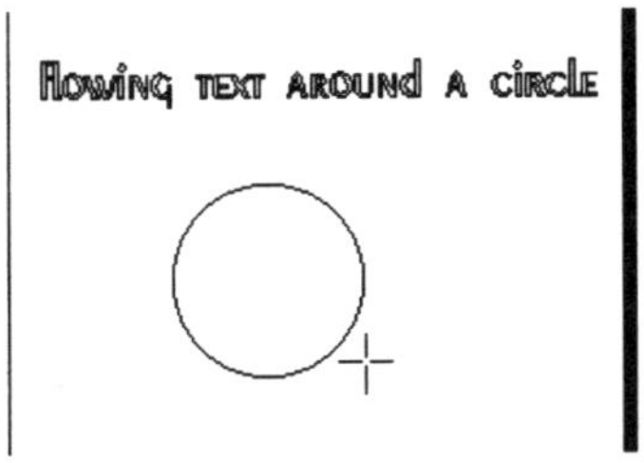

4. Select both the text and the circle. Since they are the only objects on the page, you can choose the *Select All* command from the **Edit** menu to select them.

Alternatively, you could click the mouse once on both objects with the Pick Tool, while holding down the ⇧ Shift key or draw a frame around both objects with your finger on the mouse and the Pick Tool activated.

Once you have both objects selected (the Status Line reads, "2 objects selected"), choose the *Fit Text To Path* command from the **Arrange** menu.

After a moment the text will flow around the circle like this:

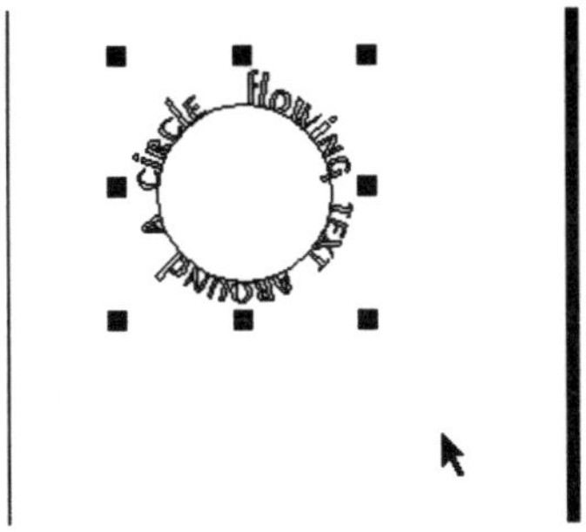

5. Click on the text and circle to activate the rotate and skew handles. Make sure you click exactly on one of the objects. If you do not, they will both become deselected. If this happens, choose the *Select All* command again, and click anywhere on a line of one of the objects.

You must select the circle and text together if you want them to rotate together. When the rotate and skew handles are present, hold the mouse over the bottom right handle so it turns into a crosshair. When this crosshair is displayed, hold the mouse down and drag it around to the right and up, counterclockwise like this:

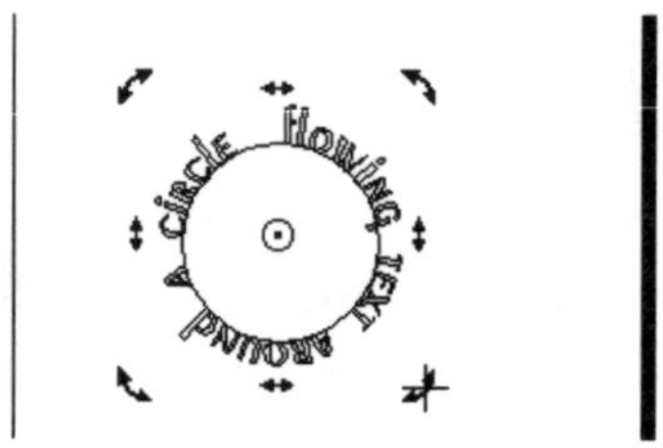

Release your finger from the mouse when the Status Line shows that you have rotated the objects approximately 90 degrees. The screen should look like this:

The text and the circle have now been successfully rotated as shown in the following illustration.

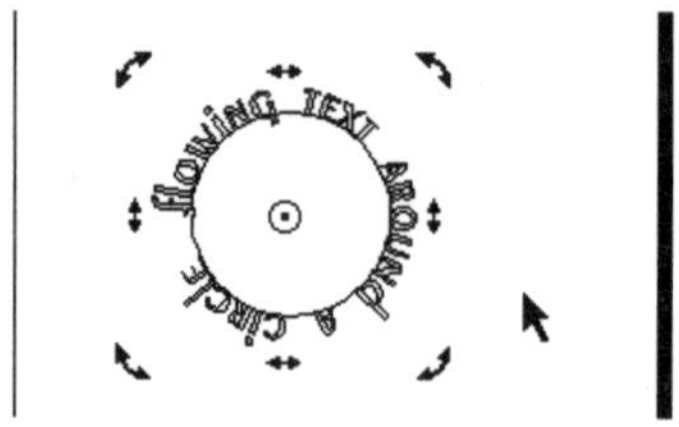

SHORTCUT

Alternatively, the circle and the text can be rotated through the *Rotate & Skew* dialog box available from the **Transform** menu. You can also rotate the circle by typing 90 degrees in the *Rotation Angle* box and selecting OK.

6. Click the mouse anywhere on the blank page to deselect both objects. Now you can safely click on the circle once with the Pick Tool, and it will be selected on its own. If you are not sure which object you have selected, look at the Status Line and it will show you. The screen should look like this:

Once you select the circle, press the delete key, or select the *Clear* command from the **Edit** menu. The circle will be deleted from the page, leaving the text still in its circular position like this:

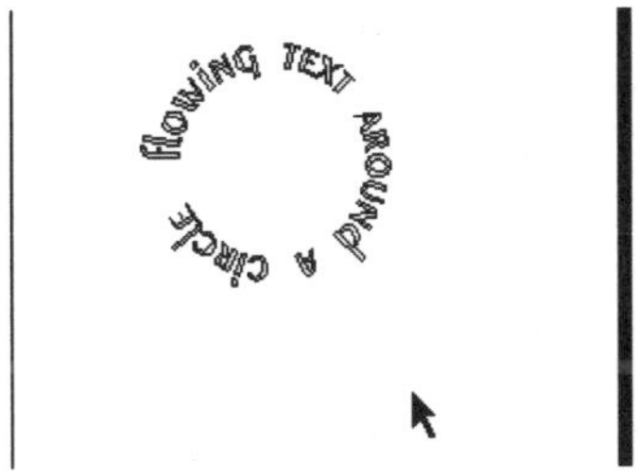

7. Select the text with the Pick Tool and use one of the corner nodes.

For this step, hold the mouse over the top right corner node to display a crosshair. Then hold the mouse down on the node, and drag it up and to the right like this:

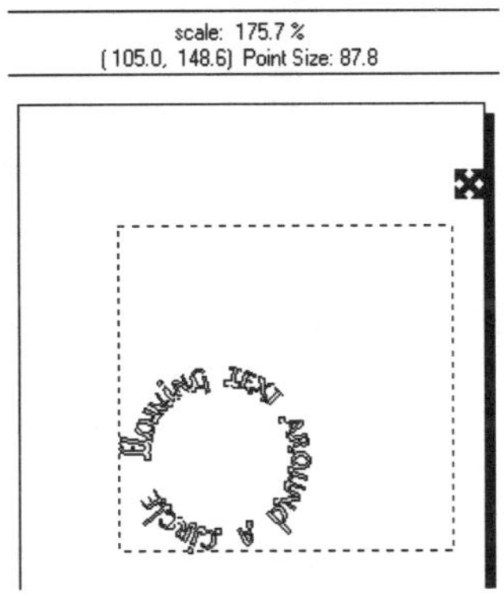

When the scale figure reaches approximately 175% in the Status Line, take your finger off the mouse. The circle will now sit on the page at the larger size.

Enlarging any object from a corner node ensures that it stays in its correct proportions. The following illustration shows the larger text.

8. Move to the **Display** menu and select the *Show Preview* command. Alternatively, you can press the Shift + F9 keys on your keyboard, to move directly to and from the Preview Screen.

Once you display the Preview Screen, you can make the window larger or smaller by moving the mouse over the left-hand wall of the Preview Window until a double-headed, horizontal arrow appears. Then hold down the mouse and drag the window to the left or right as the following illustration shows:

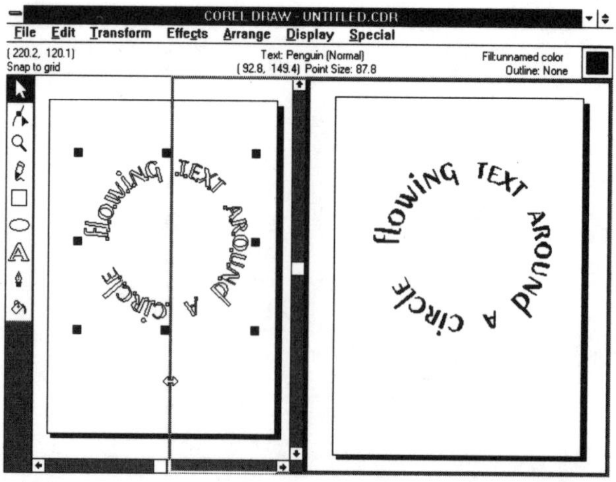

Once you change the size of the window, it remains this size every time you select the Preview Screen. To deselect the Preview Screen or keep it from displaying, select the *Show Preview* command again from the **Display** menu (or press Shift + F9). The following illustration shows the Preview Screen covering the whole screen.

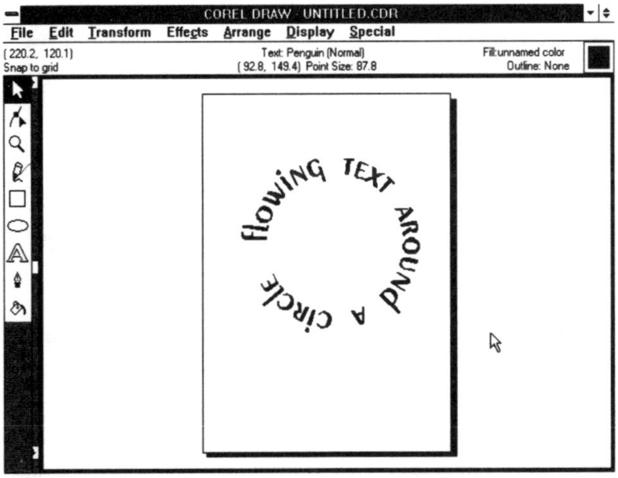

As was mentioned at the beginning of this exercise, you can flow text along any object on your page. Where text begins to flow, when rotating around circles and squares, is determined by where you began to draw the object.

If you flow text around a circle, for example, and the flow of text has begun in the wrong spot, you can still rotate it to a different position as you did in this exercise. The remaining illustrations show text being fitted to some different paths that you might like to try for yourself, replacing the circle with another object. In the following illustration, the circle on the left was drawn dragging the mouse up and left. The flowed text now starts from a different position. The circle on the right was drawn dragging the mouse up and to the right.

The following circle was drawn dragging the mouse down and to the left.

The illustration on the left has text that has been fitted to a curved line. The illustration on the right has text fitted to a square.

You can also flow a text string along another piece of text after the latter text has been converted to curves like this:

Exercise 2

Changing Character Attributes

This exercise shows you how to mix and change character attributes in the same text string. You can apply a different attribute to each piece of text you type in CorelDRAW!. The following pages contain the steps, as well as the details on how to execute this task.

The Steps in Brief

1. Create a new CorelDRAW! file.
2. Type "text" onto your page using 2" (50 mm) Homeward Bound.
3. Magnify the text so that it takes up most of the screen.
4. Change the font of the first letter "t" to Vogue and make it bold.
5. Change the size of the letter "e" to 100 points.
6. Give the letter "x" a character angle of –15 degrees.
7. Give the last letter "t" a vertical shift of 10%.

This is the result of this exercise.

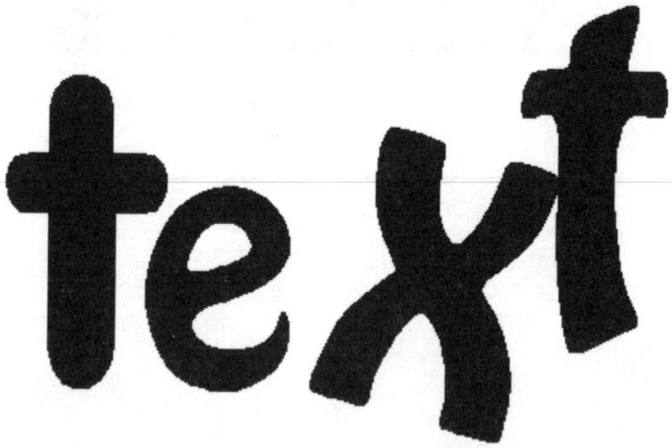

The steps for completing this exercise are on the following pages.

The Steps in Detail

1. Create a new CorelDRAW! file.

If you are already in CorelDRAW!, select *New* from the **File** menu and save changes, if applicable. If you are not in CorelDRAW!, start the program from Windows or DOS.

2. Select the Text Tool from the Toolbox, and click it onto the page where you want the text to begin to display the *Text* dialog box. The flashing text cursor is automatically in the window at the top of the dialog box so that you can type in the word "text."

After you type the text, move to the rectangle containing the list of fonts. Using the mouse, click on the down arrow until you display the Homeward Bound typeface and click on it. Now move to the *Size* box.

Click on the measurement box, beside the *Size*: rectangle until it reads inches or millimeters (depending on your preference). Once it does, double-click on the current value in the *Size* box, so that it becomes selected in reverse video, and type in 2 for inches (or 50 for millimeters). Alternatively, use the up or down arrow to the right of the box containing the Size, until it reaches the desired figure.

Once your dialog box is set up to look like the following illustration, click on OK to display the text on the page.

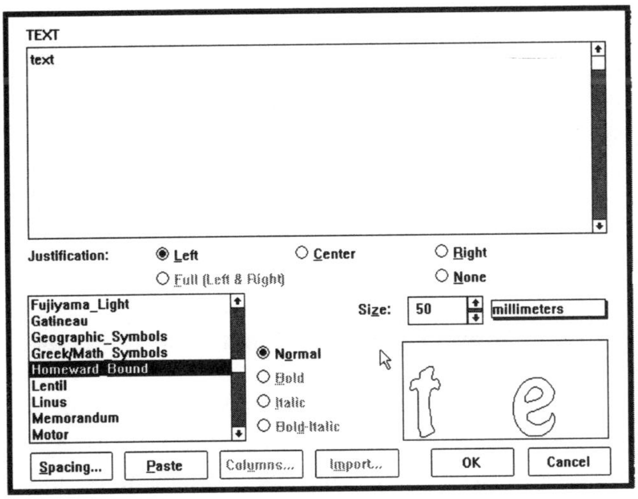

3. Select the Zoom Tool from the Toolbox. From the Zoom Tool fly-out, click on the tool with the plus symbol. Holding your finger on the mouse, draw a frame around the text with this tool, starting from the top left corner. Release your finger from the mouse once you have covered the whole text. The screen should look like this:

The section of the page that was inside the frame you drew with the Zoom Tool, now takes up the whole working screen. The text is larger as shown in the following illustration.

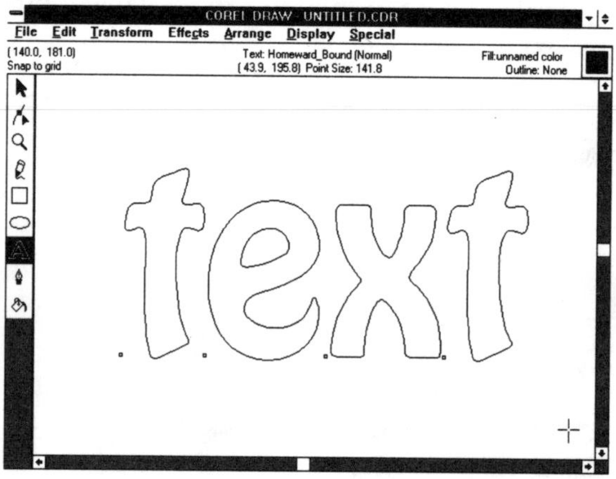

4. Select the Node Tool from the Toolbox, and if the text is not selected, click on it once with this tool. When text is selected with the Node Tool, each letter of the text string has a node at its bottom left like the following illustration. This is where the text is selected to change its attributes.

Click once inside the node at the bottom left of the first letter "t." Notice that the node becomes black like this:

This letter is now selected.

To change its attributes, select the *Character Attributes* command from the **Edit** menu. Then click on the arrow at the bottom right of the rectangle that contains the list of fonts, until the Vogue typeface is available, and click on it as shown in the following illustration:

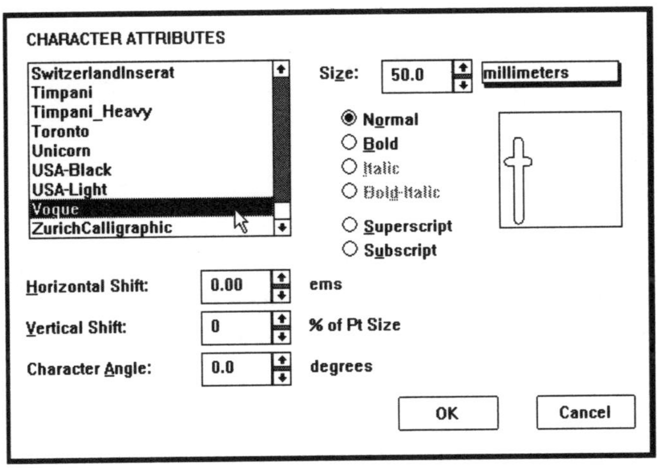

Since the first letter was the only one selected, the changes you make here only affect this letter.

To the right of the list of fonts in the previous illustration are the style options. Click in the circle corresponding to the *Bold* option to complete the second half of this step.

Once you make these changes in the *Character Attributes* dialog box, click on OK, and the first letter of your text string will reflect the changes you have just made like this:

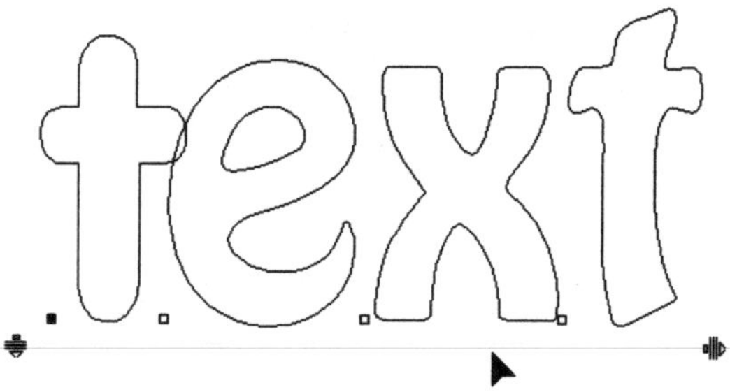

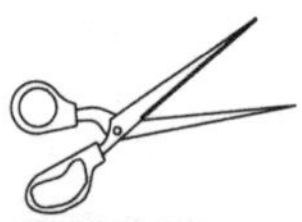

SHORTCUT

5. Activate the *Character Attributes* dialog box, however, this time instead of clicking once inside the node at the bottom left of the letter "e," double-click inside the node shown here to activate the *Character Attributes* dialog box directly.

Click on the box containing the word millimeters or inches, until it changes to points. Then change the figure in the *Size* box to 100, and then click on OK.

The following illustration shows results of the changes you made to the second letter of your text string.

6. Select the letter "x" the same way you selected the first letter "t."

Choose the *Character Attributes* command from the **Edit** menu. Alternatively, double-click inside the node at the bottom left of the letter "x" to activate the *Character Attributes* dialog box, without having to go through the menu.

Now, double-click over the current value in the *Character Angle* rectangle, which should be 0. Once it is in reverse video, type in –15.

You could have also clicked on the down arrow to the right of the frame containing the current figure, with the mouse, until it reached –15. Either way the *Character Angle* frame should read –15 degrees.

Click on OK. The letter "x" is now at a –15 degree angle. The screen should look like this:

7. Select the last letter by double-clicking inside the node to the bottom left of the letter as shown in the following illustration:

As a result, the *Character Attributes* dialog box is displayed. In the *Vertical Shift* option frame, change the current value to 10. Either select the current value by double-clicking over it and typing the new amount in, or by clicking the mouse on the up arrow to the right, until it reaches 10.

Once the dialog box is displayed, click on OK. The last letter now is a superscript character and has a Vertical Shift of 10% of the current point size like this:

Move to the Preview Screen (Shift + F9). The finished result of the changes made to the text string should look like this:

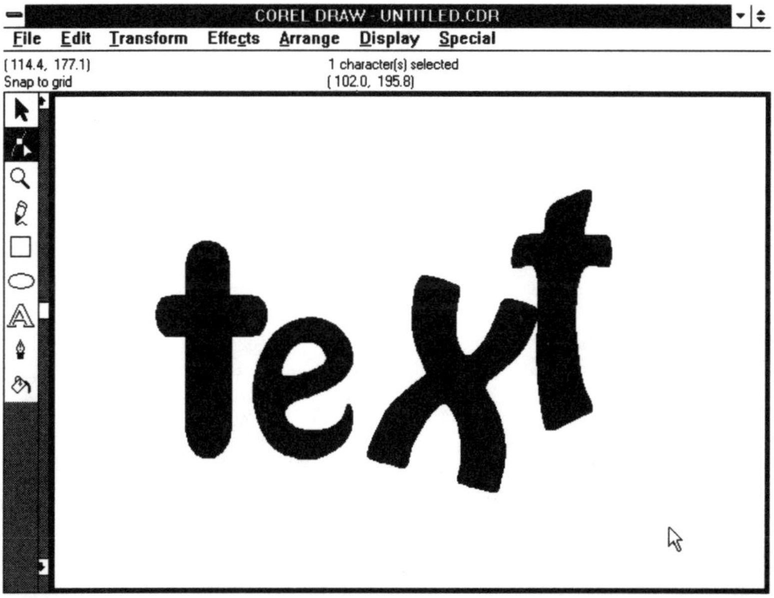

You can select more than one text character at a time by holding down the Shift key and clicking inside the number of nodes you wish to select. You can also hold your finger on the mouse and draw a frame over the nodes you wish to select. Once the required nodes are black, simply double-click inside any one of them, or select the *Character Attributes* command from the **Edit** menu. Any changes you make in the *Character Attributes* dialog box affect all the letters you selected with the Node Tool.

You can alter every piece of text placed on the page this way. The choice of being able to mix text attributes in the one text string, gives you great freedom in creating unusual text strings, logos, headings, and many other applications. Experiment for yourself and see what you can come up with using the *Character Attributes* dialog box.

Exercise 3

Changing the Shape of Text

This exercise takes you through the details of changing the shape of a text character. You can manipulate the text you type onto your page in CorelDRAW! and change it to suit your own needs. You can also alter an individual piece of text to any degree, so that it no longer resembles the original font. The following pages contain the steps, as well as details on how to execute this task.

The Steps in Brief

1. Create a new CorelDRAW! file.
2. Type "Edit" on the page using Bold 24-point Avalon.
3. Enlarge the text approximately 850%, keeping it in its correct proportions.
4. Convert the text to curves.
5. Change the shape of the letter "E" to resemble the letter "E" in the first illustration.
6. Display the Color Palette.
7. Apply a color to the text from the Color Palette.

This is the result of the exercise.

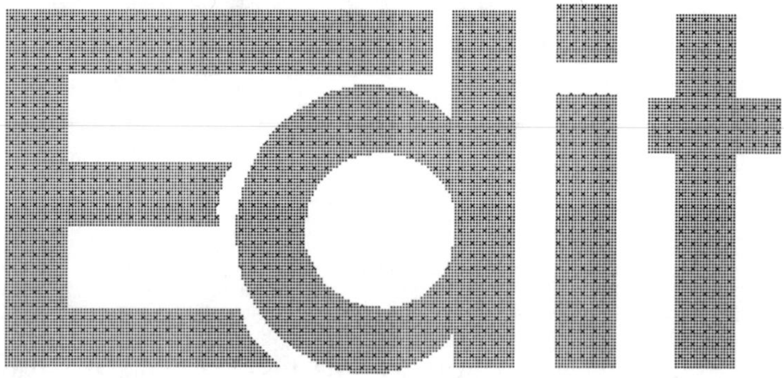

The steps for completing this exercise are on the following pages.

The Steps in Detail

1. Create a new CorelDRAW! file.

If you are already in CorelDRAW!, select New from the **File** menu and save changes, if applicable. If you are not in CorelDRAW!, start the program from Windows or DOS.

2. Select the Text Tool from the Toolbox, and click it onto the page where you would like to display the text. The *Text* dialog box will be activated.

The flashing text cursor is automatically in the window at the top of the dialog box ready for you to type the word "Edit." For this exercise, you are choosing Avalon, 24 point, with the Bold option. If your typeface and point size are different, select the Avalon font and change the size to 24 points. When your dialog box is set up, click on OK.

After setting up your *Text* dialog box and clicking on OK, the text is displayed on the page. Select the Pick Tool from the Toolbox. The text is automatically selected, ready for Step 3 like this:

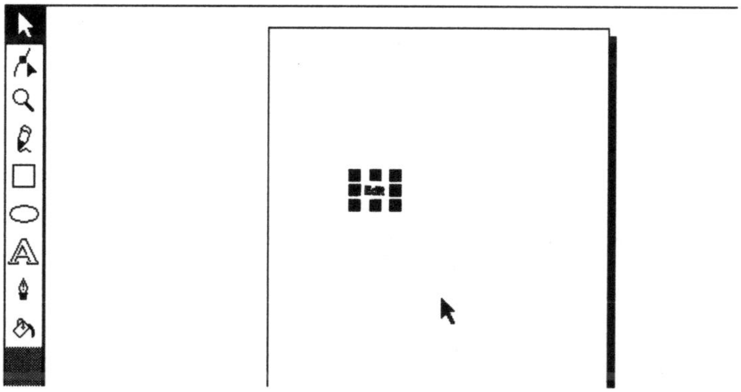

3. Hold the mouse over the bottom right-hand corner node until a crosshair appears. When it does, hold your finger on the mouse and drag it down and to the right, until the Status Line indicates a scale of approximately 850% like this:

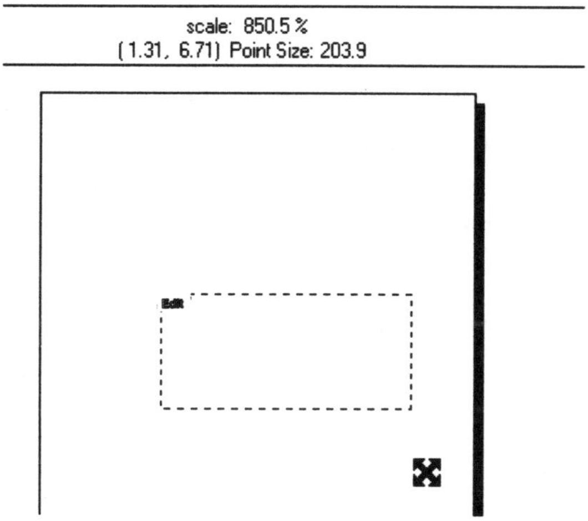

Then release your finger from the mouse. The text will now be similar to this:

For the remainder of this exercise, you might find it easier to further magnify the text. Select the fourth option in the Zoom Tool fly-out so that the text takes up the full screen like this:

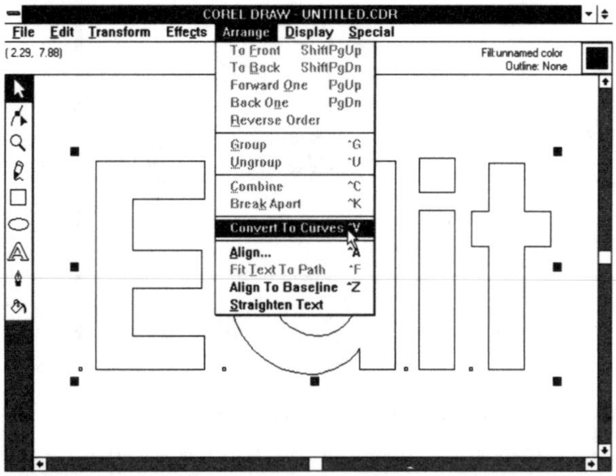

4. Select the text with the Pick Tool, and choose the *Convert To Curves* command from the **Arrange** menu.

After applying the *Convert To Curves* command to the text, you can manipulate each character. To manipulate the text, you must select the Node Tool from the Toolbox. When the text is selected with this tool, the nodes will become larger, making it easier to select them as the following illustration shows:

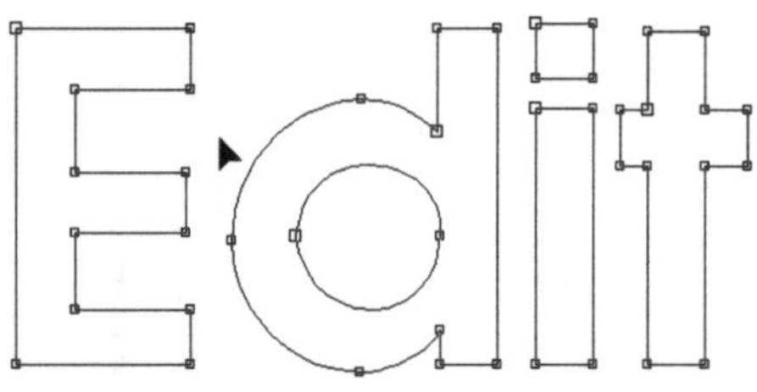

Once you convert text to curves, you cannot change it back again. Therefore, you cannot apply the *Edit Text* and *Character Attributes* commands to text that you have converted to curves.

5. First select the two nodes at the top of the letter "E" as shown here. With the Node Tool selected, hold your finger on the mouse, and draw a frame around the two nodes, and then release your finger.

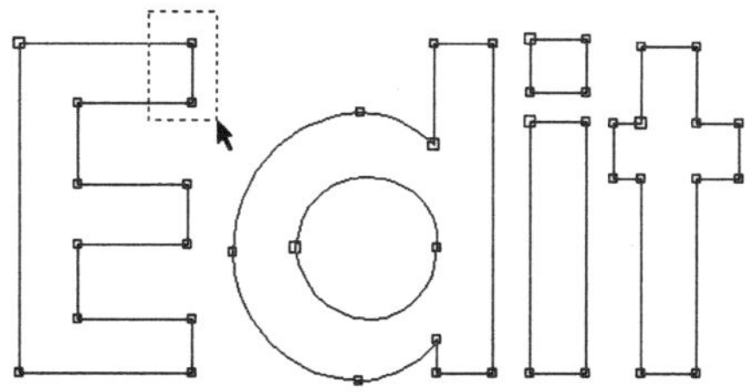

Once the nodes are selected, they become darker, and in this case, the Status Line indicates that you have two nodes selected. Now hold the mouse down inside either of the selected nodes, and drag the mouse to the right. Release your finger just before the top of the letter reaches the top of the "d" as shown here.

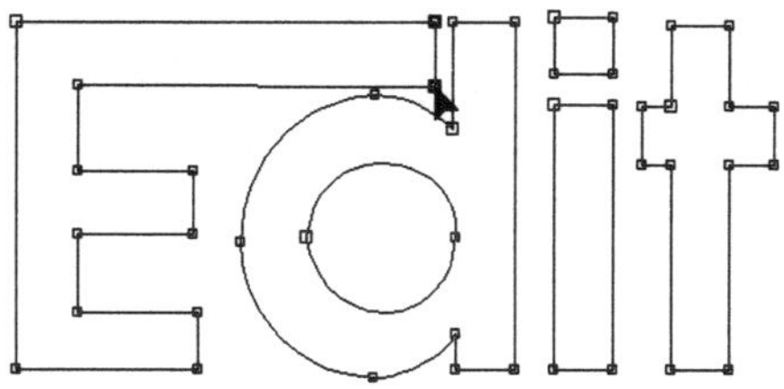

Now select the two nodes of the middle section of the letter "E," the same way you selected the two top nodes. Alternatively, you could have clicked once inside each node holding the Shift key down.

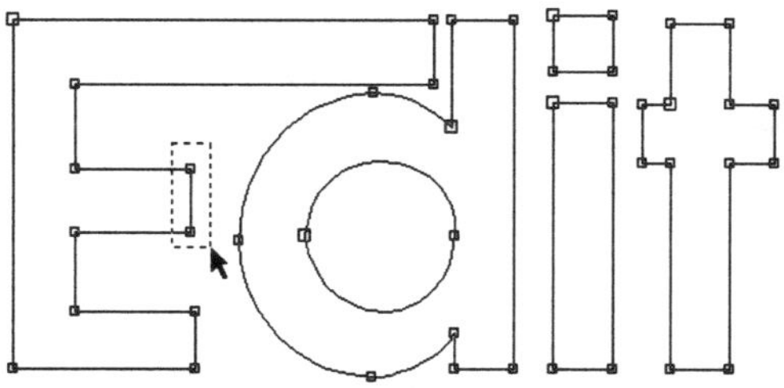

Hold the mouse down on the lower selected node and move it to the right. Since the other node is selected too, it moves as well. Release your finger from the mouse when you have moved the nodes to the correct position like this:

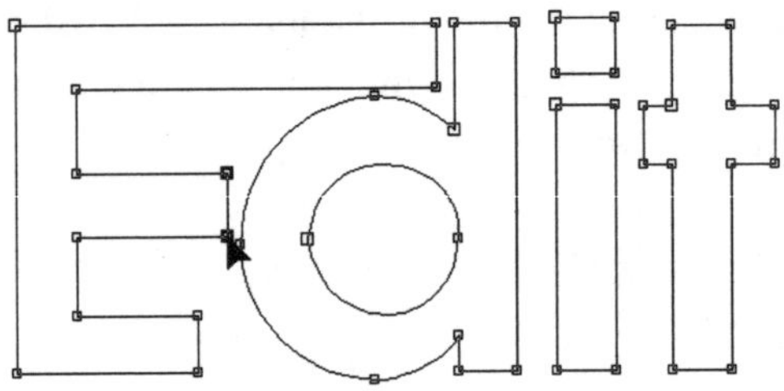

To perform the next step, you must first deselect the two currently selected nodes. This is because you are going to move one of the nodes only, and if two are selected you cannot. To do this, simply click anywhere on the blank page.

Select and move the top node of the middle section of the letter "E" closer to the curved section of the letter "d" like this:

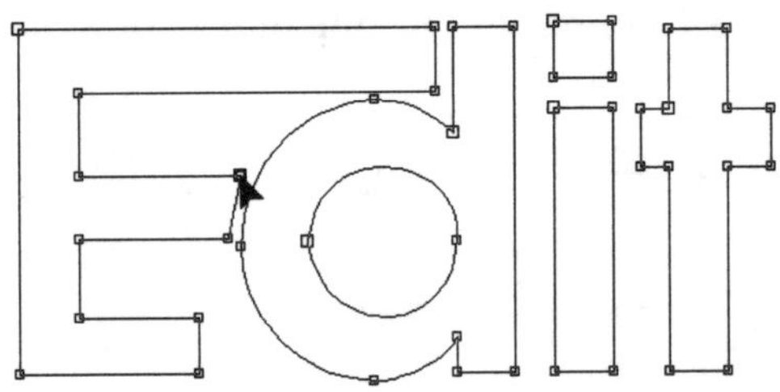

Double-click on the line indicated below to activate the *Node Edit* dialog box, so that you can apply a curved attribute to the line.

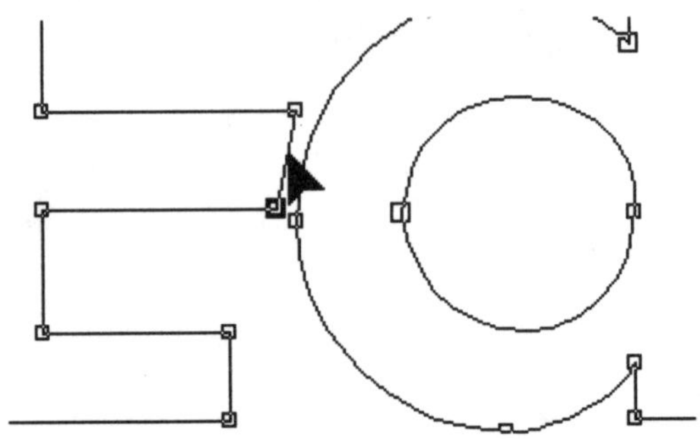

Once you have activated the *Node Edit* dialog box, select the *toCurve* option as indicated here. This gives curved attributes to the line selected.

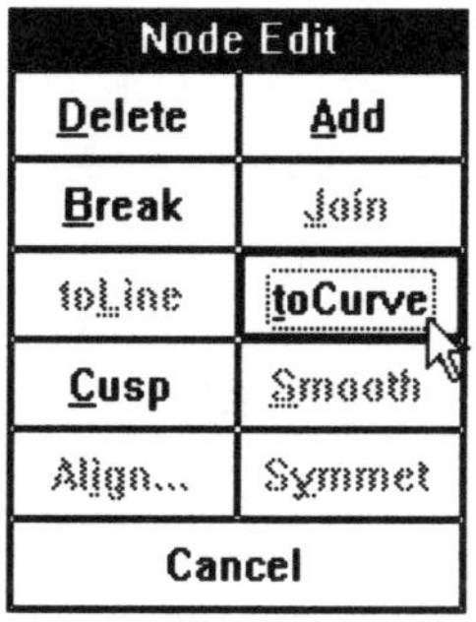

Now that you have given this line curved attributes, it has two control points running along it, coming from the nodes on the top and bottom. Drag these control points slightly to the left, to give the line a curved shape.

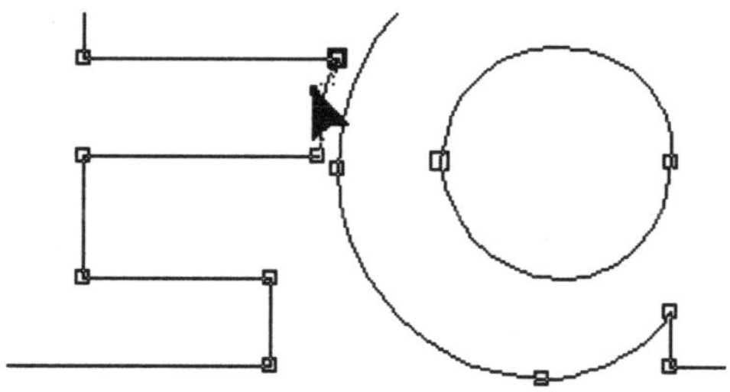

Now do the same with the control point coming out of the bottom node, as with the one above. That is, move it to the left slightly, so this section of the letter "E" fits in nicely with the letter "d" like this:

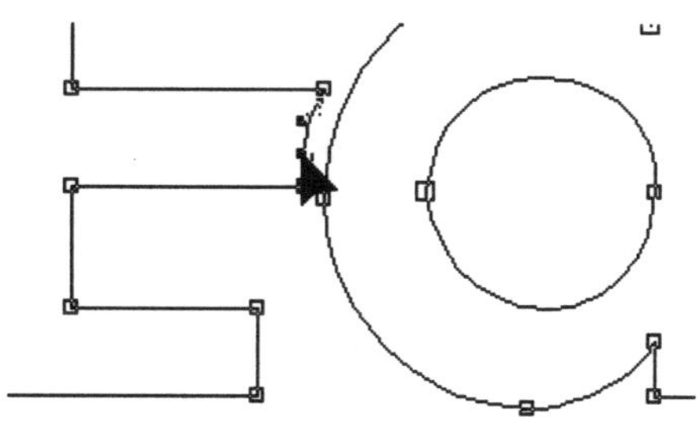

Move to the bottom of the letter "E" and select the two nodes as shown here.

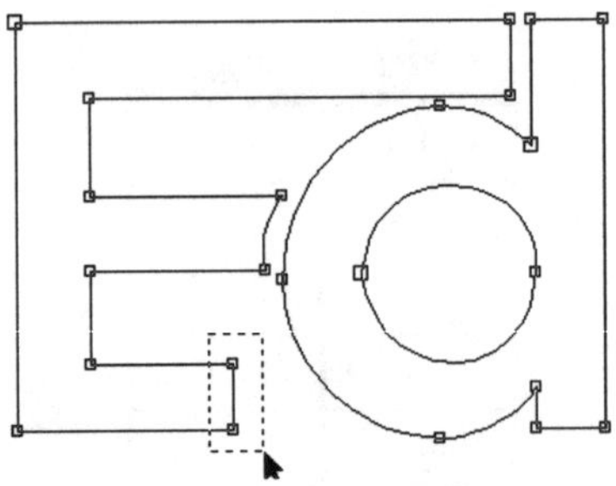

Drag the two nodes over toward the next letter, as you did with the other sections, and release the mouse just before the letter "d."

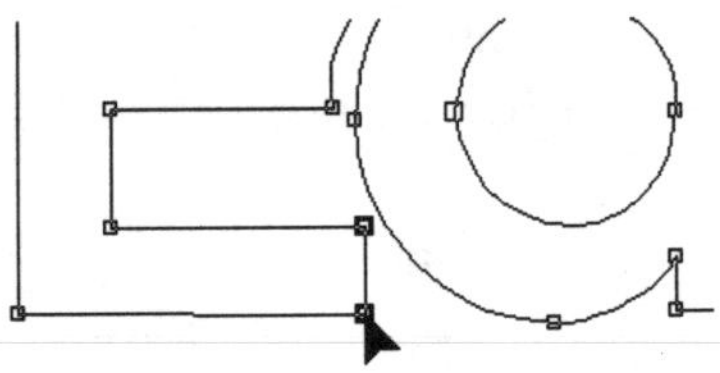

Click anywhere on the page to deselect the two nodes and move the bottom node closer to the letter "d" like this:

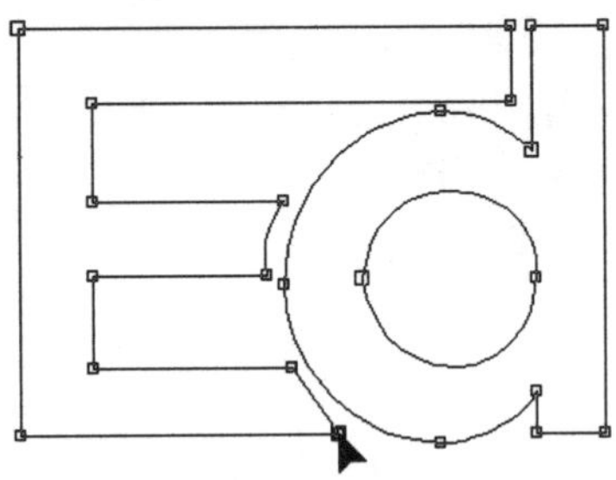

You are now going to give the line indicated here curved attributes, so double-click on it to activate the *Node Edit* dialog box.

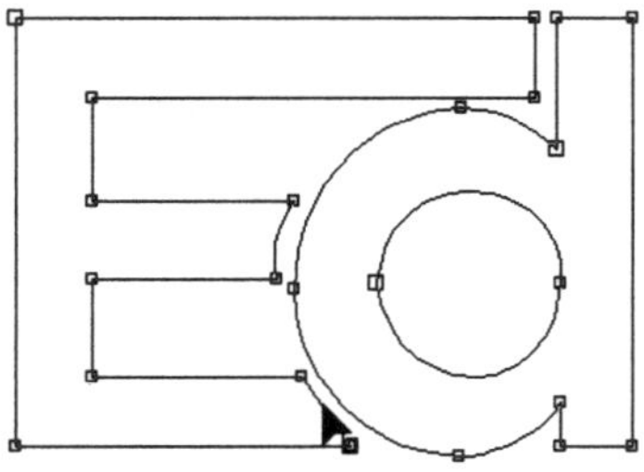

Once the *Node Edit* dialog box is activated, select the *toCurve* command. Now move the control point of the top node slightly to the left, as shown below, to give the line a curved look.

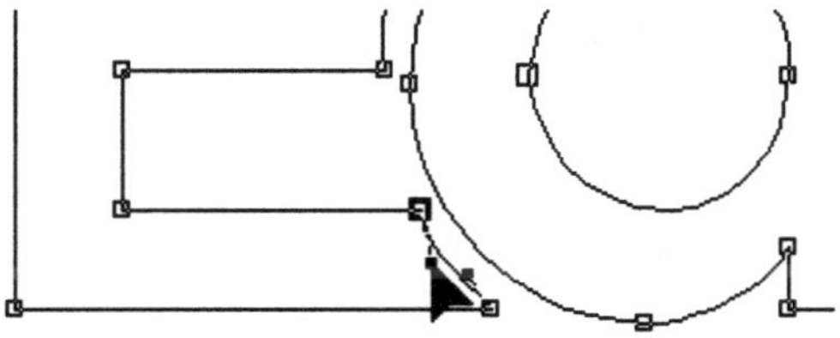

Move the control point of the bottom node to finish the curved shape like this:

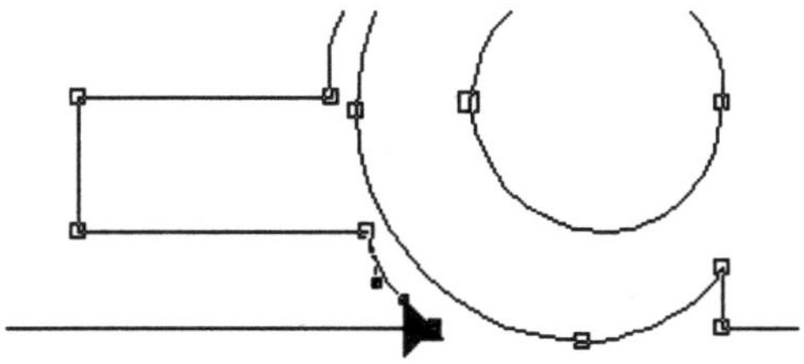

The following illustration shows the finished result of your manipulation of the letter "E."

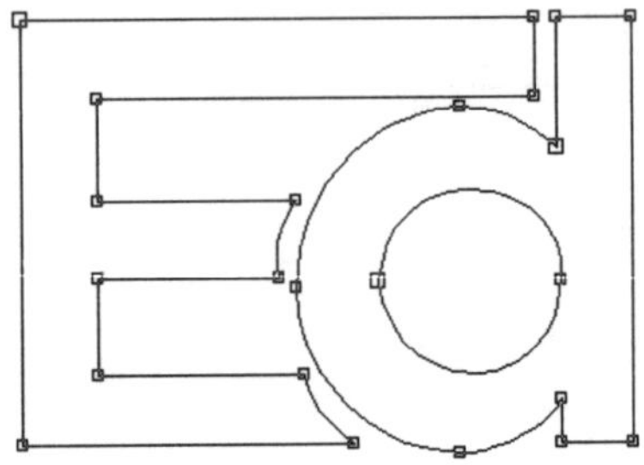

6. Select the *Show Color Palette* command from the **Display** menu as shown below.

On selecting this command, the Color Palette is displayed at the bottom of your screen underneath the scroll bar like this:

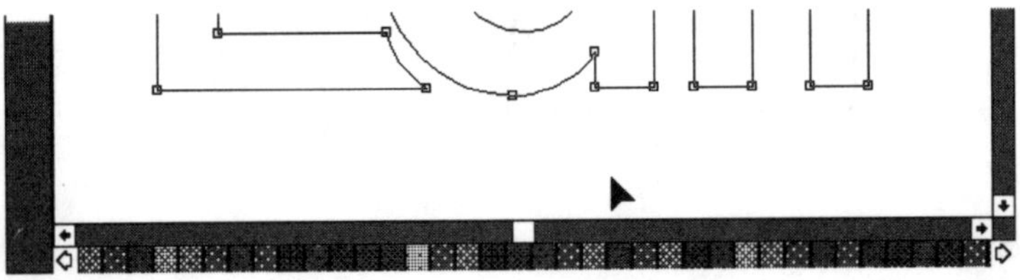

7. Select the text with the Node Tool or the Pick Tool, and click on any color from the palette.

The arrows at the right and left of the Color Palette scroll the palette along the bottom of the screen to reveal the rest of the colors in the palette.

After applying the color to the text, move to the Preview Screen to see what the changes you have made to the text really look like. Select the *Show Preview* command from the **Display** menu, or press the Shift + F9 keys.

The following illustration shows how your changes look in the Preview Screen.

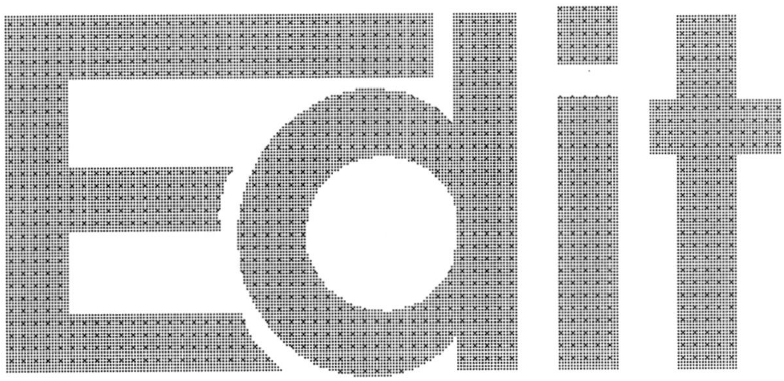

Exercise 4

Moving Text Characters

This exercise explains how to move individual text characters away from the rest of the text string. Since CorelDRAW! is an object-oriented program, you can individually move and manipulate every object on the screen, including pieces of text. The following pages contain the steps, as well as the details on how to execute the task.

The Steps in Brief

1. Open a new CorelDRAW! file.
2. Type "amazing" on the page using 24-point Prose Antique.
3. Enlarge the text approximately 575%, keeping it in its correct proportions.
4. Magnify the text so that it takes up most of the screen.
5. Adjust the inter-character spacing of the text to approximately 0.8 inches (20 millimeters).
6. Move the first letter "a" up until the *dy*: figure in the Status Line reads approximately "0.4 inches" (10 millimeters).
7. Move the letter "m" until the *dy*: figure in the Status Line reads –0.4 inches (–10 millimeters).
8. Move the letters "a" and "z" together, until the *dx*: figure in the Status Line reads –0.2 inches (–5 millimeters) and the *dy*: figure reads 0.4 inches (10 millimeters).
9. Move the remaining three letters of the text string at random so that they resemble the letters in in the illustration that follows.

This is the finished result you get at the end of the exercise.

The steps for completing this exercise are on the following pages.

The Steps in Detail

1. Open a new CorelDRAW! file.

If you are already in CorelDRAW! select New from the **File** menu and save the changes, if applicable. If you are not in CorelDRAW!, start the program from Windows or DOS.

2. Select the Text Tool from the Toolbox, and click it on the page where you would like your text to begin. The *Text* dialog box is displayed. The flashing text cursor is automatically in the window at the top of the dialog box, ready for you to type the word "amazing."

After typing the word in the window at the top of the dialog box, move to the frame containing the list of fonts. Click the mouse on the down arrow of the scroll bar, to the right of this frame, until the Prose Antique font is displayed in the list. Select the typeface by clicking on it with the mouse. Change the point size to 24 if necessary.

After selecting the relevant font for this exercise, click on OK. The text will look like this:

Once the text is on the page, choose the Pick Tool from the Toolbox, and the text should be automatically selected as the following illustration shows. If it is not, click on it once with the Pick Tool.

3. Drag one of the four corner nodes when the object is selected with the Pick Tool. To enlarge this text string, place the Pick Tool over the bottom right node of the selected text, so that it changes into a crosshair. When this crosshair appears, put your finger on the mouse and drag it down and to the right like this:

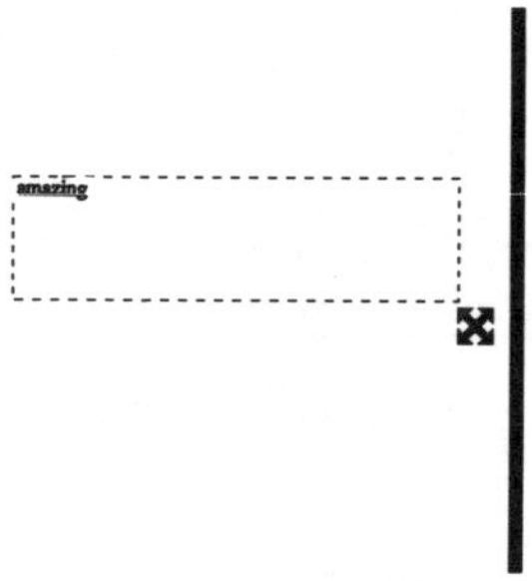

When the Status Line scale figure reads approximately 575% and looks like this illustration, release your finger from the mouse.

4. Select the Zoom Tool from the Toolbox. From the Zoom Tool fly-out, select the tool with the plus symbol in it.

Move out onto the page, and with your finger on the mouse, draw a frame around the text. Release your finger when this frame has covered the whole text like this:

The section of the page that lies inside the frame you drew with the Zoom Tool now takes up most of the screen like this:

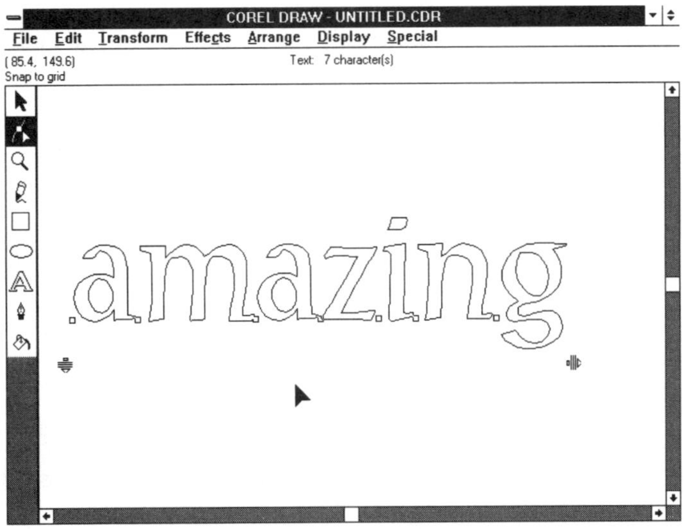

5. Move from the Pick Tool to the Node Tool. Hold the mouse over the right-facing arrow symbols so that a crosshair is displayed, as the following illustration shows:

Once the crosshair is displayed over the right-facing arrow at the end of the text string, hold down your finger on the mouse and drag it to the right. Release your finger from the mouse when the Status Line tells you that you have changed the inter-character spacing to approximately 0.8 inches (20 millimeters) as the following illustration shows:

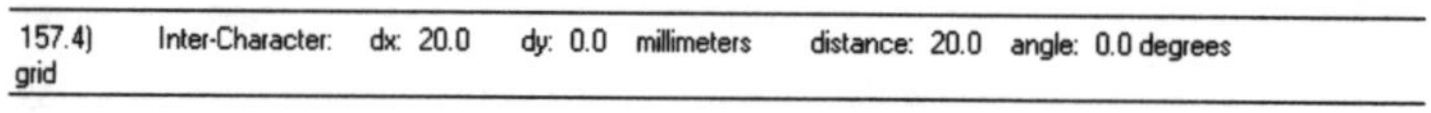

This illustration shows the result of this step. If you are working in inches, move to approximately 0.8 inches.

6. Hold the mouse inside the node at the bottom left of the first letter "a" like this:

Start dragging the mouse up (with your finger still on it), until the *dy*: figure in the Status Line reaches approximately 0.4 inches (or 10 millimeters) as the following illustration shows. Release your finger.

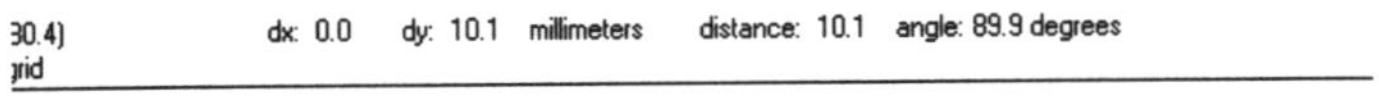

7. Hold down the mouse inside the corresponding node of the letter "m" and drag it downwards until the *dy*: figure reaches approximately 0.4 inches (or –10 millimeters).

After you release your finger from the mouse, the letter "m" will sit a similar distance below the original baseline of the text string, like the letter "a" is now sitting above like this:

8. Select the nodes of the "a" and the "z." Holding your finger on the mouse, draw a frame around the two nodes of the relevant letters like this:

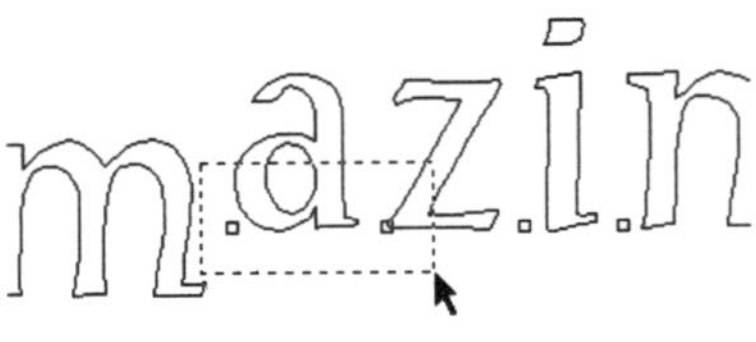

Make sure that these are the only two nodes that are inside the frame you draw because any other nodes that may happen to fall inside this frame will also be selected. Alternatively, you could click once inside both the nodes with the Shift key held down to select both nodes.

Once the two nodes are selected, you only have to hold the mouse down inside one of the nodes to move them both. For example, hold the mouse down inside the node of the letter "z," and move it up and to the left, until the dx: figure in the Status Line reads "– 0.2 inches" (–5 millimeters), and the *dy*: figure reads "0.4 inches" (or 10 millimeters) like this:

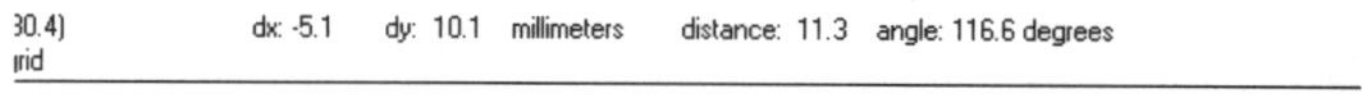

9. Move the last three letters the same way you moved the other letters, but this time, move them at random into any position you like. Remember, keep your finger held down on the mouse while you are dragging the node. The following illustrations show some examples of how you can move letters.

Drag the letter "i" at random down and to the left like this:

Drag the letter "n" at random up and to the left like this:

Move the "g" down to the left a little like this:

If you want to bring the text back, so that all the text characters sit on the same baseline, it is difficult to drag them one by one and get them to sit exactly on the baseline. If you wish to do this, however, you select the text with the NodeTool and select the *Straighten Text* command from the **Arrange** menu.

The following illustration shows the result of applying the *Straighten Text* command to the jumbled text string.

Exercise 5

Grids and Rulers

In this exercise, you use some of the grid and ruler options available in CorelDRAW! to help draw a chess board pattern. CorelDRAW! lets you set up a grid on your page to ensure that you draw these squares in the right spot, and at the right size. You also use the rulers and guidelines for more accuracy. The following pages contain the steps, as well as details on how to execute this task.

The Steps in Brief

1. Create a new CorelDRAW! file.
2. Set up a grid on the page that has a Grid Origin and a Grid Frequency of 1" for both the horizontal and vertical measurements. Show the grid on the page.
3. Display the Rulers, and change the Zero point to one grid frequency across and three grid frequencies down, on the grid that is showing on your page.
4. Place a horizontal guideline on your page on the 0" and 6" points of the ruler, and place two vertical guidelines on the 0" and 6" points of the ruler.
5. Draw a horizontal row of six 1" x 1" squares across the page adjacent to each other.
6. Set up the Place Duplicate command in the Preferences dialog box to duplicate the six squares, so that they are automatically placed below the first row on the grid. (You change the Horizontal figure to 0.00 and the Vertical figure to –1.00 to achieve this.)
7. Duplicate the first row of squares, and then each row in turn, until you have six rows of squares. Give all the squares a black fill.
8. In rows 1, 3, and 5, select the 1st, 3rd, and 5th squares, and in rows 2, 4, and 6 select the 2nd, 4th, and 6th squares with the Pick Tool, so that you have 18 squares selected together. Give these squares a shade of gray from the Fill Tool fly-out.

This is the finished result of this exercise.

The Steps in Detail

1. Create a new CorelDRAW! file.

If you are already in CorelDRAW!, select *New* from the **File** menu and save the changes, if applicable. If you are not in CorelDRAW!, start the program from Windows or DOS.

2. Make sure that the Snap To Grid option is on. If it is not on, select it now from the **Display** menu. Once selected, this option is reflected in the left-hand corner of your Status Line.

Once the *Grid Parameters* dialog box is activated, change all the measurement systems to inches, if they are not inches already. To do this, click on the frames containing the current measurement unit until they all read "inches." Then change the *Horizontal* and *Vertical* figures for both *Grid Origin* and *Frequency* all to 1". Next, select the *Show Grid* option in the bottom left of the dialog box. Once your dialog box is setup like the following illustration shows, click on OK.

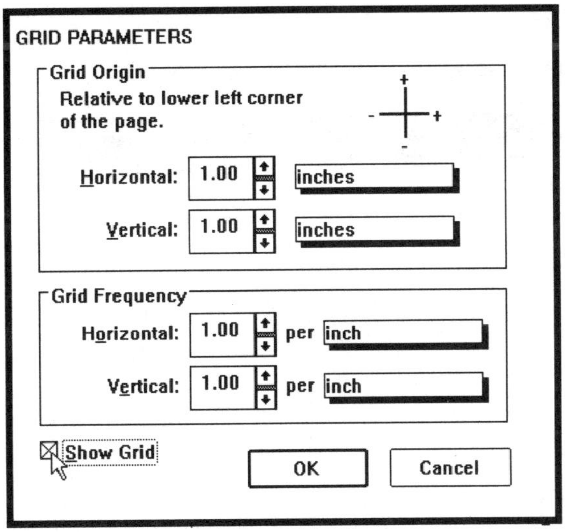

The grid you set up in the *Grid Parameters* dialog box is now displayed on the page like this:

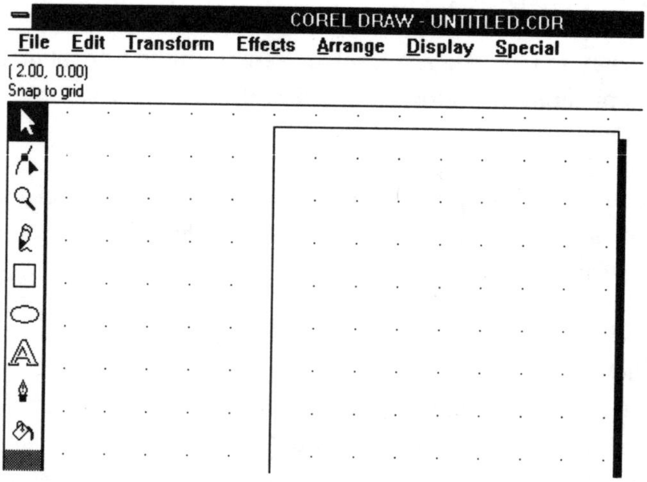

3. Select the *Show Rulers* command from the **Display** menu to display the Rulers on the page.

The rulers are now displayed on the page like this:

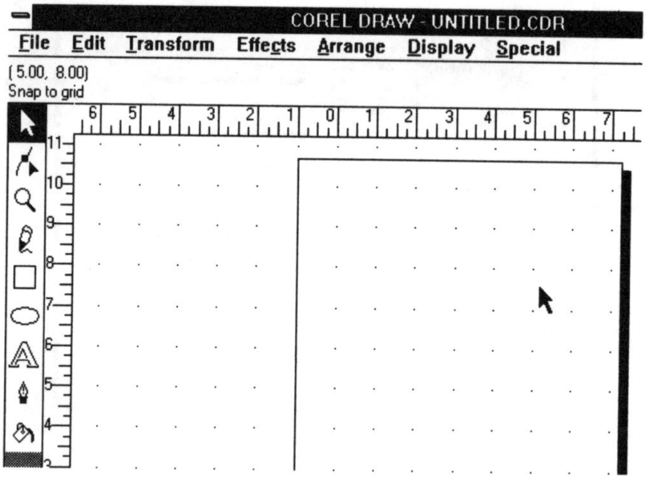

To change the zero point of the ruler, first move the mouse to the left-hand corner, where the two rulers meet like this:

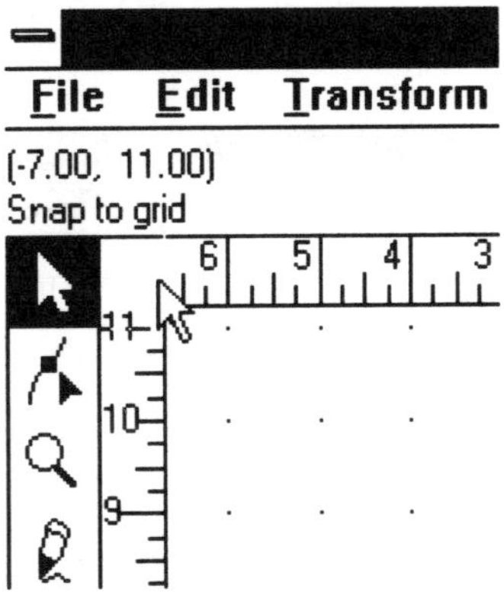

Hold the mouse down, and drag it down and to the right. Two dotted lines follow the mouse and meet at a crosspoint like this:

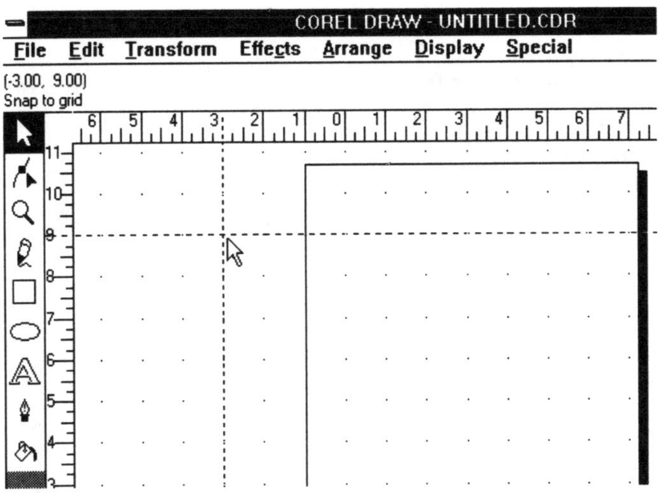

When you release your finger from the mouse, the location of this crosspoint will be the new zero point.

Since you have the *Snap To Grid* option on, when you are changing the zero point, it snaps to the grid on your page. For this exercise, you are changing the zero point of the rulers so that it sits one across and three steps down on your page like this:

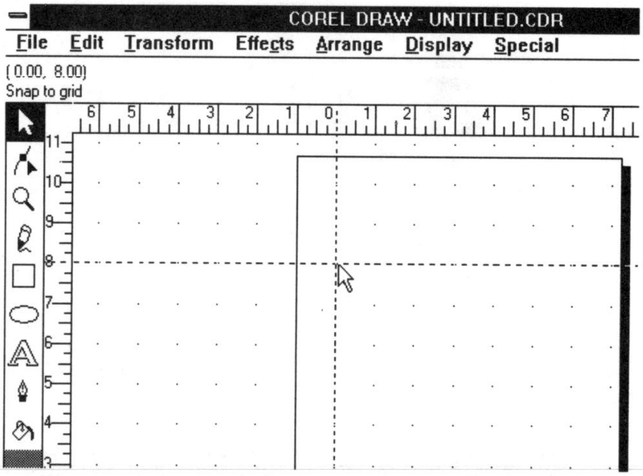

Once you release your finger from the mouse, the guidelines are not displayed, and the zero point moves to the new spot, which is shown as the intersection of the two lines like this:

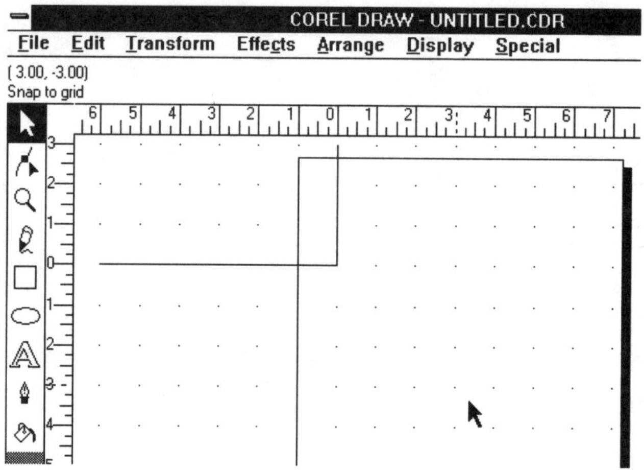

4. Place horizontal guidelines on the page by holding the mouse down on the ruler at the top, like the following illustration shows, and start to drag the mouse down. A guideline follows the mouse, but this time the location of the guideline when you release your finger is where the guideline will stay.

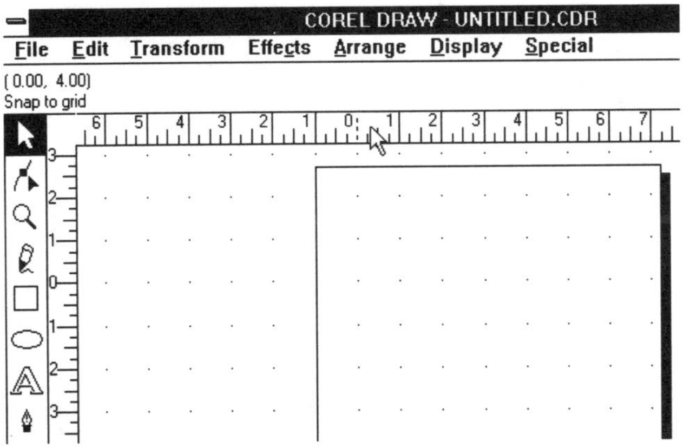

If you want to move the line around the page, hold the mouse down on the actual guideline and drag it to a new position. To remove a guideline from the page, simply drag it back up or across into the rulers.

For this exercise you are going to drag the first guideline from the top ruler to the new 0 position like the next illustration shows. Since the *Snap To Grid* feature is on, it will be easy to place the guideline exactly on the point.

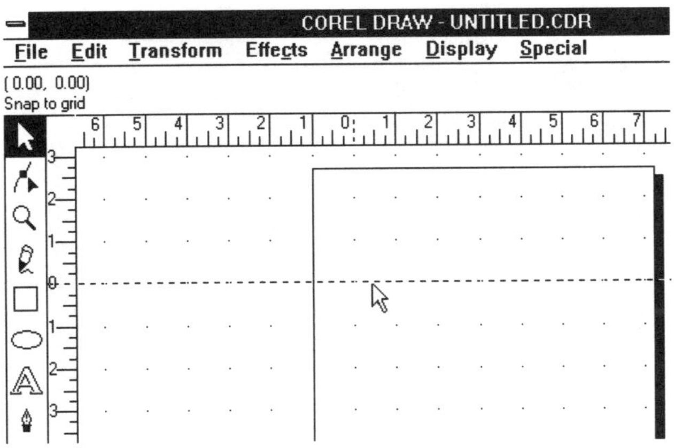

Get another horizontal guideline, and drag this one down until it reaches 6" on the vertical ruler. You do this the same way you selected the first guideline. Hold the mouse down on the top ruler, and drag the mouse down the page until the current guideline snaps in line with 6". Then release your finger from the mouse.

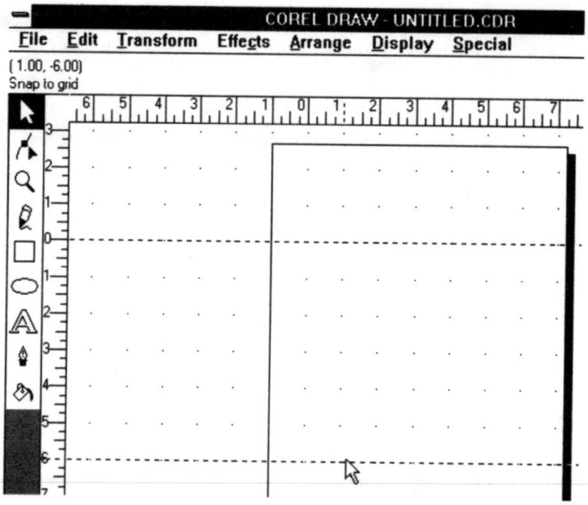

You get vertical guidelines the same way you get horizontal ones, except you drag the vertical guidelines from the ruler at the side.

Your first vertical guideline is to be set up in line with the 0 point on the horizontal ruler like this:

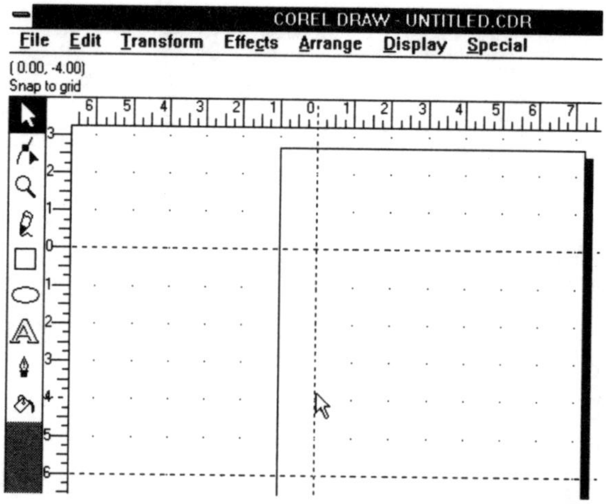

Drag the second vertical ruler out to line up with 6 on the horizontal ruler like this:

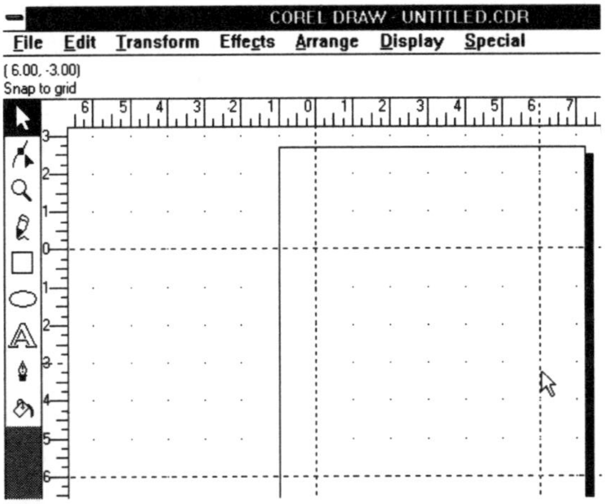

The four guidelines now make a perfect square on the page.

You can also activate guidelines through the *Guidelines* dialog box, available through the *Guidelines Setup* command in the **Display** menu. You can place as many guidelines on the page as you like, and move them round as you wish.

5. Select the Rectangle Tool. Draw the first square in the top left corner of the square that the guidelines created. That is, right on the 0 point of the two rulers like this:

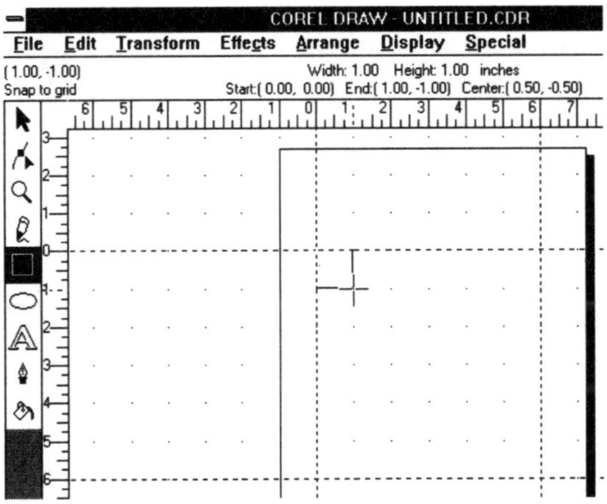

To draw this first square, hold the mouse down near the 0 point, and start to drag it down slightly and to the right. The *Snap To Grid* feature forces the drawing of the square to begin at the 0 point, and it enlarges it in 1" intervals. Since you want the square to be 1", release your finger from the mouse once the square is the size of one of the grid sections.

Continue drawing the top row of squares in the same way as you drew the first one. Start drawing the square right on, or near enough to the previous one, so that the *Snap To Grid* feature ensures that they will be perfectly lined up.

The following steps guide you through drawing the first row of squares. Stop when you have done six. This will be at the guideline you placed on the 6" point of the horizontal ruler.

Draw square number two. The *Snap To Grid* feature ensures the square is the right size and aligned with the first square. If it does not seem to work for you, make sure you have the *Snap To Grid* feature in the **Display** menu on.

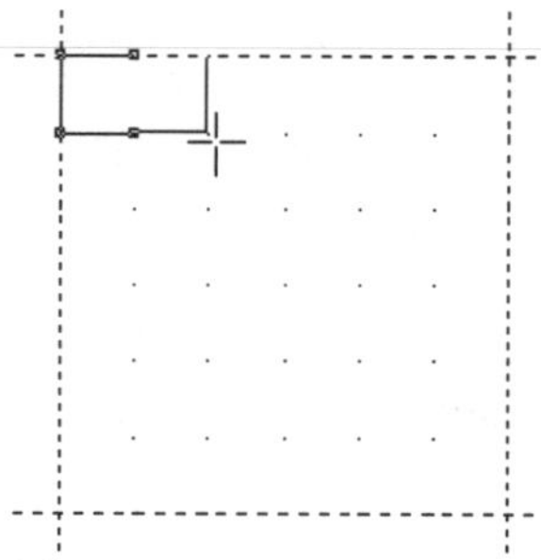

Now draw the third through sixth squares like you drew the previous two.

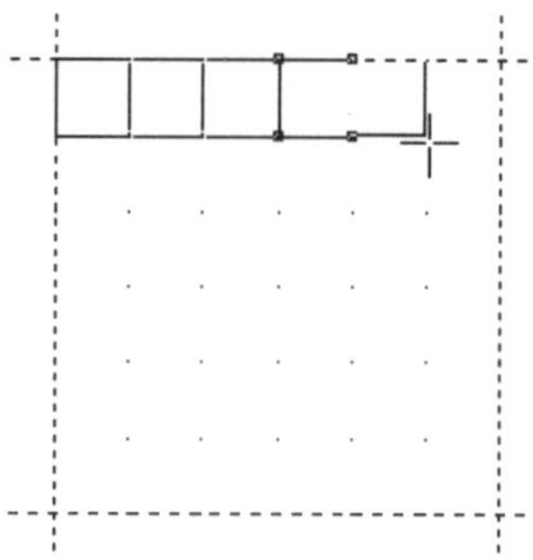

You have now drawn a row of six squares at 1" x 1". They should also be aligned with each other because of the *Snap To Grid* feature.

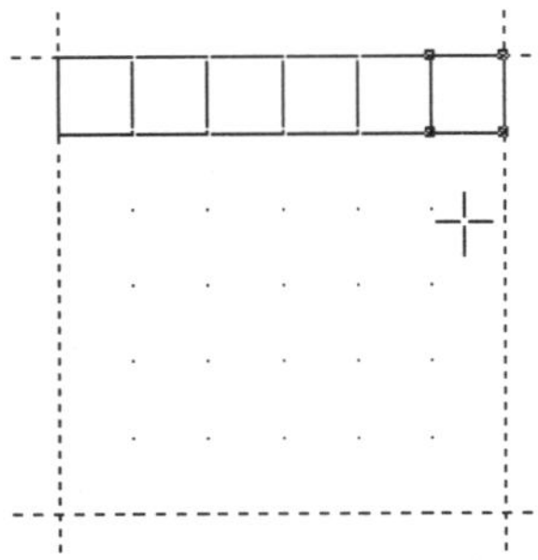

6. Select the *Preferences* command from the **Special** menu.

Note: Whenever you duplicate an object in CorelDRAW!, the duplication is displayed on the screen, according to what settings you have in the *Place Duplicate* command in the *Preferences* dialog box. You can adjust this so that you can specify where to display the duplication in relation to the object you are duplicating from. This is necessary to complete this exercise.

When you activate the *Preferences* dialog box, change the *Place Duplicate* settings to 0.00 inches for *Horizontal* and –1.00 inches for *Vertical*. Once you set up the *Place Duplicate* command in your dialog box like the following illustration, click on OK.

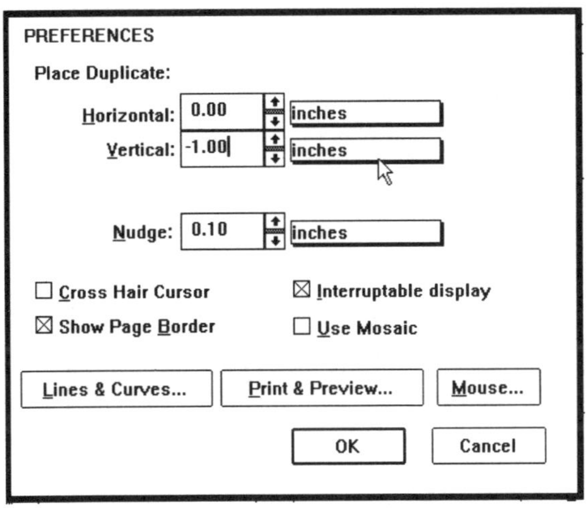

Change the settings in the *Place Duplicate* option to ensure that when you duplicate the row of squares, the duplication will be displayed one step down on the grid.

7. Select the squares with the Pick Tool and draw a frame around them with your finger on the mouse like the following illustration shows. Alternatively, since the six squares are the only objects on the page, you can use the *Select All* command from the **Edit** menu.

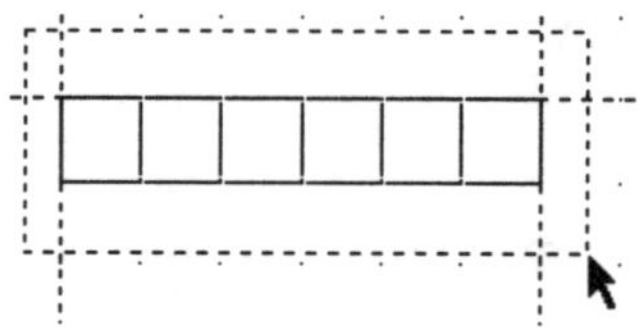

Release your finger from the mouse. The six squares are now selected like this:

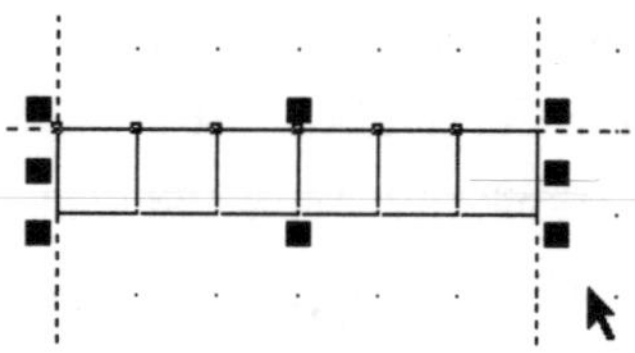

Once you select the squares, choose the *Duplicate* command from the **Edit** menu.

After a short while, a second row of squares will be displayed directly below the first row. The second duplicated row is now the selected row. This means if you choose the *Duplicate* command again, you have a third row of squares below the second one like this:

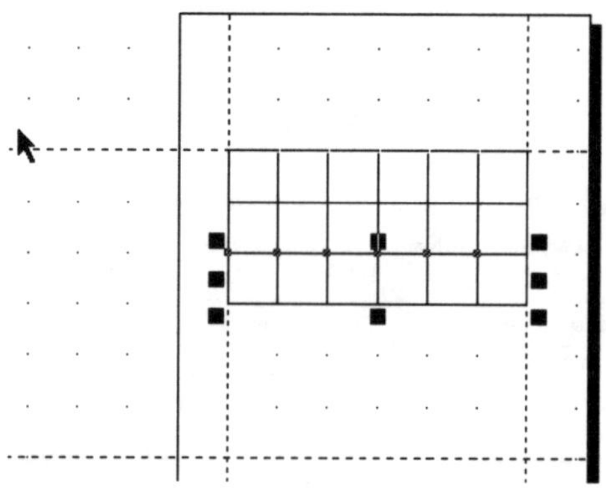

You could also select the *Repeat* command from the **Edit** menu because this repeats the last command you just applied to the selected objects, which was *Duplicate*.

Continue selecting the *Duplicate* command from the **Edit** menu, ensuring that the last duplicated object remains selected. Stop once you get six rows of squares, which end at the bottom guideline like this:

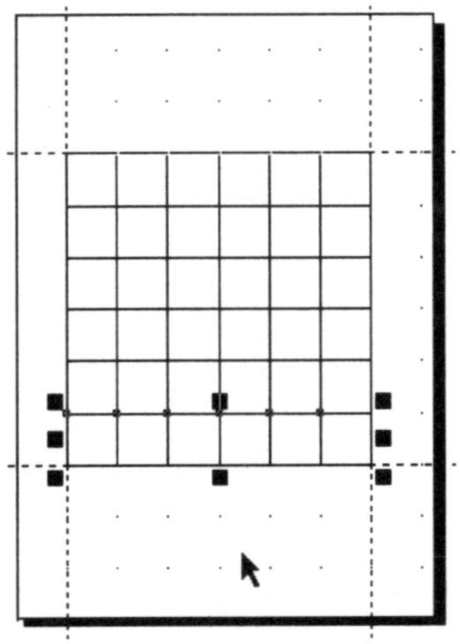

To apply a black fill to all squares on the page, you must select them all with the Pick Tool. The easiest way to select all the squares, in this case, is to execute the *Select All* command from the **Edit** menu. The *Select All* command selects all the squares with the Pick Tool. Now, activate the Fill Tool fly-out and from here, select the black option.

8. For this last step you are, in fact, selecting every second square in each row, so that when you apply a lighter fill to the selected squares, you achieve a chess board effect.

You might like to do this row by row, but for this example you will not. It is not as hard as it looks. Simply move to the first row and select the first square. Hold your finger on the [⇧ Shift] key and select the third square, and then the fifth square.

Note: A selected square has a node in its top left corner.

With your finger on the [⇧ Shift] key, move to the second row, and select the second square by clicking on the top line with the Pick Tool.

Now select the fourth and sixth squares in the same way. Move through the rows until you select all the appropriate squares. The Status Line will read "18 objects selected" and the screen will look like this:

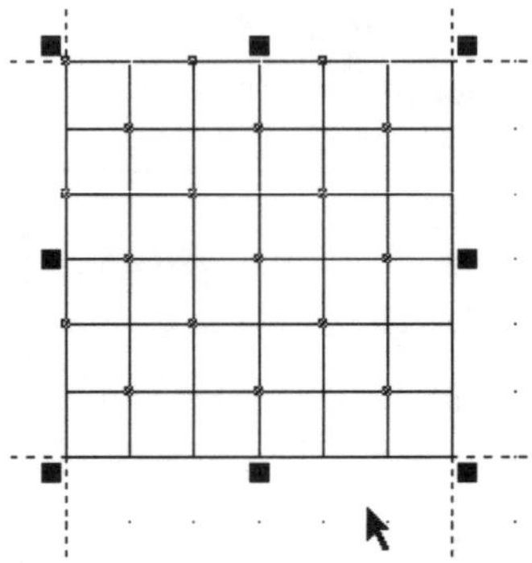

Once you have selected all the required squares for this exercise, you can apply color to them. For this exercise you are going to apply a shade of gray from the Fill Tool fly-out. Select this tool and apply one of the middle shades of gray.

It does not really matter which shade of gray you apply to the squares, as long as you can tell the difference between the black squares and the gray ones.

Now you can move to the Preview Screen (Shift + F9) to see what your chess board design really looks like. If yours did not turn out correctly, you may have had some of the wrong squares selected when you applied the gray fill. If this is the case, move back to the working screen, individually select the squares with the wrong color, and give them the correct fill. This is what your page looks like on the Preview Screen.

You can use the grid you created for this exercise, or something similar, for many things such as calendars, or any sort of chart or timetable.

The *Snap To Grid* feature in CorelDRAW!, when activated, affects resizing and moving objects around the page, and drawing squares, circles, and straight lines with the Pencil Tool. Although it does not affect the Pencil Tool when drawing freehand lines, it does affect the nodes and control points when you are trying to manipulate them. The nodes and control points snap to the grid you have set, when you try to move them. If you do not want this to happen, select the *Snap To Grid* command again from the **Display** menu to deactivate it.

Exercise 6

Calligraphic Outlines and Bitmap Fills

This exercise explains two very unique and creative features of CorelDRAW!: calligraphic outlines and bitmap pattern fills. CorelDRAW! lets you apply a calligraphic outline to any selected object, and for this exercise you will use text. You can apply bitmap pattern fills to any closed object, and you will use the same text string to show this effect. The following pages contain the steps, as well as the details on how to execute this task.

The Steps in Brief

1. Create a new CorelDRAW! file.
2. Type "HAPPY" on the page using 160-point Arabia.
3. Magnify the text so that it covers most of the working screen.
4. Give the text a calligraphic outline that is 6.5 points in width. Angle the Nib Shape of the outline 50 degrees and Stretch it 25%.
5. Give the text the "smiley" Bitmap Fill Pattern.
6. Add the word "BIRTHDAY" to the text, center it, change the font to Dawn Castle, and bold it.

This is the result of this exercise.

The steps for completing this exercise are on the following pages.

The Steps in Detail

1. Create a new CorelDRAW! file.

If you are already in CorelDRAW!, select *New* from the **File** menu and save the changes, if applicable. If you are not in CorelDRAW!, start the program from Windows or DOS.

2. Select the Text Tool from the Toolbox and click it on the page where you want the text to begin. It does not matter where you click because you can always move the text around once it is on the screen.

Click the Text Tool on the page to activate the *Text* dialog box. Here you can type the word "HAPPY" into the window at the top of the dialog box. If the flashing cursor is not in this window, click the mouse once inside it.

After you have keyed in the text, move to the frame containing the list of fonts and click on Arabia to select it. Now, change the current font size to 160 points. To do this, double-click inside the *Size* frame, so that the current value is selected in reverse video, and type in 160. Alternatively, click on the up arrow to the right of the frame containing the current value, until it reaches 160. After you have set up your *Text* dialog box, select OK to display the text on the page.

Depending on where you originally clicked the Text Tool, and because of the large point size selected, your text may be hanging over the page. This is easily adjusted by first selecting the Pick Tool from the Toolbox. If you have not done anything, or clicked the mouse anywhere else on the page, the text will be automatically selected. To move the text onto the middle of the page, hold the mouse down on the outline of one of the text characters and drag it into the new position like this:

Release your finger from the mouse. The text will be in the middle of the page like this:

3. Select the fourth option (All) in the Zoom Tool fly-out. Now the text takes up most of the screen.

4. Make sure the text is still selected with the Pick Tool, and activate the Outline Tool fly-out. From this fly-out, select the *Custom Outline Pen* option as shown in the following illustration:

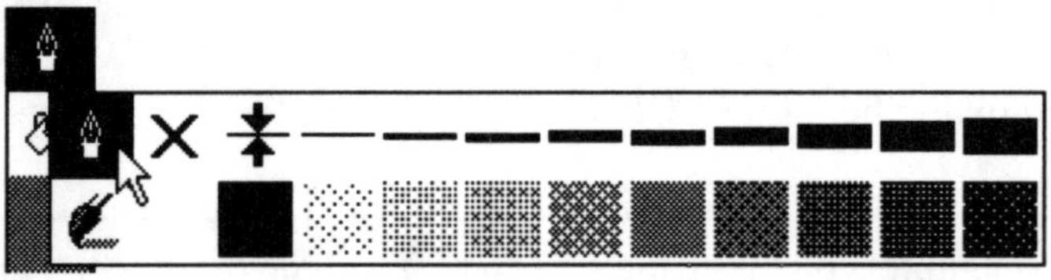

This activates the *Outline Pen* dialog box where you can give the selected text a calligraphic outline. Select the rounded option from the corners section and the second option for line caps. Then, change the nib angle to 50 and stretch it 25%. The screen should look like this:

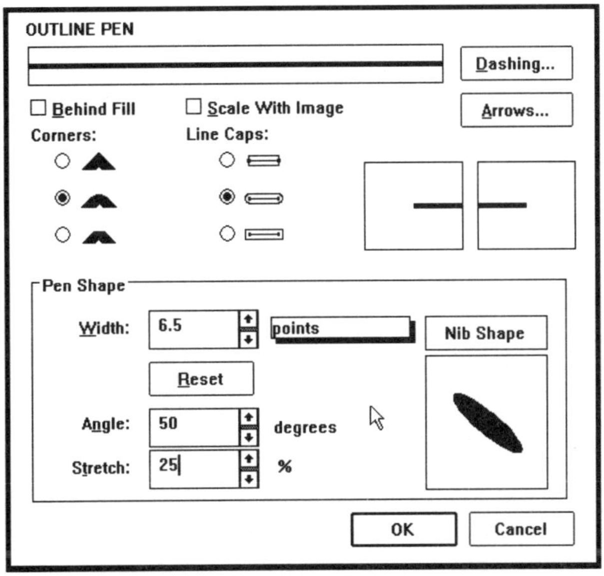

Once your dialog box is set up like the previous illustration, click on OK. When you return to the screen, there will be no visible change to the text. You can only see the result of this step by moving to the Preview Screen, which you will do at the end of this exercise.

5. With the text still selected with the Pick Tool, choose the checkered *Bitmap Fill Pattern* from the Fill Tool fly-out.

Selecting the *Bitmap Fill Pattern* option from the Fill Tool fly-out activates the *Bitmap Fill Pattern* dialog box.

The *Bitmap Fill Pattern* dialog box has a whole range of patterns that you can apply to a fillable object. To select the smiley pattern, click the mouse on the down arrow to the right of the frame containing the bitmap patterns. When the smiley pattern becomes available, click on it once with your mouse. The pattern will now fill the large rectangle in the top left of this dialog box like this:

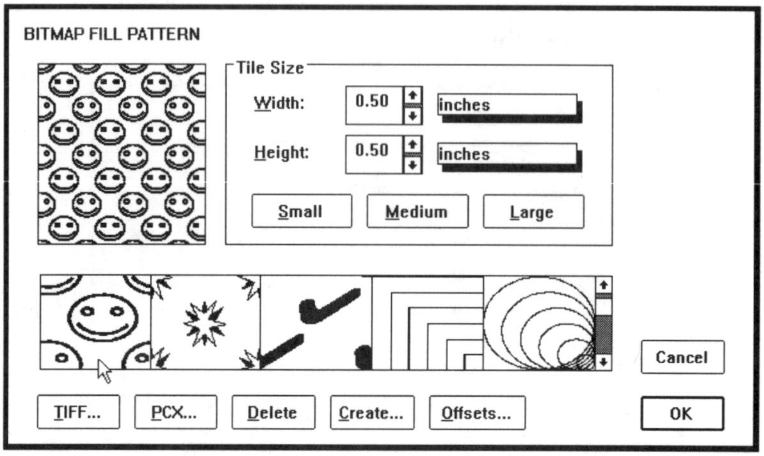

There are three sizing options you can give the *Bitmap Fill Pattern* in this dialog box. Choose the *Large* option. When you select the *Large* option, the pattern increases its size inside the big frame at the top left of the *Bitmap Fill Pattern* dialog box.

Select OK in the dialog box to activate the *Bitmap Pattern Color* dialog box. This color dialog box lets you choose a color for both the background and the actual pattern of the Bitmap Fill.

This color dialog box works the same way that all color dialog boxes work in CorelDRAW! You can either select a color of your choice from the two available palettes in the *Bitmap Pattern Color* dialog box, or click on the *Others* button to get to the other color choices. See **Chapter 3**: **Outline and Fill Tools,** for more information. The following illustration shows the *Bitmap Pattern Color* dialog box:

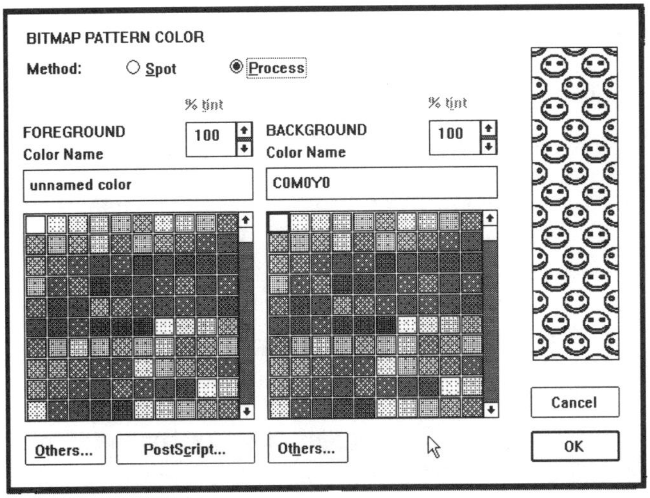

For this exercise, you are not going to change the color of your Bitmap Fill, so when the *Bitmap Pattern Color* dialog box is displayed, click on OK.

Return to the screen. The text has no visible change. The right-hand corner of the Status Line indicates the thickness of the outline you applied. It also tells you that the selected text has a *Bitmap Pattern Fill* by displaying the *Bitmap Fill* icon that appears in the Fill Tool fly-out as shown below:

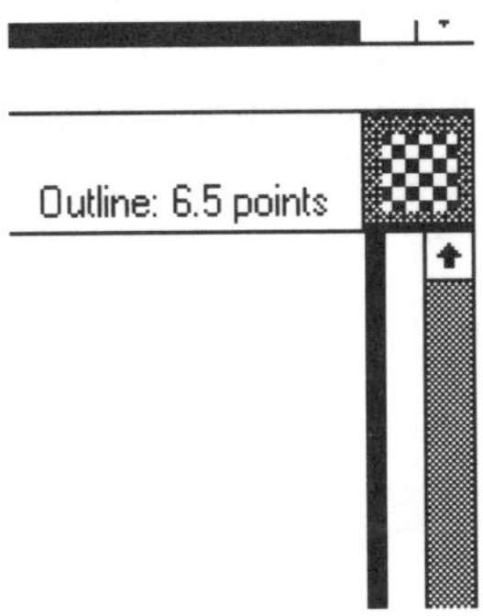

6. Make sure that the text is still selected with the Pick Tool and select the *Edit Text* command from the **Edit** menu. If the text is currently not selected, click on it once.

Selecting the *Edit Text* command activates the *Text* dialog box. This dialog box is identical to the *Text* dialog box you get when you first click the Text Tool on the page, although this time the information in it reflects the currently selected text.

If the flashing cursor is not in the window at the top of the dialog box, click next to the word "HAPPY." Now press the Enter key, so that the flashing cursor is sitting on the line underneath the word "HAPPY."

Next, type the word "BIRTHDAY." From the list that contains the fonts, scroll down to the Dawn Castle font and click on it. Select the *Center* choice from the *Justification* option and the *Bold* choice from the style option, and click on OK.

Since you magnified the first piece of text, the text now added may not all fit on the screen. To view it all, select the fourth option from the Zoom Tool fly-out.

Once all the text is showing, select the *Show Preview* command from the **Display** menu or press the Shift + F9 keys, to view the text on the Preview Screen. This is the final result you wish to achieve.

Exercise 7

More Bitmap Fills

In this exercise, you will use a combination of CorelDRAW! features, including the *Fit Text To Path* and the *Bitmap Fill* options. The following pages contain the steps, as well as the details on how to execute this task.

The Steps in Brief

1. Create a new CorelDRAW! file.
2. Type "golden triangle" on the page using 100-point Dawn Castle.
3. Draw a triangle about 3/4 the size of the page, starting from the bottom left corner of the page.
4. Flow the text along the left side of the triangle.
5. Give the triangle a Bitmap Fill Pattern of bricks, and send it to the back.
6. Create your own Bitmap Pattern in the Bitmap Fill Pattern dialog box and apply it to the text.

This is the result of this exercise.

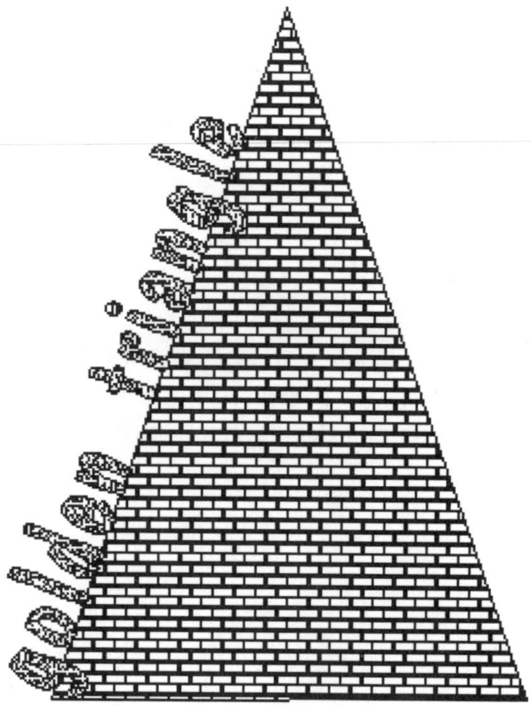

The steps for completing this exercise are on the following pages.

The Steps in Detail

1. Create a new CorelDRAW! file.

If you are already in CorelDRAW!, select *New* from the **File** menu and save changes, if applicable. If you are not in CorelDRAW!, start the program from Windows or DOS.

2. Move your cursor onto the page, and click the mouse once somewhere in the top left of your page to invoke the *Text* dialog box.

When the *Text* dialog box is displayed, type the words "golden triangle." Change the point size to 100 and highlight the Dawn Castle font.

Also make sure it is left-aligned (see *Justification*). Click on OK. The following illustration shows the result.

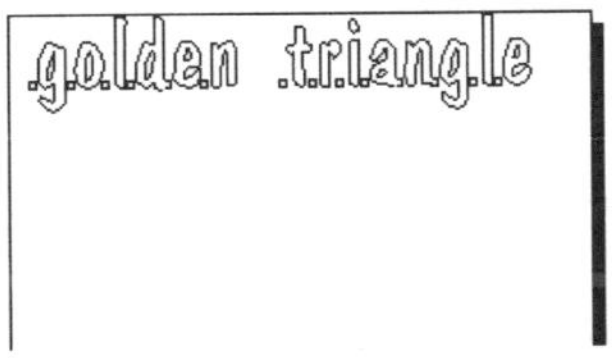

Note: If your text is not totally on the page, select it with the Pick Tool and readjust its position.

3. Select the Pencil Tool, and position it in the bottom left section of the page. Click the mouse once, and move the mouse to the top middle of the page to create the first side of the triangle. Double-click the mouse when you reach the top of the page like this:

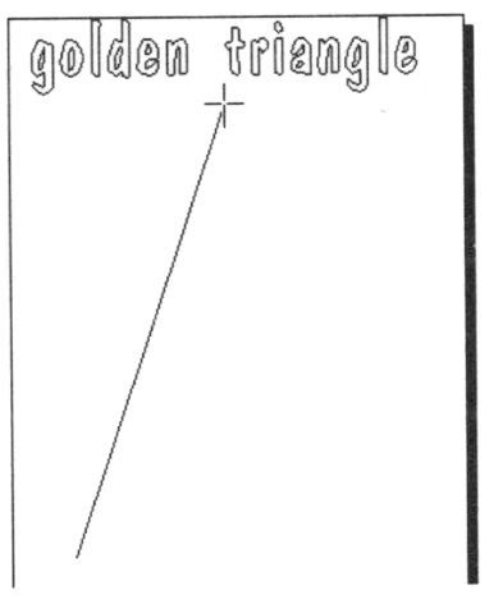

To ensure that the text flows along the left side of the triangle, you must draw it from the bottom left corner of the page. This exercise describes drawing with the Pencil Tool in Freehand mode. If you currently have Bezier mode active, click the mouse once where it says to double-click. Finish off the drawing the same way. The following three illustrations show how.

Move down to the bottom right of the page and double-click the mouse again like this:

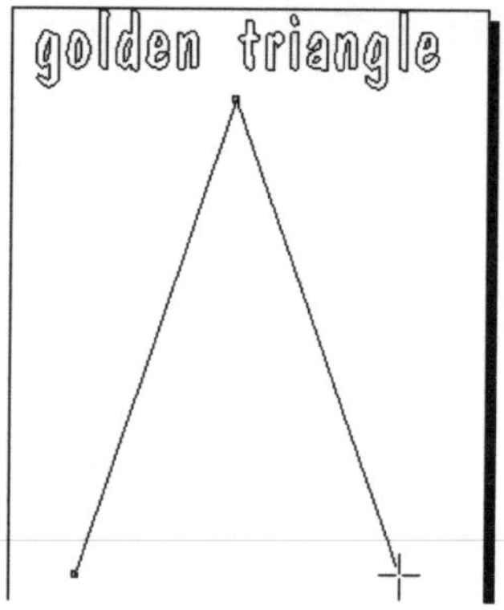

Move the mouse to the left to meet the bottom line. Click the mouse once on the first node to close the shape like this:

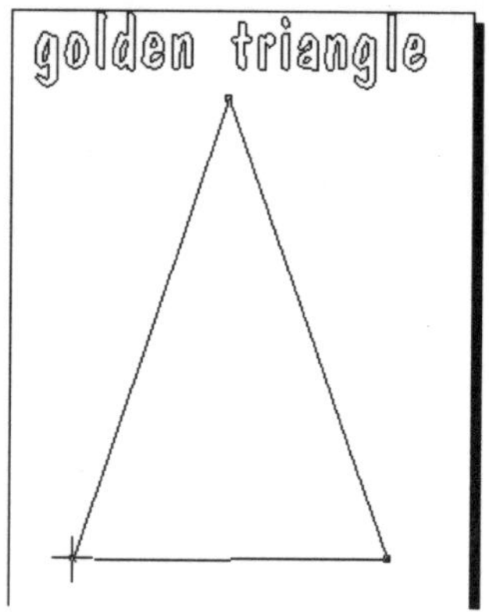

4. Select both the text and the triangle. To do this accurately, execute the *Select All* command from the **Edit** menu. You can activate this command only when the Pick Tool is selected. Now select the *Fit Text To Path* command in the **Arrange** menu.

After you have invoked this command, the text will have aligned itself to the shape of the triangle like this:

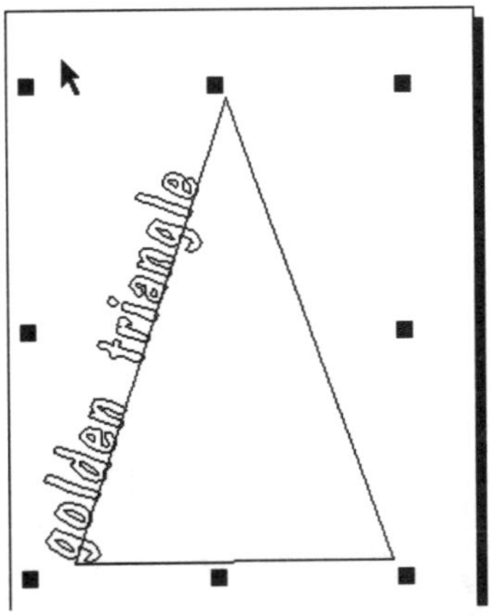

5. Deselect both objects by clicking somewhere off the page. Then select the triangle with the Pick Tool. Once the triangle has been selected, activate the *Bitmap Fill* option in the Fill Tool fly-out. The *Bitmap Fill* dialog box will be displayed like this:

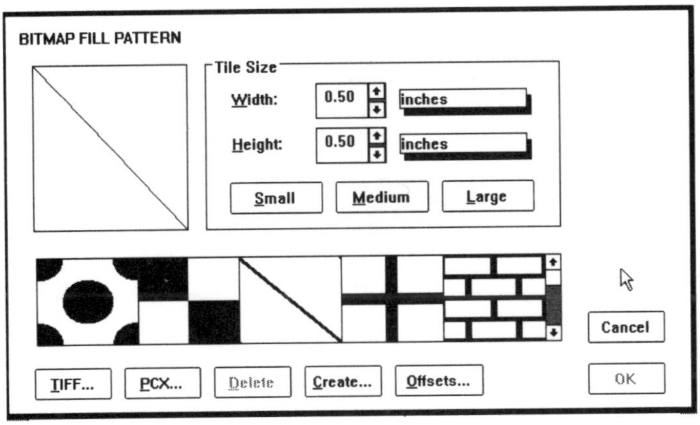

Note: The *Bitmap Fill* option in CorelDRAW! allows you to select any closed object and give it a variety of patterned fills. It also allows you to create your own fills.

If the brick pattern is not currently displayed, click the mouse up or down on the scroll bar to locate it. Then click on the pattern, and it will be displayed in the large frame at the top left of the dialog box. Now click on OK.

After you have selected OK, this color dialog box will be displayed. Select OK again to return to the screen, as you are not changing the color of the bitmap.

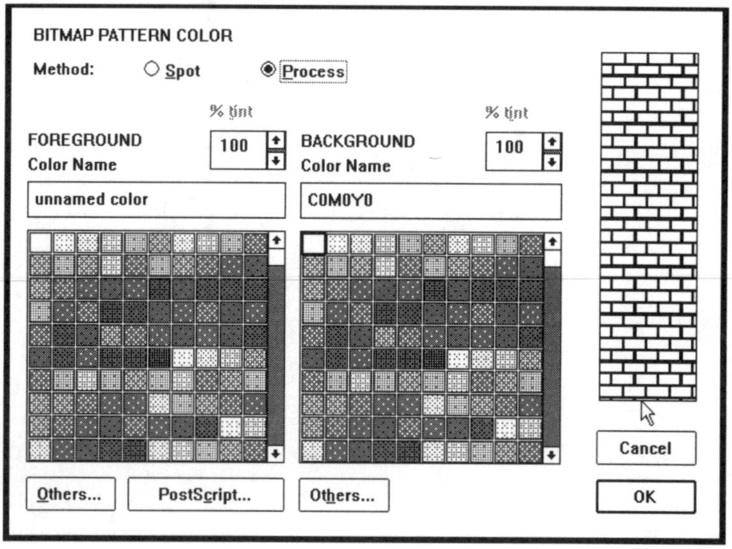

No noticeable changes occur to the triangle on returning to the screen, until you activate the Preview Screen.

Making sure that the triangle is still selected, choose the *To Back* command from the **Arrange** menu. Again, the effect of this will not be visible on the working screen. The following illustration shows how the Preview Screen looks at this stage.

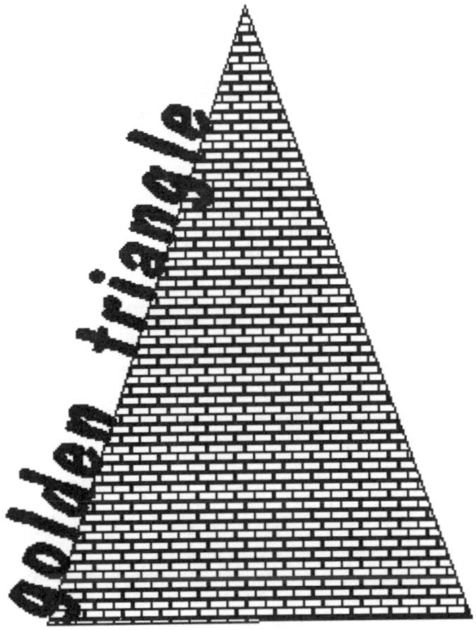

6. Select the text with the Pick Tool and select the *Bitmap Fill* option in the Fill Tool fly-out. Inside the *Bitmap Fill Pattern* dialog box, select the *Create* option, and the *Bitmap Pattern Editor* dialog box will be displayed like this:

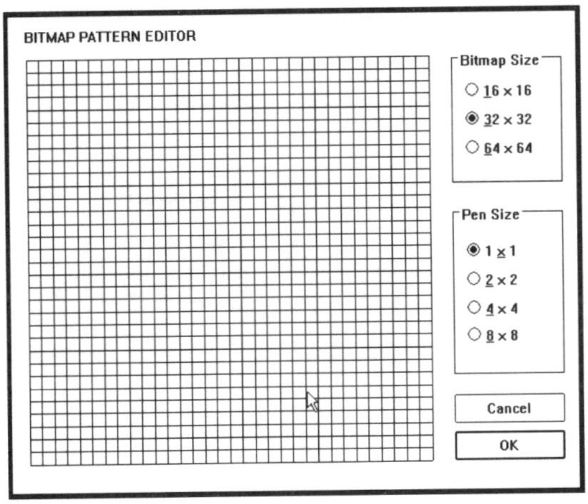

In the *Bitmap Pattern Editor* dialog box, you can create any pattern you like, simply by clicking on the squares to fill them. (Use the left mouse button to fill a square, and the right button to delete a square.) Create your own pattern by randomly selecting squares as shown below:

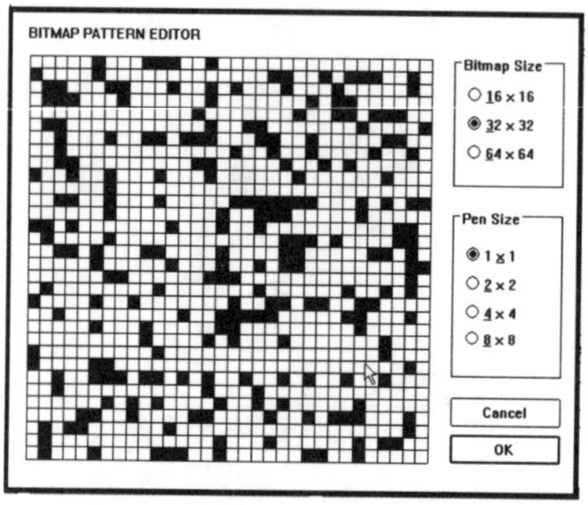

The *Bitmap Size* option determines the size of the final bitmap, and the *Pen Size* option lets you alter the size of the pen used to draw in this dialog box. The larger the pen size, the more squares are filled or deleted at once. Experiment with this to see the effect.

Once you are satisfied with your pattern, select OK. This takes you back to the *Bitmap Fill Pattern* dialog box.

The pattern you created will be displayed in the next available frame in the *Bitmap Fill Pattern* dialog box. Click on the newly created Bitmap so that it appears in the large viewing area like this:

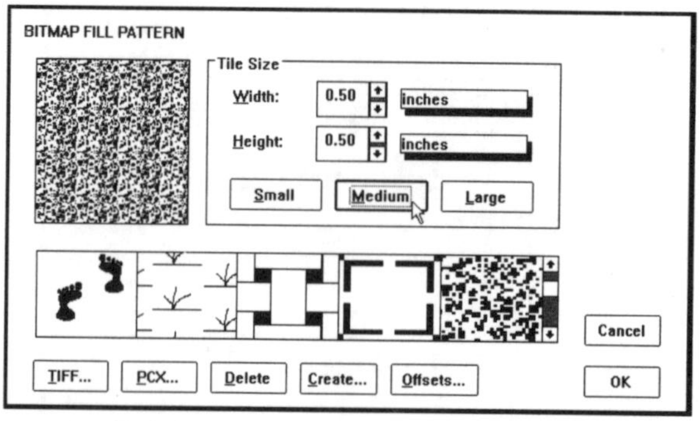

By clicking alternately on the *Small*, *Medium,* and *Large* options in the *Tile Size* section, you will see the size of the bitmap changing. For this exercise, select *Medium* for your bitmap size, and click on OK. When the *Bitmap Pattern Color* dialog box is displayed, select OK because you are not going to change the color of the *Bitmap Fill Pattern.*

On completion of the exercise, compare your result with the following illustration, by selecting the *Full Screen Preview* command from the **Display** menu, or by pressing F9.

This is the finished result viewed on the Preview Screen.

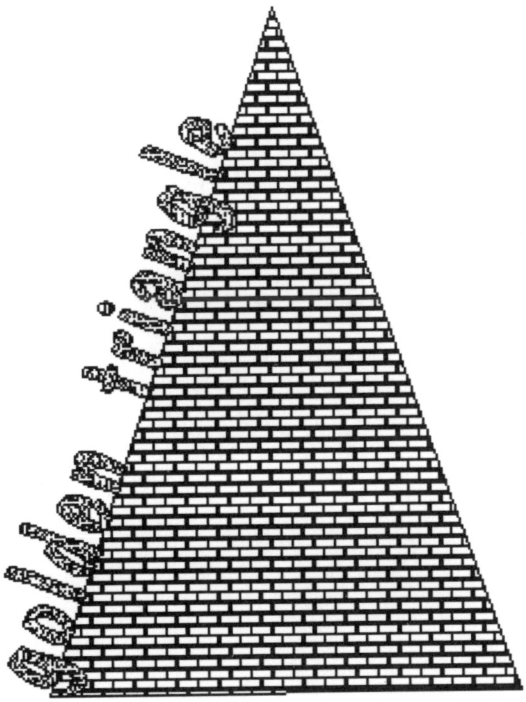

Exercise 8

Changing the Shape of Text (Advanced Version)

This exercise takes you through the details of changing the shape of a text string. You will learn how to manipulate all of the letters in the text string, and use more advanced features of CorelDRAW! than you used in **Exercise 3**.

The steps in this exercise show you how to use the *Node Edit* dialog box, and how to maneuver nodes and their control points. The following pages contain the steps, as well as details on how to execute this task.

The Steps in Brief

1. Create a new CorelDRAW! file.
2. Type "drip" on the page using 100-point Homeward Bound.
3. Magnify the word so it takes up most of the working screen.
4. Convert the text to curves.
5. Manipulate the letters, one at a time, so they resemble the letters in the following illustration.

The steps for completing this exercise are on the following pages.

The Steps in Detail

1. Create a new CorelDRAW! file.

If you are already in CorelDRAW!, select *New* from the **File** menu and save changes, if applicable. If you are not in CorelDRAW!, start the program from Windows or DOS.

2. Select the Text Tool. Move it out onto your page and click where you would like your text to be displayed.

The *Text* entry dialog box is now displayed ready for you to type in the text. Type "drip" in the text entry rectangle. Hold the mouse on the down arrow at the bottom right of the box containing the list of fonts. Once Homeward Bound is visible, select it with the mouse. Next, double-click inside the *Size* rectangle, so the current point size is displayed in reverse video, and key 100 over the top of the current setting. Alternatively, keep clicking on the up arrow until you reach 100. Select OK to display the text on the page.

3. Click on the Zoom Tool to display the associated fly-out. From this fly-out, select the tool with the plus symbol on it.

Now that you have the Zoom Tool, draw a box around the text so that it takes up most of the working page. Alternatively, you can select the fourth option from the Zoom Tool fly-out () and, since the text is the only current object on the page, it achieves this effect:

4. Make sure the text string is selected with the Pick Tool. Then move to the **Arrange** menu, and choose the *Convert To Curves* command.

5. This part of the exercise shows the manipulation of the text using the control points of selected nodes, and the nodes themselves. Control points are the little black dots at the end of the thin straight lines that are displayed after you select a node.

Select all the nodes of the object with the Node Tool. To do this, select the Node Tool and draw a box around the whole word like the following illustration shows. Make sure it covers the whole object so that all the nodes are selected.

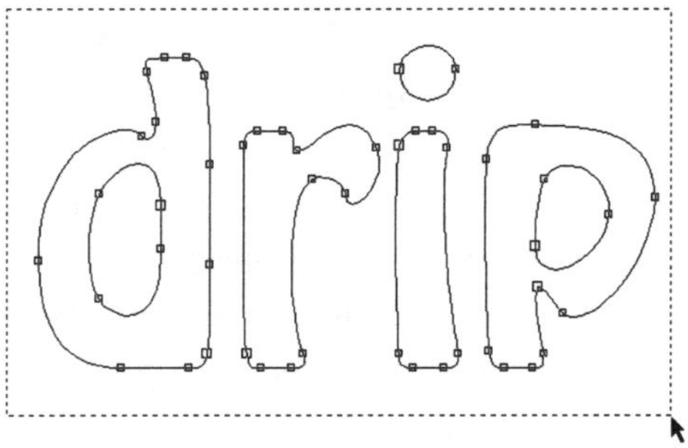

When you select a node, it becomes darker in appearance, as shown in the following illustration:

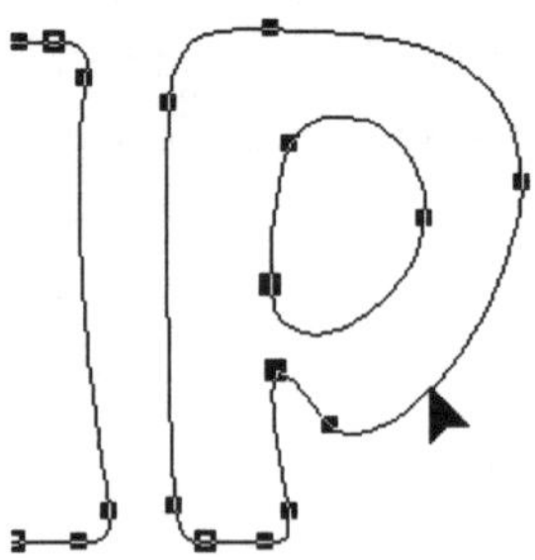

Once all the nodes are selected, double-click anywhere on the path of the object to activate the *Node Edit* dialog box.

You can apply different attributes to nodes. For this exercise you will use the *Cusp*, *Add,* and *toCurve* options from the *Node Edit* dialog box. Some of the options in this dialog box, for example *Smooth* and *Cusp*, when selected, affect the way you use a node's control points to manipulate a line.

Select the *Cusp* option. This option ensures that all nodes you will be working with move independently of each other. That is, when manipulating a certain line controlled by a node, the lines on either side are not affected. Deselect the text, by clicking anywhere on the page, in preparation for the next step.

To manipulate the letter "d," you need to make sure the bottom line of the letter can be curved. With the Node Tool, double-click on the bottom line of the letter like this:

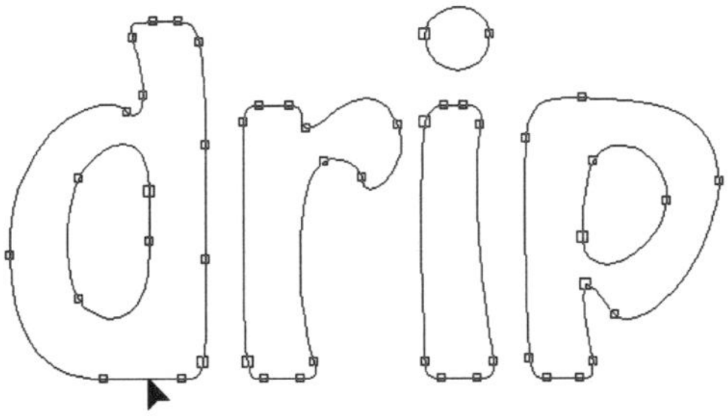

This activates the *Node Edit* dialog box. From this dialog box, select the *toCurve* option.

The dialog box is no longer displayed, and nodes on either side of the line you double-clicked on have control points lying parallel to this line.

With the Node Tool, drag either one of the control points (parallel to the bottom line) away from the bottom line. The following illustration shows the right control point of the left node being dragged first. Move your control point down and to the left, so it resembles this illustration:

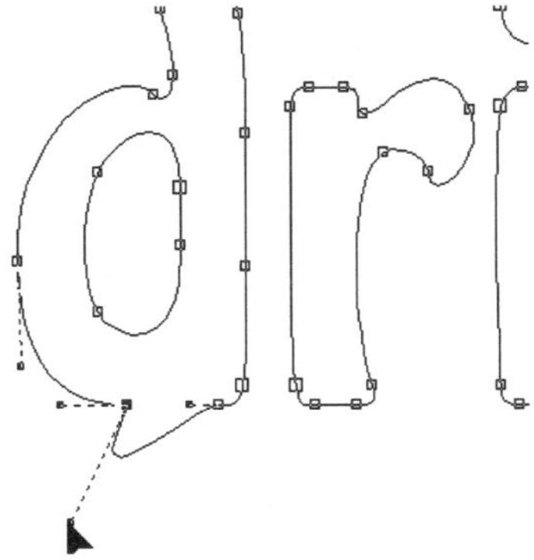

Do the same with the left-hand control point of the right node. Drag the control point down, and to the right, to get that curved shape. It does not matter if your work does not match the figure exactly, as long as you are able to maneuver control points and nodes in a similar fashion. This may take a little experimenting at first. Your drawing should look similar to the following illustration:

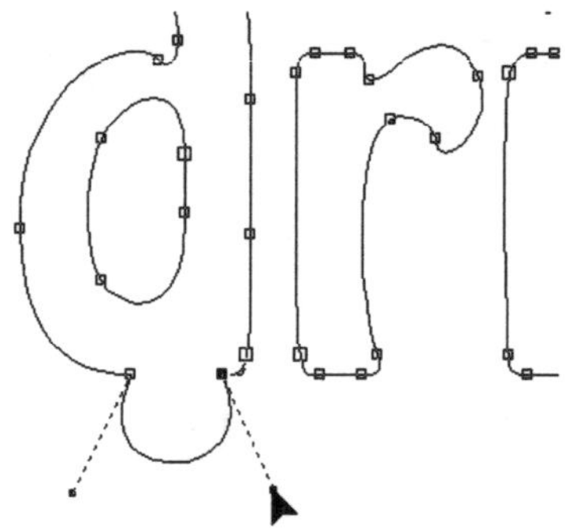

The next step is to move the right-hand node closer to the left one. To do this, make sure the right-hand node is the only one selected. If any other nodes are selected, they move as well. To deselect all nodes, move away from the object and click the mouse. Then move the Node Tool so its tip is inside the right side node, hold the mouse down, and drag it to the left like this:

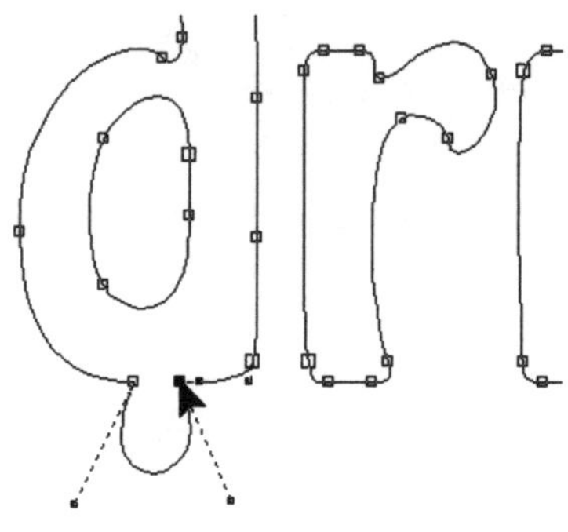

Now do the same with the left-hand node, only move it to the right like this:

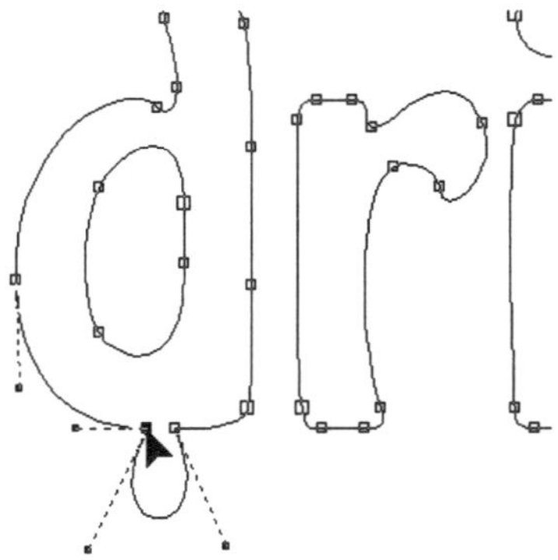

Since you moved the left and right nodes closer together, you lost part of the curve shape. To get this back again, simply maneuver the bottom left and right control points as you did before. That is, move them, one at a time, away from each other.

When you manipulate objects with nodes and control points, you can move back and forth between control points and nodes as shown in the next illustration. This is so you can accurately achieve the desired shape you want.

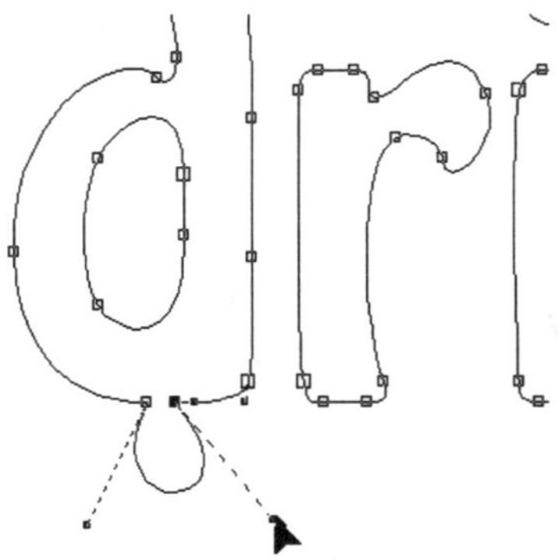

You are now ready to move onto the next letter. With the Node Tool, move to the part of the object that is indicated in the following illustration, and double-click on this line.

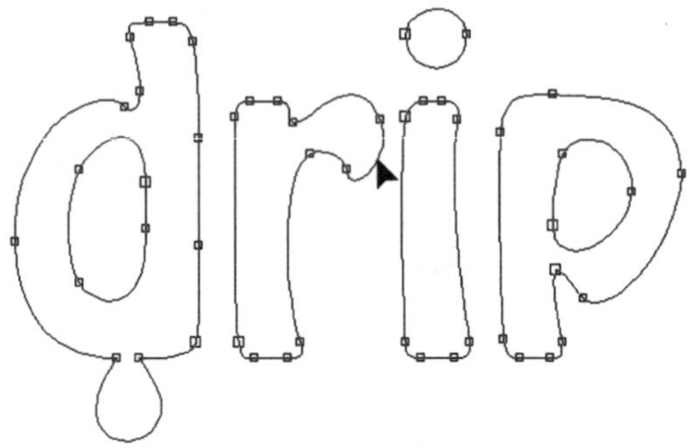

To make this easier, you need to add a node to this part of the object. Double-click on the line to display the *Node Edit* dialog box. From this dialog box click on the *Add* option as shown below:

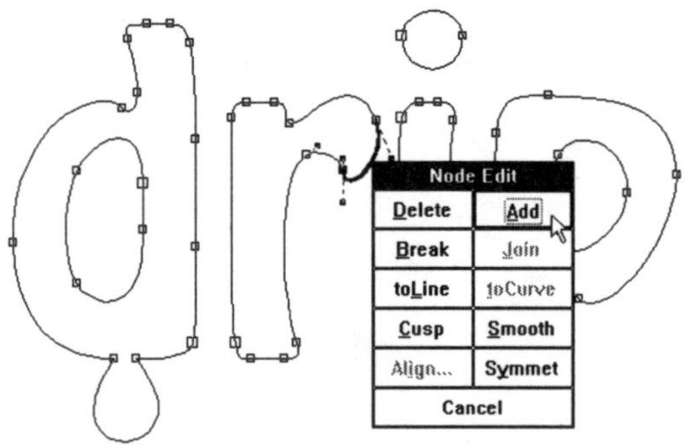

Once you have added this node, you want it to be the only one selected. Click the mouse away from the letter, and then with the Node Tool, click inside the newly added node.

When you select the node you just added, the control points of the nodes both above and to the left are displayed, but these nodes remain unhighlighted. Move to the bottom control point of the selected node, and drag it down and to the right like the following illustration shows. This affects the section above the node, but this can be useful in the overall look you want to achieve.

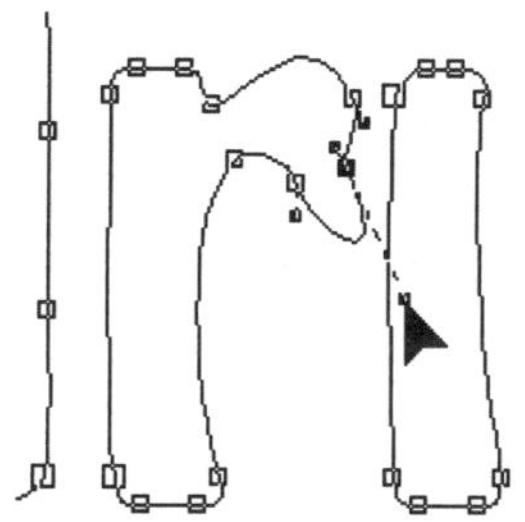

Now move to the control point of the node at the left of the selected node. Drag this control point down and to the left to get that curved, circular shape of a drip-like object like this:

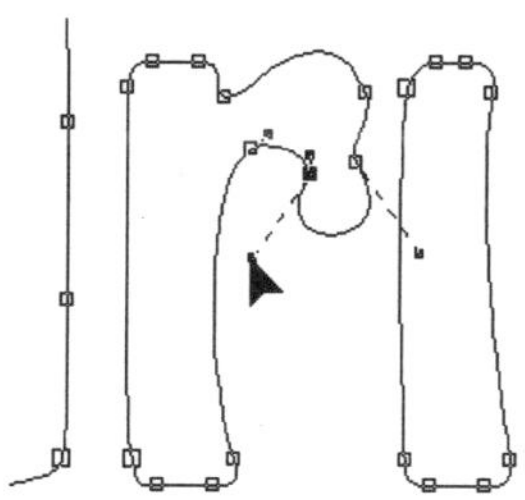

The following illustration shows the finished result of what you achieved as shown in the previous two illustrations. Now you are ready to create the drip-like object between the letters "r" and "i."

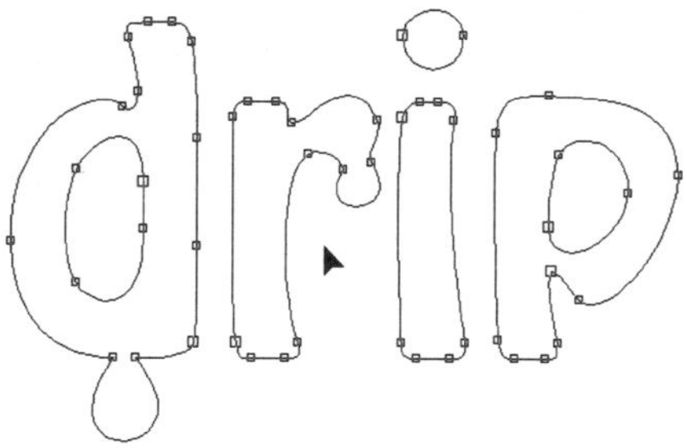

Select the Pencil Tool, and move out to the area of the page under the letter "r" to begin drawing. Click the mouse once at the starting point of your drawing. As you begin moving the mouse, a line follows your movement from the beginning of your drawing.

Move the mouse so that the line makes up one side of a triangle and then double-click the mouse. This ensures that you get the line to follow your mouse again. If you do not get the drawing line, move the cross back to where the first line ended, and click once directly on the node at the end of this line. For this exercise draw the triangle with the Pencil Tool in Freehand mode. If you have Bezier mode active, click the mouse once instead of double-clicking it. For more information on the differences between Freehand and Bezier mode, see the Pencil Tool in **Chapter 2: The Toolbox**.

Move the mouse across so that you have a line representing the bottom side of the triangle and double-click the mouse. Now move the drawing tool crosshair directly over the position, where you began your triangle, and click the mouse once to complete the drawing like this:

You must click the mouse directly over the first node of your drawing to ensure the triangle is a closed object that can have fills applied to it. If it was not clicked directly over the first node, the Status Line displays "Open Path" when you select the drawing with the Pick Tool. If this is the case, select both the nodes that began and ended your drawing, by dragging the Node Tool over both nodes. The Status Line will read "2 selected nodes."

Double-click inside one of the nodes with the Node Tool to display the *Node Edit* dialog box. From this box choose the option *Join*. This option is only available if you correctly selected the two nodes. Only two nodes from the same object can be joined. You cannot join nodes from separate objects.

Once you are sure you have a closed object that is not already selected, select it by clicking on it with the Pick Tool. Next give it a black fill from the Fill Tool fly-out.

Now select the triangle with the Node Tool, and draw a box around it. All three nodes then become highlighted like this:

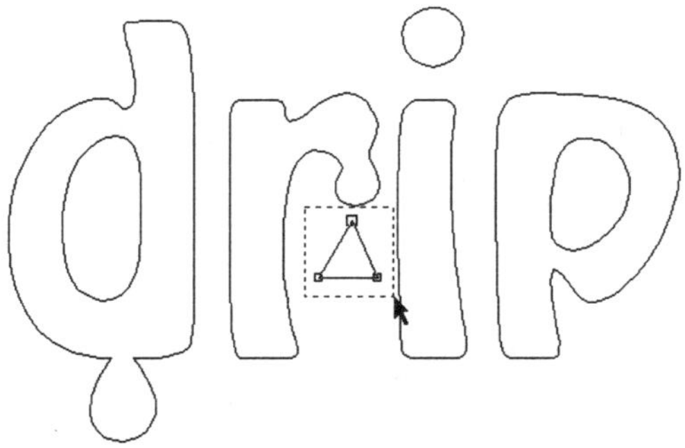

Double-click on one of the three selected nodes to display the *Node Edit* dialog box. From this dialog box choose the *toCurve* option.

All three nodes now have control points, which you can use to manipulate the triangle into a drip shape. The following four illustrations explain this process in visual detail. First, you must deselect the three nodes by clicking elsewhere on the screen to select each one individually.

Using the control points of selected nodes again, manipulate the object so it begins to look like this:

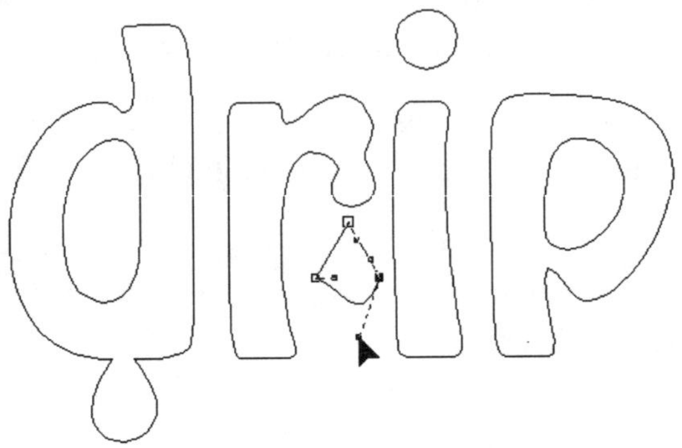

Using the control points of selected nodes again, manipulate the object so it becomes even more circular in shape.

Move the upper control points of the selected nodes, one at a time, to give the object a more curved appearance like this:

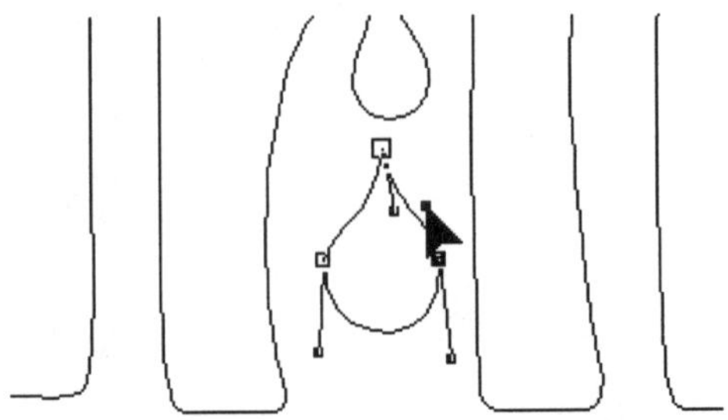

The triangle you created now resembles a drip like this:

You are now ready to manipulate the third letter. Move to the point indicated in the following illustration, and double-click on the line with the Node Tool.

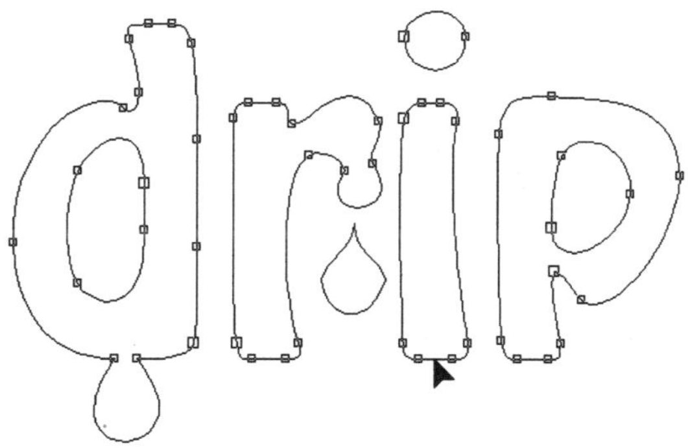

From the *Node Edit* dialog box, again select the *toCurve* command.

Select the furthest left node at the bottom of the letter "i" as indicated in the following illustration. Now move the control point away from the object as you did with the previous letters.

Select the node as shown below, and move the control points similar to the previous letters. Maneuver and experiment with your nodes, and control points of your nodes, to get the best shape for the drip. Once you have gained the desired effect, or your drip resembles what is shown here, you are ready to move onto the "p."

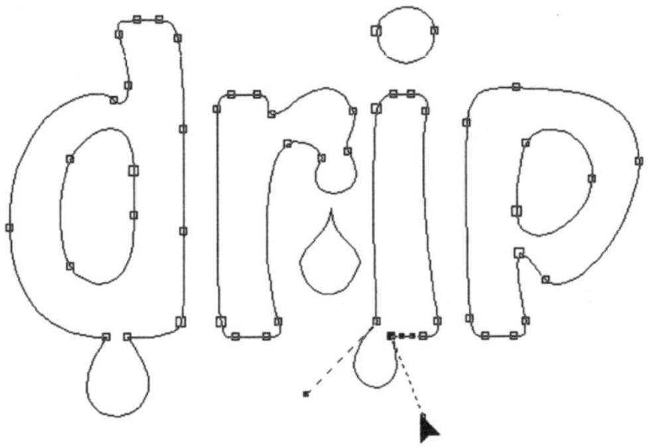

Select the nodes, one at a time, at the bottom right of the letter, as you did at the bottom left of the previous letter. Maneuver them in a similar fashion, and you again achieve this curved, circular shape.

The following illustration shows the final result of this exercise on the Preview Window. You achieve this by choosing *Show Preview* from the **Display** menu, or by pressing [Shift] and [F9]

Exercise 9

Creating a Logo

This exercise takes you through the steps of creating a logo. It uses some of the CorelDRAW! options and commands that you have used in previous exercises, but for this exercise you are applying these options and commands to applications that you can use in everyday situations. The following pages contain the steps, as well as the details on how to execute this task.

The Steps in Brief

1. Create a new CorelDRAW! file.
2. Type "webster & associates." using 45-point, bold Vogue.
3. Draw a circle on the page approximately 2.2" (55mm) in diameter. Draw the circle by dragging the mouse down and to the right.
4. Wrap the text around the circle and delete the circle.
5. Magnify the text so that it covers most of the screen.
6. Give the text a white fill and the third thinnest black outline from the Outline Tool fly-out.
7. Edit the perspective of the text.
8. Drag the top left node of the perspective frame down so that the Horizontal vanishing point is approximately –9.85" (–250mm).
9. Extrude the text so that the X and Y offsets are both 1" with the Absolute coordinates off, a scaling factor of 80, and the Perspective on.
10. Give the extrusion a Linear Fountain Fill ranging from 75 to 25 black using CMYK color method. Give the fill a 110 degree angle.
11. Display the Preview Screen and enlarge it so that it covers the whole screen.

This is the finished result of this exercise.

The steps for completing this exercise are on the following pages.

The Steps in Detail

1. Create a new CorelDRAW! file.

If you are already in CorelDRAW!, select *New* from the **File** menu and save changes, if applicable. If you are not in CorelDRAW!, start the program from Windows or DOS.

2. Select the Text Tool from the Toolbox and click it once on the page where you want the text to begin. This activates the *Text* dialog box. The flashing cursor is automatically in the window at the top of this dialog box, so you can type the text.

Type "webster & associates." Then, move down to the box containing the list of available fonts. Using the down arrow to the right of this box, scroll down the list until the Vogue typeface is available. Click on it once with the mouse. To the right of the box that contains the list of fonts, select the *Bold* option.

Change the point size to 45 by double-clicking over the current figure in the *Size* frame, so that it is selected in reverse video; then key in 45. Also confirm that your *Justification* setting is *Left*. Click on the OK button to display the text on the page.

3. Make sure the Status Line is activated. If it is not, select the *Show Status Line* command from the **Display** menu. Now select the Ellipse Tool from the Toolbox to draw a circle on the page. To make sure you are actually drawing a perfect circle, hold down the Ctrl key on your keyboard while you are drawing the object. Draw it in the middle of the page.

Keeping your finger on the Ctrl key, hold down the mouse and drag it down and to the right. You must draw it in this direction for this exercise. The text flows automatically from the first node, which is at the top of the ellipse.

Watch the Status Line and release the mouse when it reaches approximately 2.2" (55 mm) by 2.2". It does not have to be exactly this dimension. Take your finger off the mouse and release the Ctrl key.

You now have a circle on the page proportionate to the one in the following illustration:

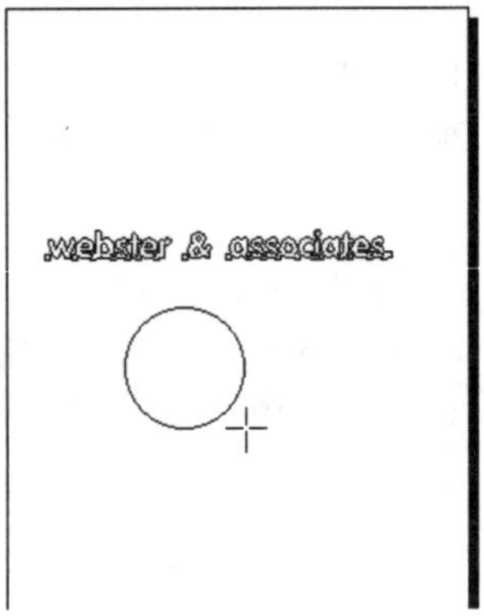

4. Select both the text and the circle using the Pick Tool. Use the *Select All* command from the **Edit** menu, or hold the [⇧ Shift] key down and click on both objects once. You can also draw a frame (marquee) around them using the Pick Tool.

Note: To make sure you have them both selected, check the Status Line to see that the two objects are selected.

Now select the *Fit Text To Path* command from the **Arrange** menu. After a few moments, the text will flow around the circle like this:

The last part of Step 4 is to delete the circle. If you have not clicked the mouse anywhere else, the circle and the text will both still be selected. To delete the circle you must select it by itself. If you try to select it now with the text and circle still selected, you will get the rotation and skew handles.

First deselect the text and the circle. Click the mouse elsewhere on the page. Then click the circle once more with the Pick Tool. If you are unsure whether you have actually selected the circle, since it is so close to the text, check the Status Line. It should read "Ellipse."

Once you are sure that you have selected the circle only, press the delete key on the keyboard, or choose the *Clear* command from the **Edit** menu. The text will now be the only object left on the page as the following illustation shows:

5. You are now going to use the Zoom Tool to magnify the text so that it takes up most of the screen. Select the Zoom Tool from the Toolbox, and from the Zoom Tool fly-out, select the *All* option.

Since the text is currently the only object on the page, it will cover most of the screen like this:

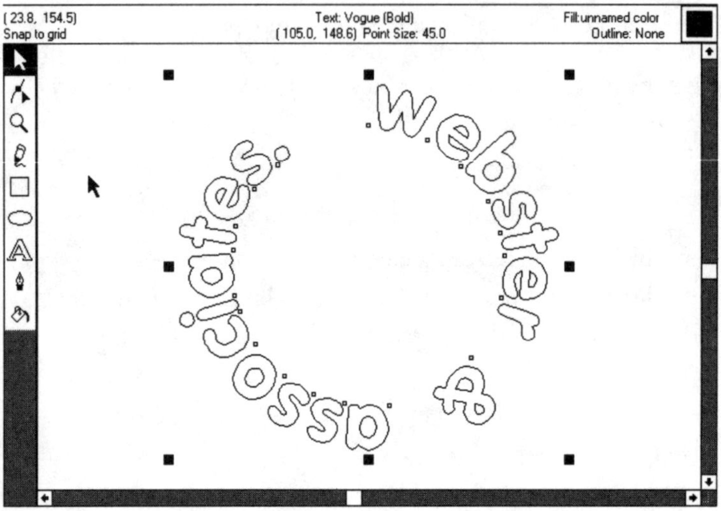

6. Select the text with the Pick Tool. Click on it once or hold down the mouse and draw a frame over it. Select the Fill Tool from the Toolbox, and from the Fill Tool fly-out, click on the white fill option.

Now select the Outline Tool fly-out. Note from this fly-out that there are 10 different thickness options that you can apply to an object. Give the text the third thinnest outline.

7. You are now ready to edit the perspective of the text. This gives the impression that it is getting smaller or larger, depending upon which way you look at it.

You can select the text with the Pick Tool or the Node Tool when executing the *Edit Perspective* command from the **Effects** menu. If you choose this command, and the text is selected with the Pick Tool, it automatically moves to the Node Tool after you select the command.

Once you use the *Edit Perspective* command, you can only use the Node Tool to edit, alter, or move a frame that surrounds an object.

Select the *Edit Perspective* command from the **Effects** menu. The text will have a dashed frame around it, and the Node Tool will be activated like this:

Now you are ready to alter the current perspective of the text.

8. With the Node Tool still selected, hold the mouse over the top, left node of the perspective box until a crosshair is displayed. Then, press the mouse and drag it down until the Horizontal Vanishing Point (Horiz) reads approximately "–9.85 inches" (or –250mm) in the Status Line as shown below:

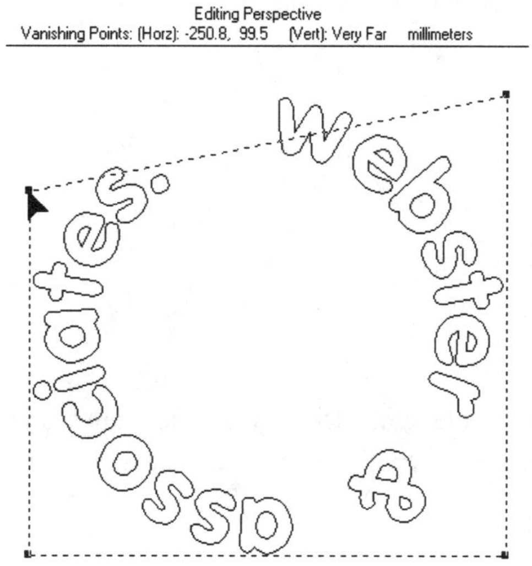

Take your finger off the mouse. After a moment, the text will have a new perspective, and will be displayed as though it is leaning over slightly.

9. Select the text with the Pick Tool. Choose the *Extrude* command from the **Effects** menu. This activates the *Extrude* dialog box.

Alter the *X* and *Y Offsets* to one inch. If the current measurement is not in inches, click on the frame that informs you what the current measurement system is, until it reads "inches."

In the boxes containing the current measurement for the *X* and *Y Offsets*, change them to 1". To do this, double-click over the current value and type a 1. Alternatively, click on the arrows to the side of the box containing the measurements, until each measurement reaches 1".

The *Absolute Coordinates* option, by default, will be off, so leave it this way. Leave the *Scaling Factor* option at 80. Also, turn the *Perspective* option on, if necessary (it is on by default). Once your dialog box is set up, click on OK.

After you click on OK, the extrusion will take a moment or two to work. Once the command works you can see that it gives the text a three-dimensional look. The same applies to any object that uses this command. The text and the text extrusion are two separate objects, so different fills can be given to them individually. Your drawing should look like this:

10. If the extruded object is not currently selected, click on it once with the Pick Tool. The Status Line tells you how many extruded parts make up the group of selected objects.

Once you select the extruded group of objects, activate the Fill Tool in the Toolbox, and select the *Fountain Fill* option. The *Fountain Fill* dialog box will now be displayed.

By now you know just how many choices CorelDRAW! gives you with color. The initial *Fountain Fill* dialog box gives you a choice between Spot and Process.

In this exercise, you are going to use the CMYK method for the *Fountain Fill*, so underneath the palette to the left, select the *Others* button. This activates another color dialog box where you can use the CMYK method.

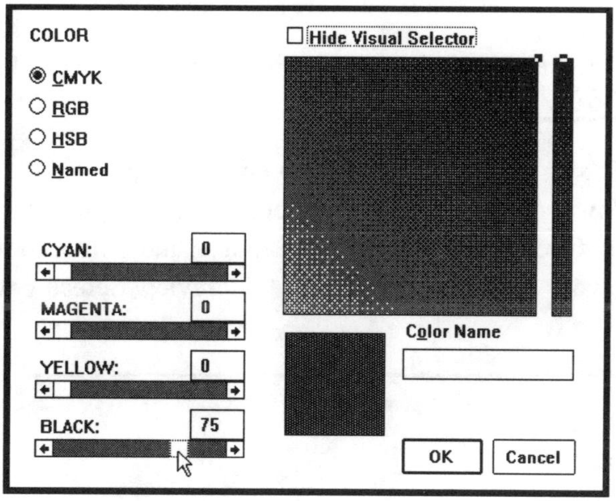

Double-click over the figure in the frame holding the current Black setting so that it is selected in reverse video, and type 75. Alternatively, hold the mouse down on the horizontal scroll bar representing the color Black and move it over until it reaches 75. Click on OK to return to the *Fountain Fill* dialog box.

Make sure Cyan, Magenta, and Yellow are all set to zero.

Now click on the *Others* button to the right in the *Fountain Fill* dialog box, under the second palette. This activates a second CMYK dialog box, where you will change the current Black setting to 25. Again, ensure the other colors are all zero.

After you have changed these settings, you activate the first *Fountain Fill* dialog box again. Notice the vertical color bar to the right reveals the two color settings previously made displaying from 75% to 25% black.

Now move up to the *Angle* option that is above the two color palettes. In the box that contains the current setting (it should read 90 by default), double-click the mouse so that it is selected in reverse video, and type the new figure of 110.

Alternatively, you could click on the up arrow to the right of the frame holding the current setting, until it reaches 110. Notice that the vertical bar to the right of the dialog box changes the angle of its fill to give you an example of the settings you have just made. After you have done this, click on OK.

11. Select the *Show Preview* command from the **Display** menu. Alternatively, you can press the [⇧ Shift] + [F9] keys.

The Preview Screen is now displayed. To enlarge it, move the mouse over the left-hand window wall of the Preview Screen, until a two-headed, horizontal arrow is displyed. Once it is, hold down the mouse and drag it to the left, so that when you take your finger off the mouse, the Preview Screen covers the whole screen like this:

You can create professional-looking logos easily following these or similar steps. By experimenting with CorelDRAW!, you can come up with your own amazing design or company header.

Exercise 10

Molding Text into Shapes

In this exercise, you will use a combination of CorelDRAW! features, including *Fountain Fills* and the *Edit Envelope* command to mold text into a circle. The following pages contain the steps, as well as the details on how to execute this task.

The Steps in Brief

1. Create a new CorelDRAW! file.
2. Draw a circle approximately the width of the page while holding down the Ctrl key.
3. Give the circle a Radial Fountain Fill, using Spot color, 100% to 0% black.
4. Type "circle" in the center of the circle using 100-point Prose Antique.
5. Use the Node selection option to create the circle.
6. Give the text a white fill and a white outline.

This is the finished result of this exercise.

The steps for completing this exercise are on the following pages.

The Steps in Detail

1. Create a new CorelDRAW file.

If you are already in CorelDRAW!, select *New* from the **File** menu and save changes, if applicable. If you are not in CorelDRAW!, start the program from Windows or DOS.

2. Select the Ellipse Tool. Press the Ctrl key, and position the cursor somewhere in the top left of the page. Now hold the mouse down, and drag it until the circle is approximately the width of the page like this:

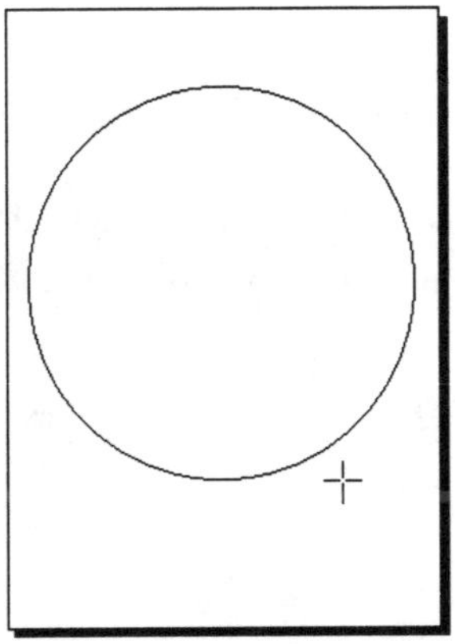

3. Activate the Pick Tool to select the circle. To give it a Fountain Fill, select the *Fountain Fill* option from the Fill Tool fly-out.

In the displayed *Foutain Fill* dialog box, select *Spot color* and *Radial* options by clicking the mouse inside the relevant circles. Leave the color settings at 100% Black (left palette) and 0% Black (right palette), and then select OK. The result will only be visible on the Preview Screen.

4. Select the Text Tool. Move your cursor onto the page, and click the mouse close to the center of the circle, to invoke the *Text* dialog box. Type the word "circle." Change the point size to 100 by either using the arrows to the side of the *Size* box, or double-clicking the mouse inside the box, and typing in the new value. Click the mouse on the down arrow of the scroll bar, to the right of the font frame, until you see Prose Antique. Click on OK.

When you return to your page, it will look similar to the following illustration.

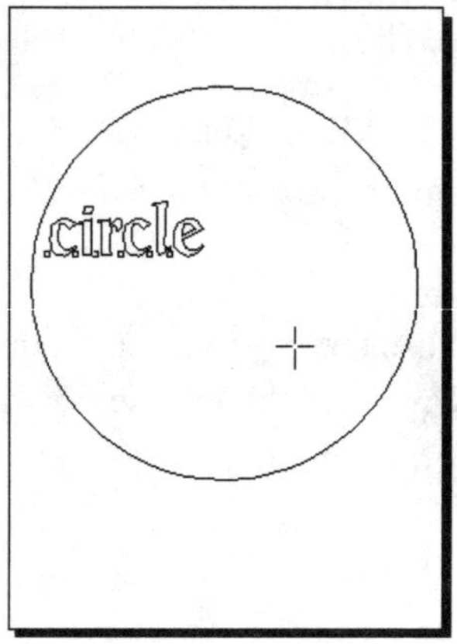

Select the Pick Tool, and move the text into the middle of the circle, if necessary. When you return to your page, the text will have a dotted outline around it and the Node like this:

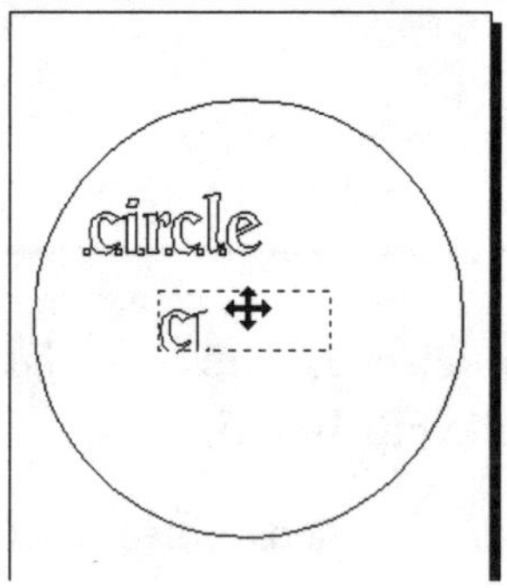

5. With the text still selected with the Pick Tool, go to the **Effects** menu, highlight the *Edit Envelope* command, and select the Node Edit shaped option from the Fly-out.

When you return to your page, the text will have a dotted outline around it, and the Node Tool will be selected as shown in the following illustration. This outline contains nodes which you will move in order to reshape the text inside the circle.

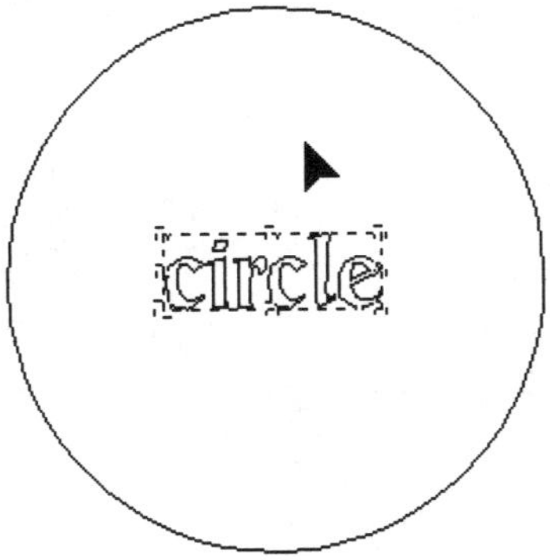

Hold the mouse down on the middle node and drag it to the circle edge like this:

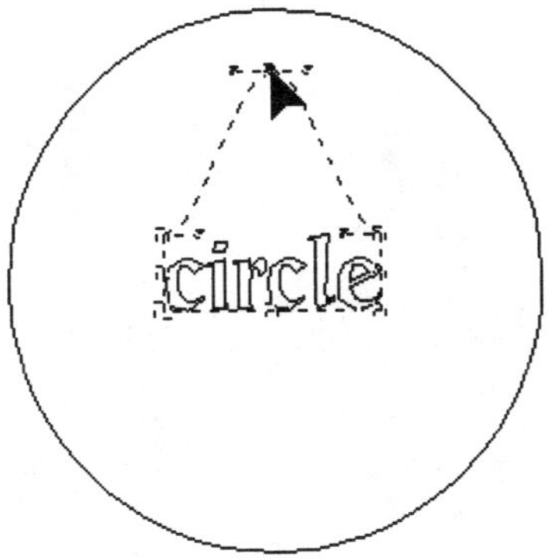

Repeat for the opposite node like this:

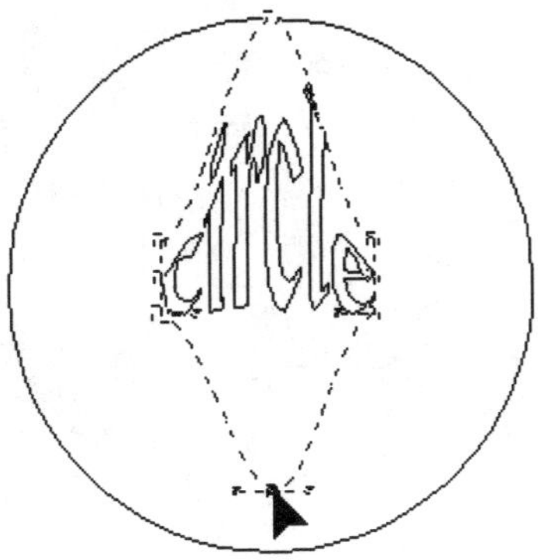

Select the top right corner node and move it to the circle edge like this:

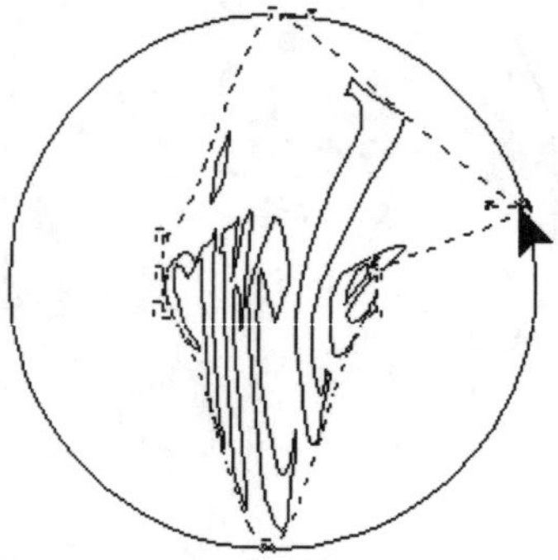

Select the bottom right corner node and move it to the circle edge like this:

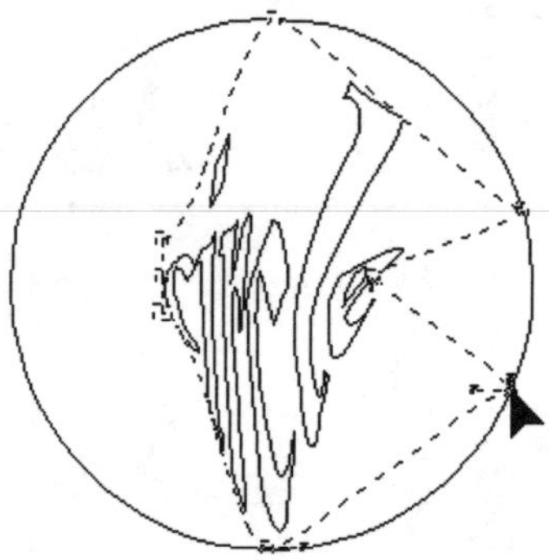

Select the middle right node and move it to the circle edge like this:

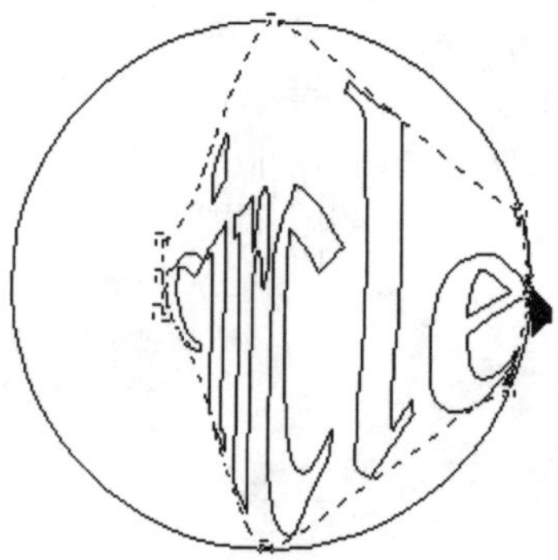

Repeat this process for the opposite side. It will look like this:

Now you are going to select nodes individually and manipulate their control points, so the envelope frame fits the inside of the circle better.

Select the top node so that its control points are visible. Select the right control point, and move it to the right, so that the envelope boundary fits the circle edge.

Select the top right node and move its control point to align the dotted line with the circle edge like this:

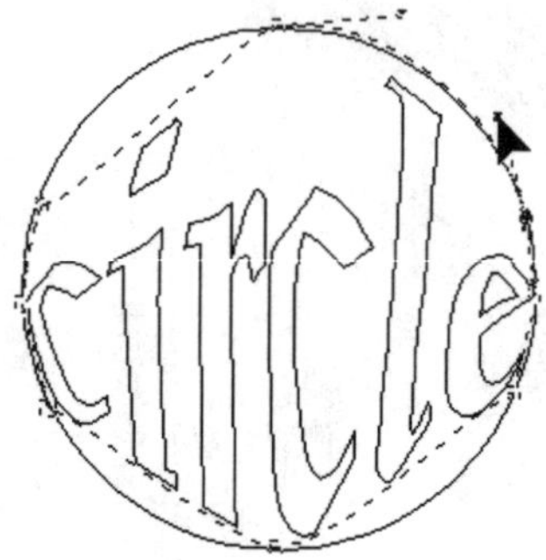

You may need to readjust control points to align exactly with the circle edge like this:

Repeat this process for the bottom right corner like this:

Repeat this process for the left side. When finished, your text will look like this illustration.

6. Select the Pick Tool to automatically select the text. To give it a white fill, select the Fill Tool, and click on the white selection from the fly-out.

To give it a white outline, select the Outline Tool, and click on the white selection from the fly-out.

To view the final result of the exercise, move to the Preview Screen, by either selecting the *Show Preview* command from the **Display** menu, or pressing the Shift + F9 keys.

This is how your final result looks on the Preview Screen.

Exercise 11

Change of Perspective

In this exercise, you will combine the *Stretch & Mirror*, *Extrude*, and *Perspective* commands to change the perspective of a text string. The following pages contain the steps, as well as the details on how to execute this task.

The Steps in Brief

1. Create a new CorelDRAW! file.
2. Type "perspective" on the page using 80-point Bangkok.
3. Change the perspective of the text.
4. Use the Extrude command on the text with the Absolute Coordinates turned off, both X and Y values at 1.2" (30mm), Perspective on, and a Scaling Factor of 50%.
5. Give the extrusion a white fill and a black outline.
6. Mirror the original text and its extrusion vertically, and leave the original.
7. Move the mirrored image below the original.

This is the finished result of this exercise.

The steps for completing this exercise are on the following pages.

The Steps in Detail

1. Create a new CorelDRAW! file.

If you are already in CorelDRAW!, select *New* from the **File** menu and save changes, if applicable. If you are not in CorelDRAW!, start the program from Windows or DOS.

2. Select the Text Tool to type the text. Move your cursor onto the page, and click the mouse once somewhere in the middle of your page to invoke the *Text* dialog box.

When the *Text* dialog box is displayed, type "perspective." Change the point size to 80 by either using the arrows to the side of the box, or double-clicking the mouse inside the box, and typing in the new value. Highlight Bangkok with the mouse and click on OK.

It's probably a good idea at this stage to use the Zoom Tool to enlarge the section of the screen around the text.

3. Select the text with the Pick Tool, go to the **Effects** menu, and select the *Edit Perspective* command.

When you return to your page, the text will have a dotted line around its edges, and the Node Tool will be selected. Hold down the mouse on the top right corner of the dotted square, drag it upwards and release the mouse like this:

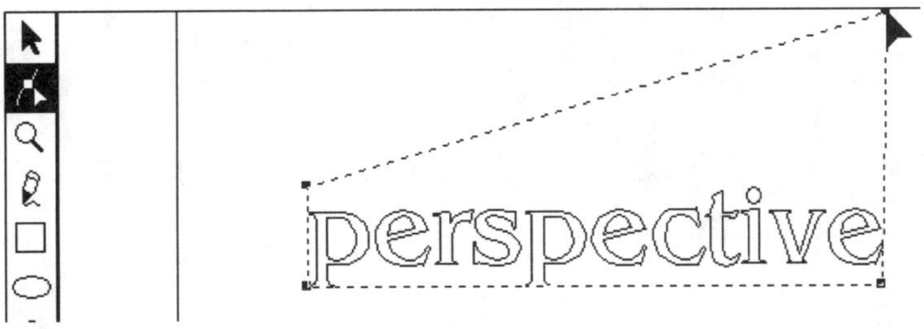

In a few seconds, the text will reformat according to its newly created perspective like this:

4. Give the text a three-dimensional look, by using the *Extrude* command. Make sure the text is still selected with the Node Tool. Then, select the *Extrude* command from the **Effects** menu.

Once the *Extrude* dialog box is on the screen, change the values so that they match the ones in the following illustration. You can also change from millimeters to inches here, by clicking on the measurement unit.

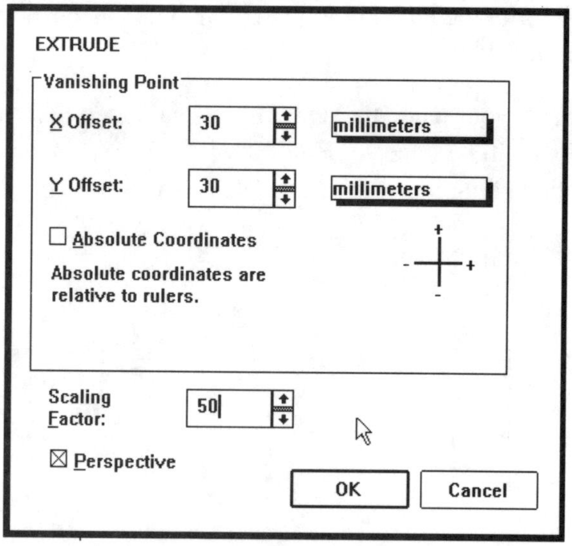

Click on OK and your text will now look like this:

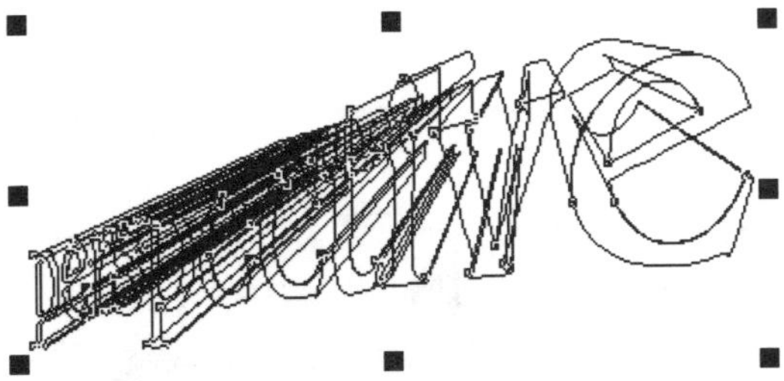

5. Make sure the extrusion is still selected with the Pick Tool (it is selected by default after an extrusion). The Status Line reflects the group of objects of the extrusion. If only the text at the front is selected, the Status Line will read "Text: Bangkok (Normal)." If the extrusion is not selected, click on it once with the Pick Tool.

Note: Whenever an object is extruded, the actual extrusion is several grouped objects, which you can select as one, or ungrouped and manipulated like any other object.

Select the *White* option from the Fill Tool fly-out. Then, from the Outline Tool fly-out, select a black outline of any thickness.

6. Select the original text and the extension with the Pick Tool by holding down the ⇧Shift key. You may find it easier to choose the *Select All* command from the **Edit** menu, so all objects are correctly selected. The following illustration shows the selected text:

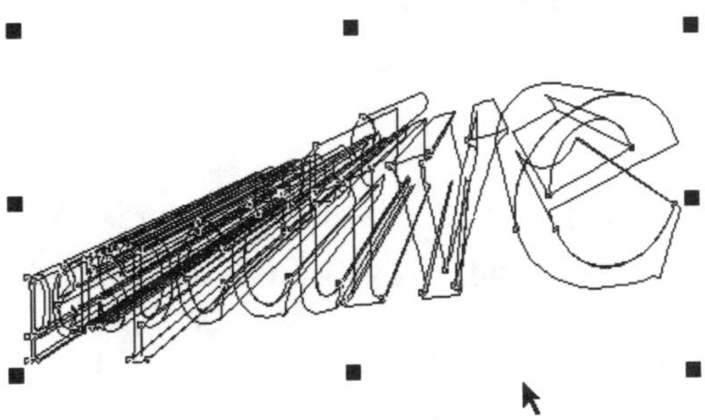

When you select the two objects, the Status Line reads "2 objects selected." Now select the *Stretch & Mirror* command from the **Transform** menu. The *Stretch & Mirror* dialog box will be displayed like this:

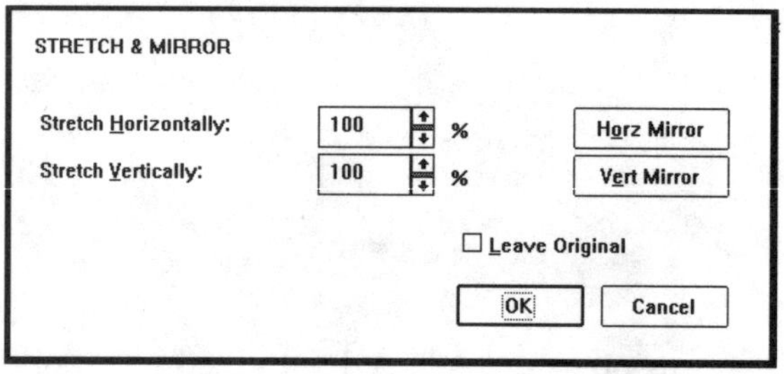

In the *Stretch & Mirror* dialog box, click your mouse on the *Vertical Mirror* option. When you select this option, the figure in the *Stretch Vertically* frame automatically reverts to –100, which is what you need. Now select the *Leave Original* option, and click on OK.

The mirrored objects are now displayed on the screen directly on top of the original objects like this:

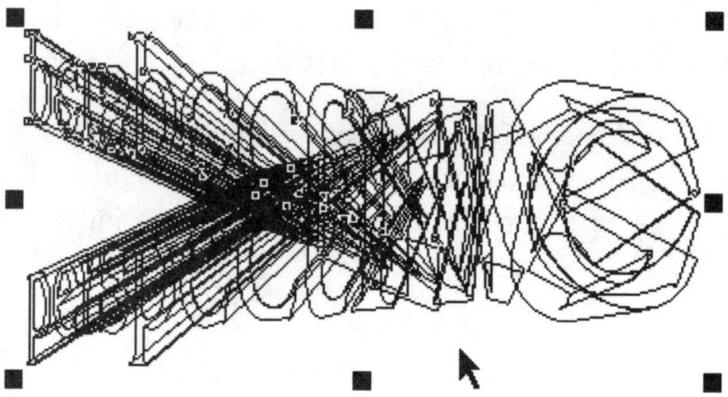

7. The mirrored text that is now displayed on screen is automatically selected. To move it away, make sure it stays selected. Do not click your mouse elsewhere on the page, or you will deselect it, and it is very hard to reselect. If you do deselect it, you will have to hold down the Shift key and click on the mirrored text and the mirrored extrusion with the Pick Tool.

When you are sure the mirrored objects are selected, hold the mouse on one of the selected objects and drag it down. Release the mouse when the mirrored objects are directly below the original objects. If they are not in the right position, pick them up again and move them. They should look like this:

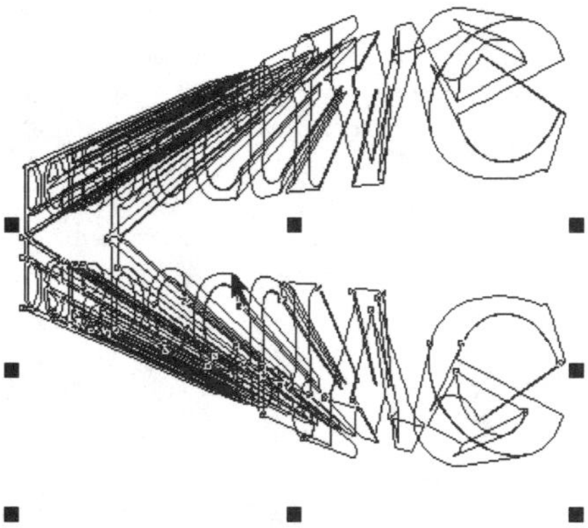

Now that you have completed the exercise, either select the *Full Screen Preview* command from the **Display** menu, or press the F9 key to view what you have done. The result in the Preview Screen is shown below:

Exercise 12

Creating and Saving Patterns

This exercise shows you how to create bitmap and vector fill patterns that you can save and use again as fills for whole objects. CorelDRAW! has a wide range of bitmap and vector patterns that you can apply to a fillable object. The following pages contain the steps, as well as details on how to execute this task.

The Steps in Brief

1. Create a new CorelDRAW! file.
2. Draw a star on the page, any size, with the Pencil Tool and give it a black fill.
3. Save the star as a high-resolution bitmap pattern.
4. Draw a square on the page, at any size, and give it the Bitmap Pattern fill you just created. Make the star white and the background black.
5. Delete everything from the screen.
6. Draw a rectangle on the page approximately 5" (127mm) wide x 1" (25mm) high.
7. Rotate the rectangle 25 degrees and leave the original.
8. Repeat the last step until the last rectangle has rotated back to the beginning.
9. Select all the rectangles, combine them, and give them a yellow CMYK fill.
10. Save the combined rectangles as a vector pattern.
11. Draw a rectangle on the page, at any size, and apply the vector pattern fill you just created.

The following illustration shows the result of the bitmap pattern created and applied to a rectangle.

The following illustration shows the result of the vector pattern created and used as a rectangle fill.

The Steps in Detail

1. Create a new CorelDRAW! file.

If you are already in CorelDRAW!, select *New* from the **File** menu and save the changes, if applicable. If you are not in CorelDRAW!, start the program from Windows or DOS.

2. Select the Pencil Tool from the Toolbox and move out onto the page. You use the Pencil Tool to draw the star in Freehand mode, rather than Bezier mode. If you have Bezier mode currently active, click the mouse once where the exercise says click it twice. Click once to end the drawing.

The following illustrations demonstrate how to draw the star. To start drawing the star, click the mouse once and move it down and to the left, and double-click it at the next point. Double-clicking the mouse ensures that the straight line of the Pencil Tool follows the mouse.

The left-hand side of the star is almost complete by moving the mouse around and double-clicking at each change of direction. Note the nodes along the star. This is where you double-clicked the mouse.

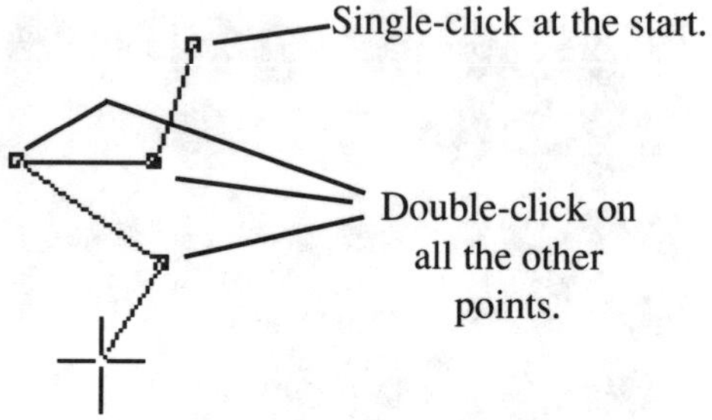

Move further around the star. This way of drawing makes it easy to draw a simple shape, instead of holding your finger on the mouse and trying to draw it freehand.

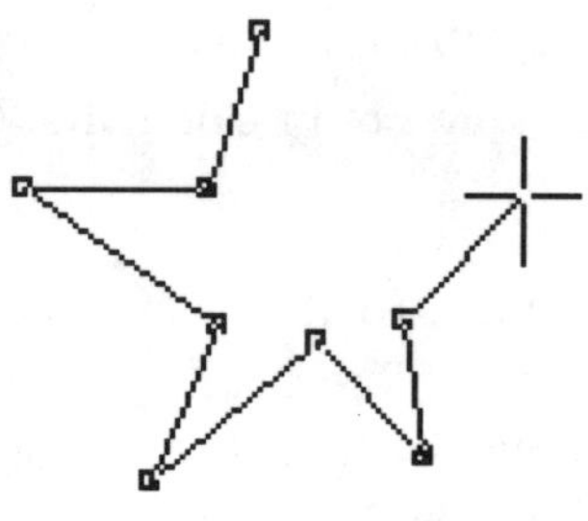

To end the star, click once on the beginning node. Make sure you click the mouse right on the first node, so the star will be a fillable, closed object.

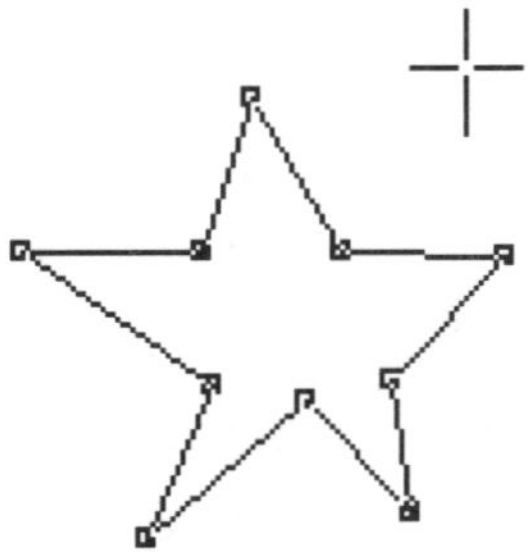

The above star was drawn using a mix of straight lines. If you draw with the Pencil Tool in a completely freehand way, you will usually get a very uneven shape, with a lot of nodes along the lines.

Note: You can also draw a curved shape the same way you drew this star. Once you have completed the shape, curve the lines through the *Node Edit* dialog box. A drawing with the least amount of nodes along its lines is a lot easier to manipulate and edit.

After drawing your star, select it with the Node Tool, and move the nodes around a bit to straighten the object. This is not really necessary, as any shape would do for this exercise. If you would like yours to be a bit more aligned, you may like to move it round a bit as shown in the following illustration:

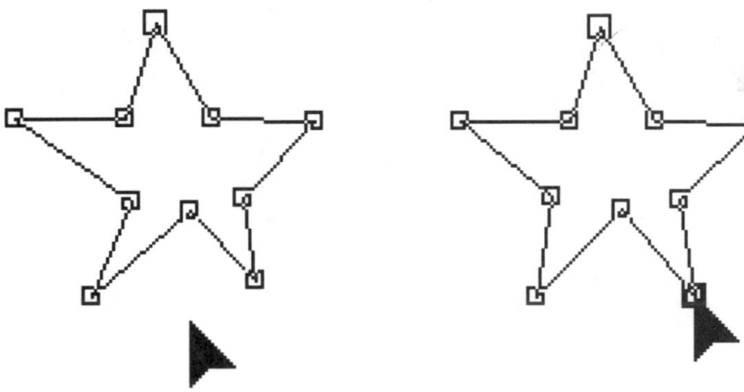

While the star is still selected with the Node Tool, you can select it with the Pick Tool and apply a black fill to it from the Fill Tool fly-out.

3. Now that you have drawn a shape on the page, you are going to save it as a bitmap pattern. CorelDRAW! lets you create and save a bitmap image that sits beside all the other bitmap fills in the *Bitmap Fill Pattern* dialog box. Select the *Create Pattern* command from the **Special** menu.

Selecting the *Create Pattern* command activates the *Create Pattern* dialog box. The type of pattern you are creating is *Bitmap*, which is selected. Click on *High* for *Resolution*. The message in the dialog box indicates that after selecting OK, you are to select the area on your page with a marquee that you want saved as the pattern, as shown below:

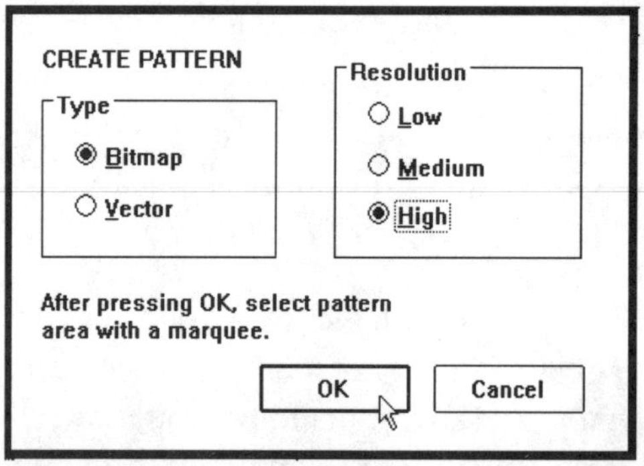

Set up your dialog box and click on OK. When you return to the screen, the mouse changes into a large crosshair (the point at which the two lines meet being the center of the mouse movement) like this:

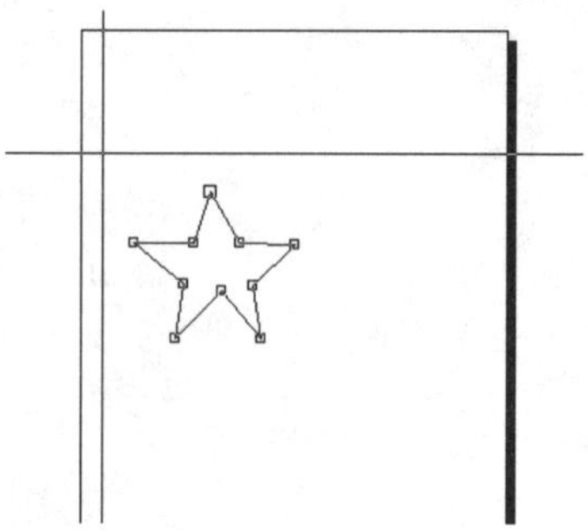

Select the star with the crosshair (marquee) by holding your finger on the mouse and dragging it right over the star like this:

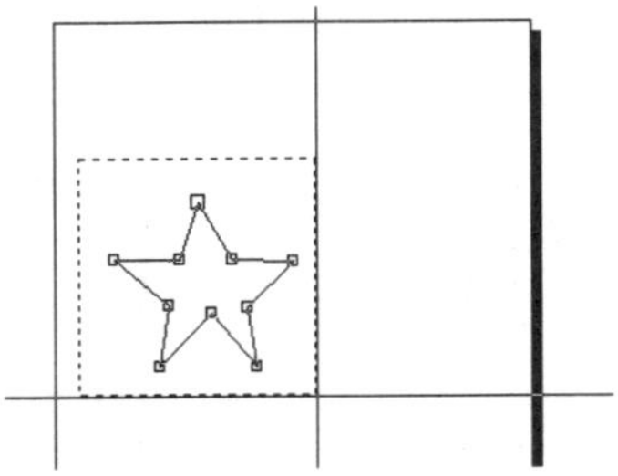

Note: Make sure you cover the whole star, because only what falls inside the frame you draw will be included in the creation of the pattern. Once you have covered the whole star, release your finger from the mouse.

After selecting the star with the marquee, a screen prompt asks if you want to create the pattern with the area you just selected. If it is right, select OK. If you selected the wrong area, select *Cancel* and start the *Create Pattern* process again.

No apparent change takes place after you have concluded this procedure. You can see what has happened in the next step.

4. Select the Rectangle Tool from the Toolbox and move out onto the page like this:

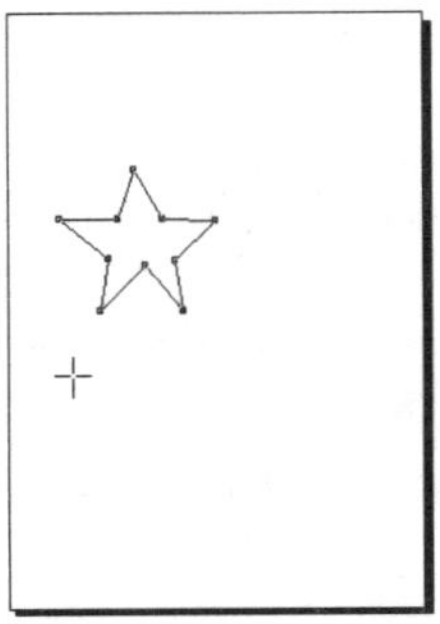

To draw a perfect square, hold your finger on the Ctrl key while you are drawing. It does not matter where you draw it on the page, but make it quite large.

To draw the square, hold your finger on the mouse and drag it down and to the right, until it is proportionate to the one in the following illustration:

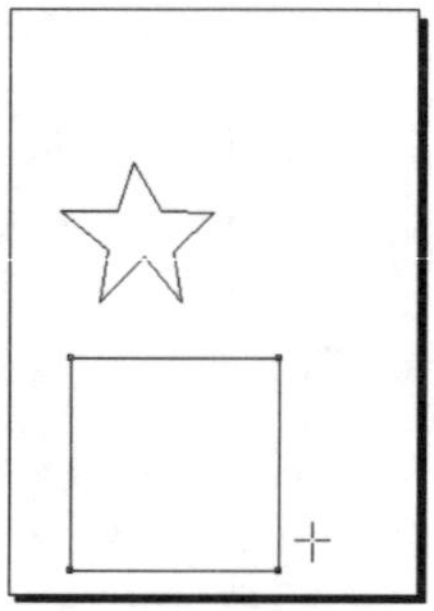

Release your finger from the mouse when it is the size you want, and then take your finger off the Ctrl key.

You can fill this square with the bitmap pattern you created, so select the square with the Pick Tool like this:

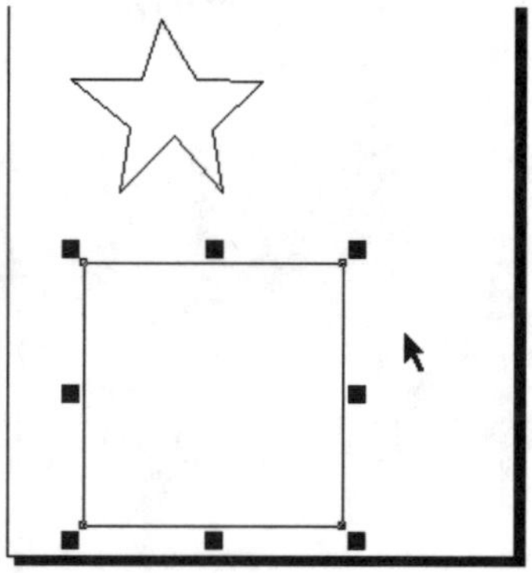

Once the square is selected with the Pick Tool, select the *Bitmap Fill Pattern* option from the Fill Tool fly-out.

Selecting this option activates the *Bitmap Fill Pattern* dialog box. Once the *Bitmap Fill Pattern* dialog box is activated, you can see your star pattern in the frame containing all the bitmap fill patterns. If you cannot see it, use the scroll bar to the right of this frame, and scroll down until you see the star you drew.

When it is available, click on it, and the pattern will be displayed in the larger frame at the top left of the dialog box as shown below:

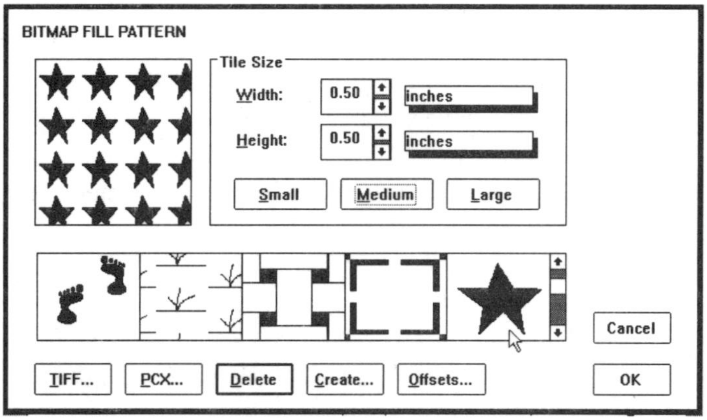

When you have done this, select OK.

The *Bitmap Pattern Color* box will be displayed as shown below.

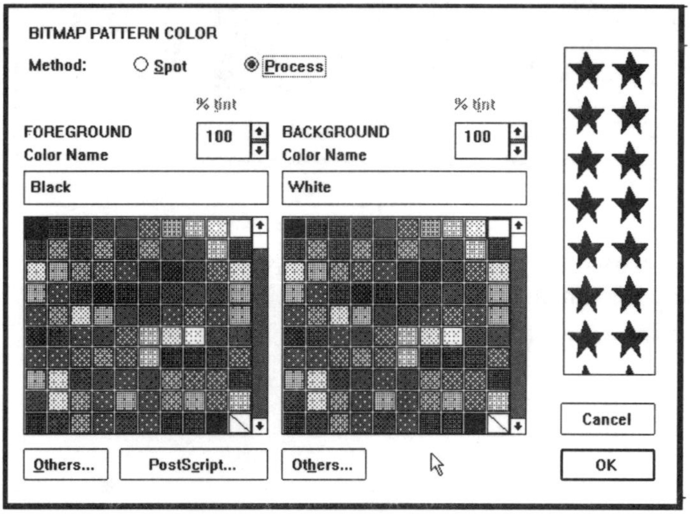

Here you can assign a color to both the foreground and background of your Bitmap Pattern.

To give the *Foreground* a different color, select one from the palette to the left of the dialog box. For this exercise you are going to reverse the current colors. In the *Foreground* palette, select the white option.

For the *Background,* select black. Do this by clicking on the black square in the palette to the right. Once you have selected a color from each palette, the selected color will be named in the frames above the palettes. The frame at the right of the dialog box, reflecting the pattern, will change to the selected colors like this:

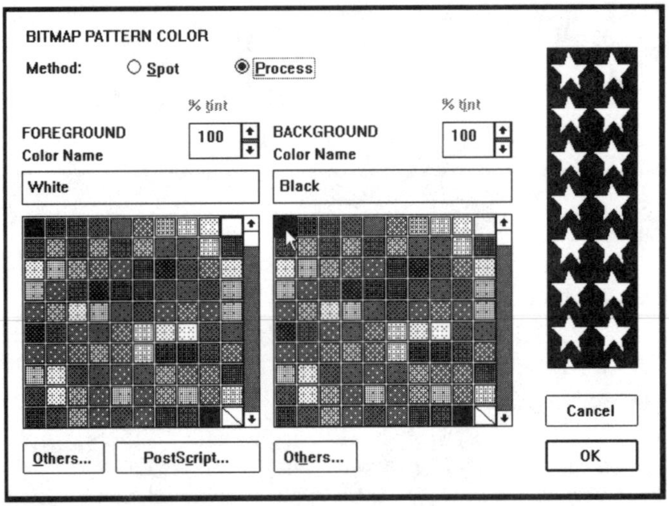

Click on OK when you return to the screen. No apparent change will have occurred, until you view the square through the Preview Screen. Before you do this, magnify the square so that it covers most of the screen by selecting the first option from the Zoom Tool fly-out.

With the Zoom Tool, draw a frame over the square with your finger on the mouse. Release your finger from the mouse when the square is completely covered like this:

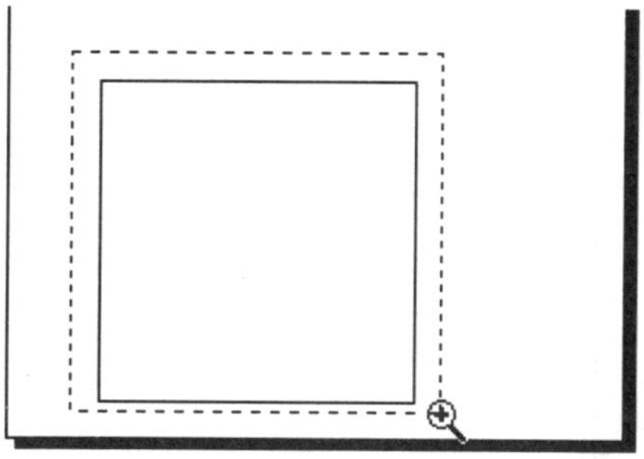

After magnifying the square, activate the Preview Screen (Shift + F9), to get a detailed look at the Bitmap Pattern you created as shown below:

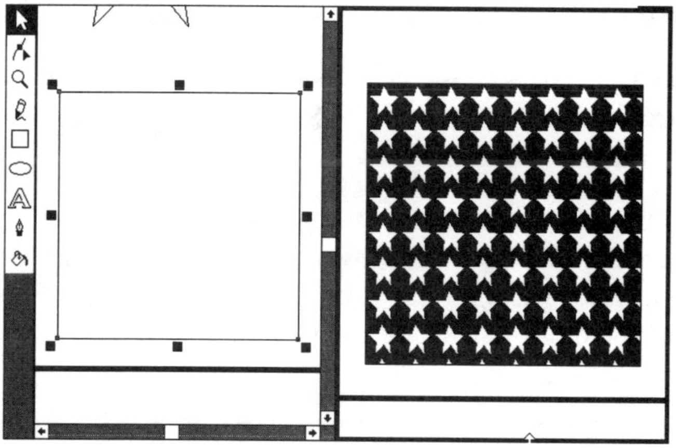

Once you have viewed the square in the Preview Screen, deactivate the Preview Screen by pressing Shift + F9 keys again. Then, from the Zoom Tool fly-out, select the last option, which changes the view of the screen so the whole page is displayed.

5. Delete everything from the screen. To do this, select the star and the square with the Pick Tool while you hold down the Shift key. Once they are both selected, press the delete key. Alternatively, you can choose the *Select All* command from the **Edit** menu, and press the delete key.

6. Select the Rectangle Tool from the Toolbox and move out onto the page. Holding your finger on the mouse, drag it down and to the right until the Status Line tells you that the rectangle you are drawing is approximately 5" (127 mm) wide by 1" (25 mm) high as shown below:

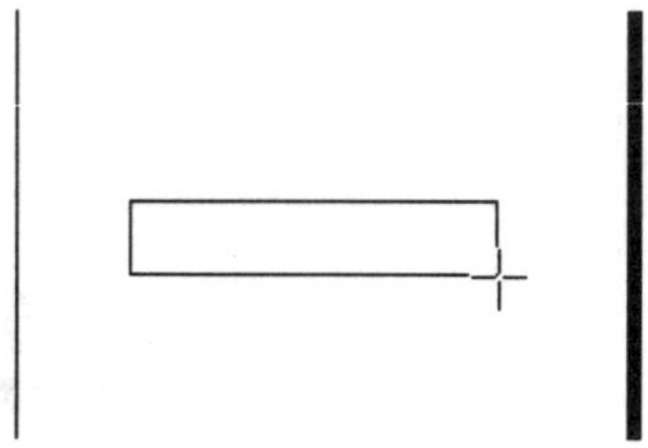

Note: The unit of measurement currently active in the Status Line is the unit of measurement currently selected in the *Grid Parameters* dialog box. You activate this dialog box when you select the *Grid Setup* command from the **Display** menu.

7. Select the rectangle with the Pick Tool and then choose the *Rotate & Skew* command from the **Transform** menu. Selecting this command activates the *Rotate & Skew* dialog box.

Once you activate the *Rotate & Skew* dialog box, change the *Rotation Angle* to 25. To do this, double-click the mouse inside the frame containing the current setting, so that it is selected in reverse video, then type 25. Alternatively, use the up arrow to the right of the frame until you reach 25. Also, check the *Leave Original* option by clicking on it with the mouse as shown below:

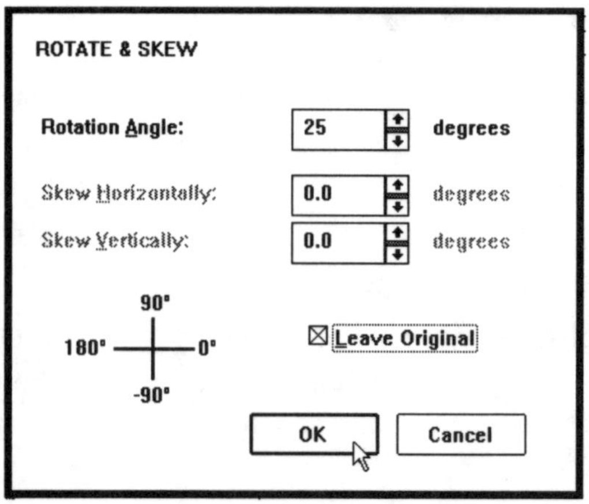

Click on OK. You now have a rectangle on the page that has been rotated 25 degrees from the original rectangle as shown below:

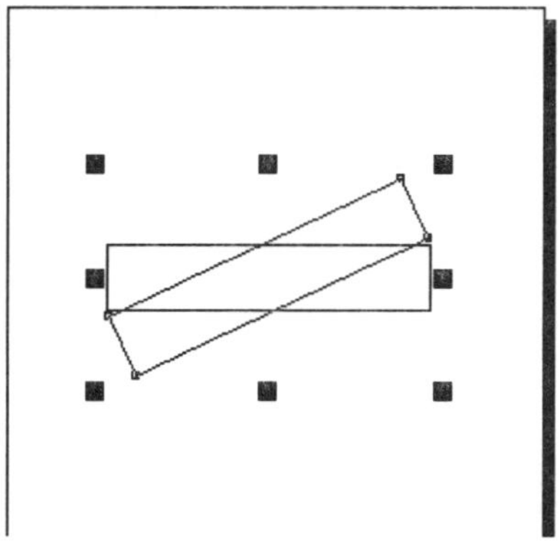

For the next part of the exercise to work correctly, do not click the mouse anywhere on the blank page, or you will deselect the second rectangle. If you do, select it by clicking on it once with the Pick Tool.

8. Repeat the last step until the last rectangle has rotated back to the beginning.

Use the *Repeat* command from the **Edit** menu to display another rectangle that will be rotated 25 degrees from the second rectangle and 50 degrees further on the first rectangle as shown below:

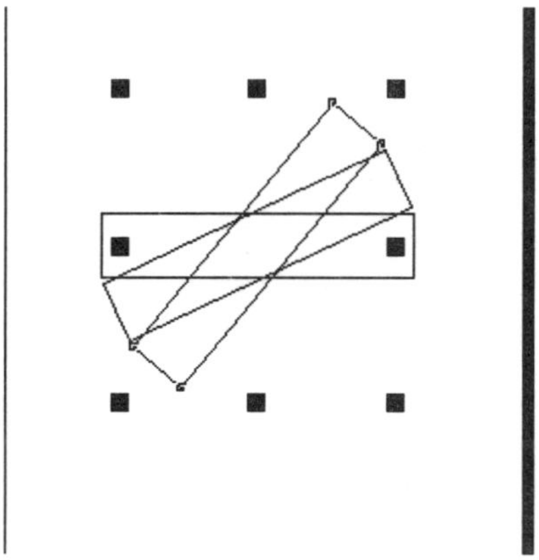

You can now keep using the *Repeat* command until the rectangles are in almost a complete circle. Alternatively, you can press the Ctrl + R keys giving you the same effect. The following illustration shows the result of using the *Repeat* command a number of times, until the last rectangle lands almost on top of the first one.

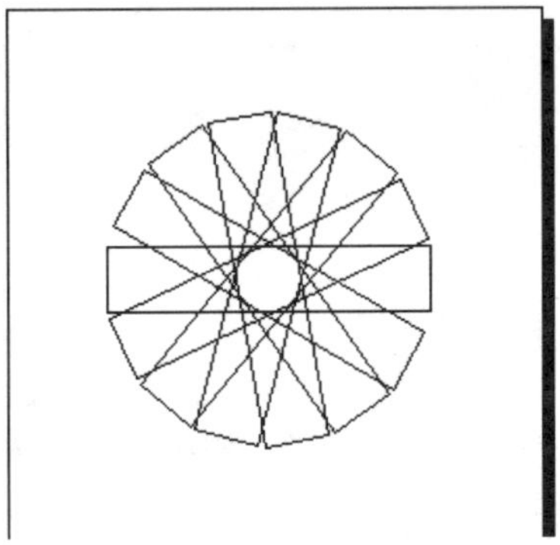

9. Select all the rectangles. You can either choose the *Select All* command from the **Edit** menu or draw a frame around the rectangles with the Pick Tool like this:

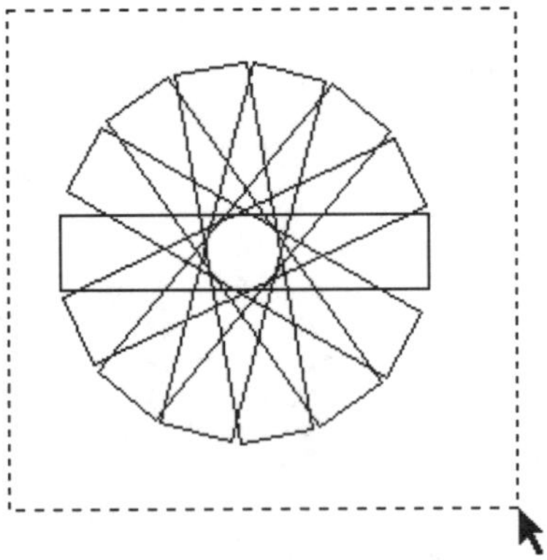

Once you select all the rectangles, you are going to combine them. Do this by selecting *Combine* from the **Arrange** menu. Since these rectangles are overlapping, combining them results in an interesting effect. Wherever the rectangles overlap, there is no fill or gap, which is actually see through. You can see anything behind the objects through these gaps.

Now that you have combined the rectangles, give them a CMYK fill of 100 percent yellow. To do this, make sure they are still selected with the Pick Tool, and choose the *Uniform Fill* option from the Fill Tool fly-out.

Once the *Uniform Fill* dialog box is displayed, select the CMYK option. This is the first available option at the top left of the dialog box. If the *Palette* dialog box is displayed instead, click on the *Others* button at the right of this box, to activate the *Uniform Fill* color options dialog box.

With the CMYK option selected, move to the frame containing the current setting for Yellow. Double-click over the current setting, so it is selected in reverse video, and type100.

Alternatively, hold the mouse on the horizontal scroll bar representing the color yellow, and drag it to the right until it reaches the end, where the setting is 100. If you are using any other colors, drag their scroll bars furthest to the left, or type 0 in the frames representing each color. The color selected will be displayed in the frame to the right of the scroll bars, and the color name will be displayed to the right of this as shown below:

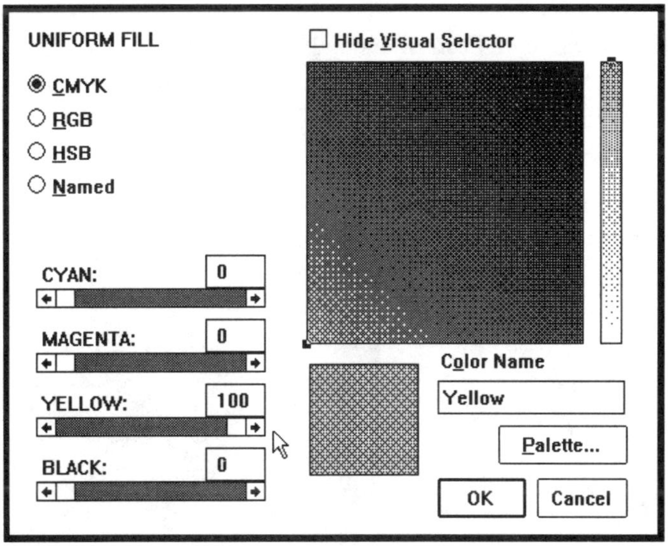

An optional approach to apply a color to objects is to activate the *Color Palette* from the **Display** menu, and from this click on the required color.

Click on OK. The following illustration shows the progress of the Preview Screen.

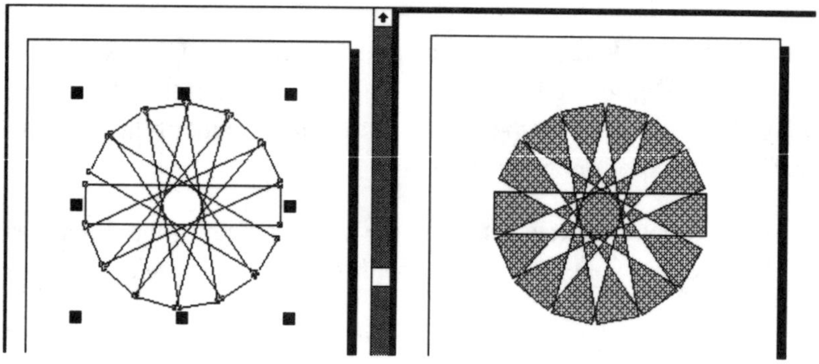

10. Follow almost the same steps as you did when saving the star as a bitmap pattern. The first thing to do is select the *Create Pattern* command from the **Special** menu.

Once you display the *Create Pattern* dialog box, select *Vector* in the *Type* option by clicking in the circle to the left of the word *Vector*.

Click on OK in the *Create Pattern* dialog box to display the large crosshair, which you use to select the rectangles. Holding your finger on the mouse, drag the crosshair over the rectangles, and release your finger from the mouse when they are completely covered as shown below:

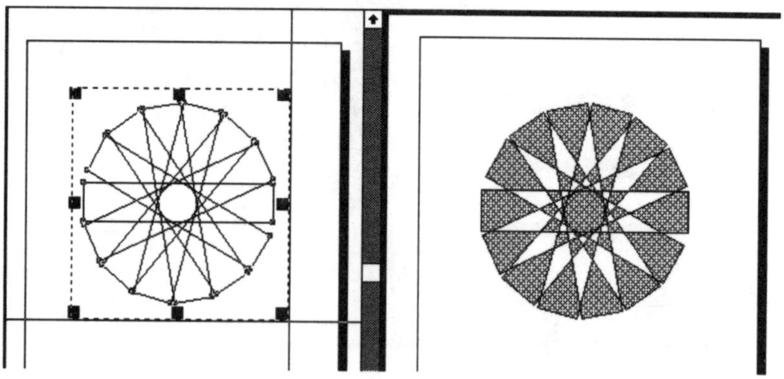

After you select the rectangles, you will see the *Create Pattern* screen prompt. If you are sure you selected the right area of the page, click on OK.

You will then see the *Save Vector Pattern* dialog box. Here you can move through the computer's drives and directories to where you would like to save the pattern. You also have to give the pattern a name. The following illustration shows the *Save Vector Pattern* dialog box:

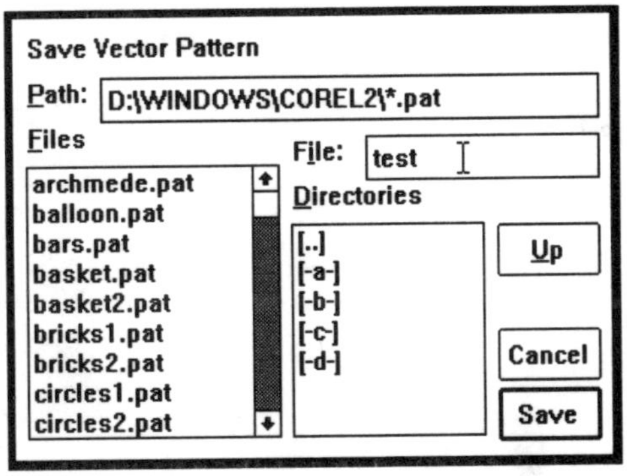

After you name the pattern, decide where you are going to save it, and click on OK. For this exercise, save the pattern with the other vector patterns that come with CorelDRAW!, and call it "test." If you choose not to save your pattern in this directory, remember that vector pattern files have an exstension of .PAT, which makes it easier to find them in the future.

11. Select the Rectangle Tool from the Toolbox and move it onto the page. Hold your finger on the mouse, and drag it down and to the right. Release your finger from the mouse when your rectangle is porportinate to the one in the following illustration:

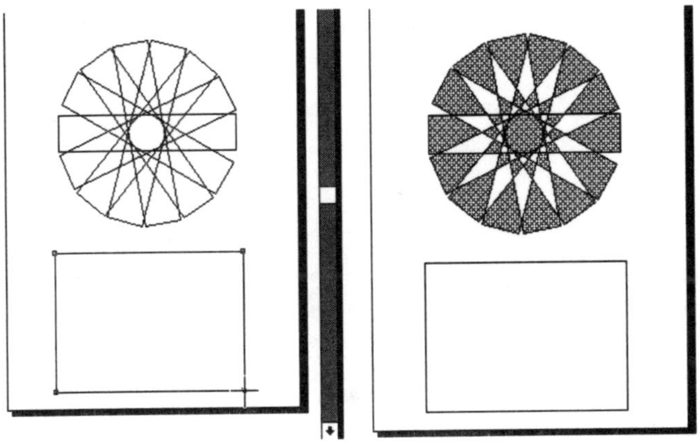

Immediately after drawing the rectangle, select the *Load Vector Pattern* option from the Fill Tool fly-out.

On selecting the *Load Vector Pattern* option from the Fill Tool fly-out, you will see the *Load Vector Pattern* dialog box as shown below:

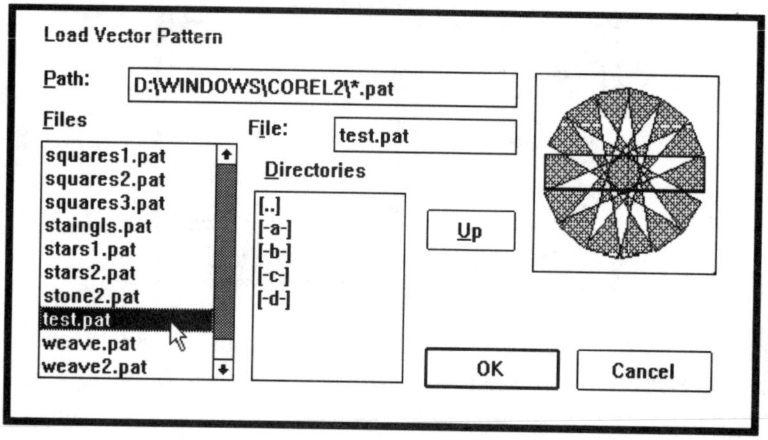

Here you can scroll down the list containing the vector pattern files, until the one you saved ("test") becomes available, and then select it. Remember, if you did not save your pattern in the directory with all the CorelDRAW! vector patterns, you must go to the directory where you did save it.

Once you have selected a pattern from the list, a low resolution version of the pattern will be displayed in the frame at the right of the dialog box. This allows you to verify that you are selecting the right one from the list. Now click on OK.

After you select OK in the *Load Vector Pattern* dialog box, the *Vector Fill Pattern* dialog box is activated as shown in the next illustration. For this exercise, you are not going to make any changes to this dialog box, so click on OK.

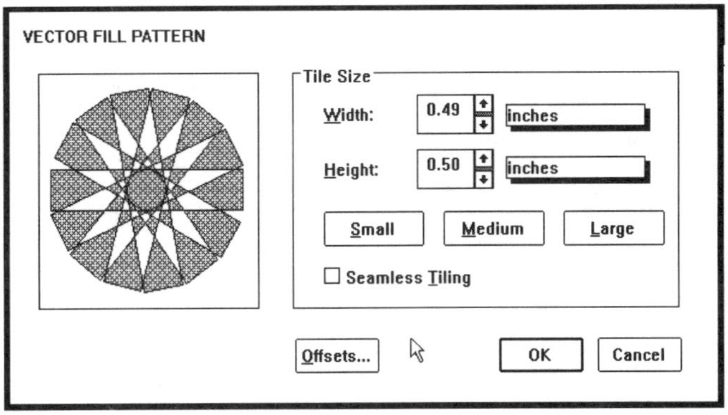

The *Vector Fill Pattern* dialog box is the last one you work with in this exercise. After you click on OK in this dialog box, the rectangle contains the vector pattern fill you created. To view it, magnify the rectangle and look at it in the Preview Screen as shown below:

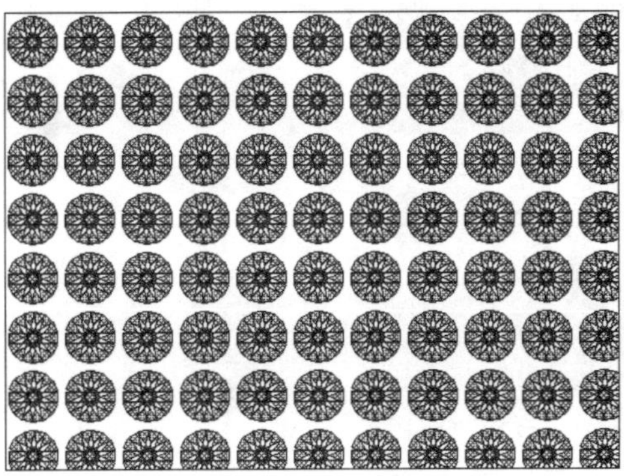

For more information on bitmap and vector fills, see **Chapter 3: The Outline and Fill Tools**. The difference between vector and bimap fills is that vector fills are of a higher quality and a higher resolution. The vector fills supplied with CorelDRAW! are also full color, and have to be opened in a separate CorelDRAW! file to edit (See Chapter 3). You can edit bitmap fills in the *Bitmap Fill Pattern* dialog box, and you can apply a color to the foreground and the background.

In this illustration, the four images on the left are some examples of vector patterns that are supplied with CorelDRAW!, while the images on the right are bitmap patterns.

Exercise 13

Masking

This exercise shows you how to create a mask or hole in an object on your page, so that anything you place underneath it will show through. For this exercise, you use text for the actual mask. You will rotate rectangles, each with a different fill, and place them behind the object to create a striped effect. The following pages contain the steps, as well as the details on how to execute this task.

The Steps in Brief

1. Create a new CorelDRAW! file.
2. Change the page layout to Landscape.
3. Draw a row of five rectangles, one above the other, approximately 8" wide by 1" deep (or 200mm by 20mm if using millimeters).
4. Rotate all five rectangles together approximately –30 degrees.
5. Give the rectangles no outline.
6. Give each of the five rectangles a different shade of gray from the Fill Tool fly-out, ranging from the darkest shade of gray for the top rectangle, to the lightest shade for the bottom rectangle.
7. Type “mask” on the page, across the rectangles, using 140-point Switzerland-Black.
8. Draw a rectangle that covers the whole area taken up by the rotated rectangles and text.
9. Combine the large rectangle and the text.
10. Give the combined objects no outline and a white fill.

This is the finished result of this exercise.

The steps for completing this exercise are on the following pages.

The Steps in Detail

1. Create a new CorelDRAW! file.

If you are already in CorelDRAW!, select *New* from the **File** menu and save changes, if applicable. If you are not in CorelDRAW!, start the program from Windows or DOS.

2. Select the *Page Setup* command from the **File** menu. This displays the associated dialog box shown below:

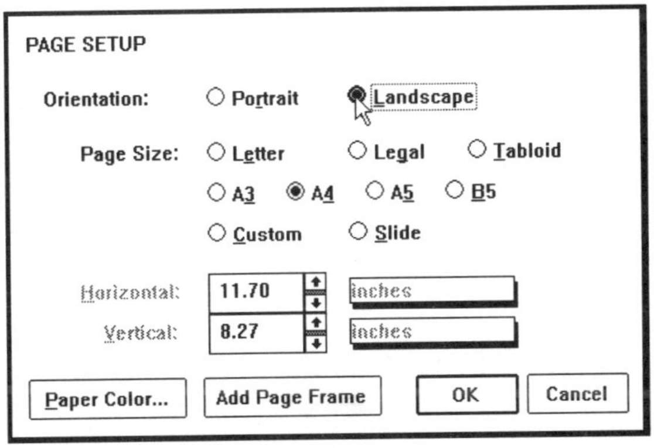

Note: By default, a CorelDRAW! page is in portrait format, unless the previous page in which you were working was a different setup, and you did not exit, but just created a new file.

From the *Page Setup* dialog box, click the mouse inside the circle in front of the word *Landscape*. After clicking on OK, the page will be in Landscape format.

3. Select the Rectangle Tool. Now move out onto the page. With your finger on the mouse, drag it down and to the right until you get a rectangle that is approximately 8" wide by 1" deep as shown in the following illustration. If using millimeters, choose 200mm wide by 20mm deep.

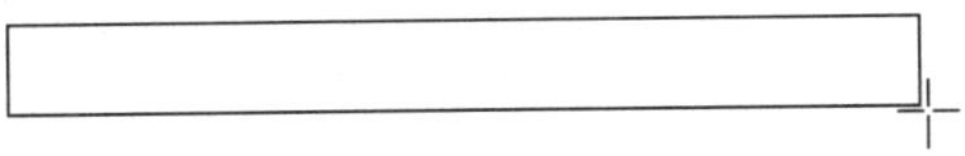

Once you have drawn the first rectangle, draw all others the same way. For this exercise, it does not matter if the rectangles are not exactly the same size. The five completed rectangles should look like this:

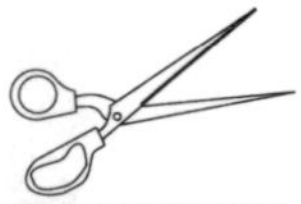

SHORTCUT

Note: You can also use the *Duplicate* command to do this.

4. Select all rectangles together to rotate them. To do this, draw a box around them all, using the Pick Tool, with your finger on the mouse like this:

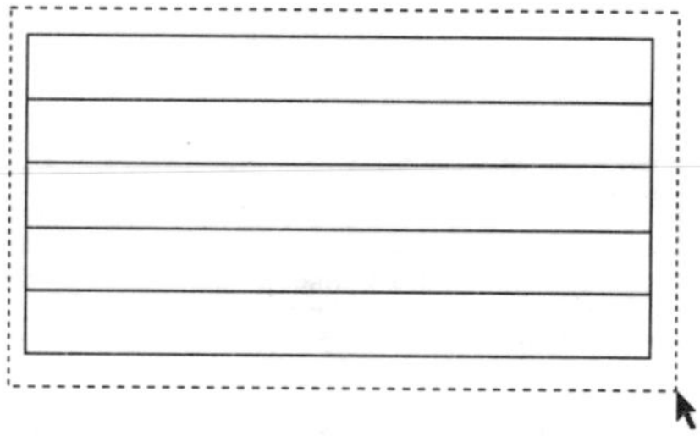

Alternatively, since they are the only objects on the page, you could choose the *Select All* command from the **Edit** menu.

Once all the rectangles are selected, click on them again to get the rotation handles like this:

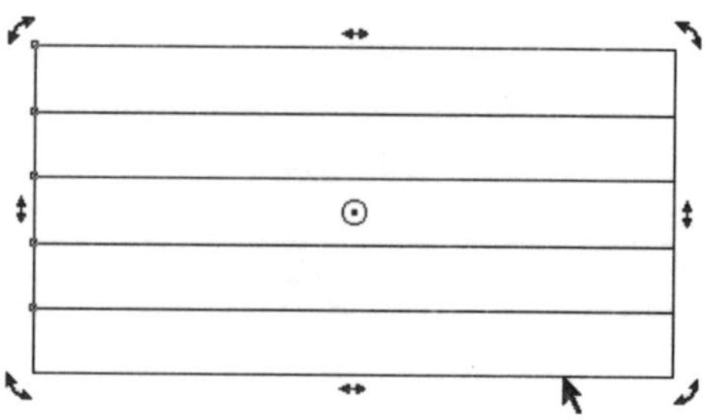

To rotate the rectangles, move the mouse over one of the handles until it changes into a cross. In this illustration, the bottom right handle is changed.

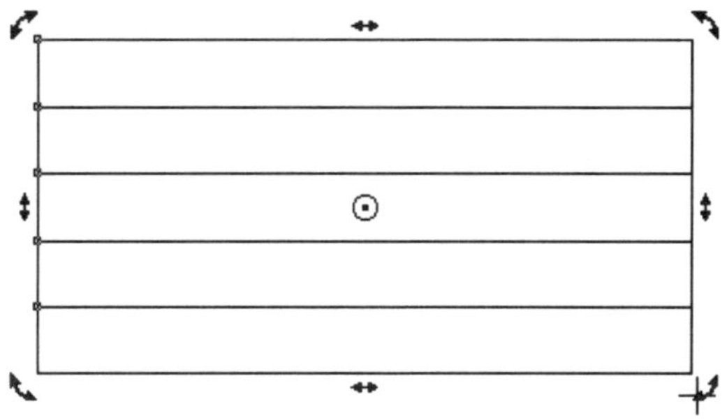

Once the cross is displayed, hold the mouse down and drag it down and to the left like this:

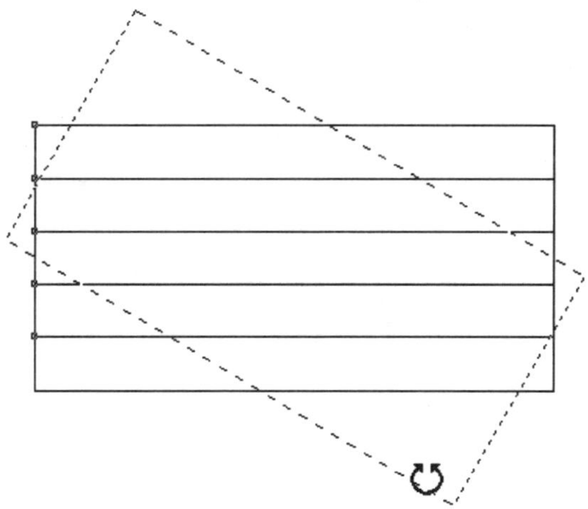

Watch the Status Line until it reaches approximately –30 degrees. Once you release your finger from the mouse, the rectangles will stay rotated at this new location like this:

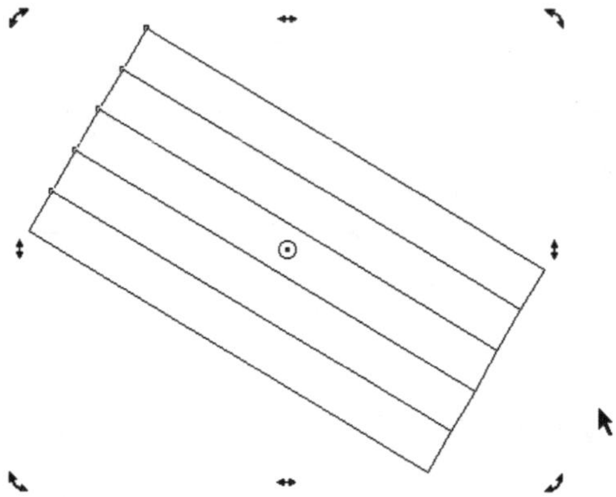

Note: If the total object has been moved off the page, select it once with the Pick Tool, and move it back onto the page.

5. With all five rectangles still selected, click on the Outline tool. From the Outline Tool fly-out, select the **X** mark. This makes the selected rectangles outline free.

6. Separately deselect the five rectangles. Do this by clicking the mouse on the page away from the rectangles. Then select the first rectangle by clicking on its top line like this:

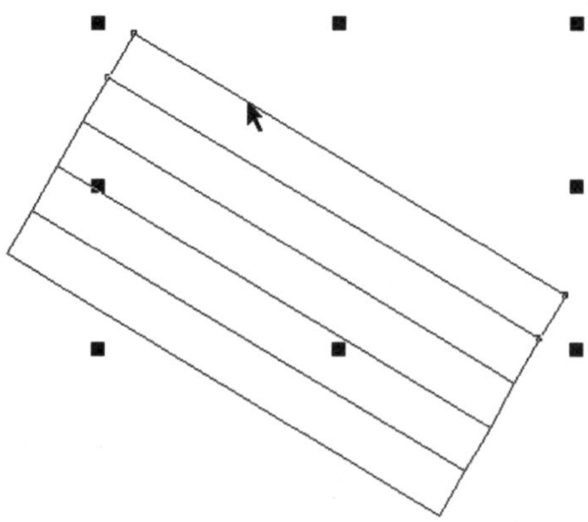

Now that you have the top rectangle selected, choose the darkest shade of gray (not black) from the Fill Tool fly-out.

Next, select the second rectangle by clicking on it with the Pick Tool. Give it the next lightest fill from the Fill Tool fly-out.

Keep moving down the rectangles, selecting one at a time, and applying the next lightest shade of gray as you go.

When you have applied the fills to the rectangles, move to the Preview Screen by selecting *Show Preview* from the **Display** menu. The following illustration shows the Preview Screen displayed.

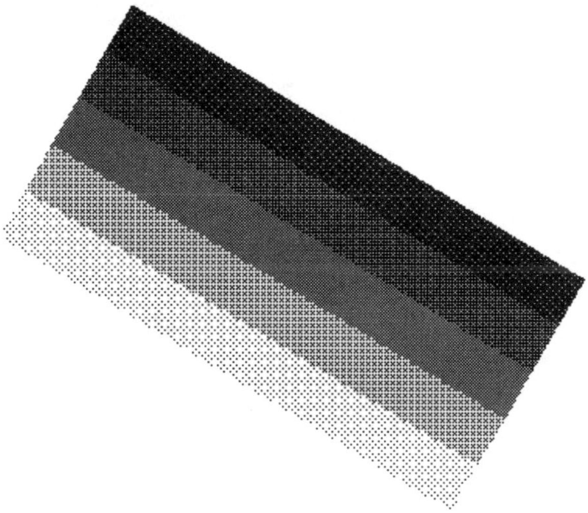

7. Select the Text Tool and click it on the page where you want the text to begin.

When the *Text* entry dialog box is displayed, type the text into the window at the top of the box. Scroll down the list of fonts, by clicking the mouse on the down arrow, until you reach the Switzerland-Black typeface and select it. Then select the current point *Size* by double-clicking in the *Size* box and typing 140. Click on OK.

The text is now on the page sitting across the rectangles like this:

8. Select the Rectangle Tool and move to the top left corner of the page like this:

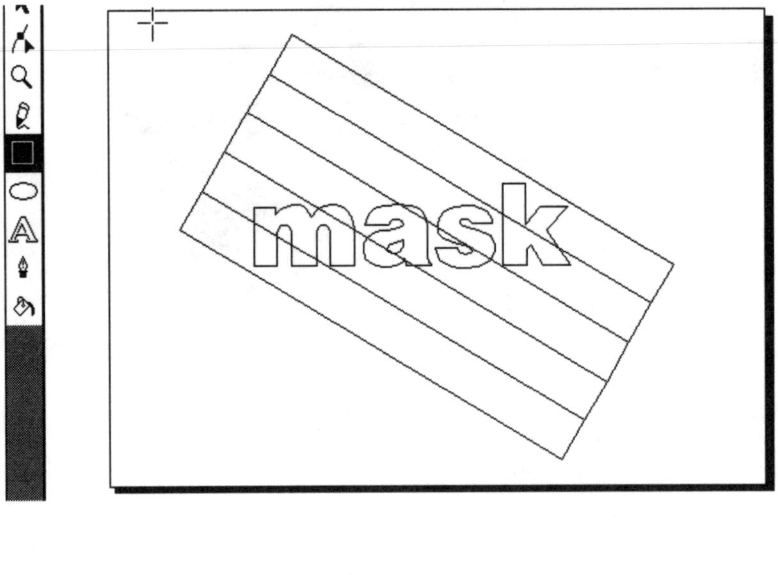

Keep your finger on the mouse, and drag it down and across so that it covers just about the whole page like this:

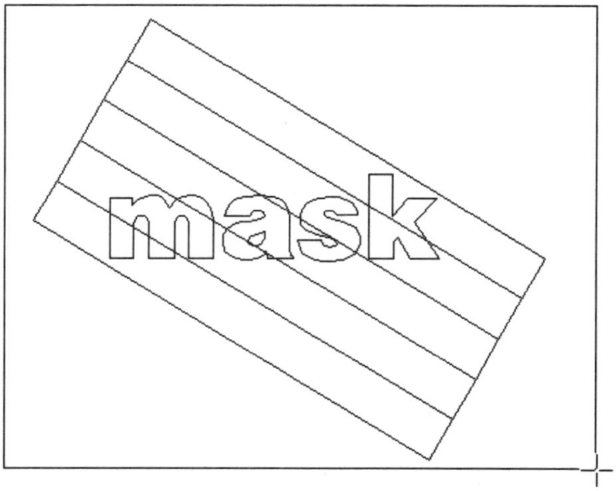

9. Combine the large rectangle and the text. You do this by selecting both of them with the **Shift** key held down and clicking the mouse on both objects, one at a time.

When you have selected both the text and the large rectangle, choose the *Combine* command from the **Arrange** menu.

10. Select the **X** mark from the Outline Tool fly-out to give the combined objects no outline. Then from the Fill Tool fly-out, select the white option.

To get a better look at what you have just done, use the Zoom Tool with the plus symbol on it, to magnify the word like this:

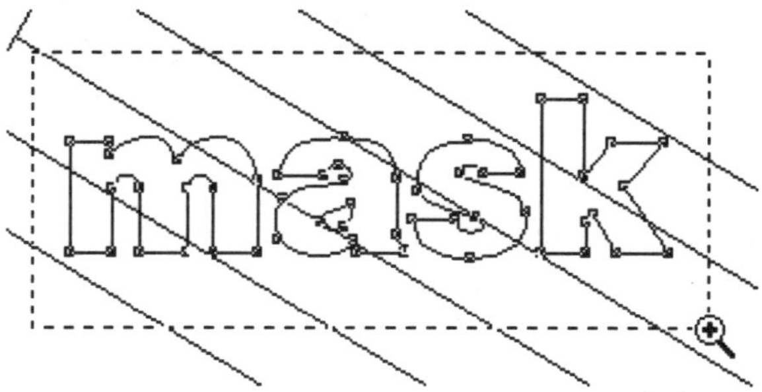

The text now takes up most of the screen.

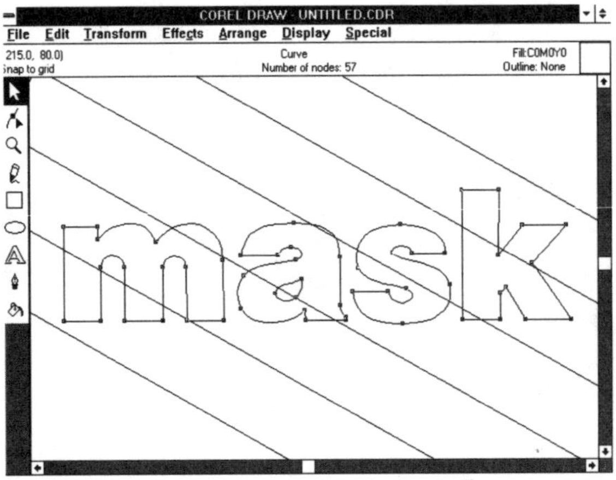

Once you have magnified the word, move again to the Preview Screen to see what the printable page looks like.

Since you gave the combined text and the square a white fill, you will not see them on the Preview Screen. Also, since they were combined, the actual text acts as a cutout, and whatever is underneath shows through.

In doing this exercise, the text and the large rectangle were created last, so they are actually sitting on top of the rotated rectangles. If you had put them on the page before the rectangles, you would need to select them, and choose the *To Front* command from the **Arrange** menu.

Whatever you put behind your mask is up to you. You may like to choose a more simple backdrop than the one created for this exercise. Or if you have a color screen, you could substitute the shades of gray for colors. It is also possible to put clip art, drawings, and bitmaps behind your mask or cutout. You do not have to use text for the mask.

Exercise 14

Copying Styles

The following exercise illustrates how you use the *Copy Style From* command. This command lets you apply the attributes of one object to another without repeating the same steps. You will copy styles from one object to another using the *Outline Pen*, *Outline Color*, *Fill*, and *Text* attributes. You can use all or one of these commands at any one time. The following pages contain the steps, as well as details on how to execute this task.

The Steps in Brief

1. Create a new CorelDRAW! file.
2. Type "copy style from" on your page using 50-point Homeward Bound.
3. Enlarge the text approximately 130% so that it takes up most of the page.
4. Give the text the fifth thickest outline from the Outline Tool fly-out.
5. Give the text a Linear Fountain Fill at a 45-degree angle using the CMYK color selection, ranging from 25% black to 100% black.
6. Activate the Preview Screen Toolbox, and magnify the text on the Preview Screen.
7. Type "that to this" using 45-point Timpani Heavy.
8. Give the second text string the same outline, fill, font, style, and size as the first text string, without invoking all the commands you used for the first text string.
9. Draw a rectangle of any size on the page below the text.
10. Give the rectangle the same fill and outline pen as the text.

This is the finished result of this exercise.

The steps for completing this exercise are on the following pages.

The Steps in Detail

1. Create a new CorelDRAW! file.

If you are already in CorelDRAW!, select *New* from the **File** menu and save changes, if applicable. If you are not in CorelDRAW!, start the program from Windows or DOS.

2. Select the Text Tool and click it on the page where you would like to type your text.

Once the *Text* dialog box is displayed on screen, type "copy style from" into the window at the top of the dialog box.

From the list of fonts in the *Text* dialog box, scroll down by clicking the mouse on the down arrow until you reach the Homeward Bound font. Once it is visible, select it with the mouse.

Change the current number in the point *Size* dialog box to 50. Check the dialog box to make sure you have done this correctly. Click on OK.

This illustration shows the result on your page:

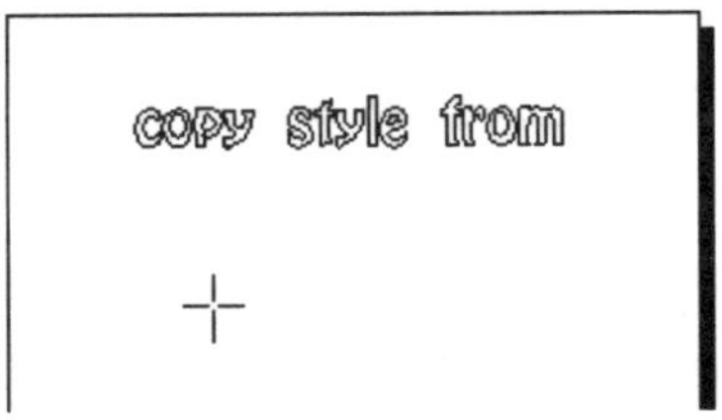

3. Move to the Pick Tool and make sure the text string is still selected. Move the cursor over the top right handle until a cross is displayed. Then holding your finger on the mouse, drag it to the right, and up as shown below, until the Status Line reads approximately "scale: 130.0%."

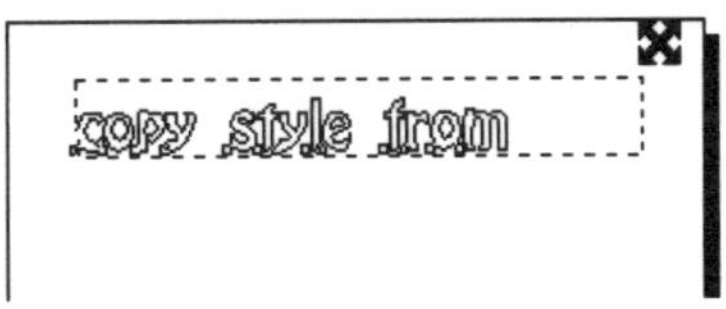

Move the text wholly on the page by holding the mouse down on the text, and dragging it into position (if necessary).

As the following illustration shows, the text is now larger.

4. Ensure that the text is still selected, and click the mouse on the Outline Tool icon to get the Outline Tool fly-out. From this fly-out, select the fifth thickest black outline.

5. Now move to the Fill Tool and select it to get the Fill Tool fly-out. From this fly-out, select the *Fountain Fill* option. This displays the *Fountain Fill* dialog box.

In the *Fountain Fill* dialog box, select *Linear*. Change the *Angle* of the Linear fill to 45, by selecting the current measurement with the cursor and typing the new number over the top.

To get to the position of selecting a CMYK color for your fountain fill, click on the *Others* button at the bottom left of the color palette of the *Fountain Fill* dialog box. This displays another dialog box where the CMYK option should already be selected. If it is not, click inside the circle to the left of the letters CMYK with the mouse.

In the box containing the current setting for black, double-click the mouse to select the figure, and change it to 25. Alternatively, use the horizontal scroll bar that represents the color black and move it over until it reaches 25. After you have done this, select OK. You will now return to the *Fountain Fill* dialog box. Now click on the second *Others* button under the palette to the right to return to the *Color* dialog box. This time, change the setting for black to 100, the same way you changed the setting to 25, and click on OK. (It may already be on 100.) Once you are back in the *Fountain Fill* dialog box again, select OK.

SHORTCUT

6. Activate the Preview Screen Toolbox by displaying the Preview Screen as shown in the next illustration. To show the Preview Screen, select the *Show Preview* command from the **Display** menu (or just press the Shift + F9 keys).

Once the Preview Screen is displayed, select the *Show Preview Toolbox* from the **Display** menu.

The following illustration shows the Preview Screen Toolbox in the Preview Screen:

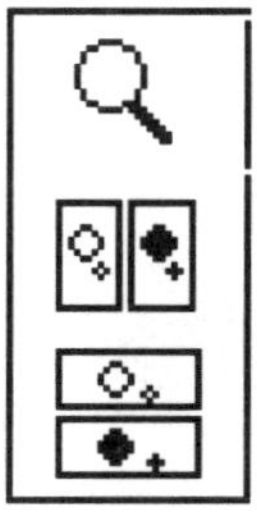

The Preview Screen Toolbox has a Zoom Tool that works the same way the Zoom Tool does on the working page. To magnify the text on the Preview page, select this new Zoom Tool and from the fly-out, select the tool with the plus symbol in it like this:

Once you have selected the tool with the plus symbol in it, draw a box around the text on the Preview Screen with your finger on the mouse like this:

Once you take your finger off the mouse, the text will be magnified like this:

7. Return to the working screen by pressing the [Shift] + [F9] keys to remove the Preview Screen. Select the Text Tool again and click on the screen underneath the first text string like this:

This activates the *Text* dialog box.

Type "that to this" in the window at the top of the dialog box. From the list of fonts, select the Timpani Heavy font and change the point *Size* to 45. When you do this, click on OK and select the Pick Tool in preparation for the next step.

The following illustration shows the result:

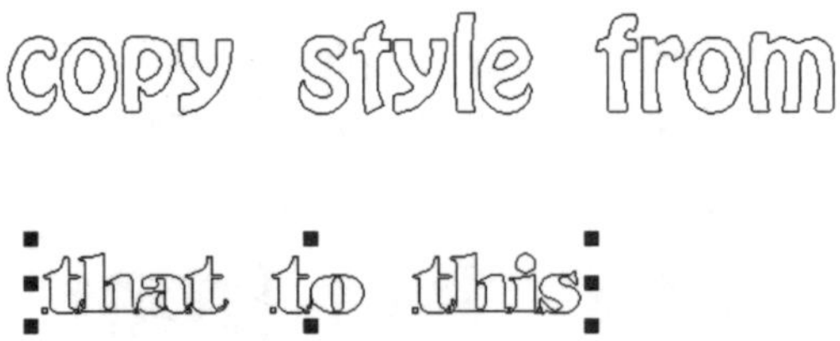

8. Give the second text string the same attributes you applied to the first text string. Instead of going through all the same steps, you can do this with one command.

With the second text string selected with the Pick Tool, choose the *Copy Style From* command from the **Edit** menu. This displays the *Copy Style* dialog box shown below:

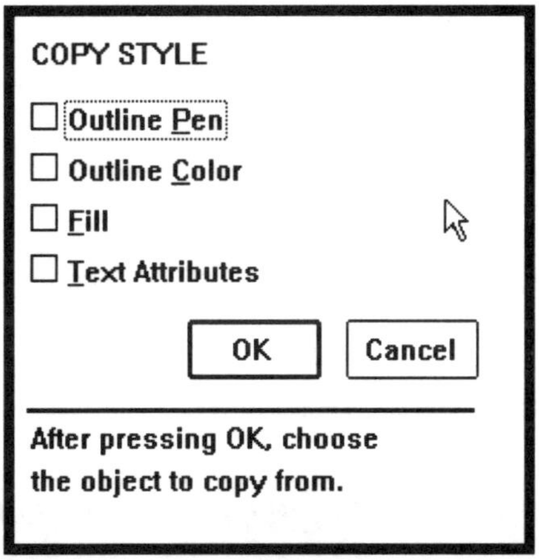

From the *Copy Style* dialog box, select all the available options by clicking inside the boxes to the left of the options. After doing this, click on OK. The cursor becomes an arrow with the word *From?* inside it like this:

Since you want the second text string to have the attributes of the first text string (that you selected in the *Copy Style* dialog box) click on the first text string with this arrow like this:

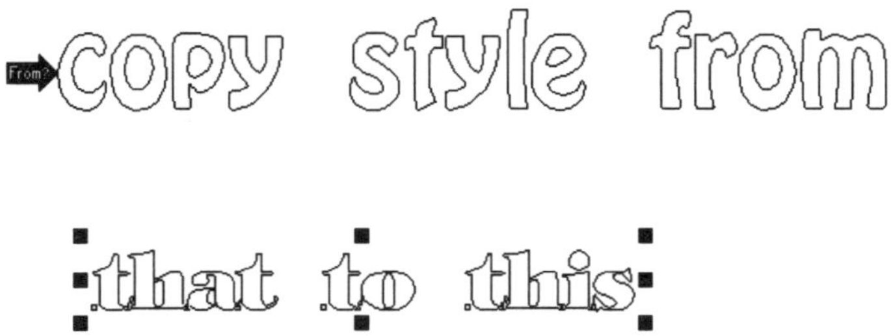

After you click this arrow on a line of the top text, the selected text underneath will take on its attributes like the following illustration shows. The cursor then becomes the Pick Tool again.

The following illustration shows the result.

9. Select the Rectangle Tool and move out onto the page. Draw a rectangle on the page underneath the text at any size you want like this:

10. Select the Pick Tool. The rectangle should be selected unless you have done something else. If it is not currently selected, click on it with the Pick Tool. Then from the **Edit** menu, choose the *Copy Style From* command again.

The *Copy Style* dialog box will still have all the attributes selected from the last time you used this dialog box. You do not need to have all the attributes selected for this part of the exercise. Deselect *Text Attributes* and *Outline Color* by clicking the mouse inside the check boxes to their left. Click on OK.

With the *Copy Style* arrow, click on the text above the rectangle. You must click directly on a line, or a dialog box asks you to try again. You could also click the arrow on either text string, since they both have the same Fill and Outline attributes.

With the From? arrow, click on the text above the rectangle like this:

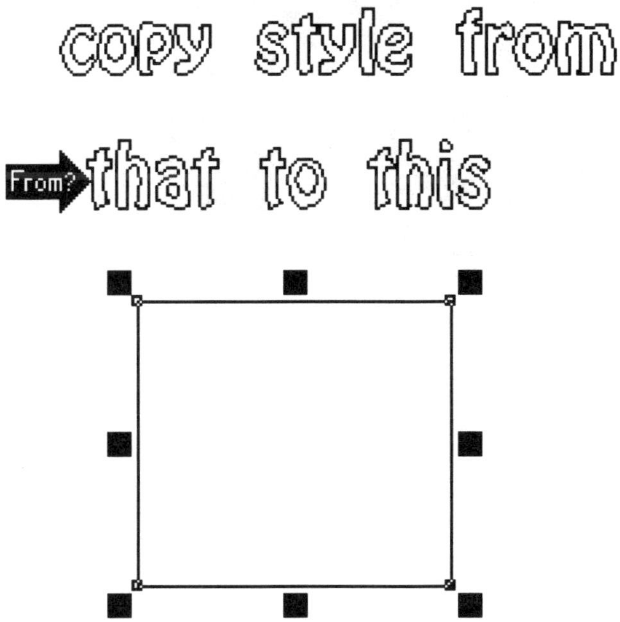

To check whether this worked, select the Preview Screen again. Since you have the Preview Screen Toolbox activated, the page will be in a different position. To view all the objects on the Preview Screen, select the ALL option from the Preview Screen Zoom Tool fly-out.

The rectangle has now taken on the Fill and Outline Pen attributes of the text.

Exercise 15

Drawing, Extruding, and Blending Objects

In this exercise, you will use a combination of some of the features of CorelDRAW!, including the *Extrude* and *Blend* commands. You will create a text string, draw an object, and extrude and blend the two. The following pages contain the steps, as well as the details on how to execute this task.

The Steps in Brief

1. Create a new CorelDRAW! file.
2. Draw a square on the lower section of your page that is approximately 1.6" x 1.6" (40mm). Give it a gray fill from the Fill Tool fly-out.
3. Use the Extrude command to create a three-dimensional, rectangular cube with both X and Y offsets at 2", Absolute Coordinates turned off, Scale Factor of 60%, and Perspective turned on.
4. Ungroup the extrusion and change the fills, so that the top part of the box is white with a thin black outline, and the right side of the box is dark gray.
5. Create a lid for the box and give it a black fill.
6. Draw a circle inside the box that is approximately 0.78" (20mm) in diameter. Send this circle to the back.
7. Type "Pandora's box" at the top of the page using 80-point Bangkok.
8. Use the Extrude command on the text with the Absolute Coordinates turned off, Perspective on, and a Scaling Factor of 60%. Give this a white fill and a 1-point black outline.
9. Blend the text and the circle together. There are 10 blended steps, and the rotation is 0%. Give the blended objects a thin black outline.
10. Select the front square of the box and bring it to the front.

This is the finished result of this exercise.

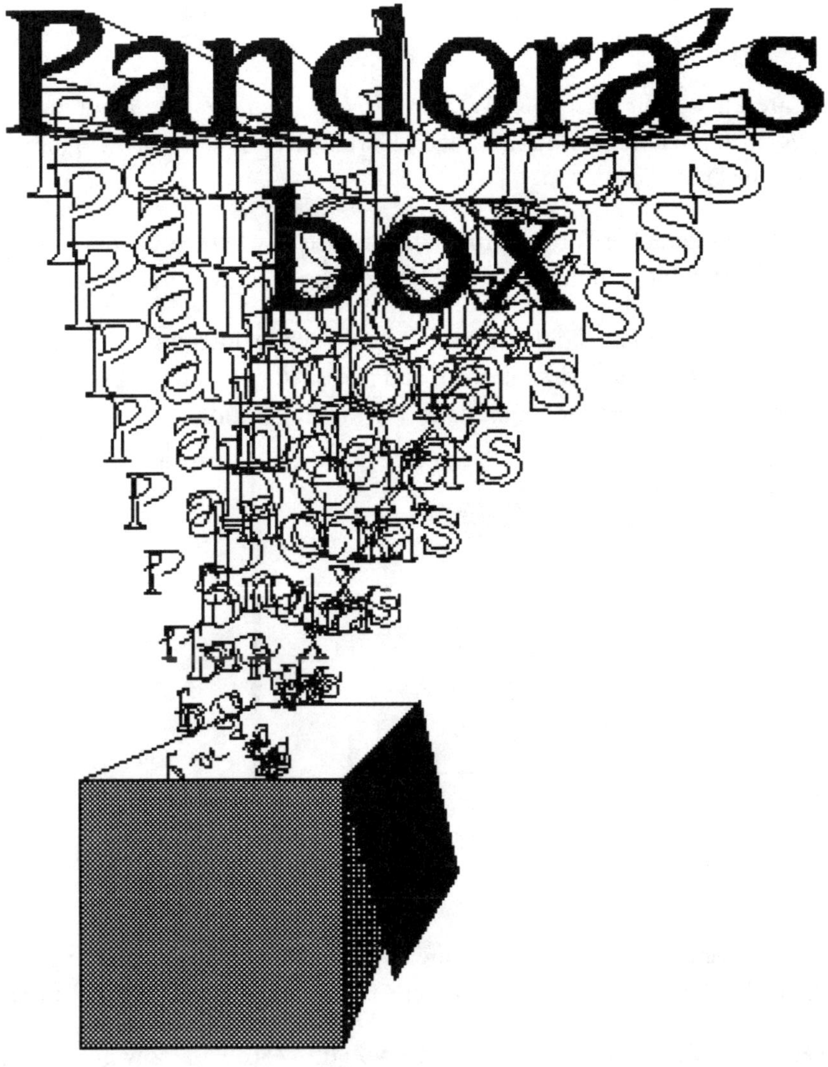

The steps for completing this exercise are on the following pages.

The Steps in Detail

1. Create a new CorelDRAW! file.

If you are already in CorelDRAW!, select *New* from the **File** menu and save changes, if applicable. If you are not in CorelDRAW!, start the program from Windows or DOS.

2. Select the Rectangle Tool and move the mouse to where you would like your square to start, which, in this case will be near the bottom of your page.

To draw a perfect square, hold down the Ctrl key while dragging the mouse. With your finger on the mouse, drag it down and across until you have a square that is proportionate to the one shown in the following illustration.

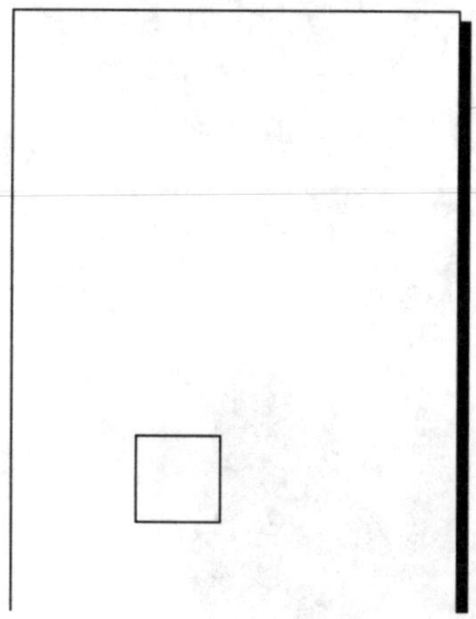

You can also draw rectangles and squares by dragging the mouse in the opposite direction. Check the Status Line to estimate the size at approximately 1.6" (40mm).

Activate the Pick Tool to select the square you drew. You are now going to give the square a gray fill. To do this, select any shade of gray from the Fill Tool fly-out.

3. With the square still selected with the Pick Tool, activate the *Extrude* command from the **Effects** menu, which invokes the dialog box.

To obtain the effect as shown in the first illustration in this exercise, turn the *Absolute Coordinates* off. If there is not a cross in its check box, it is already off. (You can activate it only if the *Perspective* option is on.)

Make both the *X* and *Y Offset* values 2". If "inches" is not currently displayed, click on the box containing the current system of measurement until you display it.

Change the *Scale Factor* value to 60%, and make sure that *Perspective* is turned on. The box to the left of the word *Perspective* has a cross in it when it is on. When your dialog box is set up like the following illustration, select OK.

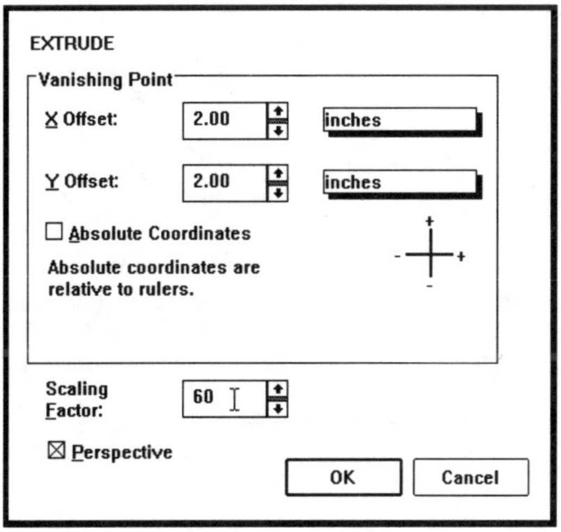

The following illustration shows the result.

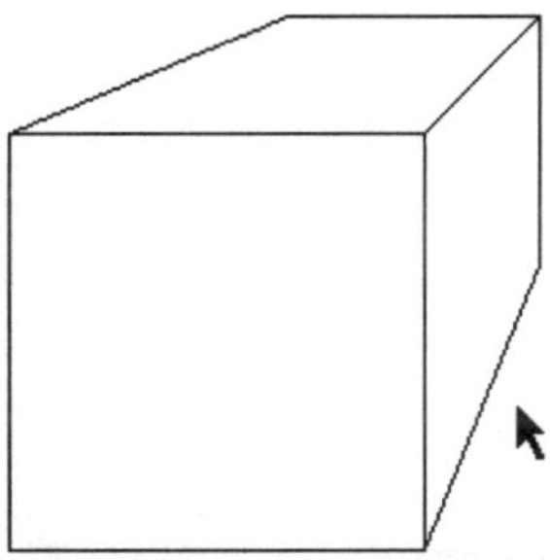

Note that you can enlarge the box with the Zoom Tool.

4. Ungroup this extrusion, so that you can select them individually to give each a different fill. Whenever an object has been extruded, the actual extrusion is a group of objects that can be selected together, or ungrouped and edited as any other object. Select the extrusion with the Pick Tool. If you have not performed any other step since the extrusion, it will automatically be selected. If it is not, click on it once at the back of the extrusion so that you are sure to select it, and not the actual square. When it is selected, the Status Line will read "Group of 2 objects."

Next, select the *Ungroup* command from the **Arrange** menu. The extrusion will now be two separate objects like this:

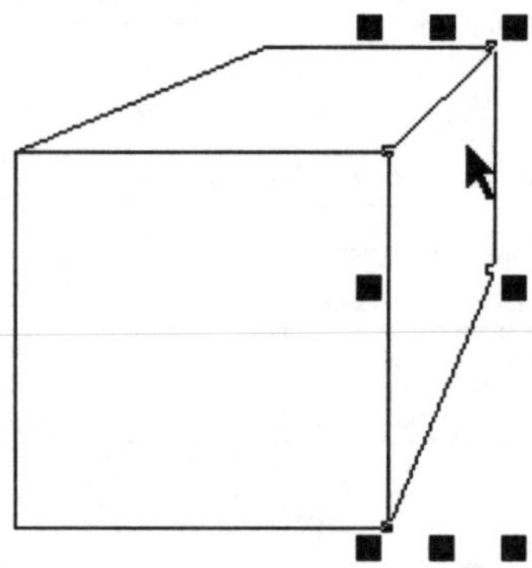

Change the fills of these two separate objects by first selecting the top rectangle with the Pick Tool. From the Fill Tool fly-out, select the white option. To change the outline, activate the Outline Tool fly-out, and choose one of the thin outline options as shown below:

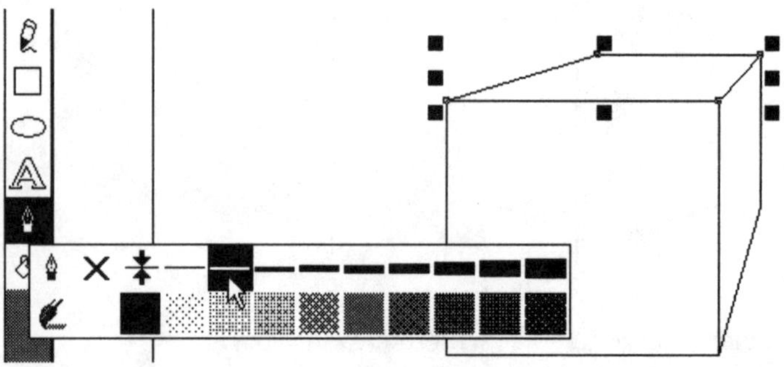

You cannot see the Fill and Outline attributes you just applied to the square until you activate the Preview Screen. If the square is still selected, however, you can see these attributes on the right of the Status Line. Use the same procedure to change the right-hand side rectangle and give it a dark gray fill.

5. Create the lid for the cube. Do this by using the Pencil Tool to draw the shape, followed by the Node Tool to make any modifications.

This exercise assumes you are using the Pencil Tool in Freehand mode. If you currently have Bezier mode active, click the mouse once where this exercise says twice. End the drawing the same way.

Select the Pencil tool and position the mouse on the top right-hand corner of the front box, click the mouse once, and move the mouse to the top far corner of the cube as shown here.

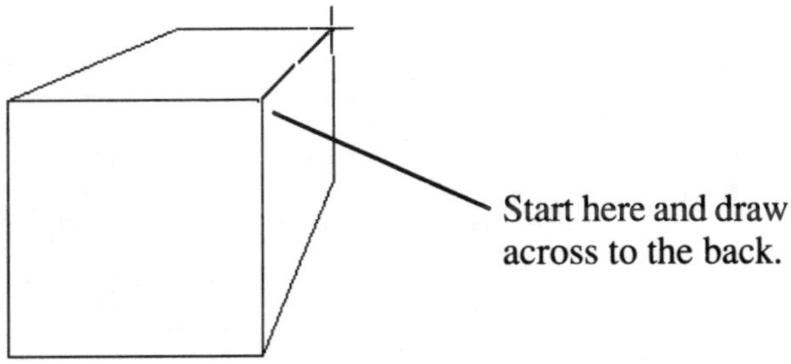

Double-click the mouse in this second position, which will create another node, and allow you to continue drawing the rectangle. Now move the mouse to the third position as shown in this illustration:

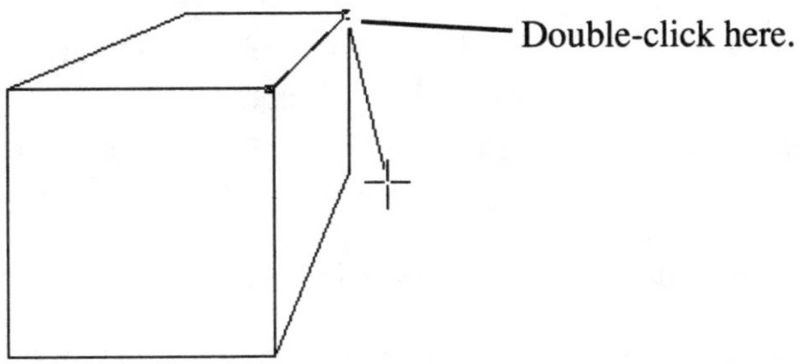

Double-click the mouse again to create a second node, and then move the mouse to the third position as shown here. Double-click the mouse at the node.

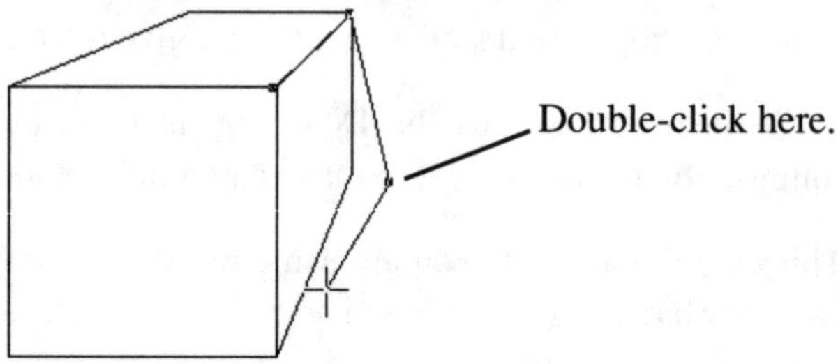

Double-click again in the third position, and carefully position the mouse this time on top of the first node. Click the mouse once to create a closed object. Click the mouse only once at the node on the top.

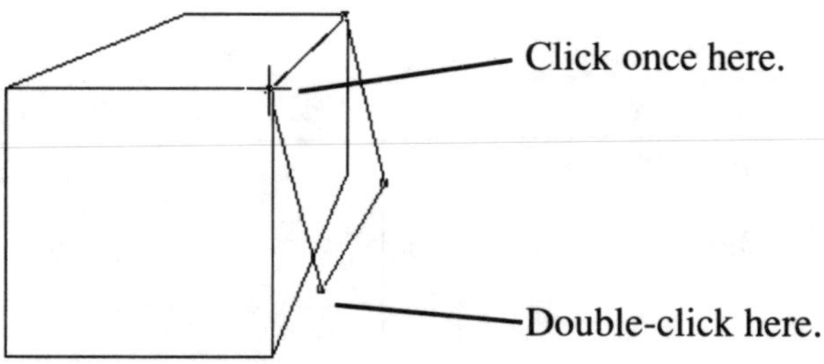

To end the shape you are drawing, click directly on top of the first node of the object so it becomes a closed, fillable object. If it is not, delete it and start again. Alternatively, you can use the Node Tool and the *Node Edit* dialog box to join the two nodes.

To make sure it is a fillable, closed object, activate the Pick Tool and the object should already be selected. If it is not, click on it once with the Pick Tool. When it is selected, the right side of the Status Line indicates if it is a closed object. The Status Line also indicates what sort of fill the object has.

Note: Only closed objects can have fills.

There will either be an X in the square at the right of the Status Line, which means it has no fill, or it will specify the color with which you have filled it. To give it a black fill, select the black option from the Fill Tool fly-out while the object is still selected. The following illustration shows the result:

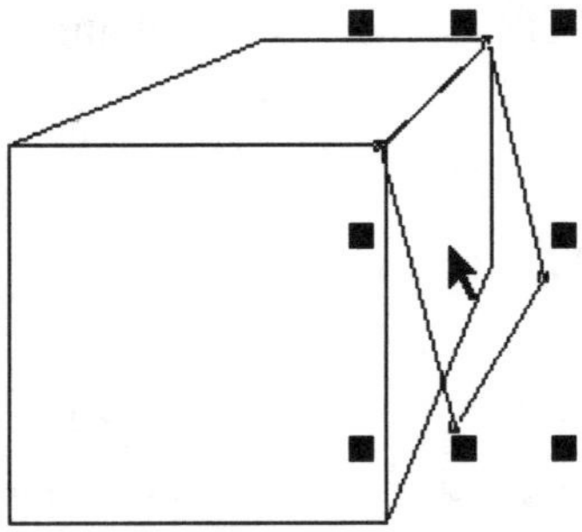

6. Select the Ellipse Tool, and position it on the page where you would like the circle to start. Holding the mouse button down, and the Ctrl key, drag the mouse diagonally downwards to draw a small circle. Release the mouse when you have reached the size like this:

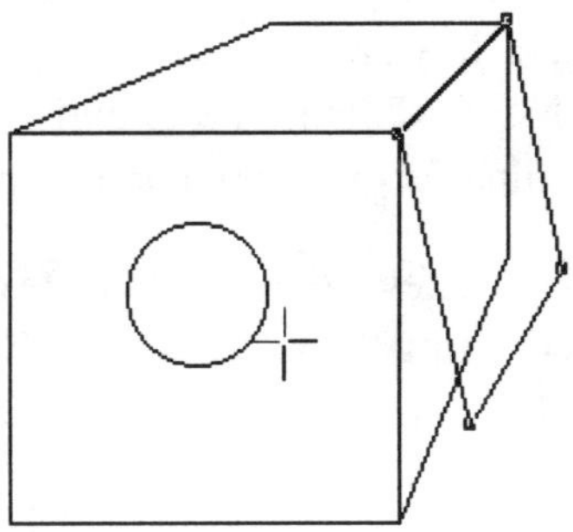

Once you have drawn the circle, activate the Pick Tool. On doing this, the circle is automatically selected. If it becomes deselected for any reason, simply click on it with the Pick Tool. Once it is selected, choose the *To Back* command from the **Arrange** menu, and give it a thin black outline from the Outline Tool fly-out.

7. Use the Zoom Tool to bring the whole page in view. Create a line of text by first selecting the Text Tool, and clicking it somewhere near the top of your page.

The *Text* entry dialog box is now displayed on your screen. Type "Pandora's box" **on two lines**. Select *Center* for the *Justification* option by clicking on it with the mouse. To change the point size, double-click in the *Size* box and type in 80.

Alternatively, you may use the up or down arrow to the right of the *Size* box by clicking on it until you reach the desired value.

Finally, before you select OK, locate and highlight the Bangkok font. Once on the page, move your text with the Pick Tool so that it is sitting at the top of the page, directly over the box.

The text will be displayed on the page like this:

8. Give this text a three-dimensional look. Do this by using the *Extrude* command. First, make sure you have the text selected with the Pick Tool. Then go to the **Effects** menu and select the *Extrude* command, to invoke the *Extrude* dialog box. Change the values to 0 inches for X and Y offsets, Absolute Coordinates relative to rules, a scaling factor of 60, and Perspective on.

Return to your page and wait a few seconds. Your text will look similar to the following illustration. By changing the values in the *Extrude* dialog box, you can create an infinite number of effects on any object you desire.

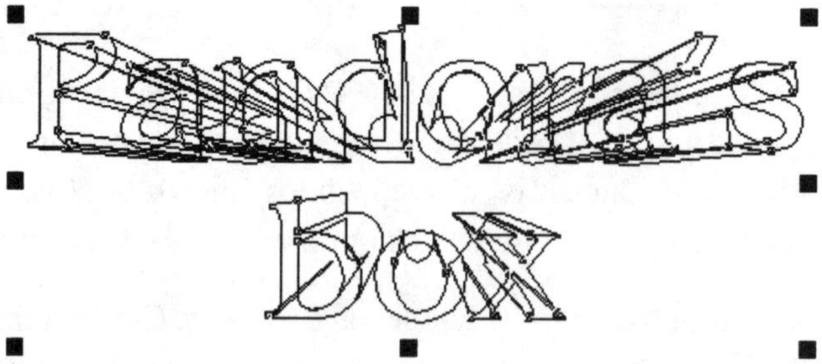

With the extrusion still selected, which it will be by default, give it a white fill and a thin black outline using the procedures described earlier in this exercise.

9. Create the effect of the text coming out of the box. Do this by using the *Blend* command from the **Effects** menu. First, select both the original text block and the circle with the Pick Tool, by holding down the Shift key. Select the text first. To make sure you have the text selected, and not the extruded objects, check the Status Line and it will indicate the font and the size of the text. Now with your finger on the Shift key, select the circle like this:

From the **Effects** menu, activate the *Blend* command to get the *Blend* dialog box and fill it in like the following illustration shows:

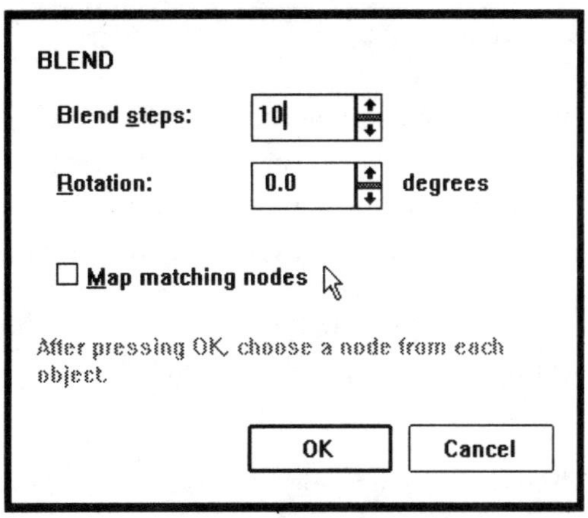

The blended steps, by default, are automatically selected with the Pick Tool after using the *Blend* command. While they are still selected, give them a thin black outline from the Outline Tool fly-out. The following illustration shows the blended text and circle.

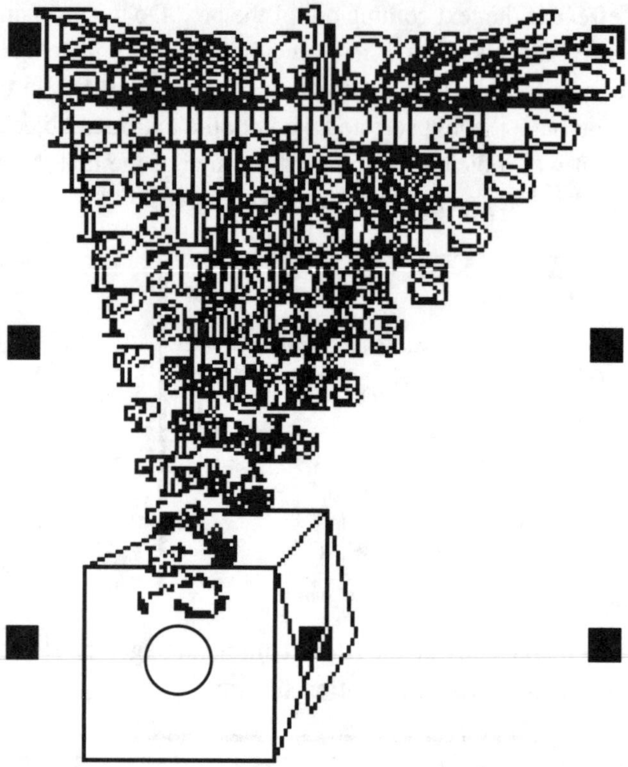

10. Move down to the square you drew earlier in the exercise, and select it with the Pick Tool. When you are sure you have it selected, choose the *To Front* command from the **Arrange** menu. This ensures that the blended objects are behind it, which provides the effect of text coming out of the box.

You are now ready to view the result in the Preview Screen. If your whole screen is not showing, select the fifth option from the Zoom Tool fly-out, which displays the whole page.

Now, to activate the Preview Screen, select the *Show Preview* command from the **Display** menu, or press the Shift + F9 keys.

Alternatively, you can activate the *Full Screen Preview* option from the **Display** menu, which you can also do by pressing F9 on the keyboard. Either way, you can view what you have done in preview to see how it will look when printed.

This is how the final graphic looks on the Preview screen.

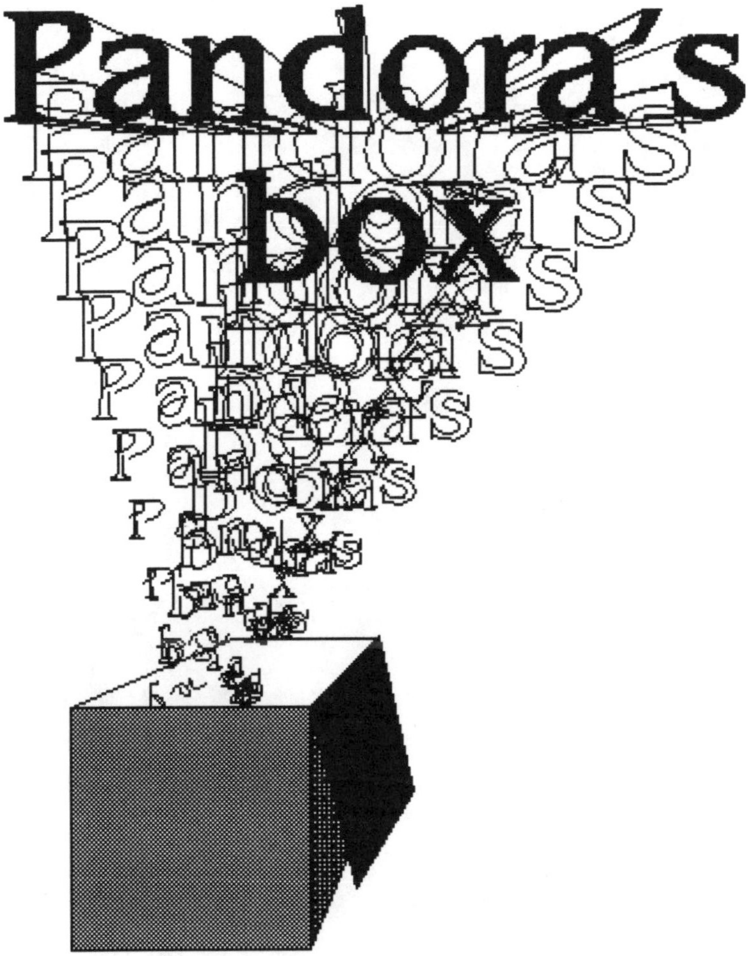

Index